# Multiplayer Gaming and Engine Coding for the Torque Game Engine

# Multiplayer Gaming and Engine Coding for the Torque Game Engine

## A GarageGames Book

### Edward F. Maurina III

A K Peters, Ltd.
Wellesley, Massachusetts

Editorial, Sales, and Customer Service Office
A K Peters, Ltd.
888 Worcester Street, Suite 230
Wellesley, MA  02482
www.akpeters.com

**Library of Congress Cataloging-in-Publication Data**

Maurina, Edward F., 1969–
  Multiplayer gaming and engine coding for the Torque Game Engine /
Edward F. Maurina III.
     p. cm.
  "A GarageGames book."
  Includes bibliographical references and index.
  ISBN 978-1-56881-422-3 (alk. paper)
  1.  Computer games--Programming.  I. Title.
  QA76.76.C672M363 2008
  794.8'1526--dc22                                                2008005991

Printed in the United States of America

12  11  10  09  08                          10 9 8 7 6 5 4 3 2 1

To my wife Teresa, for her encouragement, her advice, and most of all for her tolerance [again] of the odd hours I kept while locked away in my office writing this [second] book.

# Contents

**Contents**

**Contents**

# Acknowledgments

I give special thanks to Jerry for sitting through numerous lunches listening to me complain about "topic ordering" and "chicken or egg" dilemmas.

I also thank the many members of the GarageGames community for their unfailing interest in the guide and their encouragement. Without the community there would have been no need or reason to write this book. Thanks for waiting.

Lastly, I would like to thank the editors and reviewers who helped me clean up the mess that was my original draft. You each did a wonderful job, and I really appreciate the feedback you gave me.

# Introduction

# Chapter 1
# Introduction

## 1.1 About This Guide

### 1.1.1 Multiplayer Gaming and Engine Coding for the Torque Game Engine

You are reading *Multiplayer Gaming and Engine Coding for the Torque Game Engine,* a follow-on to my last book, *The Game Programmer's Guide to Torque* (GPGT).

In short, the purpose of this guide is to extend your knowledge of the Torque Game Engine (TGE) such that you are prepared to write, modify, and debug your own multiplayer games.

Whereas GPGT functioned as both a tutorial/learning guide and a reference, this book tends more towards the latter. The discussions you will find in this guide are a bit more terse and assume a higher level of experience than those discussions found in my last book.

In this guide, I assume that you have read GPGT or have acquired an equivalent level of experience elsewhere. Be warned: you will not make very good progress in this book if you are not familiar with TorqueScript language and the ins and outs of running TGE games/mods. A full list of the things you should know is provided in Section 1.4.

> Much of what you will learn in this guide can also be directly applied to Torque Game Engine Advanced (TGEA).

It is important to understand that this guide does not attempt to paint a coherent picture of what a multiplayer Torque game is. Instead, it provides discussions and descriptions of the parts that go into multiplayer Torque games. It will become clear as you learn more about the engine that there is no single right way to assemble a multiplayer Torque game. Instead, there are many.

At the end of your journey, having read this guide and having done the exercises (on the accompanying CD), you should be well prepared to modify standard Torque game mods like "Starter.FPS" and "Starter.Racing" to take your first steps towards designing a new multiplayer Torque game.

## 1.2 What This Guide Contains

This book is split into two major pieces, the printed guide (which you are reading now) and the accompanying CD.

### 1.2.1 The Printed Guide

This book contains the following parts and chapters.

➤ **Part I: Introduction**

- **Chapter 1: Introduction.** This is the chapter you are reading now. It discusses what this book will teach you and how the book is organized.

➤ **Part II: Multiplayer Games.** Before now, our focus was on basic scripting, engine tools, and single-player game design. To complete the picture, we learn how multiplayer games are implemented using Torque.

- **Chapter 2: Torque Multiplayer Games Primer.** In this chapter, we learn how TGE enables and implements various game types using a client-server architecture. We also build a vocabulary of important terms and concepts.

- **Chapter 3: Game Connections.** In this chapter, we examine the connection class used as the backbone in both multiplayer and single-player games.

- **Chapter 4: Servers.** In this chapter, we learn how game servers advertise their presence on a local-area network and the Internet. We also learn how clients can locate servers.

- **Chapter 5: Communications.** In this chapter, we learn about the three fundamental networking communications methodologies used in Torque multiplayer games.

- **Chapter 6: Game Phases and Organization.** In this chapter, we learn about the standard organization of a Torque multiplayer game and examine the phases that all such games pass through between the time they start up and when game play commences.

➤ **Part III: Advanced Scripting.** We covered a number of basic and intermediate scripting concepts in GPGT. Here, we will supplement our Torque scripting knowledge by discussing a few additional advanced topics.

- **Chapter 7: Artificial Intelligence.** In this chapter, we examine the three AI classes TGE provides and learn how to use them in our own games.

- **Chapter 8: Collision Detection and Response.** This chapter looks more closely at how and when collision detection and response events occur.

- **Chapter 9: Containers and Ray Casting.** In this chapter, we discuss how to use the built-in container searches and ray-casting features that Torque provides for finding objects and predicting collisions in the game world.

➤ **Part IV: Engine Coding.** Having advanced beyond making simple mods, we will often find ourselves wanting to enhance and/or add to engine behavior. Towards that end, a large part of this guide is spent introducing you to the (C++) engine code.

- **Chapter 10: Introduction to Engine Coding.** In this, the first of two engine coding chapters, we roll up our sleeves and dive into the guts of the engine, laying a foundation for a number of programming tasks.
- **Chapter 11: Creating and Using Game Classes.** After getting our bearings in the previous chapter, we learn how to inherit properties from all the primary game classes to create our own new classes. We also cover the hows and whys of using the features these classes provide.

➢ **Part V: Debugging and Improving Performance.** This part deals with debugging scripts, engine code, and miscellaneous engine behaviors. During this debugging discussion, we also learn about performance profiling.

- **Chapter 12: It's Broken!** Here, we learn tools and techniques for debugging the engine when things aren't working the way they should.
- **Chapter 13: It's Slow!** Next, we learn how to profile and otherwise measure engine performance.
- **Chapter 14: I'm Stuck!** Lastly, we talk about what to do and where to go when we have exhausted our own capability to solve a TGE problem.

➢ **Appendices**

- **Appendix A: Glossary.** Throughout this guide, I expect you to have a fairly complete understanding of terms related to game development and TGE, but to help you out and to clarify certain discussions, this appendix lists and defines what I consider the most important and relevant terms.
- **Appendix B: Essential References.** It is possible to dump function and method references from the console. However, I feel it is important to supplement those materials with a printed document containing the most-referenced scripting and C++ topics. That is the role this appendix fills.

## 1.2.2 The Accompanying CD

To supplement the printed guide, a CD is included that contains the following directories/materials.

➢ **exercises/.** This directory contains PDF documents, each of which is a series of exercises supplementing printed chapters. If you do not examine these documents and try the exercises therein, you will miss out on a significant portion of the value of this guide. Nearly all of these exercises require you to edit and modify files and are suitable as homework assignments.

➢ **answers/.** This directory contains matching PDF documents for every exercise. The difference is that these documents show all of the finished code and necessary steps to complete the exercises.

> ➤ **C++ Samples(Finished)/.** This directory contains all of the finished C++ files that we will write together in chapters 10 and 11. It does not contain any sample code for exercises.

> ➤ **C++ Templates/.** I am a big fan of starter code and templates. Therefore, this directory contains basic templates that you may use for creating a variety of new game classes. These templates are discussed in Chapter 11.

> ➤ **engine/.** No, this directory doesn't contain the engine. It actually contains the C++ code (starters and answers) that you will need to do the exercises for Chapters 10 and 11.

> ➤ **Kit/.** This directory contains a slightly modified copy of the standard TGE mod "Starter.FPS." This kit is referenced extensively throughout the printed guide and used in most of the exercises. Both Windows and Macintosh OS X executables are present in this directory.

> ➤ **MasterServer/.** This directory contains a Perl-based master server implementation that you can use in your own game development work. (See the Chapter 4 exercises to learn how to use it.)

> ➤ **More?** By the time you get this book, additional materials may have crept onto the CD. So, for a complete listing of what the CD contains, refer to the "readme.pdf" file on the disk.

Of course, you will need more tools than this to make a game, but only a few tools are really required to use this guide.

## 1.3 Tools Used in This Guide

Before you start reading this guide, it will serve you well to get tools to fill each of the needs listed in Table 1.1.

**Table 1.1.**
Tools you will need.

| Tool | Description and Suggestions |
|---|---|
| TorqueScript editor | We will modify a number of scripts while progressing through this guide, and you will need an editor for that purpose.<br>**Windows users:** I use and discuss the Torsion TorqueScript IDE in Chapter 12. I suggest that you buy a copy of this tool from the GarageGames site.<br>**OS X users:** I suggest either jEdit with the TIDE (Torque IDE) plug-in, or the free XCode tools from Apple. |
| model viewer | Although it is not required for this guide, I do suggest you buy a copy of the Torque ShowTool Pro. It is quite useful, even for the non-artist. (Be warned: I use this tool a little in Chapter 9.) |
| model editor | We don't do any modeling, but I do provide some simple models for you to examine in Chapter 9. For those examples, I use MilkShape 3D. However, for pro users, there is no substitute for 3ds Max. |

| Torque Topic | Suggested Knowledge Level |
|---|---|
| running the engine | Before reading this book, you should already know how to start the engine and how to run the sample missions. |
| editing the scripts | You should know how to open and edit the scripts found in the Demo and/or in the FPS Starter Kit. You do not need to know how everything works (especially the multiplayer parts) because we will be learning about multiplayer scripting in this guide. |
| Torque tools | You absolutely must understand how to use the eight World Editor tools (Manipulator, Inspector, Creator, etc.). It will also be helpful to know your way around the GUI Editor. |
| TorqueScript | We will be making heavy use of the Torque scripting language (TorqueScript) throughout this guide. You will be severely hampered if you do not already know this language well. |
| ShapeBase classes | In my first book, we discussed many of the ShapeBase (and ShapeBaseData) classes. If your knowledge of this area is weak, you will probably struggle a bit as you work your way through this guide. |

**Table 1.2**
*Torque skills you will need for this guide.*

## 1.4 What You Should Know Before Reading This Guide

### 1.4.1 There Ain't No Such Thing As A Free Lunch

Understand that this guide is here to start you on a learning journey. You still have to do some real work in order to learn the things it has to teach you. So, as I said in my first book, and as Robert Heinlein says in his:

**"TANSTAAFL:** *There ain't no such thing as a free lunch."*    —Robert Heinlein

### 1.4.2 A Basic Understanding of Torque

Although I would like to assume that everyone has read my first book, I know that some folks have not.

So, if you are not familiar with the topics in Table 1.2, I strongly suggest that you read my first book or learn about these topics in some other way.

### 1.4.3 Knowledge of the C++ Language

It would benefit you greatly if you were already a knowledgeable C++ user. However, as long as you have a fundamental grounding in C++, you will be just fine. If you haven't learned C++ and are hoping to catch up as you go, I suggest you take a pause and read through a C++-specific book first. Then, you can come back and dig into the guts of Torque.

### 1.4.4 Knowledge of Your C++ Tools

Torque is a cross-platform engine. This means that at some time you will need to compile the engine at least once per operating system (OS) that you wish to target.

At a minimum, you will need to know how to operate an editor and a compiler in at least one OS.

Although I would like to assume that you are already an expert in your chosen OS, I cannot and will not. Because I'm not a mean guy, I provide two compiling exercises (listed at the end of Chapter 10) showing how to compile on Windows and on OS X.

After these short tutorials, the onus is back on you to learn your tools.

## 1.5 Conventions

Throughout the guide, I will attempt to align my naming conventions and terminology with those you will encounter in the official Torque software development kit (SDK) documents and otherwise on the GarageGames site. In the cases where this is not possible, I will make it clear that the names/terms in use are of my own invention.

### 1.5.1 Warnings, Notes, and Expert Tips

Throughout this guide, you will be presented with side notes of various forms. Some of these will be warnings of odd or misleading behavior, others will be notes on interesting bits or facts, and some will be expert tips for those who want to explore the edges of Torque's behaviors. You will be able to recognize these side notes by looking for the following icons.

**Warning**          **Note**          **Expert Tip**

## 1.6 Copy Accompanying CD to Your Hard Drive

Before you go any further, take the opportunity to copy the entire contents of the accompanying CD to your hard drive. You may place the copy anywhere you wish. Just remember where you've placed it and you'll be fine. I am asking you to do this because you cannot edit files on or run the kit from the CD, and because you're about to do your first exercises.

| Exercise Summary | Location on Disk |
|---|---|
| Using the kit for the first time. | /exercises/ch1_001.pdf |

**Table 1.3.**
Introduction exercises.

## 1.7 Exercises

Because it just wouldn't be any fun to read through a chapter without having to do at least some work, the exercise in Table 1.3 has been provided for your pleasure. Enjoy!

# Multiplayer Games     Part II

# Chapter 2
# Torque Multiplayer Games Primer

## 2.1 Introduction

The Torque Game Engine (TGE) is a multiplayer (MP) game engine that supports single-player (SP) games as the degenerate case (one player.) In Torque, both SP and MP games are implemented using the same game architecture. In either case, there is a single game-state controller and one or more participants that connect to the controller.

SP game connections are supported internally and MP game connections are supported both on a local-area network (LAN) and across the Internet.

In order to improve efficiency, the controlling and participating agents in a Torque game each have distinct roles. Additionally, the controlling agent uses a variety of techniques to limit the amount of data transmission between itself and the game participants, thus reducing the overall network bandwidth requirements for a game.

There is no theoretical limit on the number of players that can participate in a Torque MP game. Because the engine utilizes an efficient game architecture and exceptional network code, the practical simultaneous multiplayer limit is quite high (128 or more players.)

## 2.2 Client-Server

Torque implements what is commonly referred to as a client-server architecture. In this game architecture, there is a single server and one client per player. So, at the highest level, a client-server game engine has two basic parts, the server and one or more clients. At this level, we are talking about purely conceptual objects. In practice, the server and the clients are conglomerates of several engine classes, various functions, globals, and scripts working together. Figure 2.1 shows the symbols we will use to represent the client(s) and the server in future illustrations.

**Figure 2.1**
The client and server.

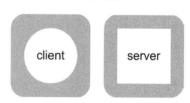

### 2.2.1 Server Responsibilities

The server in a client-server game engine architecture is the game master (or owner). It is responsible for creating the game world and for tracking every-

13

**Table 2.1**

Division of labor between
TGE client and server.

| Task | Client Responsibilities | Server Responsibilities |
|---|---|---|
| sound | 2D sounds | 3D sounds |
| input | capture and pre-process | post-process and determine response |
| GUI rendering | all processing and rendering | none |
| game rendering | all | none |
| animations | non-authoritative prediction | authoritative calculations and interactions |
| collision detection | non-authoritative prediction | authoritative calculations and responses |
| game decisions and calculations | limited to things that *do not affect* gameplay directly | all decisions regarding object creation, deletion, movement, damage, etc. |

thing that happens in that world (the game state). See Table 2.1 for a list of server responsibilities.

In a standard Torque game, there is only one server.

## 2.2.2 Client Responsibilities

The client in a client-server game engine architecture is merely a game participant. It has no direct means of modifying the game state. Instead, it take inputs from a player and feeds them back to the server. Subsequently, the server updates the game state and notifies the client as to the new game state. The client acts on these updates, rendering images and playing sounds to represent the game player's position, view, and actions in the world. See Table 2.1 for a list of client responsibilities.

In a standard Torque game, there is one client per player.

## 2.3 Game Hosting

In order to fully grasp the next two topics, engine modes and engine connections, we need to understand the concept of hosting. Fortunately, it is a simple one.

With Torque, when someone plays an SP game, he runs a single copy of the game. In this scenario, the individual is self-hosting. As we will learn shortly, both the server and client roles are handled by this single game copy.

On the other hand, when people play an MP game, each player will (generally) run his own copy of the game. Then, in order to play together, the individuals connect (over a network) their game copies to a single copy of the game that then acts as the game server.

As was noted by my use of the word "generally," there is one exception to the game-copies rule for MP games. One person in the group may both host and participate in an MP game using the same copy of the game. We will learn more about this below.

In summary, you just need to remember, that all Torque games require a game host and game participant(s). Whether the participants connect locally or across a network is dependent on the engine modes and the engine connections in use.

## 2.4 Engine Modes

Standard TGE games operate (run) in any of three modes: dedicated-client, dedicated-server, and client-server.

In *dedicated-client mode* (Figure 2.2), the engine is only executing client tasks. It parses user inputs, sends these (processed) inputs to the server, and does any rendering necessary to present the game.

To participate in a game, the engine must connect to another copy of the engine running in either dedicated-server or client-server mode.

In *dedicated-server mode* (Figure 2.3), the engine is only executing server tasks. It receives user inputs (from clients), maintains the game state, and updates clients regarding that state.

External copies of the engine running in dedicated-client mode may connect to this server to participate in an MP game.

In *client-server mode* (Figure 2.4), the engine is executing both client and server tasks.

An engine running in this mode can be used to implement either an SP game or an MP game. We will examine both instances below when we discuss connections.

> In my first book, I mentioned a single-player mode and a listen-server mode. Each of these is actually the same mode. Their differences are the result of connection decisions. So, to simplify the discussion, I decided to combine these two modes and rename them as the client-server mode.

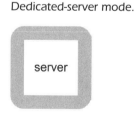

**Figure 2.2**
Dedicated-client mode.

**Figure 2.3**
Dedicated-server mode.

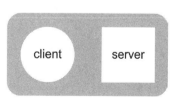

**Figure 2.4**
Client-server mode.

## 2.5 Engine Connections

In addition to the three engine modes, there are three ways that clients and a server can be connected: single-player, listen-server, and dedicated-server.

**Figure 2.5**
Single-player connection.

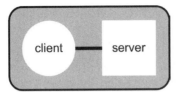

**Figure 2.6**
Listen-server connection.

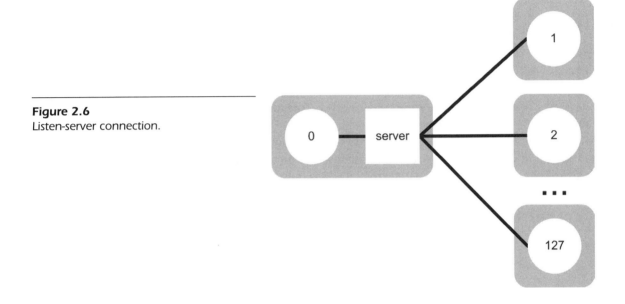

**Figure 2.7**
Dedicated-server
connection.

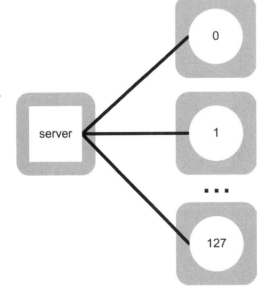

The *single-player connection* (Figure 2.5), as you may have guessed, is used for SP games. In this case, we run a single copy of the engine in client-server mode. The engine is then told to ignore all external connection requests and the server and client are connected internally.

The *listen-server connection* (Figure 2.6) is the first of two connections that allow us to run an MP game. In this case, we run a single copy of the engine in client-server mode, and any number of additional copies (on other machines) in dedicated-client mode.

The engine running in listen-server mode hosts the game and allows any number of external connections. Additionally, one player participates in the game using the client in this engine copy.

The *dedicated-server connection* (Figure 2.7) is the second of two connections that allow us to run an MP game. In this case, we run a single copy of the engine in dedicated-server mode, and any number of additional copies (on other machines) in dedicated-client mode.

The engine running in dedicated-server mode hosts the game and allows any number of external connections.

## 2.6 Server Objects and Ghosts

In the Torque implementation of a client-server architecture, the game world is controlled by the server. Game objects representing the game state are created and maintained on the server. For that reason, these objects are often called *server objects*.

During a game, individual clients are provided with copies of server objects. These copies are called *ghosts*. Figure 2.8 shows the symbols we will use to represent the server objects and ghosts in future illustrations.

All game calculations are done using server objects. Thus, only server objects affect the game and its outcome.

In order to keep clients up to date, the server will send information across the individual server-to-client connections, updating the ghosts on each client.

Clients then render the game based on the state of their own ghosts. Figure 2.9 depicts the concept of server objects and copies of those objects being ghosted to a client.

The server is aware of all server objects and all ghosts. Individual clients are only aware of their own ghosts. This provides a strong measure of security and prevents a number of game cheats involving clients having direct access to server objects and/or knowledge of other clients' objects.

**Figure 2.8**
Symbols for server objects and ghosts.

From now on, when I use the term "render," I am referring both to the rendering of images to a player's screen and to the playing of sounds through their speakers.

**Figure 2.9**
Server objects and ghosts.

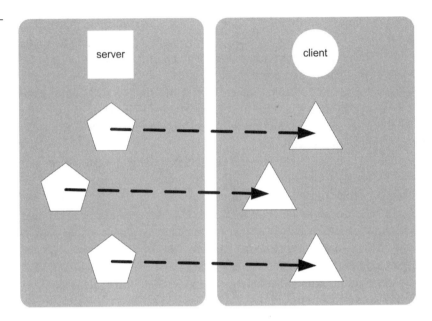

## 2.7 Control Objects and Scoping

Of course, it would be very wasteful if all server objects were copied (ghosted) to all clients. Fortunately, the folks who designed Torque implemented a means to optimize this interaction. This optimization involves the use of control objects and scoping calculations.

For every client attached to a server, there is a server object specified as that client's *control object*. Usually, this control object is a `Player`, a `Vehicle`, or a `Camera`, but it can be any of the `GameBase`-derived objects. (We will talk more about `GameBase` and its children in Chapters 10 and 11).

The primary purpose of marking an object as a control object is to enable *scoping* calculations. The result of a scoping calculation tells the server which server objects need to be ghosted to which clients. In this context, an object is in scope if it should be rendered on the current client for which the scoping calculation is being done.

This may seem a little confusing, at first, so let's make up a hypothetical example demonstrating the concepts of control objects and scoping, illustrating their effects on ghosting.

## 2.7.1 Control Object and Scoping Example

In this example, we have two players, each using dedicated clients and connecting to a dedicated server. On the server, there are two player objects (A

**Figure 2.10**
Scoping example.

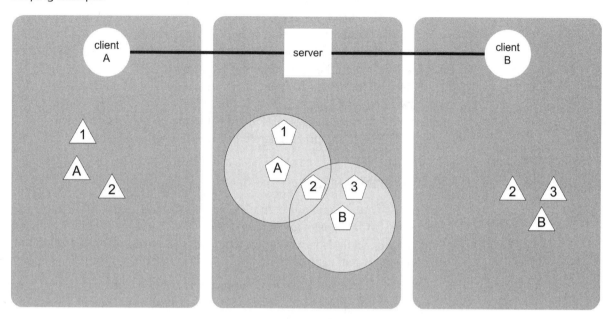

and B) and three other objects (1, 2, and 3). Objects A and B are the control objects for client A and client B, respectively. Figure 2.10 illustrates these relationships.

In practice, Torque implements an elaborate set of scoping equations. So, to keep this example simple, we will pretend that it only calculates scope based on radius; that is, if an object is within some specified radius of a control object, it is considered to be in scope.

Figure 2.10 shows the radius for a control object's scope as a circle around the control object. Examining the figure, you should see that both object A and object B have a circle around them. After applying the aforementioned scoping rule, you should see that we have the following scoping relationships:

➢ Control object A scopes server objects A, 1, and 2.

➢ Control object B scopes server objects B, 2, and 3.

Therefore, objects A, 1, and 2 will be ghosted to client A, and objects B, 2, and 3 will be ghosted to client B.

**Multiplayer Games**

## 2.7.2 Server Object IDs and Ghost IDs

There is no correlation between ghost IDs on different clients, nor do ghost IDs necessarily match the IDs of server objects that the ghosts are copying.

In other words, if we look at the example above, the numeric IDs for ghost 2 on client A and ghost 2 on client B don't need to match. Neither do they need to match the corresponding server object's ID.

Later, when we learn about the `GameConnection` class, we will find out how to correlate ghost IDs with server IDs and vice versa. For now, just remember that none of these IDs are likely to match and that the server is the only agent that is able to correlate ghost IDs and server object IDs.

## 2.8 Datablocks

There is one more game object that we need to discuss, namely the *datablock*. We discussed datablocks to some extent in GPGT, and I will assume you are familiar with them. I only mention them here because I want to remind you of a few important attributes:

1. All datablocks are copied from the server to every client.

2. Unlike ghosts and server objects, individual datablocks have the same numeric ID on the server and on each of the clients.

3. The primary purpose of datablocks is to provide a static store of data that is available to all clients and the server. This information is used for initialization when creating objects and saves network bandwidth (since datablocks are only sent once per mission).

4. Datablock names can be used to scope console methods.

Figure 2.11 shows the symbol we will use to represent datablocks in future illustrations.

**Figure 2.11**
Symbol for datablocks.

# Chapter 3
# Game Connections

## 3.1 Introduction

In Torque games, the connections between clients and the server are all created using the same engine class, `GameConnection`. In this chapter, we will learn about this fundamental class and see how it is used in Torque games, as well as how it interacts with scripts and game objects. Our discussions of `GameConnection` will be in the context of completing a specific task or handling a specific event. In Chapter 6, we will complete our understanding of this class and its interactions by examining it in the context of running games.

## 3.2 Instances

For every player in a Torque game (SP or MP), there are two instances of `GameConnection`.

Instances of `GameConnection` are frequently named, stored (in variables), and referred to based on the direction of their connection, be it client-to-server or server-to-client. In this guide, and in the standard Torque scripts, you will find a number of different names and variables referring to instances of `GameConnection`. Table 3.1 lists the names and variables used in this guide and in the standard game examples that come with TGE.

| Name | Meaning |
|---|---|
| clientConnection | A named instance of `GameConnection` on the server and connected to a client. |
| serverConnection | A named instance of `GameConnection` on a client and connected to the server. |
| %serverConn | A local variable containing the ID of a server connection. |
| localClientConnection | A named instance of `GameConnection` on a listen server and connected to a local client. |
| %clientConn | A local variable containing the ID of a client connection. |
| %conn | A generic local variable holding the ID of a `GameConnection` instance which may be either a client or server connection. |

**Table 3.1**
**GameConnection** names.

21

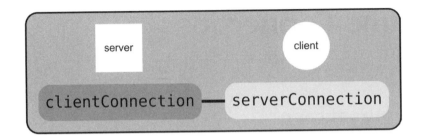

**Figure 3.1**
SP game (two instances of
`GameConnection`).

### 3.2.1  Examples of Instances

I realize that the first time you start to associate instances of `GameConnection`, their names, and their relationship to clients and the server that it can be a little confusing. So, let's examine a couple of examples to clarify these relationships.

### SP (One Local Connection)

In an SP game, there is one copy of the engine running. Furthermore, this copy of the engine operates in client-server mode and uses a single-player connection. By the time the game is started, two instances of `GameConnection` will have been created, as shown in Figure 3.1. As you can see, the server owns `clientConnection`, and the client owns `serverConnection`.

### LAN Party (One Local Connection and Two Remote Connections)

Our second example is somewhat more elaborate.

Imagine that you have invited two friends over to your home to play a new Torque game (made by you, of course.) These two friends bring over their own machines and hook them into your home network. You are hosting a small LAN party (just three players.)

In this scenario, there are three copies of the engine running, each on a separate machine. Between the three copies, the engines are using two different modes and one connection type.

➤ **Your machine (the host).** This machine has a copy of the engine running in client-server mode and has enabled a listen-server connection.

➤ **Friend #1's and #2's machines.** Each of these machines are running their own copies of the game (engine). These copies are each running in dedicated-client mode and are connected to your listen server.

By the time the game is started, four instances of `GameConnection` will have been created on your copy of the engine and one each on your two friends' copies, for a total of six instances of `GameConnection`. Figure 3.2 illustrates this.

**Figure 3.2**
Three-person LAN party (six instances of **GameConnection**).

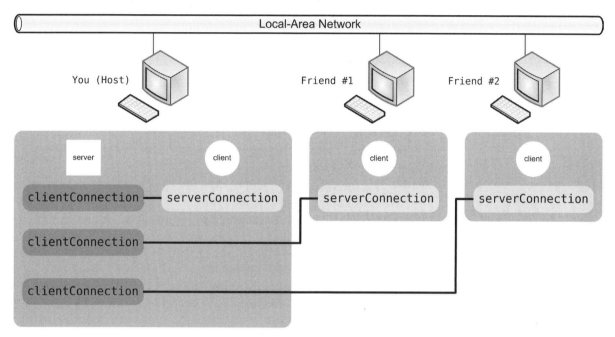

## 3.2.2 Creation

Instances of GameConnection are created both manually and automatically. For reasons that I will make clear shortly, client instances of GameConnection are always created manually, while server instances of GameConnection are always created automatically.

### Manual Creation

In all Torque games, it is the clients that request a connection to the game server. Therefore, we must create our client instances of GameConnection manually.

To manually create a GameConnection (on a client), we simply write the following code.

```
%serverConn = new GameConnection( serverConnection );
```

Subsequently, we can refer to this instance of GameConnection by the name serverConnection.

## Automatic Creation

GameConnection instances are automatically created on the server when a client successfully connects to it.

The server-to-client connection will be named localClientConnection in any game utilizing a listen server where the local client has connected to the game server. In all other cases (remote clients attaching to a game server), the server-to-client connections will be unnamed.

## Finding Client Connections on the Server

"So, how do I find these server-side GameConnection instances (client connections)?" you may ask.

Easily. The standard server scripts store the ID of every client connection in a special SimGroup named clientGroup.

So, looking up client connections on the server simply requires us to write some code like this.

```
%count = ClientGroup.getCount();

for (%i = 0; %i < %count; %i++)
{

  %cl = ClientGroup.getObject(%i);

  // Do something with client ID (%cl) here

}
```

## 3.2.3 Deletion

Most game connection deletions are automatic. Both the client and the server will delete a game connection if some fatal error occurs on that connection (we discuss this in Section 3.4). The engine will also automatically delete a connection if the connection on the other end disconnects. In fact, the only time we manually delete a connection is if we wish to force a disconnect. Clients do this when they want to quit a game, and servers do this to shut a game down, or to kick a player. The code for deleting a connection is simple.

```
%clientConn.delete("Kicked");
```

Here, a server is disconnecting a client and passing an optional argument to the GameConnection delete() method specifying that the client was kicked.

# 3.3 Connections

Once we have instances of `GameConnection`, we must connect them. As we learned above, there are both internal and external connections. Here we will learn how to create both.

# 3.3.1 Before Connecting

Before we connect instances of `GameConnection`, we may find it necessary to set up a few details, such as a password, the player name, and possibly extra arguments that should be passed in our client-to-server connection request.

### Setting a Password on the Server

It is possible for game servers to specify a connection password. To do this, simply set the `$Server::Password` global variable.

```
$Server::Password = "Bingo"; // Password is Bingo
```

Once this global variable is set, no client will be allowed to attach to the server without supplying the proper password. Alternately, if you don't want a password, set this global to the null string.

```
$Server::Password = ""; // No password
```

### Providing a Password on the Client

A client can provide a password by calling the method `setJoinPassword()` on its server connection before connecting to the game server.

```
%serverConn.setJoinPassword( "Bingo" ); // Provide password of "Bingo"
```

By default, the password is cleared, but you can manually clear it by passing the null string to `setJoinPassword()`.

```
%serverConn.setJoinPassword( "" ); // Clear the password
```

### Providing a Player Name on the Client

Although passwords are optional, names are not; that is, all client-to-server connections need to supply a player name prior to connecting to the server. You may supply a name by calling the method `setConnectArgs()` and then passing a string as the first argument.

```
%serverConn.setConnectArgs( "Big Dog" ); // This is player "Big Dog"
```

### Providing Extra Connection Arguments on the Client

Although we don't do it very often, the function `setConnectArgs()` can be used to pass up to 15 arguments. These arguments will be passed to the server during the connection request and, as we will see later, subsequently provided to the server's `onConnect()` callback.

In the following example, we modify the previous code to pass three arguments as part of the connection request:

1. Argument 1 (player name)—"Big Dog"
2. Argument 2 (extra argument 1)—10
3. Argument 3 (extra argument 2)—"Cool"

```
%serverConn.setConnectArgs( "Big Dog" , 10 , "Cool" );
```

### Enabling Connections on the Server

To allow remote clients to connect to an engine running in client-server or dedicated-server mode, we need to do two things. First, we need to specify a port address for the server to accept connections on. Second, we need to enable remote connections.

```
setNetPort( 10000 ); // Open port 10000

allowConnections( true ); // Allow clients to connect
```

By running the above snippet on either of the two server types, we will open port 10000 for connections and allow the engine to accept connections coming in on that port.

## 3.3.2 Connecting

Once the prep work is done, how do we connect to a local or a remote server? Easily.

### Local Connections

A local connection is an internal connection used when both instances of `GameConnection` are running in the same copy of the engine (client-server mode).

To make this connection, we write the following code.

```
%error = %serverConn.connectLocal(); // Connect to local server

if( "" !$= %error )
{
  error("Failed to connect locally: ", %error);
}
```

Notice that the `connectLocal()` method returns a non-null string if the connection attempt failed and a null string if it succeeded.

## Remote Connections

Remote connections are also easy to establish and require just a small amount of code.

```
%addr = "192.162.12.1:10000"; // Address of game server

%serverConn.connect( %addr ); // Connect to remote server
```

In the snippet above, you will notice that the server address (`%addr`) incorporates both an Internet protocol (IP) address and a port number. In this example, the IP is 196.162.12.1, and the port is 10000. To initiate the remote connection, we take this address and pass it to the appropriately named `connect()` method.

Unlike the `connectLocal()` method, the `connect()` method does not return a value. Instead, callbacks are used to determine if this connection request succeeded or failed. We will discuss these callbacks shortly.

> Don't forget: clients need to specify a port number as part of their connection request, and that port number should match the value used by the server in its `setNetPort()` call.

## 3.3.3 Disconnecting

Once a connection has been established, either the client or the server may sever that connection at any time. Severing a connection is as simple as deleting the instance of `GameConnection` that is providing that connection.

For example, if a server wanted to kick a player, it would simply delete the client's instance of `GameConnection`.

```
%clientConn.delete( "Kicked" );
```

In this snippet, we are passing an argument to `delete()`. This is optional but encouraged since it helps distinguish between a purposeful disconnect and an accidental disconnect. When an argument is provided during deletion, the client will receive that argument in a callback.

As another example, if a client wanted to quit, it could simply delete its server connection.

```
%serverConn.delete( "Quitting" );
```

Executing the above snippet would send a message to the server notifying it that this client is "Quitting" and then sever the connection.

## 3.4 Callbacks

The GameConnection class provides a small set of callbacks that are critical to the establishment, maintenance, and proper severance of game connections. Some of these callbacks are called only on the clients, and others are called only on the server. So, for clarity, I have ordered the following discussions accordingly.

## 3.4.1 Client-Only GameConnection Callbacks

The following callbacks are only called on server connections.

### Successful Connection

When the client successfully connects to a server, either locally or remotely, the onConnectionAccepted() callback will be called.

```
function GameConnection::onConnectionAccepted( %serverConn )
{
  echo(%serverConn , " successfully connected to server.");
}
```

### Initial Control Object Set

Some time after a client has connected to a server, that server will send datablocks and ghosts to the client. One of the ghosts that the server sends will be a client's control object.

Once the initial control object has been received, the client may safely join the game and start displaying the game world.

To tell the client that the control object has been received, the engine calls the initialControlSet() callback.

```
function GameConnection::initialControlSet( %serverConn )
{
  // Add this client to clientGroup
  if( !isObject( clientGroup ) )
  {
   new SimGroup( clientGroup );
  }

  clientGroup.add( %clientConn );
}
```

### Failed Connection

If we attempt to connect to a non-existent (remote) server, or if the server ignores our request, we will eventually get a request timeout. When this occurs, the `onConnectRequestTimedOut()` callback is called, and then the server connection is deleted.

```
function GameConnection::onConnectRequestTimedOut( %serverConn )
{
  echo( %serverConn , " failed to reach the server." );
}
```

Alternately, a server may deny our connection request, and the callback `onConnectionRequestRejected()` is called instead, then the server connection is deleted.

Below is an example implementation of this callback with some possible rejection reasons.

```
function GameConnection::onConnectRequestRejected(
%serverConn, %reason )
{
  switch$( %reason )
  {
  case "CHR_PASSWORD":
   if ($Client::Password $= "")
     %error = "Server requires a password.";
   else
     %error = "Incorrect password.";

  case "CR_SERVERFULL":
   %error = "The server is full, try another one.";

  default:
   %error = "Connection error. Please try another server." @
       "Error code: ( " @ %reason @ " )";
  }

  error(%error);
}
```

## Dropped Connection

Once a connection has been established, the server may disconnect a client at any time. When it does so, the `onConnectionDropped()` callback is called with the reason for the drop, and then the server connection is deleted.

```
function GameConnection::onConnectionDropped( %serverConn, %reason )
{
  echo("Server dropped the connection because: " , %reason );
}
```

## Connection Errors

During a game, fatal connection errors may be encountered. In such a case, the onConnectionError() callback is called with a description of the error, and then the server connection is deleted.

```
function GameConnection::onConnectionError( %serverConn, %error )
{
  echo( "This connection [" , %serverConn ,
    "] has encountered, an error: ", %error
    );
}
```

## Lagging Connections

The last client-only callback is the lag callback, setLagIcon(). This very specialized callback is called when the client has detected significant lag in the connection to the server. Whether you relay this information (visually) to the player is up to you.

```
function GameConnection::setLagIcon( %serverConn, %lagging )
{
  if( %lagging )
  {
   // Enable lag notification for the player
  }
  else
  {
   // Disable previously enabled lag notification
  }
}
```

Be aware that the onDatablockReceived() callback is **not** scoped to the GameConnection class. It is a console function that is called as part of the datablock exchange process.

The global variable $Pref::Net::LagThreshold is used to specify the maximum time (in milliseconds) that a connection can go without notification before setLagIcon() is called.

## Receiving Datablocks

So, how does a client know if datablocks are being transmitted? Well, there is a callback (called on the client) that can be used to track the receipt of datablocks. This callback is aptly named onDatablockObjectReceived(). Implementing this callback is purely optional. It is usually used to update a progress indicator so the player knows that something is happening (while datablocks are being sent).

```
function onDatablockObjectReceived( %index ,
                                    %total )
{
  echo( %index , " of ", %total , " total datablocks received");
}
```

## Connections That Time Out

Sometimes, a server may crash, or the link between the server and its clients may be severed. In either of these cases, the clients' server connections just go dead. In such instances, the engine will detect this and call the callback onConnectionTimedOut() and then delete the server connection.

```
function GameConnection::onConnectionTimedOut( %serverConn )
{
  echo("The server may have died!");
}
```

# 3.4.2 Server-Only GameConnection Callbacks

The following callbacks are only called on client connections.

## Connection Requests

When a client attempts to connect to an active server, the server will automatically create a GameConnection. Then, the engine will call the callback onConnectRequest().

In this callback, you may apply any number of connection constraints you wish, to include such things as player counts, banned connection checks, etc.

If the client requesting a connection does not meet the requirements specified by this callback, simply return a string containing the rejection reason, and the engine will automatically reject the connection. Otherwise, return a null string (""), and the client will be allowed to connect.

```
function GameConnection::onConnectRequest( %clientConn, %address, %name )
{

  // Check for too many players
  //
  if( clientGroup.getCount() > $Pref::Server::MaxPlayers )
  {
   return("CR_SERVERFULL");
  }

  // Do whatever other checks you need
  //


  // Return "" to signify an accepted connection.
  return "";
}
```

In the above example, a client connection is rejected if too many clients are already connected to this server.

**Multiplayer Games**

Remember:
`onConnect()`
receives up to 14 extra
arguments that might
have been specified
when the client called
`setConnectArgs()`
on its server
connection.

It is worth noting that the callback receives the address of the connecting client and the name the client provided. This information is useful for building ban lists (among other things).

## Successful Connections

Assuming that we did not reject the connection request in the prior callback, the engine will now call the `onConnect()` callback. At this point, any initial maintenance for the client connection should be done. This maintenance usually includes putting the client ID in a `SimGroup` where we will track all clients. The standard name for this group is `clientGroup`.

```
function GameConnection::onConnect( %clientConn , %name
                                       [ , %arg1 , .. , %arg14 ] )
{
  // Add this client to clientGroup
  //
  if( !isObject( clientGroup ) )
  {
   new SimGroup( clientGroup );
  }

  clientGroup.add( %clientConn );
}
```

## Done Sending Datablocks

Sending datablocks to a client takes time. During this time, the server should not send any other information or commands to the client. Therefore, the standard mission upload scripts are designed to initiate the datablock transfer for every client and then to wait.

Later, when the engine finishes sending datablocks to a client, it will issue the callback `onDatablocksDone()` on that client connection. This callback indicates that the server has finished sending datablocks to the specified client and is ready to continue processing that client.

```
function GameConnection::onDatablocksDone( %clientConn , %sequence )
{
  // Various accounting code
}
```

Note that the above callback implementation receives a sequence number. This number should match the `$missionSequence` value that the server passed to `transmitDataBlocks()`. If these values do not match, an error has occurred, and the connection should be aborted.

## Dropped Connections

There are several reasons that a server might choose to disconnect a client, mostly involving errors. Additionally, a server may purposely kick a client, or that client may quit by deleting its server connection.

In all of these cases, the client connection is deleted, and the onDrop() callback is called as a result.

```
function GameConnection::onDrop( %clientConn , %reason )
{
  echo("Client ", %clientConn, " dropped for reason: ", %reason );
}
```

# 3.5 Control Objects and Scoping

As we learned above, a control object is a special object existing on the server, and ghosted to the client, that is used by the server to scope that client's connection. We also learned that scoping refers to the calculations required to determine which other server objects should also be ghosted to this client. As a rule, every client has to have a control object. While creating games, we will run into situations where we need to get or set a client's control object.

## 3.5.1 Getting a Client's Control Object

We can get a client's control object using the method GameConnection:: getControlObject(). When called on a client connection, this method will return the ID of the server object that is currently being used to scope the connection.

```
%controlObj = %clientConn.getControlObject();
```

## 3.5.2 Setting a Client's Control Object

We can set a client's control object with the method GameConnection:: setControlObject().

```
%OK = %clientConn.setControlObject( %controlObj );
```

Here, the server will attempt to change the control object for the selected client connection (%clientConn) to the server object (%controlObj). If the change is successful, the local variable %OK will be set to true, and false otherwise.

## 3.5.3 Forced Scoping

Once a control object is set, scoping is done automatically, but in some cases, you may wish to keep an object in scope all of the time. We call this scope-always.

**33**

To set an object to scope-always on a specific client connection, we use the method `NetObject::scopeToClient()`.

In case you missed it, this method is called on a server object ID where that server object is a `NetObject` child of some type. Additionally, we pass in the ID of the client connection for which this shape should be marked as scope-always. This object will continue to be scoped as normal on all other connections.

```
%objID.scopeToClient( %clientConn );
```

Alternately, we can force an object to be scope-always for all clients by calling the method `NetObject::scopeAlways()`.

```
%objID.scopeAlways( %clientConn );
```

Subsequently, we may clear the scope-always setting for an object at any time by calling the method `NetObject::clearScopeToClient()`.

```
%objID.clearScopeToClient( %clientConn );
```

## 3.6 Ghosting and Ghost Resolution

As we discussed before, when we are playing a Torque game, server objects are ghosted to individual clients based on scoping calculations.

### 3.6.1 Start Ghosting

Once a client has gotten all the datablocks it needs and once the path manager has been updated, the server enables ghosting for that client by calling the `activateGhosting()` method.

```
// Start ghosting on a client connection
%clientConn.activateGhosting();
```

As soon as the above code is executed, the server will start sending ghost information to the client specified by `%clientConn`.

Be sure to call `resetGhosting()` **before** calling `clearPaths()` or you may crash the client(s).

### 3.6.2 Stop Ghosting

To stop ghosting, we call the reciprocal method `resetGhosting()`.

```
%clientConn.resetGhosting(); // Stop ghosting on a client connection
```

## 3.6.3 Counting Ghosts

At any time, it is possible for a client to determine how many objects the
server has ghosted to it.

```
%activeGhosts = serverConnection.getGhostsActive();
```

> The server
> cannot count
> ghosts using this
> method. Calling
> `getGhostsActive()`
> on a client connection
> will always return 0.

## 3.6.4 Resolving Ghost IDs

Imagine, if you will, the following scenario. In this scenario, we have an MP
game with one server and two clients. Between the server and the two clients,
there are ten game objects (see Table 3.2), three server objects, three ghosts,
and four GameConnection instances. Remember that not all objects are
ghosted to all clients, so it is entirely possible that some clients will be
ghosted objects that are not ghosted to other clients. That is the case in
Table 3.2.

   In addition to the object IDs (on the server and clients), there is another
kind of ID we have not yet discussed. This ID is called a ghost index. These
values are used to index arrays of ghosted objects, where there is one array per
client connection (GameConnection instance on the server.) Ghost indexes
start at 0 and are sequentially incremented to $n$, where $n$ is the number of
ghosts for a connection minus one. Figure 3.3 depicts our current example,
including the index arrays.

> I have chosen
> simple numeric
> values for this exam-
> ple, and the actual IDs
> could be anything.
> There is no direct
> relationship between
> game object IDs on
> the server and clients.

**Table 3.2.**
Ghost resolution: object IDs.

| Object IDs | Descriptions |
|---|---|
| 100 | A GameConnection object connected to client 0. |
| 101 | A GameConnection object connected to client 1. |
| 102 | The control object for client 0. |
| 103 | The control object for client 1. |
| 104 | A world object. |
| 200 | A GameConnection on client 0 connected to the server. |
| 201 | A ghost of the control object for client 0. |
| 202 | A ghost of the world object. |
| 300 | A GameConnection on client 1 connected to the server. |
| 301 | A ghost of the control object for client 1. |

**Figure 3.3.**
Object IDs and ghost indexes.

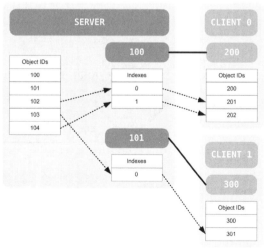

At times, we may find it useful to convert (server) object IDs into ghost indexes, and subsequently to convert ghost indexes into (ghost) object IDs on client. Or, we may find it useful to convert indexes in (server) object IDs. How do we do this?

Out of the box, Torque provides three methods for resolving ghost IDs.

### Resolving Server IDs to Ghost Indexes

The first method we need to discuss is named `getGhostID()`. This method is called by the server and is used to acquire ghost indexes from client connections. We use this method by passing it a server ID, and it returns an index corresponding to the ghost; otherwise, it returns –1 if the server object was not ghosted or if we pass an invalid ID.

Calling `getGhostID()` on a server connection may crash the engine.

For example, if we wanted the ghost index for server object 102 (as ghosted by client connection 100), we could write the following code.

```
%index = 100.getGhostID( 102 ); // Returns 0
```

After executing, the local variable `%index` will contain the index value 0.

### Converting Ghost Indexes into Server Object IDs

The second method is named `resolveObjectFromGhostIndex()`. This method is called by the server and is used to acquire server object IDs. We use this method by passing it an index value, and it returns an ID for a corresponding server object, otherwise it returns 0 if the server object was not ghosted or if we pass an invalid index.

For example, if we wanted to get the server object ID of the first ghosted object (index 0) on client 0 (client connection ID 101), we could write the following code.

```
%ID = 101.resolveObjectFromGhostIndex( 0 ); // Returns 103
```

After executing, the local variable `%ID` will contain the index value 103.

Calling `resolveObjectFromGhostIndex()` on a server connection may crash the engine.

### Converting Ghost Indexes into Ghost Object IDs

The third method we need to discuss is named `resolveGhostID()`. This method is called by the client(s) and is used to acquire ghost object IDs. We use this method by passing it an index value, and it returns an ID for a corresponding ghost object, otherwise it returns 0 if the index is invalid.

For example, if we wanted to determine the ghost ID of ghost index 0 on a client, we could write the following code.

```
%ghostID = serverConnection.resolveGhostID( 0 );
```

After running this code on client 0, the local variable `%ghostID` will contain 201. Likewise, if we ran the same code on client 1, the local variable `%ghostID` would contain 301.

> Running the function `resolveGhostID()` on a client connection may crash the engine.

## 3.7 Field of View and Point of View

A common requirement we encounter while writing games is the need to get and set information about our camera or camera proxy.

### 3.7.1 Camera Proxies

You may find my use of the term "camera proxy" confusing, so let me explain.

There is a special `CameraData` datablock. This datablock is designed specifically for setting view parameters. In turn, a `Camera` object may be used as a control object. However, you are not required to use either of these. In fact, the `ShapeBaseData` datablock and all of its children have fields for setting up the field of view (FOV), camera distances, etc. Therefore, any `ShapeBase` object and its datablock may be used as a control object to control the view settings. I refer to these as camera proxies.

### 3.7.2 Current Camera Object

We can get the current camera object with the function `GameConnection:: getCameraObject()`.

```
%camera = %clientConn.getCameraObject();
```

The above code will return the ID of the `ShapeBase` child that is currently acting as the camera. We can switch to a new camera object with `GameConnection::setCameraObject()`.

```
%clientConn.setCameraObject( %newCamera );
```

### 3.7.3 Field of View (FOV)

If we need to check the current FOV setting for a client's control object, we can request this information by calling the function `GameConnection:: getControlCameraFOV()`.

```
%FOV = %clientConn.getControlCameraFOV();
```

The above code will return a value between 0.0 and 180.0. Alternatively, we can set FOV by calling `GameConnection::setControlCameraFOV()` and by passing in a value in the same range.

```
%clientConn.setControlCameraFOV( 45 );
```

The above code will set the client's control object's FOV to 45 degrees as long as that value is in the range defined by that control object's current datablock.

Remember that the `ShapeBase` datablock fields `cameraMinFov` and `cameraMaxFov` control the minimum and maximum FOV, respectively. These values act as range caps.

## 3.7.4 Point of View

We can query a client's POV by calling `GameConnection::isFirstPerson()`.

```
// In first-person POV?
%isFirstPOV = %clientConn.isFirstPerson();
```

When executed, if the control object for the selected client (connection) is in first-person POV, the local variable `%isFirstPOV` will be set to `true`, and `false` otherwise.

We can set POV by calling `GameConnection::setFirstPerson()`.

```
// Switch to third-person POV
%clientConn.setFirstPerson( false );
```

## 3.8 Networked Sound

You may recall that there is a mission object (`AudioEmitter`) for playing 3D sounds in the game world. Many times, this object will suit our needs, but on occasion, we may want to play a sound without needing to place an object first. Torque allows us to do this by supplying two sound methods.

The first method, `GameConnection::play2D()`, is used to play 2D sounds. This method is often used for playing background music, voice-overs, and other sounds that do not need to originate from a position within the world.

```
%clientConn.play2D( %anAudioProfile );
```

The above code will play the audio datablock specified in the local variable `%anAudioProfile` on the client connected to `%clientConn`.

The second method, `GameConnection::play3D()`, is used to play 3D sound. It is often used for sounds like creaking doors, or other triggered positional ambient sounds.

```
%doorPos = %theDoor.getPosition();

%clientConn.play3D( %doorSound , %doorPos );
```

The above (hypothetical) example gets the position of our creaky door and then plays the audio profile datablock specified by the `%doorSound` local variable at the position `%doorPos`.

## 3.9 AI Connections

Torque provides two other `GameConnection` classes, `AIConnection` and `AIClient`. These classes are used to create server connections that are controlled by client scripts.

These classes behave like `GameConnection` and can be used as a substitute if you wish. We will discuss this option further in Chapter 7. For now, let's learn how to detect whether a connecting client is utilizing one of these classes.

Previously, we talked about the callback `GameConnection::onConnectRequest()`. As you will recall, every time a client tries to connect to the server, this callback is automatically called. In the body of this callback, we can add code for detecting an AI-controlled client.

```
function GameConnection::onConnectRequest( %clientConn )
{
  // Check for too many players
  //
  if( clientGroup.getCount() > $Pref::Server::MaxPlayers )
  {
   return("CR_SERVERFULL");
  }


  // Don't allow AI connections
  //
  if( %clientConn.isAIControlled() )
  {
   return("CR_AICONN_NOT_ALLOWED");
  }
  return "";
}
```

The above code calls the method `GameConnection::isAIControlled()`. This method will return `true` if the client is using either an `AIConnection` or `AIClient` instance to connect to this server. It returns `false` otherwise.

## 3.10 Paths

As part of the mission upload process, the server needs to update each client's path manager with all of the path information in the level. The server accomplishes this by calling the `transmitPaths()` method for each client connection.

```
%clientConn.transmitPaths();
```

Because path information is maintained by the path manager and because the path manager is not directly aware of the current mission, we need to clear all path data for every client when we exit a mission and before we load another one. The server does this by calling the `clearPaths()` method on every client connection.

Be sure not to call this method until after you call `resetGhosting()` or you may crash the client's engine.

```
%clientConn.clearPaths(); // Get ready for fresh path data
```

## 3.11 Datablocks

One of the jobs of the `GameConnection` class is to transmit datablocks from the server to each client that connects to it. This is accomplished by using two methods and two callbacks. We have already talked about the callbacks. Now, let's discuss the methods.

## 3.11.1 Sending Datablocks (Server Only)

Initially, when a client connects to a server, the server needs to tell the client about the datablocks that are currently in use. To do this, the server will call the `transmitDataBlocks()` method.

```
%clientConn.transmitDatablocks( $missionSequence );
```

"What," you may ask, "is `$missionSequence` for?"

This number is used for bookkeeping purposes. Basically, it starts at zero and is incremented once each time the server loads a mission. By sending this number to clients, we have created a simple mechanism that allows the engine to check if they (the clients) are receiving new data or data that they already have. If you use the standard Torque networking scripts, you can simply forget about this feature as the scripts are already set up to use it.

## 3.11.2 Deleting Datablocks

At the end of a mission, we will likely wish to delete all of the current datablocks so that we can load a new set before loading the next mission.

This is easy to do. When a mission ends, the server (and the clients) can call the `deleteDataBlocks()` function.

```
deleteDataBlocks(); // Deletes all datablocks on client or server
```

## 3.12 Blacking Out The Screen

A minor yet useful feature is the ability to fade the screen in and out. When fading out, the screen turns black. When fading in, the screen returns to the original view.

This feature can be used while switching between special areas in a mission, while loading new missions, or for whatever other reason we may want.

`GameConnection::setBlackout()`, the method used for screen fading, is different from most other `GameConnection` methods in that it is called on the client's server connection; that is, clients control fading in and out, not the server.

```
// Fade out over %fadeOutTime milliseconds
//
serverConnection.setBlackout( true , %fadeOutTime );

// ... later

// Fade back in over % fadeInTime milliseconds
//
serverConnection.setBlackout( false , %fadeInTime );
```

| Exercise Summary | Location on Disk |
|---|---|
| Examine the named connections `localClientConnection` and `serverConnection` in the context of a single-player game. | /exercises/ch3_001.pdf |
| Examine `ClientGroup` and learn to search it. | /exercises/ch3_002.pdf |
| Experiment with ghost resolution. | /exercises/ch3_003.pdf |
| Play 2D and 3D sounds. | /exercises/ch3_004.pdf |
| Black the screen in and out. | /exercises/ch3_005.pdf |

Table 3.3. **GameConnection** exercises.

## 3.13 Exercises

At this point, mostly because we lack a framework to operate in, it is still a little difficult to examine and to try out the individual features that we have learned about. This problem will be remedied in Chapter 6. However, there are still a few exercises you can try that will be useful in progressing your knowledge of the engine. Try out the following examples and then move on to the next chapter when you are ready.

# Chapter 4
# Servers

## 4.1 Introduction

In Chapter 2 we learned that TGE supports MP network connections on a LAN and across the Internet. Although never mentioned, it was implied that TGE provided a way for servers to advertise their presence and a way for clients to find them. In this short chapter, we will learn how servers advertise their presence on a LAN and the Internet, and how clients find these "advertising" servers.

## 4.2 Advertising Game Servers

Before any MP game can begin, the game server needs to make its presence known to clients that wish to connect to it. In order to achieve this goal, a server needs to set up some global variables and to define one console function as a callback. Then, once the appropriate setup is complete, advertising on a LAN is as simple as following three steps (advertising on the Internet involves one additional step).

## 4.2.1 Configuring to Advertise—Globals

To enable a server to advertise itself on a LAN or the Internet (and to receive connections), we need to configure the following globals.

- ➤ **$Pref::Server::Info**. An optional global containing a short string describing this server.
- ➤ **$Pref::Server::MaxPlayers**. An integer value specifying the maximum number of players (clients) the server will allow to connect.
- ➤ **$Pref::Server::Name**. A string containing the name of this server.
  - Example: "Lesson Server"
- ➤ **$Pref:Server::Password**. An optional password value (see Chapter 3 for more details on passwords).
- ➤ **$Server::GameType**. A string containing the game type (or name).
  - Example: "Lesson Kit"
- ➤ **$Server::MissionName**. A string containing the currently playing mission name.
  - Example: "Lava Level 100"

**Table 4.1**
Server global locations.

| Global | Location |
|---|---|
| `$Pref::Server::Info` | "~/server/defaults.cs" |
| `$Pref::Server::MaxPlayers` | "~/server/defaults.cs" |
| `$Pref::Server::Name` | "~/server/defaults.cs" |
| `$Pref:Server::Password` | "~/server/prefs.cs"<br>(only appears here after you set the variable) |
| `$Server::GameType` | "~/server/defaults.cs" |
| `$Server::MissionName` | Not automatically provided. |
| `$Server::MissionType` | Set in the `onServerCreated()` function, which is located in two different places.<br>➤ "common/server/game.cs"<br>➤ "~/server/scripts/game.cs" |
| `$Server::Status` | Set in the `initServer()` function, which is located in the file "~/server/init.cs." |

The `$Server::Status` variable is incorrectly documented in the standard "Starter. FPS" mod. This value should be passed back on the `onServerCreated()` callback. The lesson kit has been modified to do this.

➤ **$Server::MissionType.** A string containing a name describing the type of gameplay the current mission is enabling/providing.

• Example: "DeathMatch", "Rabbit", "CTF", "Exercise", etc.

➤ **$Server::Status.** A short string containing the current status of the server.

• Example: "OK"

To assist you in setting these globals, Table 4.1 provides their locations (as found in a standard Torque game/mod.)

Don't forget to stop the game you are running and delete all preference (prefs.cs) files before setting the server globals; otherwise, your preference settings may override your new default values.

## 4.2.2 Configuring to Advertise— `onServerInfoQuery()`

As was mentioned above, you also need to define a single callback to enable the server to respond to info queries (from clients and master servers.)

The body of the necessary callback is quite simple.

```
function onServerInfoQuery()
{
    return $Server::Status;
}
```

Since the `$Server::MissionName` variable is not automatically set, you should set it yourself when you create a new game. A good place to do this is in the `loadMission()` function found in the file "common/server/missionLoad.cs."

## 4.2.3 Advertising on a Local-Area Network

With the above-mentioned globals initialized, and the `onServerInfoQuery()` callback implemented, we are ready to advertise our server.

To advertise a server, do these three things.

1. Initialize a port to listen for connections on.
2. Optionally, set a password.
3. Call the function `allowConnections()`.

```
portInit( 10000 );

$Server::Password = "Bingo";

allowConnections(true);
```

Now, assuming that the proper `GameConnection` callbacks are in place, our server is ready to accept connections and is advertising itself on the LAN that this game's machine is attached to.

## 4.2.4 Advertising On the Internet

Advertising a server on the Internet isn't significantly more difficult than advertising on a LAN, but it does requires the use of a master server to work.

### The Master Server

The job of a the master server is to act as a clearing house for game-server addresses. It does this by allowing game severs to poll it and to then provide it with their respective addresses and information on the game they are running.

Later, when a client wants to find a game server, it can query the master server. The master server will send its current list of known game servers back to the client. With this information, a player can select the server he or she wishes to play on.

A play-by-play visual representation of the game server, master server, and client interactions would look something like Figure 4.1.

### Master-Server Addresses

Before a game server can advertise its address on a master server, it must know where the master server(s) lives. Therefore, we must provide a list of master servers to the (game) server. This can be done by specifying an address list in the " ~ /server/defaults.cs" file as shown below.

```
$pref::Master[0] = "2:192.162.123.15:28002";
$pref::Master[1] = "2:192.162.123.2:28002";
// ...
```

> The accompanying CD contains a simple master-server implementation (in Perl) that you can use for testing, but the design of a full-fledged master server is beyond the scope of this guide. We will use this master server in an exercise associated with this chapter.

**45**

**Figure 4.1**
Master server in action.

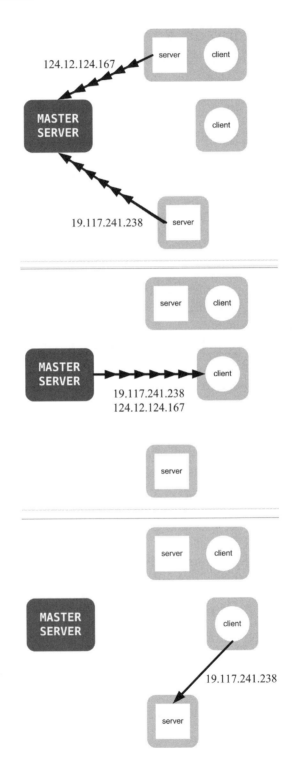

| Address Element | Description |
|---|---|
| Region Number | A nonzero number describing the region this master server exists in. For example, if your game became a worldwide hit, you might have master servers in North America, Europe, and Asia. You could give each of these regions a number (1, 2, 3), and then clients could restrict master queries to just those master servers in their region. |
| IP address | This is a standard four-part IP address (e.g., 192.168.123.1). |
| port | This is the port that the master server has enabled for queries. Legal values are in the range 1000 to 65536. |

**Table 4.2**
Master-server address elements.

In the above code, each address contains three elements.

```
Region Number : IP Address : Port
```

These elements are described in Table 4.2.

### Internet/Master-Server Advertising Code

Now, to advertise a game server to a master server(s), and thus to any machine that can locate the master server(s), we do the following.

1. Initialize a port to listen for connections on.
2. Optionally, set a password.
3. Call the function `allowConnections()`.
4. Start a heartbeat.

```
portInit( 10000 );

$Server::Password = "Bingo";

allowConnections(true);

schedule( 0 , 0 , startHeartbeat );
```

The heartbeat interval is controlled by the C++ variable `gHeartbeatInterval`. If necessary, you can modify this in C++, or expose it to the console for manipulation by scripts. See Chapter 12 to learn about exposing C++ globals to the console.

The only step that is different than for LAN servers is the starting of the heartbeat. This heartbeat is an automated feature that will re-send the game server's data to the master server every two minutes, until that heartbeat is stopped.

```
stopHeartbeat();
```

## 4.3 Finding Game Servers

For a client to participate in a LAN or Internet multiplayer game, that client must locate at least one game server that is hosting a game. To accomplish this, the client calls one of two possible console functions, `queryLanServer()` or `queryMasterServer()`.

Don't forget to stop the game you are running and delete all preference (prefs.cs) files before (or after) setting the master server addresses in "~/server/defaults.cs," otherwise your preference settings may override your new default values.

## 4.3.1 Finding LAN Servers

The `queryLanServers()` console function allows a client to search a LAN for game servers and filter those servers against a variety of criteria. Those criteria are listed below, in the order in which they are passed to `queryLanServers()`.

> **port**. Find any servers on the LAN that have enabled this port.
>
> - Servers specify the port they use in the preference variable `$Pref::Server::Port`.
> - A standard value for this setting is 28000.

> **flags**. Not used. Just set this to 0.

> **gameType**. Specifies the game type to filter on.
>
> - Servers specify the game type they are playing in the global `$Server::GameType`.
> - To match any available game, set this to`"ANY"`.

> **missionType**. Specifies the mission type to filter on.
>
> - Servers specify the mission type they are playing in the global `$Server::MissionType`.
> - To match any available mission type, set this to `"ANY"`.

> **minPlayers**. This is the minimum number of players to filter on.
>
> - If the server has fewer players than this, it is ignored.
> - A standard value for this is 0.

> **maxPlayers**. This is the maximum number of players to filter on.
>
> - If the server has more players than this, it is ignored.
> - A standard value for this is 128.

> **maxBots**. Maximum bots the server can have.
>
> - Server scripts should track the current bot count in the global variable `$ServerInfo::BotCount` (the standard example scripts don't set this variable).
> - If the server has more bots than this, it is ignored.

> **regionMask**. Not used by the engine for LAN games (only for Internet games), so just set this to 0.

> **maxPing**. Maximum ping time allowed before latency is considered too high.
>
> - Setting this value to 0 disables the test.

> **minCPU**. Minimum speed (in MHz) of server CPU.
>
> - Setting this value to 0 disables the test.

> **filterFlags**. See "The Special Filter—`filterFlags`" below.

A sample call to `queryLanServers()` designed to find all servers on port 2800 with 128 or fewer players and no bots would look like this.

```
queryLanServers(2800,0,"ANY","ANY",0,128,0,0,0,0,0);
```

## The Special Filter—`filterFlags`

Very few people use the `filterFlags` feature, and thus it is normally set to 0. However, it is perfectly OK to use, and it does provides useful filtering features. This flag is a bitmask and can take any OR'd combination of these bit values.

> **0x1**. Dedicated servers *only*.

> **0x2**. Servers not requiring passwords *only*.

> **0x4**. Linux servers *only*.

> **0x80**. Servers matching engine version of querying engine *only*.

For example, if you wanted to locate non-password protected Linux servers, you could pass `0x6` as the `filterFlags` value.

$$( 0x2 | 0x4 ) == 0x6$$
```
QueryLanServers(2800,0,"ANY","ANY",0,128,0,0,0,0,0x6);
```

> There are no special named globals provided by the engine for these bitmask values, so you will have to make your own or simply use numeric values.

## 4.3.2 Finding Internet Servers

As we learned above, game servers advertise themselves on the Internet with the help of master servers. In order for a client to query these master servers, it must do two things.

First, it needs to set up a list of master-server addresses. Second, it needs to call the function `queryMasterServer()`.

## Master-Server Addresses

Most games are set up so that the client's list is the same as the master's list. That is, the client's addresses are set in the file "~/server/defaults.cs." Additionally, the client uses the same globals as the master server.

```
$pref::Master[0] = "2:192.162.123.15:28002";
$pref::Master[1] = "2:192.162.123.2:28002";
// ...
```

## Using `queryMasterServer()`

The `queryMasterServer()` function is quite similar to the function `queryLanServers()`. This function takes virtually the same arguments as `queryLanServers()` with two exceptions. It is not passed a port number, and it does use the region-mask argument. The arguments it takes are listed below, in the order they are passed.

> **flags**. Same as for queryLanServers().

> **gameType**. Same as for queryLanServers().

> **missionType**. Same as for queryLanServers().

> **minPlayers**. Same as for queryLanServers().

> **maxPlayers**. Same as for queryLanServers().

> **maxBots**. Same as for queryLanServers().

> **regionMask**. An integer value used to separate master servers geographically. When your game goes global, this will be a concern. For now, just use a default value like 2.

> **maxPing**. Same as for queryLanServers().

> **minCPU**. Same as for queryLanServers().

> **filterFlags**. Same as for queryLanServers().

A sample call to queryMasterServer() designed to find all servers on the Internet in region 2 with 128 or fewer players and no bots would look like this.

```
queryMasterServer(0,"ANY","ANY",0,128,0,2,0,0,0);
```

## 4.3.3 Retrieving Query Results

So far, we know how to run queries, but we haven't discussed how to get the information that the queries produce.

Each time a query is run, a list of addresses and other information is stored away (in the engine.) To retrieve this information, we use two console functions, getServerCount() and setServerInfo(). The former retrieves the number of servers found, while the latter sets a series of global values with information about a specific server when we pass in the number of that server as an argument. The following code demonstrates the use of these two functions.

```
%numServers = getServerCount( );

for( %count - 0 ; %count < %numServers; %count ++ )
{
  setServerInfo( %count );

  // Do something with the $ServerInfo::* variables
}
```

In this sample code, the first function getServerCount() takes no arguments and returns the number of servers that were found by a prior search.

| Global | Description |
|---|---|
| $ServerInfo::Status | Current status for this server. |
| $ServerInfo::Address | Address for this server including IP and port. Example: "192.162.123.1:10000" |
| $ServerInfo::Name | Server name. |
| $ServerInfo::GameType | Type of game currently playing. |
| $ServerInfo::MissionName | Name of current mission (map name). |
| $ServerInfo::MissionType | Type of current mission. |
| $ServerInfo::State | A message relaying the state of this server. |
| $ServerInfo::Info | Info string describing server. |
| $ServerInfo::PlayerCount | Number of players currently attached to server. |
| $ServerInfo::MaxPlayers | Maximum number of players allowed on server. |
| $ServerInfo::BotCount | Number of bots acting as players on server. |
| $ServerInfo::Version | Version number of server. |
| $ServerInfo::Ping | Ping latency for server in milliseconds. |
| $ServerInfo::CPUSpeed | Speed of server host machine in MHz. |
| $ServerInfo::Favorite | 1 if this is a favorite, 0 otherwise. |
| $ServerInfo::Dedicated | 1 if this server is running dedicated, 0 otherwise. |
| $ServerInfo::Password | 1 if this server requires a password, 0 otherwise. |

**Table 4.3**
`getServerInfo()` globals.

The second function `setServerInfo()` takes an integer value specifying the index of the server info we wish to access. This function will then grab all the data for that server and place the data into global variables in the console. Table 4.3 lists the names of these globals and the values that they contain.

Armed with these features, we can easily access the list of found servers and provide that information to the player so that he or she may choose a server to connect to.

### 4.3.4 `$ServerInfo::*` Data Sources

In Section 4.2, we discussed setting various server globals, and now that you have seen the results of a server query, you may see that some `$ServerInfo::*` values come directly from these server globals. So as not to leave you guessing, I am supplying a table of all `$ServerInfo::*` globals and the source of the data that is put into them in Table 4.4.

### 4.3.5 Refreshing Server Data

Once a query has been done, the data from the query is kept around. Because game servers are active entities, the data in our list will become stale. To fix

**Table 4.4**
Server sources for the
**getServerInfo()**
globals.

| getServerInfo() Global | Server Source |
|---|---|
| $ServerInfo::Status | onServerInfoQuery() return value |
| $ServerInfo::Address | Address of machine hosting server. |
| $ServerInfo::Name | $Server::Name |
| $ServerInfo::GameType | $Server::GameType |
| $ServerInfo::MissionName | $Server::MissionName |
| $ServerInfo::MissionType | $Server::MissionType |
| $ServerInfo::State | Calculated by server. |
| $ServerInfo::Info | $Pref::Server::Info |
| $ServerInfo::PlayerCount | Calculated by server. |
| $ServerInfo::MaxPlayers | $Pref::Server::MaxPlayers |
| $ServerInfo::BotCount | Calculated by server. |
| $ServerInfo::Version | Calculated by server. |
| $ServerInfo::Ping | Calculated by server. |
| $ServerInfo::CPUSpeed | Calculated by server. |
| $ServerInfo::Favorite | Calculated by server. |
| $ServerInfo::Dedicated | $Server::Dedicated |
| $ServerInfo::Password | Result of this calculation: ($Pref:Server::Password !$= "") |

this, we can either re-issue a full query, or we may refresh just a single server by re-querying just it.

To re-query a single server, we use the querySingleServer() function as shown below.

```
querySingleServer( $ServerInfo::Address );
```

This will refresh the info for the last server we examined by calling setServerInfo().

## 4.3.6 Canceling a Query

Sometimes a query can hang, or for whatever reason we may wish to kill any oustanding queries. To do this, simply call the cancelServerQuery() function.

```
cancelServerQuery( );
```

This cancels the last issued query (of any type.)

## 4.3.7 Query Callbacks

The folks who wrote Torque understand that it is a good idea to provide users with (visual) feedback during any process that takes more than a few seconds. Because the query process can sometimes be quite long (due to long lists of servers or slow connections to master servers), we need some way to let the user know that things are progressing. Also, having some kind of feedback mechanism will help us when we write our scripts.

The feedback we are discussing comes in the form of query callbacks, one primary callback and four (advanced) extra callbacks.

### `onServerQueryStatus()`

The primary query callback used by all standard Torque games is `onServerQueryStatus()`. During a query, the engine calls this callback repeatedly, each time passing in new arguments. To use this callback, we create a callback like the following in script.

```
function onServerQueryStatus( %status , %message , %value )
{
}
```

As can be seen, this callback takes three arguments. Table 4.5 below lists these arguments and gives examples of the values they will receive at various times.

| Argument Name | Possible Values |
|---|---|
| `%status` | ➤ `"start"`. Starting new query.<br>➤ `"update"`. `querySingleServer()` was called. Updating data.<br>➤ `"ping"`. The engine is pinging a server to see if it will respond to queries.<br>➤ `"done"`. Query is finished.<br>➤ `"query"`. Query is (still) in progress. |
| `%message` | This variable provides additional messages, clarifying details regarding the current status.<br>➤ `"Query favorites..."`<br>➤ `"Refreshing server..."`<br>➤ `"Switching master servers..."`<br>➤ `"Retrying the master server..."`<br>➤ `"No master servers found."`<br>➤ `"No servers found."`<br>➤ `"One server found."`<br>➤ `"N servers found."` (where $N > 1$) |
| `%value` | If the status is set to `"done"` and this value is set to `"1"`, it indicates that a server(s) was located. |

**Table 4.5**
`onServerQueryStatus()` arguments.

At first, these arguments and values may seem kind of arbitrary, but they are meant to be fed directly into text fields on a feedback GUI. Of course, how you use this information is entirely up to you.

## Advanced Query Callbacks

As I mentioned above, there are three additional (advanced) callbacks. The standard Torque games/mods included with the TGE SDK do not implement them. However, I will discuss them here because I think you may find them useful if your game ends up going global (or at least becomes a big hit).

All of these callbacks are associated with master server queries and will be called for each master server that is queried.

➤ `onClearGameTypes()`. This callback takes no arguments and is called when the engine is preparing to process a list of game servers (received from a master server) sorted by game type.

➤ `onAddGameType( %type )`. This callback is executed once for every new game type the master server has passed back. In other words, for every unique game type that this master server finds, this callback will be called. Game servers are sorted by game type and then processed in that order.

➤ `onClearMissionTypes()`. This callback takes no arguments and is called when the engine is preparing to process a list of game servers sorted by mission type.

➤ `onAddMissionType( %type )`. This callback is executed once for every new mission type the master server has passed back within the current set of game types. Game servers of a specific game type are further sorted by mission type and then processed in that order.

This all may seem confusing, but consider the following hypothetical situation.

You've finished writing your game and it is immensely popular, so much so that your zealous user community has created four new game types, giving you a total of five game types (your original game type and their four new ones). Furthermore, your game supplies eight mission types ("CTF", "Deathmatch", "Team DM", etc.).

Now, imagine that hundreds of servers are running your game worldwide and that every combination of the above game types and mission types is represented.

When a user goes to query master servers, he or she may get back a list containing up to 40 different combinations of game type and mission. If so, the above callbacks will be called like this.

➢ **onClearGameTypes()**. Called once per master server that replies.

➢ **onAddGameType( %type )**. Called up to five times per master server that has replied, once per each of the four user game types and once for the default game type.

➢ **onClearMissionTypes()**. Called up to five times per master server that has replied, once per each of the four game types and once for the default game type.

➢ **onAddMissionType( %type )**. Called up to eight times per game type, once for each of the eight mission types that that game might be running at the time.

Don't forget that the whole point of these callbacks is to give you more tools with which to implement your game and the user interface that goes with it. They have been placed in the engine for your convenience only.

| Exercise Summary | Location on Disk |
|---|---|
| Experiment with server queries. | /exercises/ch4_001.pdf |

**Table 4.6**
Server query exercises.

## 4.4 Exercises

This chapter has one long exercise. In this exercise, you will learn to run LAN queries and do experiments with various settings. You will also learn to start a master server and to advertise your game on it. Lastly, you will see the results of doing limited Internet queries and huge (find any game style) queries. Table 4.6 lists the pertinent information for locating this exercise.

# Chapter 5
# Communications

## 5.1 Introduction

TGE provides three primary scripted means of sending information from clients to server and vice versa. Each of these three communication types (styles) has a specific purpose and an intended use. These three communication types and their purposes are listed in Table 5.1.

## 5.2 Commands

Torque provides a simple and robust methodology for sending commands between clients and a server (and vice versa.) This method relies upon two functions, `commandToServer()` and `commandToClient()` (see Table 5.2).

These functions operate using a simple mechanism. When one of these functions is called, a network message (containing the command name and arguments) is assembled by the caller and transmitted to the recipient. When the recipient receives this transmission, it attempts to find a function matching the one it has been issued. If it finds such a function, that function is called with the arguments it has been passed; otherwise, the command is ignored.

Actually, when a server or client receives a command that it doesn't have defined, the engine will print a message (to the console) saying it "can't find **XYZ** function", and no action will be taken.

| Communication Type | Description |
|---|---|
| Commands | TGE provides two functions to send commands across a network, one for sending commands from a server to its clients and one for sending commands from clients to their server. |
| User Datagram Protocol (UDP) | TGE provides a scripted class specifically designed to allow any running copy of Torque to attach to any other running copy of Torque and to subsequently send string data back and forth. It is worth noting that these running copies do not need to be running the same game. |
| Hypertext Transport Protocol (HTTP) | TGE provides a second scripted class that is designed to allow Torque games to send GET and POST commands to a web server. This advanced feature is used to create persistent X servers, where X is any data that the game developer chooses to persist. |

**Table 5.1**
Scripted communication types.

| Function Name | Description |
|---|---|
| commandToServer() | Issue a command from a client to a server. |
| commandToClient() | Issue a command from a server to a client. |

**Table 5.2**
Command functions.

## 5.2.1 Client-to-Server Commands

The client-to-server command function, `commandToServer()`, has the following basic signature.

```
commandToServer( COMMAND [ , ... ] );
```

COMMAND can be any word enclosed either in double quotes or in single quotes (making it a tag) and representing the command to execute on the server. Additionally, this command may be followed by any number of comma-separated arguments. These arguments may be numeric values, strings, or tags.

An example call to `commandToServer()` might look as follows.

```
commandToServer( "DoSomething" , 10 , 20 ,30 );
```

You might interpret this example as telling the server, "run the command `DoSomething` and pass it 10, 20, and 30 as arguments." This interpretation is close, but not quite correct.

### Server-Command Naming

When we issue a command to the server, TGE takes the name of that command and modifies it slightly by adding the string "serverCmd" to the front if it. Additionally, the server will pass the ID of the requesting client as the first argument to this function.

So, in our example above, the function that the server will try to find (and to execute) would look like this.

```
function serverCmdDoSomethinng( %clientConn , %arg0 ,
                                %arg1 , %arg2 )
{
  // Do something
}
```

### Tags

"So, what are tags?" you ask. Tags are a network bandwidth saving mechanism that Torque employs.

In our example above, we passed our command as a double-quote enclosed string.

```
"DoSomething"
```

We could just as easily have used a single-quote enclosed string.

```
'DoSomething'
```

Then, if we had used single quotes, TGE would do something interesting. The first time it sent the string `"DoSomething"` across the network to the server, it would calculate a number (an index) for that string and send the index along as well. It would also tell the server that, "This is a tag." Subsequently, when this client wanted to send the string `"DoSomething"` to the server, it would only send the numeric tag. As you might guess, a number takes up significantly less network bandwidth (space) than a long string.

Note, however, that you do not need to use tags if you do not wish to. It is an optional optimization.

## 5.2.2 Server-to-Client Commands

The server-to-client command function, `commandToClient()`, has the following basic signature.

```
commandToClient( %clientConn, COMMAND [ , ... ] );
```

This function has a very similar signature to `commandToServer()`, as you can see. In fact, the only difference is that we pass the ID of the client (connection) to which this command is being sent as the first argument.

An example call to `commandToClient()` might look as follows.

```
commandToClient( 100, "DoSomething" , 10 , 20 ,30 );
```

This call will send the command `"DoSomething"` to client `100` and pass three additional arguments in (`10`, `20`, and `30`.)

The function the client will try to execute should be written like this.

```
function clientCmdDoSomethinng( %arg0 , %arg1 , %arg2 )
{
  // Do something
}
```

Notice that this function uses the prefix `"clientCmd"` and only three arguments are passed in. Because this command is from the server, the client doesn't need to know the sender's connection ID. It already has this information in the named `GameConnection` instance of `serverConnection`.

## 5.3 `TCPObject`

Torque provides a special class that can be used to connect any two running copies of Torque. This class, `TCPObject`, generates User Datagram Protocol (UDP) network transmissions. As such, it should only be used for sending non-critical data.

*Actually, if you try to connect two copies of the engine that are of (very) different versions, say 1.1 trying to connect to 1.5.2, the connection may fail.*

> The Torque implementation of UDP does not guarantee data will be sent within any time frame, nor that all of the data will be sent. However, the key word here is "guarantee." Don't worry. I will show you how to ensure decent latency and how to ensure that all data is sent.

## 5.3.1 `TCPObject` Terminology

Having learned about `GameConnection` (in Chapter 3), you have a head start on the following discussion. However, as you will soon see, `TCPObject` behaves somewhat differently than `GameConnection`. With that said, I will couch this discussion in slightly different terms.

When we talk about instances of `GameConnection`, we use the terms "client" and "server." The server is in essence a controller, while the client is a participant. Similarly, `TCPObjects` have servers and clients.

A `TCPObject` client is responsible for issuing connection requests and for sending messages once it has established a connection. It is also responsible for receiving messages from the `TCPObject` it is connected to.

A `TCPObject` server is responsible for listening on a network port and for accepting connections from clients. Then, when it decides to accept a connection, it is responsible for creating a new instance of `TCPObject`. This new instance, which we will subsequently refer to as a `TCPObject` proxy, is then connected to the client that requested the connection. At this point, the server's job is done. It now goes back to listening for connections. A key difference between `GameConnection` servers and `TCPObject` servers is that, whereas `GameConnection` servers send and receive data, `TCPObject` servers do not. `TCPObject` servers only handle connection mechanics.

Completing the picture, a `TCPObject` proxy is responsible for sending and receiving messages to/from the client that it is connected to.

Figure 5.1 illustrates the steps I outlined above.

## 5.3.2 `TCPObject` Callbacks

The `TCPObject` class provides seven unique callbacks. In this section, we will discuss a simple implementation of each callback. However, before we start, I need to introduce what may be a novel concept. We will be implementing more than one copy of some callbacks, and in total, we will be using three different namespaces to write these implementations.

Because of the unique process that `TCPObject` uses to enable and handle connections, I find it simplest to define three namespaces, `TCPServer`, `TCPClient`, and `TCPProxyConnection`. Respectively, these match the

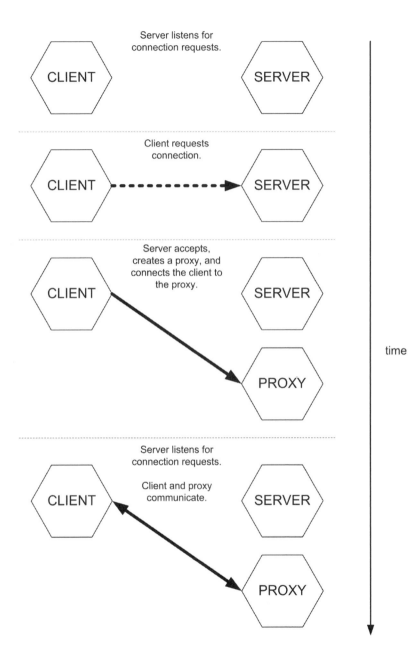

Server listens for
connection requests.

Client requests
connection.

Server accepts,
creates a proxy, and
connects the client to
the proxy.

Server listens for
connection requests.

Client and proxy
communicate.

time

**Figure 5.1**
Generalized **TCPObject**
connection process.

**Table 5.3**
Suggested **TCPObject**
callback scoping.

| TCPServer | TCPClient | TCPProxyConnection |
|---|---|---|
| onConnectRequest() | onDNSResolved() | onDisconnect() |
| | onDNSFailed() | onLine() |
| | onConnected() | |
| | onConnectFailed() | |
| | onDisconnect() | |
| | onLine() | |

TCPObject server, client, and proxy concepts we discussed above. I then implement my TCPObject callbacks in one or more of these spaces. In Table 5.3, I have listed the callbacks that we will be implementing and the namespaces they will be implemented in.

### onConnectRequest()

This callback is used by a TCPObject server to respond to connection requests. Within the body of such a callback, you may implement any code you want, and you can create any criteria necessary for accepting or denying connections. However, the simplest implementation will accept any and all connection requests.

```
function TCPServer::onConnectRequest( %obj , %addrBuf , %idBuf )
{
  new TCPObject( TCPProxyConnection , %idBuf );
}
```

A quick look at this callback's implementation will show that it receives three arguments, %obj, %addrBuf, and %idBuf, where these arguments contain the ID of the server, the address of the client, and a generated ID, respectively.

The first argument should be no surprise since you should be accustomed (by now) to the concept that the engine (usually) executes callbacks on some instance of an object (we will talk about creating instances of TCPObject shortly).

The second argument should also make sense since it is useful for the server to know the address of any incoming requests. With this information, we can easily build and implement a banning system, where some addresses are not allowed to connect and others are.

The last argument, the generated ID, is probably a bit puzzling. This argument is an internal bookkeeping mechanism that TCPObject uses. The way it uses it is as follows. When the engine receives a TCPObject connection request, it immediately starts tracking it. As part of the process, the engine assumes that the connection will be allowed and thus assigns it a speculative connection ID. This is the value that is passed as our third argument. Now, if we choose to allow the connection, we can simply create a new instance of TCPObject and pass the ID as a second argument in the creation line.

```
new TCPObject( TCPProxyConnection , %idBuf );
```

The engine looks at this second argument and compares it to the list of IDs it knows about. It matches this ID to the client that requested the connection and establishes a connection.

### onDNSResolved()

Torque is smart enough to allow either numeric addresses or name addresses, where a numeric address would be "192.168.123.1" and a name address would be "www.garagegames.com".

You may not be familiar with how name addresses are handled, but the process is called dynamic name resolution. Let me explain by way of a familiar example.

When we use names in a browser, the browser will attempt to resolve the name to a numeric address by sending the name to a Domain Name System (DNS) server. The DNS server will examine name and see if it has a number to go with it. If it finds such a number, that number will be used for the remainder of the transaction.

Because we can use names in our TCPObject connection requests, we need a callback to let us know that the address was resolved. That is what this callback does.

A simple implementation of this callback looks like this.

```
function TCPClient::onDNSResolved( %Obj )
{
}
```

### onDNSFailed()

This callback serves the reciprocal purpose to that provided by onDNSResolved() and tells us when a name lookup failed. When this callback is issued, it is Torque's way of telling us to use a number instead of a name, or to check the spelling of the name. Maybe it was spelled incorrectly.

A simple implementation of this callback looks like this.

```
function TCPClient::onDNSFailed( %Obj )
{
}
```

### onConnected()

This callback is provided to tell us when a connection request succeeded. It doesn't provide any additional data beyond that.

A simple implementation of this callback looks like this.

```
function TCPClient::onConnected( %Obj )
{
}
```

### onConnectFailed()

Of course, not all connection attempts will work. So, we need a callback to tell us when they fail. This callback serves that purpose. Unfortunately, due to the simple nature of TCPObject connections, no reason is provided.

A simple implementation of this callback looks like this.

```
function TCPClient::onConnectFailed( %Obj )
{
}
```

### onDisconnect()

As we will learn shortly, it is possible to close a connection without deleting the TCPObject. When this happens, the TCPObject will send a disconnection notice to the TCPObject it is connected to.

This callback is called when a TCPObject on the other end of a connection disconnects.

Because a client is connected to a proxy object and either of these two TCPObjects may initiate the disconnection, we need to implement this callback in two namespaces.

The simple implementations of this callback looks like this.

```
// Called when proxy disconnects
function TCPClient::onDisconnect( %Obj )
{
}

// Called when client disconnects
function TCPProxyConnection::onDisconnect( %Obj )
{
}
```

### onLine()

Another eventuality (the goal of this entire operation) that we have to be ready for is the transmission of data from a client to a proxy and vice versa.

This callback serves that purpose.

Again, this callback should be implemented in two namespaces, one for the client and one for the proxy.

Simple implementations of this callback looks like this.

```
// Called when the proxy sends data to the client
function TCPClient::onLine( %Obj , %line )
{
  echo("TCPClient::onLine( " @ %Obj @ " , " @ %line @ " ) " );
}

// Called when the client sends data to the proxy
function TCPProxyConnection::onLine( %Obj , %line )
{
  echo("TCPProxyConnection::onLine( " @ %Obj @ " , " @ %line @ " ) " );
}
```

As can be seen, this callback receives two arguments, %Obj and %line. The first argument is merely the ID of the TCPObject that received the message. The second argument is the message itself.

## 5.3.3 TCPObject Usage and Methods

Now that we've learned about the callbacks that we need to enable connections and message receipts, let us learn how to create instances of TCPObject, how to establish connections, how to send messages, and how to disconnect.

### Creating TCPObject Instances

In order to enable a connection between two TCPObjects, we need, well... two TCPObjects. To create a client, we simply do this.

```
new TCPObject( TCPClient );
```

And to create a server, we do this.

```
new TCPObject( TCPServer);
```

Lastly, lest you forget, when you create a proxy object in your onConnectRequest() callback, you should do this.

```
// Only pass second (ID) argument for creating proxies
new TCPObject( TCPProxyConnection , %idBuf );
```

### Listening for Connections

We tell a server to listen on a port by writing code like this.

```
TCPServer.listen( 5000 );
```

A `TCPObject` can listen on any single port between 10000 and 65536. Additionally, you can have multiple `TCPObjects` listening on different ports if you want.

One thing you cannot do is tell a `TCPObject` to stop listening. The only way to do this is to adjust your callback (so it won't accept connections) or to delete the `TCPObject` (server.)

> You can create as many `TCPObjects` and `TCPObject` connections as you wish, but only one `TCPObject` can be connected to any other `TCPObject` at a time.

## Requesting a Connection

To request a connection, using your client, simply write some code like this.

```
TCPClient.connect("IP:127.0.0.1:5000");
```

Notice that the `connect()` method we just used takes a single argument. This may take one of three basic forms.

1. Numeric Internet Protocol (IP) address. In this variant (shown in example), the address is provided in numeric form.

2. Named IP address. In this variant (see first example below), the address is a name and requires a successful DNS lookup to work.

3. Localhost. This final variant is really a sub-variant of named IP address, except we are using the special name `"localhost"`. In this case, the address will be a loop-back address (usually 127.0.0.1) for whatever machine the engine is running on. This is the simple way to create `TCPObject` connections on the same machine.

Here are the other two variants.

```
TCPClient.connect("IP:www.myhost.com:5000"); // Named IP

TCPClient.connect("localhost:5000");
```

You should notice that in the above IP examples, the address is preceded by the string `"IP:"` and followed by `":port"`, where **port** is some value in the range [1000, 65536]. The `localhost` variant of the address doesn't require the `"IP:"` prefix.

## Sending Messages

Assuming that we've got two `TCPObjects` ( a client and a proxy) connected, we will eventually want to send messages between them. Sending data is simple, but there are a few disclaimers you need to aware of.

To send data from one `TCPObject` to another, you would write code like this.

```
%obj.send("Hi there!\n");
```

In this snippet, you can assume that `%obj` contains either the ID of a client or a proxy object. You should also notice that we are sending a newline (\n) terminated string.

This is very important. If you do not add a newline to the end of your string, it won't be sent. It will be buffered instead. Buffered data is only sent when new data is added and that data is newline terminated, or when the sending `TCPObject` is disconnected.

## Buffering Data

If we want to buffer data and send large packets, we can simply send messages without a newline at the end.

```
for(%i = 0; %i < 100; %i++ )
    %obj.send("Message #" @ %i @ ";");

%obj.send("\n");
```

This code would end up sending a very long message with a pattern like this.

```
Message #0;Message #1; ...;Message #99;\n
```

Notice that the only separator between message elements is the semicolon we inserted ourselves.

## Flushing Data

At the end of the above buffering sequence, we sent a newline. In addition to this technique, we can flush the buffered data by disconnecting.

```
for(%i = 0; %i < 100; %i++ )
    %obj.send("Message #" @ %i @ ";");

%obj.disconnect();
```

This code would end up sending a very long message with a pattern like this.

```
Message #0;Message #1; ...;Message #99;
```

Once the last of this data was sent, the engine would disconnect from the `TCPObject` on the other end of this connection.

## Connection Latency

There is one behavior of `TCPObject` that is easily missed, but when it occurs, it can be very frustrating and confusing.

**Multiplayer Games**

If you were to execute the following code, your data would (most likely) be lost.

```
TCPClient.connect("IP:127.0.0.1:5000");

TCPClient.send("My first message!\n");
```

The reason might not be immediately apparent, but it has to do with connection latency. It takes some time for a connection to be established, and until a connection is established, instances of `TCPObject` do not buffer data—they simply drop it.

So, the lesson is to not start sending data until after you have received the `onConnected()` callback for the `TCPObject` that wishes to send data.

### Limit Send Size

The `TCPObject` is capable of transmitting up to (about) 4000 bytes of data in one transmission. Trying to send more than this will crash the engine or cause bad behavior, so be sure to track the size of your sends if you are buffering and to appropriately split large messages that exceed this limit.

### Disconnecting `TCPObject` Connections

If you read the above section, the cat has been let out of the bag. To disconnect an established connection, you simply write some code like this.

```
%obj.disconnect();
```

Now, you may optionally delete the `TCPObject`.

```
%obj.delete();
```

> You might assume that simply deleting a connected `TCPObject` would be equivalent to disconnecting and then deleting, but it is not. If you don't call `disconnect()`, no data flushing event will occur before the connection is terminated. That is, if you have messages buffered and you delete the sending object without flushing, that data will be lost. So, unless you don't need to send all of your data, always be sure to flush `TCPObjects` before deleting them.

I say "optionally" because `TCPObjects` can be connected, disconnected, reconnected, etc. That is, they can be reused, so you don't have to delete them until you are finished with them.

## 5.4 `HTTPObject`

Torque provides a second special class, derived from `TCPObject`, that is used to enable the transmission and receipt of data from a web server. The purpose of this is to enable the creation of persistent servers, where it is up to you to decide what data is to be persisted. Because the creation of such a server is well beyond the scope of this guide, and because the syntax of working with one is, too, I will only elaborate on a few details about this class.

| HTTPClient |
|:---:|
| onDNSResolved() |
| onDNSFailed() |
| onConnected() |
| onConnectFailed() |
| onDisconnect() |
| onLine() |

**Table 5.4**
Suggested **HTTPObject**
callback scoping.

## 5.4.1 Basic Usage

This class inherits from TCPObject, but it is not used in the same fashion.

### HTTPObject **Creation**

If you decide to use HTTPObject, you only need to create a single instance to use it.

```
new HTTPObject( HTTPClient );
```

### HTTPObject **Callbacks**

You only need to implement six of the callbacks, and you can place them under the same namespace (see Table 5.4). Additionally, all of these callbacks function the same way as they do for TCPObject, except that onLine() will be called when the web server responds to a call to get() or post().

## 5.4.2 get() and post()

HTTPObject communicates with a web server using two commands, get() and post(). The former is designed to query the web server for data, and the latter is designed to send data to the server for storage. They each have the following call signatures.

```
HTTPClient.get( %address, %requestURI [ , %query] );

HTTPClient.post( %address, %requestURI , %query, %post );
```

➢ **%address**. A suitable address pointing to the web server.
  • Example: "IP:www.myserver.com:80"
➢ **%requestURI**. A string containing the path to a PHP file on the server.
➢ **%query**. A string containing a query to run on the server.
  • Optional for get().
➢ **%post**. The data to send in a call to post().

**69**

**Table 5.5**
Additional **HTTPObject**
reading.

| Plan / Resource | Discusses |
|---|---|
| "Persistant Character Server" | This resource gives a great starting point for creating your own persistent character server. (Yes, "persistent" is misspelled in the resource name.) |
| "An interesting question...." | Search for this exact string (including the "....") to find an excellent plan by "LabRat" wherein he outlines the use of TCPObject as a more versatile substitute for HTTP object. |

## 5.4.3 More Reading

That is about all I have for you on HTTPObject, but I do want to point you in the direction of a couple of good threads on the subject which can be found on the GarageGames site (see Table 5.5).

**Table 5.6**
Communication exercises.

| Exercise Summary | Location on Disk |
|---|---|
| Learn to use both command functions in combination with features we discussed in previous chapters. | /exercises/ch5_001.pdf |
| An in-depth exploration of the TCPObject features and issues to beware of. | /exercises/ch5_002.pdf |

## 5.5 Exercises

This chapter is supplemented by two exercises as listed in Table 5.6.

# Chapter 6
# Game Phases and Organization

## 6.1 Introduction

The Torque Game Engine, as a product, is magnificent. It comes with the full engine source code and a myriad of starter kits, including "Starter.FPS", "Starter.Racing", and "tutorial.base". It also comes with the demo, which includes additional features not used in the starter kits. However, this mass of scripts and source code is, in its own way, problematic.

The problem is one of complexity.

If we ignore (for now) the source code (which is covered in Chapters 10 and 11), we still have to admit that the starter kits are themselves huge and complicated. There are a couple of reasons for this.

First, they come with lots of script files. Determining which scripts execute when and for what purpose is a challenge. Without a basis for examination, these scripts seem to run in a convoluted order.

Second, these starter kits include scripts, GUIs, and other content that you don't necessarily need for the game idea you might be working on. They do this because the designers of the Torque Game Engine wanted to provide full examples of the many things you can do with their engine. The side effect of this is that, for any part you don't need, you have to learn to strip it out, or to ignore it, during your development cycle.

Again, without a basis for examining and using these kits, without the big picture, it can be a real uphill slog.

This chapter is about getting that big picture.

## 6.2 The Standard TGE Software Developer Kit (Organization)

In this chapter, we will be using the exercise kit that comes with the book, but before we talk about it, let's first examine the standard TGE Software Developer Kit (SDK).

In this chapter, I will refer to the install directory of the SDK as "SDK/". You will need to translate this to your own install directory to find the files we are discussing.

For example, if you are using a Windows install and your SDK is installed in "C:\Torque\TGE_1_5_2\", then you will find the file "SDK/example/main.cs" at this location on your machine: "C:\Torque\TGE_1_5_2\example\main.cs".

## 6.2.1 SDK/

Assuming that you have installed TGE 1.5.2 on your system, you should have all of the following subdirectories in the installation directory.

> ➢ **"SDK/bin/"**. Binaries for tools of compiler(s) during engine compilation.
> ➢ **"SDK/doc/"**. Directory where doxygen documents are generated. Contains doxygen generation configuration file "doxygen.html.cfg" in a subdirectory.
> ➢ **"SDK/engine/"**. Engine source code.
> ➢ **"SDK/example/"**. Starter kits and demo.
> ➢ **"SDK/lib/"**. Source for various non-Torque libraries used in compilation.
> ➢ **"SDK/mk/"**. Makefiles.
> ➢ **"SDK/tools/"**. Source code for Torque tools such as buildWad, map2dif, and various exporters.
> ➢ **"SDK/vc6/"**. Visual Studio 6 build files. Builds with this tool are now deprecated. Use Visual Studio 7 (2003) or 8 (2005) to build the engine.
> ➢ **"SDK/vc7/"**. Visual Studio 7 (2003) build files.
> ➢ **"SDK/VS2005/"**. Visual Studio 8 (2005) build files.
> ➢ **"SDK/xcode/"**. OS X Xcode build files.

## 6.2.2 SDK/example

During this chapter, we will be operating on files and directories that normally reside in the "SDK/example/" subdirectory.

> ➢ **"SDK/example/common/"**. Common mod files used by all kits.
> ➢ **"SDK/example/creator/"**. World Creator mod. This directory contains the files necessary to run the World Creator. By not installing this mod, you can remove the user's ability to edit a game. We won't be discussing the contents of this directory any further in this chapter.
> ➢ **"SDK/example/demo/"**. The TGE demo. This is primarily used to show off the features of Torque, but for advanced users, it can be a source of sample scripts. It is worth digging through these scripts at a later time to learn more about Torque. However, we won't be discussing the contents of this directory any further in this chapter.
> ➢ **"SDK/example/show/"**. This is a remnant directory containing the scripts and other files used by the original show tool. This tool has since been superseded by the separate and external ShowTool Pro. We use ShowTool Pro in an exercise for chapter 8, but we won't be discussing the contents of this directory any further in this chapter.
> ➢ **"SDK/example/starter.fps/"**. First-person shooter starter kit. This kit is the basis for many TGE users' first games. I have used it in combination

with parts of "starter.racing" and some minor modifications to produce the exercise kit we use during this guide.

➢ **"SDK/example/starter.racing/"**. Racing starter kit. This kit is very similar to the "starter.fps" kit, but it is focused on demonstrating the design of a basic racing game. Because it is so similar to "starter.fps", you can consider anything said in the subsequent pages to be equally true for this directory and its contents.

➢ **"SDK/example/tutorial.base/"**. Stripped down starter kit. This starter kit was added to provide a simpler starting point for tutorial creation. We are ignoring this directory for the remainder of this chapter, but you should feel free to examine it on your own time. It has a slightly different organization from "starter.fps" and is interesting.

➢ **"SDK/example/main.cs"**. This is the first script file that gets loaded by the engine when we start a game. It must be present in the root directory of your game ("SDK/example" in this case). As we will soon see, this file has the responsibility for initializing the game and loading all of the files needed to launch your game.

➢ **"SDK/example/console.log"**. This file will not be present until you run a game for the first time, but once you do, starter kits are all set up to produce this log file. It contains a log of all data that was dumped to the console.

This directory also contains additional files we won't be discussing, such as command/batch files, docs, etc.

## 6.2.3 Games versus Mods

In Torque, there are the concepts of a game and of a mod.

A game is the primary directory that is loaded by "main.cs". This game directory contains all of the files you need to implement your game, with the exclusion of those files and content that may have been provided by a mod.

A mod is a supplemental directory containing files (content and scripts) that are to be used by more than one game. In this way, it is possible to split out specialized and common files. With these files split out from the standard game, you can reuse them over and over in the implementation of new and different games, making this a nice time-saving and organizational mechanism.

### Overriding Mod Scripts with Game Scripts

How does a mod help in the implementation of game scripts? There are two answers.

1. A mod can help by providing a set of standard script definitions that are later overridden and/or supplemented by game-specific implementations.

2. A mod can supply scripts that are needed by a game. Subsequently, you may choose not to write game versions of these scripts and to instead use the mod versions directly.

Torque provides a number of features for overriding and supplementing scripts. Among these are the following two primary features.

➢ **Packages**. Mods and games may implement packages that can later be turned on (or not) and stacked. In this way, packaged console functions and console methods may override old console functions and console methods and still be able to access the old definitions (see package example below).

➢ **Namespaces**. Console methods all utilize namespaces to associate themselves with the proper instance(s) of objects in a game. As you know, this namespace mechanism is hierarchical and supports the ability to access parent implementations. Utilizing this mechanism, a game mod can implement a console method low in a namespace hierarchy, and a game can implement the same console method higher in the namespace hierarchy. This way, the game version of the console method overrides the mod version, and the game version can still make use of the mod definition (see namespaces example below).

## Packages in Use

To put the package discussion in concrete terms, let's look at a real example of packages in use in the "starter.fps" game.

By default, when "starter.fps" is loaded, the "common" and "creator" mods are also loaded. Furthermore, between "SDK/example/main.cs", the game "SDK/example/starter.fps/main.cs", and the two mods ("SDK/example/common/main.cs" and "SDK/example/common/main.cs"), there are four implementations of the function onStart(). Three of these implementations are in packages.

In "SDK/example/main.cs" we have this code.

```
function onStart()
{
  // Default startup function
}
```

In "SDK/example/common/main.cs" we have code similar to this.

```
package Common
{
  // ...

  function onStart()
  {
```

```
        Parent::onStart();

        // Do common work...
      }

    // ...
  };
```

In "SDK/example/starter.fps/main.cs" we have code similar to this.

```
    package FpsStarterKit
    {
      // ...

      function onStart()
      {
       Parent::onStart();

        // Do common work...
      }

      // ...
    };
```

In "SDK/example/creator/main.cs" we have code similar to this.

```
    package Creator
    {
      // ...

      function onStart()
      {
       Parent::onStart();

        // Do creator work...
      }

      // ...
    };
```

We'll talk about start-up and initialization in more detail later, but for now, let me just state that the three packaged and one unpackaged implementations of onStart() are stacked as shown in the following list.

1. Creator version of onStart() is on top.
2. FpsStarterKit version of onStart() is below Creator.
3. Common version of onStart() is below FpsStarterKit.
4. The "main.cs" implementation is not in a package and is at the bottom of the stack.

During initial start-up, after loading some scripts, the engine calls the function `onStart()`. Because of the stacking shown above, we get the following execution order.

1. The `Creator` version is executed first and immediately calls its parent version, `FpsStarterKit`.

2. The `FpsStarterKit` version immediately calls its parent version, `Common`.

3. The `Common` version immediately calls its parent version, the unpackaged "main.cs" version.

4. The "main.cs" version does some work.

Because each of the packed implementations call their parent before doing any work, work is done in this order.

1. "main.cs" version does work.

2. `Common` version does work.

3. `FpsStarterKit` version does work.

4. `Creator` version does work.

## 6.3 The Exercise Kit (Organization)

Now, it is time to turn our attention to the exercise kit that you should have installed while copying the accompanying disk to your hard drive in Chapter 1.

The exercise kit is a slightly modified version of the "starter.fps" starter kit and includes some assets from "starter.racing" as well as modifications I made to allow the loading of multiple chapter-separated missions. All in all, this kit is quite standard and a good example of a basic Torque game directory.

### 6.3.1 kit/

In the exercise kit directory, you should find all of the following files and subdirectories.

➤ **"kit/common/"**. A slightly modified version of the standard common mod directory.

➤ **"kit/creator/"**. A slightly modified version of the standard creator mod directory.

➤ **"kit/gpgt/"**. A more heavily modified version of "starter.fps" with aspects of "starter.racing" and my own additions.

➤ **"kit/main.cs"**. A slightly modified version of the standard "main.cs" script file.

➤ **"kit/console.log"**. A standard log file, generated anew on each run of the kit.

This directory also contains other files that don't need to be mentioned for now.

The exercise kit is located in the "gpgt/kit/" subdirectory at the location you copied the accompanying disk to. That said, in this chapter, I will refer to the install directory of the exercise kit simply as "kit/".

Because this guide is a follow-on to my first book, I have decided to continue to use the handy abbreviation "gpgt" in code and in examples.

## 6.3.2 kit/common

This is a slightly modified version of the standard common mod directory. The only modifications I have made are the addition of comments to certain files, console functions, and console methods. These comments are conditionally printed to the console and were added to assist with this chapter and learning about the script flows in general.

This directory contains the following subdirectories.

➤ **"kit/common/client/"**. Client scripts that may get overridden by the "kit/gpgt/" versions. We will dissect some of these later in the chapter while we discuss game phases.

➤ **"kit/common/help/"**. Data used by the common help dialog. We won't be discussing this further.

➤ **"kit/common/lighting/"**. Scripts and assets (PNG files) used by the Torque lighting subsystem. If you ever want to modify the general behavior of coronas, light fall-off, etc., you should look in this directory. However, we won't be discussing these topics any further in this guide.

➤ **"kit/common/server/"**. Server scripts that may get overridden by the "kit/gpgt/" versions. We will dissect some of these later in the chapter while we discuss game phases.

➤ **"kit/common/ui/"**. A base kit of frequently used GUI definitions and their support scripts. We will mostly be ignoring the contents of this directory, but you should be aware that it is here and that many of the GUIs for a standard Torque game are provided here and not in the game directory itself.

## 6.3.3 kit/creator

This is a slightly modified version of the standard creator mod directory. It provides the World Editor Creator tools and GUI editor tools.

As with the common mod, only conditionally printed comments were added to this mod. Otherwise, it matches the TGE 1.5.2 version exactly.

Beyond looking at the "main.cs" file found in "kit/creator/", we will not be discussing this mod any further in this guide.

## 6.3.4 kit/gpgt

This directory is the game directory for our exercise kit and contains the bulk of the scripts that we will be discussing in this chapter. In it, you will find the following subdirectories.

➤ **"kit/gpgt/client/"**. Client scripts and user interface implementations.

➤ **"kit/gpgt/data/"**. Game assets, including model files, textures, terrains, and mission files.

*You may freely use the HOW utility kit in any of your own projects and games. Additionally, you can find updates to this kit on the HOW website: http:// www.hallofworlds.com/.*

➤ **"kit/gpgt/HOWUtils/"**. The "Hall Of Worlds" (HOW) utility pack. I have included this pack to make it easier for me to create exercises. The pack contains a large number of scripted implementations for common scripting tasks.

➤ **"kit/gpgt/server/"**. Server scripts and game logic.

## 6.4  Game Phases

There are many ways that a Torque game can be organized and many orders in which the scripts can be executed. However, in all but the most rare cases, a Torque game can be described as having seven game phases. Each of these phases describes a set of actions that the game must execute in order to implement a game. These phases can be summarized as follows.

➤ **Start-up and initialization**. In this phase, the game engine executable is loaded into memory. Once loaded, the first thing it will do is locate and run the script file "main.cs". This file contains scripts that tell the engine what other scripts to load and how to initialize the game.

➤ **Mode selection**. At some point, usually after initialization, scripts will set some key global variables and will call key scripts to set the engine mode to dedicated-client, dedicated-server, or client-server.

➤ **Server mission loading**. If this copy of the game engine has created a server, that server will load datablocks and create server objects to prepare the game world (mission).

*When one uses the word "phase," it brings to mind the idea that some set of actions will begin and end discretely, and that there will be no overlaps. In fact, this is not true for Torque game phases. These phases can and do often overlap. Additionally, the engine will in some cases start work in one phase, switch to another operational phase, and then come back to the previous phase.*

*The purpose of the phase descriptions in this chapter and in this guide is to allow you to get your mind around the steps that a Torque game takes to run the various game types, and furthermore to see the relationship between these steps, regardless of the game type that is started.*

➢ **Connection**. At some point, at least one client will connect to the server, using one of the three standard connection types, single-player connection, listen-server connection, or dedicated-server connection.

➢ **Client mission loading**. If this copy of the game engine has created a client, that client will download datablocks and create ghosts after connecting to a server.

➢ **Game**. Once at least one client has attached to the server, and once all datablocks, server objects, and ghosts have been loaded/downloaded/created, the game will begin.

➢ **Resource purge**. When the current mission ends, the server and all clients will purge any temporary resources and prepare for another cycle of mission loading.

## 6.4.1 Exercise Kit Debug Output

In the preceding descriptions, I mentioned that I have modified some of the scripts in the common and creator mods. Additionally, I mentioned that the gpgt game itself is a modified version of the "starter.fps" starter kit. All of these have one common set of modifications, which is the addition of messages to key scripts, console functions, and console methods. These messages are conditionally printed and will help you while reading this chapter (and later) to understand and to see the order in which the scripts are run.

To enable this feature, you need to open the "kit/main.cs" file and locate the following global (by default, this global is set to `false`, disabling debug output).

```
$GPGT::MPDebug = false;
```

You simply need to set this global to `true` to start receiving additional message output. That output will always print messages of the following form.

```
====> PHASE path/filename ->: Message
```

➢ **PHASE.** This is a short string telling you which of the seven phases this message is associated with. Its possible values are START-INIT, SEL-MODE, LOAD-SERVER, CONNECT, LOAD-CLIENT, GAME, and PURGE.

➢ **path/filename**. This will show the path and the file that the call is being made in. This information is provided so you can find the line in question to investigate further if you need to.

➢ **Message**. All messages will tell us something. Most messages tell us the name of a function that was just called (with the arguments it received), but some will be status messages, telling us when something important occurs.

Keeping this in mind, let's take a look at the individual phases and talk about some of the things that happen in them.

## 6.4.2 Start-Up and Initialization

The most basic phase that all Torque games pass through is the start-up and initialization phase. In this phase, all of the following actions occur.

➤ **Executable loading**. The game is loaded into memory and begins to execute.

➤ **CPU and driver configuration**. The (optional) configuration of CPU features and the start-up of various drivers (sound, input, etc.).

```
Processor Init:
  Intel Pentium 4, ~3.35 Ghz
   (timed at roughly 3.36 Ghz)
  FPU detected
  MMX detected
  SSE detected

Math Init:
  Installing Standard C extensions
  Installing Assembly extensions
  Installing FPU extensions
  Installing MMX extensions
  Installing SSE extensions

Input Init:
  keyboard0 input device created.
  mouse0 input device created.
  joystick0 input device created.
  DirectInput enabled.
```

➤ **"main.cs" parsed**. The very first script that the engine looks for upon executing is one by the name of "main.cs". This file must exist and must be in the same directory as the executable for the file to be found.

➤ **Command-line parsing**. Most implementations of "main.cs" include scripts to parse the command line for additional arguments and to do something with those arguments. To enable this, the engine will stuff command-line arguments in a global array named $Game::argv, and the argument count will be placed in the $Game::argc global. Below is part of the body of a standard parser. In addition, individual mods may add their own parsers, named parseArgs(). This function is called as part of a normal "main.cs" parsing.

```
for ($i = 1; $i < $Game::argc ; $i++)
{
  $arg = $Game::argv[$i];
  $nextArg = $Game::argv[$i+1];
  $hasNextArg = $Game::argc - $i > 1;
  $logModeSpecified = false;

  // Check for dedicated run
```

```
if( stricmp($arg,"-dedicated") == 0 )
{
 // ...
}

switch$ ($arg)
{
 case "-log":
    // ...

 case "-mod":
    // ...

 case "-game":
    // ...

// ...

 case "-help":
    // ...

 default:
    // ...
 }
}
```

➢ **Mod loading.** Another thing that most implementations of "main.cs" do is load any mods that are specified, either as command-line arguments or as part of the script. In the case of the exercise kit, "main.cs" will load the mods Common and Creator.

```
====> START-INIT /main.cs -> --------- Loading MODS ---------
====> START-INIT /common/main.cs -> activating package: Common
====> START-INIT /gpgt/main.cs -> activating package: FpsStarterKit
====> START-INIT /common/main.cs -> activating package: Common
====> START-INIT /creator/main.cs -> activating package: Creator
```

You may notice that the Common package is getting activated twice during the mod-loading part of the start-up and initialization phase. The second load has no effect. Once a named package is loaded, subsequent attempts to load it again will have no effect. This means that for the exercise kit, we have the following mod-package stack.

➢ Creator.
➢ FpsStarterKit (re-used in gpgt game).
➢ Common.
➢ Base definitions, if any.

> ➤ **Initialize globals**. All during the above process, globals are getting set, either by "main.cs", by the mods and their scripts, or by the loading of defaults ("default.cs") and preference ("prefs.cs") files.

```
Loading compiled script gpgt/client/defaults.cs.
Loading compiled script gpgt/server/defaults.cs.
Loading compiled script gpgt/client/prefs.cs.
Loading compiled script gpgt/server/prefs.cs.
```

It is worth noting that at this point that neither the client side nor the server side of the engine is activated. The engine is modeless and ready to be set to any of the three modes, dedicated-client, dedicated-server, or client-server.

## 6.4.3 Mode Selection

The mode selection is a major branch in the code execution and is nearly invisible in terms of code. Why is this? Well, unless the currently running game is going to host the game (be the server), mode selection is made as a side-effect of the connection steps. To clarify, let's talk about the mode-selection steps a server goes through first.

### Dedicated-Server Mode

When setting dedicated-server mode, we generally do so by starting up the engine with a command-line call like this.

```
demo.exe -game gpgt -dedicated -mission gpgt/data/missions/barebones.mis
```

In this command-line call, we have supplied three arguments.

1. **-game**. This first argument specifies that the "gpgt" game is to be loaded.

2. **-dedicated**. This second argument specifies that the engine is to be started in dedicated-server mode.

3. **-mission**. This third argument specifies that the mission "gpgt/data/missions/barebones.mis" should be loaded (during the server mission loading phase.)

After the parser in "main.cs" parses this info and has finished other start-up and initialization work, it will immediately call `createServer()` (defined by the `Common` mod).

```
// common/server/server.cs
function portInit(%port)
{
 // ...
}

function createServer(%serverType, %mission)
```

```
{
 // Among other things, calls portInit() ...
}
```

The call to createServer() does the following.

➢ Calls a second function (in same file) called portInit(), which opens a port using the console function setNetPort().

➢ Assuming the port could be opened, enables connections with a call to allowConnections().

➢ If the global $pref::Net::DisplayOnMaster is not set to "Never", the engine calls startHeartbeat() to start advertising on any known master servers.

At this point, the engine is in dedicated-server mode. It then immediately jumps into the server mission loading phase. It does this when createServer() calls the onServerCreated() function to load datablocks, and then the loadMission() function to load the mission itself.

## Client-Server Mode

If we start a standard Torque game without the -dedicated command-line argument, it will load the standard splash screen(s) and then launch the main menu. From the main menu, we have two possible avenues that will actually get us to the game phase (our goal).

1. We can select a mission and cause it to be loaded (see Figure 6.1).

---

**Figure 6.1**
*Starting a mission. (a) Select a mission chapter. (b) Run the mission.*

(a)

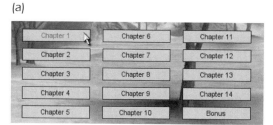

(b)

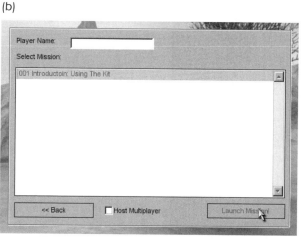

**Figure 6.2**
Joining a game. (a) Open the "Join Server..." dialog. (b) Join a game in progress.

(a)

(b)

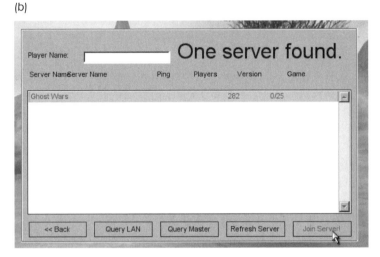

2. Alternately, we can open the "Join Server..." dialog and try to connect to a
   game in progress (see Figure 6.2).

If we make the first choice, we have effectively selected client-server mode,
although neither the server nor the client is yet active. Instead, when we click
on a mission (in the mission dialog) and select the "Launch Mission!" button
(see Figure 6.1(b)), we cause the following method to be executed (found in
"Kit/gpgt/client/ui/startMissionGui.gui").

```
function SM_StartMission()
{
  // 1
  %id = SM_missionList.getSelectedId();
  %mission = getField(SM_missionList.getRowTextById(%id), 1);

  // 2
  if ($pref::HostMultiPlayer)
   %serverType = "MultiPlayer";
  else
   %serverType = "SinglePlayer";

  // 3
  createServer(%serverType, %mission);
```

```
  // 4
  %conn = new GameConnection(ServerConnection);
  RootGroup.add(ServerConnection);
  %conn.setConnectArgs($pref::Player::Name);
  %conn.setJoinPassword($Client::Password);

  // 5
  %conn.connectLocal();
}
```

If we look at this code, we can see it does the following numbered actions.

1. It selects a mission from the list of missions and sets that as the mission to be loaded when the engine enters the server mission loading phase.

2. It selects a player mode. This will affect the connection types that are later allowed during the connection phase.

3. It calls createServer(), which, as we know from the discussion above about dedicated-server mode, will start the server side of the engine and will initiate the server mission loading phase.

4. It creates a server connection (a client), which effectively finishes setting this mode to client-server mode. It also sets up any password and name information to be used in the next step.

5. It calls connectLocal(), which connects to the local server and starts the connection phase.

## Dedicated-Client Mode

What happens if we select the second option and join a game in progress? In this case, we choose to operate the engine in dedicated-client mode.

Clicking the "Join Server!" button (see Figure 6.2(b)) will execute the following method, found in "Kit/gpgt/client/ui/joinServerGui.gui".

```
function JoinServerGui::join(%this)
{
  // 1
  cancelServerQuery();

  // 2
  %id = JS_serverList.getSelectedId();
  %index = getField(JS_serverList.getRowTextById(%id),3);
  if (setServerInfo(%index)) {

    // 3
    %conn = new GameConnection(ServerConnection);
    %conn.setConnectArgs($pref::Player::Name);
    %conn.setJoinPassword($Client::Password);
```

```
     //4
     %conn.connect($ServerInfo::Address);
   }
}
```

If we look at this code, we can see it does the following numbered actions.

1. It cancels any outstanding server queries (there is no need to keep querying if the user has already selected a server to play on).

2. It gets the server number (same as index in list) and fills the `$ServerInfo::*` globals with a call to `setServerInfo()`. This allows us to get the address of this server for an upcoming action.

3. It creates a server connection (a client). This effectively puts the engine in dedicated-client mode. It also sets up any password and name information to be used in the next step.

4. It calls `connect()`, which connects to the external server (LAN or Internet) and starts the connection phase.

## 6.4.4 Server Mission Loading

As you can see from the above discussion about the mode selection phase, there is only one case where the server mission loading phase is not overlapped with another phase, namely when dedicated-server mode is selected.

I mention this because the fact that this phase is often overlapped with the connection phase is often confusing for users. You have to remember that the engine is an event-based simulator and that there are no strict rules saying when an event can come in. In fact, the bad news is that even dedicated-server mode may see an overlap between the server mission loading phase and the connection phase. If a user attempts to connect as soon as the engine allows connections, this will happen.

In any case, the server mission loading phase is a very simple one, and it is controlled by three major functions, `onServerCreated()`, `loadMission()`, and `loadMissionStage2()`.

### onServerCreated()

This method, defined in both "Kit/common/server/game.cs" and "Kit/gpgt/server/scripts/game.cs" (which overrides the one defined in the `Common` mod), has the primary job of loading any datablock definitions that will be needed for the subsequent mission file load (next two functions).

```
function onServerCreated()
{

  // Set up some game specific globals, counters, and timers
```

```
    // Load up all datablocks
    exec("./audioProfiles.cs");
    exec("./envAudioProfiles.cs");
    exec("./camera.cs");
    exec("./markers.cs");

    // and so on ...
}
```

As can be seen by looking at this function, it basically sets up some game-specific globals, counters, and timers, then executes a bunch of scripts containing datablock definitions.

This isn't all that exciting, but it is critical that this be done before the next step.

## loadMission()

The next step is the loading of the actual mission file. In the file "Kit/common/server/missionLoad.cs", you will find the function loadMission(), which does prep before actually loading the mission. Below is a shortened version of this method (with extraneous steps removed).

```
function loadMission( %missionName, %isFirstMission )
{
  // 1
  endMission();

  // 2
  // increment the mission sequence (used for ghost sequencing)
  $missionSequence++;
  $Server::MissionFile = %missionName;

  // 3
  %count = ClientGroup.getCount();
  for( %cl = 0; %cl < %count; %cl++ ) {
   %client = ClientGroup.getObject( %cl );
   if (!%client.isAIControlled())
     sendLoadInfoToClient(%client);
  }

  // 4
  if( %isFirstMission || $Server::ServerType $= "SinglePlayer" )
   loadMissionStage2();
  else
   schedule( $MissionLoadPause, ServerGroup, loadMissionStage2 );
}
```

If we look at this code, we can see it does the following numbered actions.

1. It calls endMission(), which is a resource purge phase action. This is necessary because the loadMission() function might be called again

later to load a new mission (after this one is done) and purging resources is necessary between mission loads.

2. It increments the `$missionSequence` global (used in the client mission loading phase) and stores the name of the current mission in a global (for later use by `loadMissionStage2()`).

3. It checks to see if any clients are connected to this server. If so, it tells the client about the mission that will soon be loaded.

4. If this is not the first mission, or if it is a single-player game, this function immediately calls `loadMissionStage2()`; otherwise, it waits for a short period to allow any clients time enough to receive the data sent in Step 3. This is done because there is always a little lag time when sending data across a network.

### loadMissionStage2()

Eventually, after the last two functions have been called, this function (also located in the file "Kit/common/server/missionLoad.cs") will be called, and in this function, the server really does load the mission file. Below is a shortened version of this method (with extraneous steps removed).

```
function loadMissionStage2()
{
  // 1
  %file = $Server::MissionFile;
  if( !isFile( %file ) ) {
   error( "Could not find mission " @ %file );
   return;
  }
  exec(%file);

  //2
  $missionRunning = true;

  // 3
  $missionRunning = true;
  for( %clientIndex = 0;
    %clientIndex < ClientGroup.getCount();
    %clientIndex++ )
   ClientGroup.getObject(%clientIndex).loadMission();

  // 4
  onMissionLoaded();

  // 5
  purgeResources();
}
```

If we look at this code, we can see it does the following numbered actions.

1. It attempts to load the mission file, as was specified in the `$Server::MissionFile` global during `loadMission()`.

2. It sets a global to mark this mission as running. This is used later when clients connect to this server and need to decide if they can start loading the mission themselves.

3. Assuming success in the last step (the code that tests for success is not shown), the next step will be to tell all connected clients to load the mission (calls the `loadMission()` method on the client connection ID.) This effectively starts the client mission loading phase if there are any clients connected.

4. It calls the `onMissionLoaded()` callback to initiate the game phase.

5. It calls the engine function `purgeResources()`, which is technically a resource purge action. This may seem odd, but this particular function is a housecleaning function that deletes unused resources, making more memory available for the game to operate. Certain resources are created during the client notification and file loading process that can be unloaded at this point, so it make sense to do this.

## 6.4.5 Connection

As we have seen, the connection phase is one of those odd phases that can occur at various times and might well overlap other phases.

The connection phase is always started as the result of a call to either `connectLocal()` (single-player connection) or `connect()` (listen-server or dedicated-server connection).

### onConnectRequest()

Recall from Chapter 3 that the connect request will initiate a call (on the server) to a series of callbacks. The first of these callbacks is the `onConnectRequest()` callback. This callback is only defined in the Common mod in file "Kit/common/server/clientConnection.cs". We could of course create our own in the game files if we wanted to, but this default version is suitable for most basic games.

```
function GameConnection::onConnectRequest( %client, %netAddress, %name )
{
  // 1
  if($Server::PlayerCount >= $pref::Server::MaxPlayers)
   return "CR_SERVERFULL";

  // 2
 return "";
}
```

If we look at this code, we can see it does the following numbered actions.

1. If it detects that the current player count is greater than the value set as a maximum in `$pref::Server::MaxPlayers`, it returns a message `"CR_SERVERFULL"`, which is interpreted as a connection-denied response by the connecting client. (Recall that this will cause the client to call its `onConnectionRequestRejected()` callbacks.)

2. Assuming that there aren't too many players, this method will return the null string, meaning the connection will be accepted. This terminates the connection phase for this client-server connection attempt.

### onConnect()

The next connection phase action that will occur on the server is a call to the `onConnect()` callback (this assumes the connection was accepted in the last step). The standard version of this callback (located in the file "Kit/common/server/clientConnection.cs") does a lot of work that is specific to the "starter.fps" and "starter.racing" games, so I am presenting a bare-bones version below.

```
function GameConnection::onConnect( %client, %name )
{
  // 1
  sendLoadInfoToClient( %client );

  // 2
  if($missionRunning)
    %client.loadMission();

  // 3
  $Server::PlayerCount++;
}
```

If we look at this code, we can see it does the following numbered actions.

1. It calls the function `sendLoadInfoToClient()`, which will in turn notify the specified client about which mission it should load to participate in this game. This will trigger the client mission loading phase.

2. It checks to see if this mission is running (meaning `loadMissionStage2()` was called), and if so, it tells the client to start loading the mission. This starts the client mission loading phase for the specified client.

3. It increments the current player count so that the logic in `onConnectRequested()` continues to function properly. (As you may have guessed, this value is decremented in the `onDrop()` callback.)

At this point, the connection is established, and there isn't much else to do with regard to connections except to wait for more connection requests, wait for a disconnect(s), and watch all of the other connection events that we discussed in Chapter 3.

## The Other Connection Callbacks

There are a many other GameConnection callbacks that are part of the connection phase, but because they all have simple code in them, I am not listing their sources here. However, I want to mention what they do in the standard Torque games.

- ➢ **onConnectionAccepted().**          Calls the setLagIcon() callback.
- ➢ **onConnectionDropped().**          Calls disconnectedCleanup(), a purge phase function.
- ➢ **onConnectionError().**          Calls disconnectedCleanup(), a purge phase function.
- ➢ **onConnectionTimedOut().**          Calls disconnectedCleanup(), a purge phase function.
- ➢ **onConnectRequestRejected().** Calls disconnectedCleanup(), a purge phase function.
- ➢ **onConnectRequestTimedOut().** Calls disconnectedCleanup(), a purge phase function.
- ➢ **onDrop().**          Calls disconnectedCleanup(), a purge phase function.
- ➢ **setLagIcon().**          Sets or clears an icon indicating the connection is lagging.

There are also a few GameConnection callbacks (onDatablocksDone() and onDataBlockObjectReceived()) that are not in the connection phase but rather are in the client mission loading phase. We will discuss these shortly.

Before we continue our discussion, I want to point out the location of all files containing GameConnection callbacks. See Table 6.1 for this information.

| Callback | Located in File(s) |
|---|---|
| initialControlSet() | "Kit/gpgt/client/scripts/serverConnection.cs" |
| onConnect() | "/Kit/common/server/clientConnection.cs" |
| onConnectionAccepted() | "/Kit/gpgt/client/scripts/serverConnection.cs" |
| onConnectionDropped() | "/Kit/gpgt/client/scripts/serverConnection.cs" |
| onConnectionError() | "/Kit/gpgt/client/scripts/serverConnection.cs" |
| onConnectionTimedOut() | "/Kit/gpgt/client/scripts/serverConnection.cs" |
| onConnectRequest() | "/Kit/common/server/clientConnection.cs" |
| onConnectRequestRejected() | "/Kit/gpgt/client/scripts/serverConnection.cs" |
| onConnectRequestTimedOut() | "/Kit/gpgt/client/scripts/serverConnection.cs" |
| onDataBlocksDone() | "/Kit/common/server/missionDownload.cs" |
| onDataBlockObjectReceived() | "/Kit/common/client/missionDownload.cs" |
| onDrop() | "/Kit/common/server/clientConnection.cs" |
| setLagIcon() | "/Kit/gpgt/client/scripts/serverConnection.cs" |

**Table 6.1.**
GameConnection callback locations.

## 6.4.6 Client Mission Loading

The most complex-seeming phase is the client mission loading Phase. The reason it seems complex is because it involves a lengthy dance between a client and the server, and because it can happen many times and simultaneously for all clients as they connect to a server.

In this phase, a variety of functions and callbacks are called to initiate the transfer of data and to notify the sender that the data was received and more data can be sent.

To help you understand how this phase is a accomplished, I will discuss the steps this phase takes and refer the diagram in Figure 6.3, which illustrates the entire sequence. See Table 6.2 for a full listing of the files that contain the various functions and methods used in the client mission loading phase.

### Phase 1

#### Server

The `GameConnection` method `loadMission()` is called in one of two different places, depending on the circumstances.

➤ `loadMissionStage2()` will call this method if it detects that a client(s) is attached to the server (see Section 6.4.4).

➤ The `GameConnection::onConnect()` callback will call it if it sees that the mission is running (see Section 6.4.5).

In any case, once this method is called, it will tell the client to execute the command `MissionStartPhase1`.

#### Client

When the client receives the command `MissionStartPhase1`, it will call the `onMissionDownloadPhase1()` function to update the user interface and notify the player that it is downloading datablocks. Having done this, it immediately sends an acknowledgment back to the server in the form of a server command named `MissionStartPhase1Ack`.

#### Server

As a result of receiving the command `MissionStartPhase1Ack`, the server will start sending datablocks to the client. It will take some time for this action to complete, but when it does, the server will call the `GameConnection::onDataBlocksDone()` callback. In turn, this callback tells the client to execute the `MisionStartPhase2` command.

CLIENT MISSION LOADING PHASE

**Figure 6.3**
Client mission loading
phase diagram.

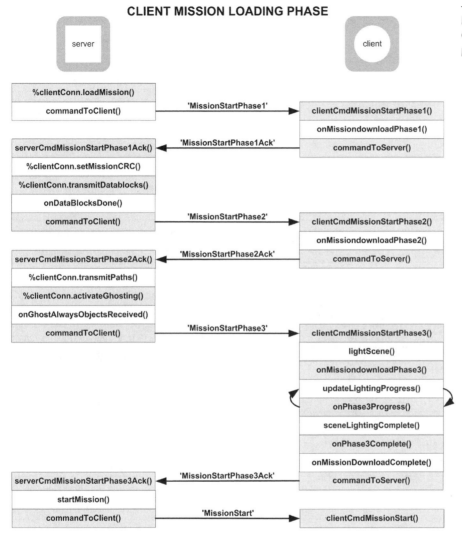

## Phase 2

### Client

Upon receiving the `MissionStartPhase2` command, the client will update its GUI, notifying the player that ghosts are being loaded. It will then immediately send an acknowledgment back to the server in the form of a server command named `MissionStartPhase2Ack`.

**Table 6.2.**
Client mission loading function, method, and callback locations.

| Function/Method/Callback | Located in File(s) |
|---|---|
| clientCmdMissionStart() | "Kit\common\client\mission.cs" |
| clientCmdMissionStartPhase1() | "Kit\common\client\missionDownload.cs" |
| clientCmdMissionStartPhase2() | "Kit\common\client\missionDownload.cs" |
| clientCmdMissionStartPhase3() | "Kit\common\client\missionDownload.cs" |
| loadMission() | "Kit\common\server\missionDownload.cs" |
| onConnect() | "Kit\common\server\clientConnection.cs" |
| onDataBlocksDone() | "Kit\common\server\missionDownload.cs" |
| onGhostAlwaysObjectReceived() | "Kit\common\client\missionDownload.cs" |
| onMissionDownloadComplete() | "Kit\gpgt\client\scripts\missionDownload.cs" |
| onMissiondownloadPhase1() | "Kit\gpgt\client\scripts\missionDownload.cs" |
| onMissiondownloadPhase2() | "Kit\gpgt\client\scripts\missionDownload.cs" |
| onMissiondownloadPhase3() | "Kit\gpgt\client\scripts\missionDownload.cs" |
| onPhase1Complete() | "Kit\gpgt\client\scripts\missionDownload.cs" |
| onPhase1Progress() | "Kit\gpgt\client\scripts\missionDownload.cs" |
| onPhase2Complete() | "Kit\gpgt\client\scripts\missionDownload.cs" |
| onPhase2Progress() | "Kit\gpgt\client\scripts\missionDownload.cs" |
| onPhase3Complete() | "Kit\gpgt\client\scripts\missionDownload.cs" |
| onPhase3Progress() | "Kit\gpgt\client\scripts\missionDownload.cs" |
| sceneLightingComplete() | "Kit\common\client\missionDownload.cs" |
| serverCmdMissionStartPhase1Ack() | "Kit\common\server\missionDownload.cs" |
| serverCmdMissionStartPhase2Ack() | "Kit\common\server\missionDownload.cs" |
| serverCmdMissionStartPhase3Ack() | "Kit\common\server\missionDownload.cs" |
| startMission() | "Kit\common\server\clientConnection.cs" |
| updateLightingProgress() | "Kit\common\client\missionDownload.cs" |

## Server

As a result of receiving the command MissionStartPhase2Ack, the server will start sending ghosts to the client by making a call to the GameConnection method activateGhosting(). It will take some time for this action to complete, but when it does, the server will call the GameConnection::onGhostAlwaysComplete() callback. In turn, this callback tells the client to execute the MisionStartPhase3 command.

## Phase 3

### Client

Upon receiving the `MissionStartPhase3` command, the client will update its GUI, notifying the player that mission lighting is underway. It will then begin lighting the mission. During this process, it will update the GUI to let the user know that progress is being made.

When mission lighting is complete, the client will tell the server that it is done by sending a server command named `MissionStartPhase3Ack`.

### Server

As a result of receiving the command `MissionStartPhase3Ack`, the server will start the mission and tell the client to start playing by sending it back a client command named `MissionStart`. At this point, the client mission loading phase is complete for the client that has been participating in this process.

## 6.4.7 Game

This second-to-last phase is composed of a number of user-defined functions and methods, most of which we will not be covering. Instead, I will introduce you to the most important functions, `startGame()` and `endGame()`.

### startGame()

In the standard Torque starter kits, once a mission is loaded, the server will immediately start the game, even if no clients have attached yet. It does this so the game is ready to go. Now, whether the game does anything during that time or just sits idle is up to your implementation changes.

The important thing to remember is that the `onMissionLoaded()` function, called during the `loadMissionStage2()` function call (server mission loading phase) will call the `startGame()` function immediately. A trimmed-down version of this function looks like this:

```
function startGame()
{
  // 1
  if ($Game::Running) {
   error("startGame: End the game first!");
   return;
  }

  // 2
  for( %clientIndex = 0;
    %clientIndex < ClientGroup.getCount();
    %clientIndex++ )
  {
```

```
%cl = ClientGroup.getObject( %clientIndex );
commandToClient(%cl, 'GameStart');

// Other client-specific set-up...
%cl.score = 0;
}

// 3
$Game::Running = true;
}
```

If we look at this code, we can see it does the following numbered actions.

1. It checks if the game is already running and aborts if it is. This error shouldn't happen, but it's a good idea to keep checks like this in your code just in case.
2. It notifies the clients (if there are any) that the game is starting, by sending each of them a client command named GameStart.
3. It marks the game as started.

### endGame ( )

As you have probably guessed, the endGame() method is not much more interesting. It is called when the mission ends, which can be for a number of reasons, most of which are dependent upon your game and its implementation, but if you want to learn more about these reasons, you should search for calls to endMission (no parentheses) and search back up the call chain in any functions that call it. For now, let's just take a look at the function and see what it does.

```
function endGame()
{
  // 1
  if (!$Game::Running) {
   error("endGame: No game running!");
   return;
  }

  // 2
  for( %clientIndex = 0;
    %clientIndex < ClientGroup.getCount();
    %clientIndex++ )
  {
   %cl = ClientGroup.getObject( %clientIndex );
   commandToClient(%cl, 'GameEnd');
  }
```

```
// 3
resetMission();
$Game::Running = false;
}
```

If we look at this code, we can see it does the following numbered actions.

1. It checks to see if the game is running, and if not, it exits. Again, this is just good basic error checking that should be present in any game.
2. It notifies any clients that are attached to the server that this game is ending by sending them each a client command named GameEnd.
3. It calls resetMision(), which is a purge phase command, and marks the game as not running.

## More Game Phase Functions and Methods

If you want to find more game phase functions to examine, you can search the code for the string "====> GAME". I also suggest running any of the exercises in single-player mode and looking at the console to see the order in which functions and methods marked with this marker are run. (Don't forget to enable the output!)

# 6.4.8 Resource Purge

This last phase includes a small set of mundane tasks that need to be done at various times. This task list includes the following actions.

➢ **Reset ghosting**. Any time a mission is unloaded, it is necessary for the server to reset ghosting for every client. It does this using the GameConnection:: resetGhosting() method. By calling this on a client connection, the server stops any ongoing ghost updates. This has to be done before the next purge step, clearing paths.

➢ **Clear path manager**. After resetting ghosting, the next thing that a server (that is unloading a mission) should do is clear all of the client connections' path managers. It can do this by calling the GameConnection:: clearPaths() method.

➢ **Delete** MissionGroup. Yet another thing that should be done when unloading a mission is to delete the special SimGroup MissionGroup. This SimGroup exists on the server and contains all of the mission's game objects.

➢ **Delete datablocks**. If the server is going to load another mission, the last thing it should do in the purge phase before entering a new server mission loading phase is to delete all datablocks. It can do this by calling the deleteDataBlocks() function.

➢ **Delete client connections**. Finally, if the server is shutting down, it should delete all client connections, thus disconnecting them.

**Multiplayer Games**

As with the game phase actions, it is easiest to learn more about this phase by simply running a single-player mission with the $GPGT::MPDebug global set to true. Then, just look for the string "====> PURGE" in the console (or the log).

# Advanced Scripting

## Part III

# Chapter 7
# Artificial Intelligence

## 7.1 Introduction

Torque provides three basic classes for implementing AI behaviors. Two of these are lightweight (with regard to networking requirements) classes where the AI entities are controlled by the server, and the third class is a heavy-weight script-controlled class used to replace the client's `GameConnection` instance.

## 7.2 `AIPlayer`

The first class provided by Torque to implement AI behaviors is the `AIPlayer` class. This derivative of the `Player` class is designed to implement autonomous non-vehicular players and opponents, sometimes referred to simply as bots. Instances of `AIPlayer` can be programmed to move to specific destinations, to aim at specific objects or positions, and to fire weapons.

### 7.2.1 `AIPlayer` Datablock Creation

The engine does not supply a new datablock class for `AIPlayer`. Instead, we use the `PlayerData` datablock to initialize instances of `AIPlayer`.

```
datablock PlayerData( BlueGuy : PlayerBody )
{
  shapeFile  = "~/data/gpgt/BlueGuy/player.dts";
};
```

> The `PlayerBody` datablock is supplied in all copies of "Starter. FPS," and the Blue Guy model is available on the GarageGames site. However, I have included a special copy of it in this kit. This special copy can swap skins, which the normal one cannot do.

In this example, we have created a new datablock (`BlueGuy`) that copies all of the features of the standard datablock `PlayerBody` and uses a new model for rendering and animations (`"~/data/gpgt/BlueGuy/player.dts"`).

### 7.2.2 AIPlayer Object Creation

Once we have a datablock to initialize our new `AIPlayer`(s) with, creating one is simple.

```
%mybot = new AIPlayer( Buddy )
{
  dataBlock = BlueGuy;

  //...
};
```

Here, we have created a new instance of `AIPlayer` named `Buddy`. `Buddy` is initialized using the datablock we created above (`BlueGuy`).

## 7.2.3 AIPlayer Movement

Out of the box, `AIPlayer` has four methods and two callbacks associated with movement. Additionally, there are resources on the GarageGames site dedicated to enhancing and evolving `AIPlayer` to do more. However, for basic AI behaviors you will find that this small set is quite sufficient.

### Basic Navigation

When I say basic navigation, I mean movement from one point to another point in the game world. All (more complex) navigation types depend on this fundamental feature.

To make an `AIPlayer` move to a specified point, we call the method `setMoveDestination()`.

```
%myBot.setMoveDestination("10 10 0");
```

In this example, we have instructed the `AIPlayer` we created above to move to location `"10 10 0"`.

As soon as we call this method, the bot will start moving towards that location, and once it reaches that location, it will stop. Easy.

### Slowing on Approach

It is possible to specify a (optional) boolean second argument when calling the `setMoveDestination()` method. If the second argument is set to `true`, the bot will slow down as it gets near its destination, where near is five or fewer world units.

```
// Go to position "10 10 0" and slow down
// when within 5 world units
%myBot.setMoveDestination("10 10 0" , true);
```

If you set this argument to `false`, or don't set it at all, the bot will always move at full speed.

### Stopping

I almost hesitate to write a section just telling you how to stop your bot because it is so simple. Simply call `stop()`, and if the `AIPlayer` is moving, it will come to rest.

```
%myBot.stop();
```

When setting move destinations, you can ignore the z-axis (elevation is ignored by `setMoveDestination()`) and leave it at zero. The engine doesn't use it.

## Setting and Adjusting Speed

When it is first created, an `AIPlayer` will assume that it should move at 100% of its datablock parameters' defined movement speed. As with any datablock parameter, these are considered static. However, there is an `AIPlayer` movement method for changing the speed at which an AIPlayer moves, `setMoveSpeed()`. `setMoveSpeed()` takes a single floating-point argument between 0.0 and 1.0, where this value attenuates the `AIPlayer`'s overall velocities.

> Section B.4 lists useful datablock movement parameters that can be modified to change an `AIPlayer`'s speed.

```
// Move at half speed
//
%myBot.setMoveSpeed(0.5);
```

## Getting Current Destination

At any time, it is possible to request an `AIPlayer`'s current destination using the `getMoveDestination()` method.

```
%destination = %myBot.getMoveDestination();

echo("Bot's current destination is: ", %destination );
```

## Resuming Motion

Calling `stop()` does not clear the current destination. It is possible to `stop()` an `AIPlayer` and then to resume motion by resetting the move destination to the previously set destination.

```
%theBot.setMoveDestination( %mybot.getMoveDesination() );
```

Also, as you might have guessed, it is possible to use the `setMoveSpeed()` method to temporarily halt an `AIPlayer` and then to resume motion at a later time.

```
// Stop moving
//
%myBot.setMoveSpeed(0.0);

// Resume full speed in 5 seconds
//
%myBot.schedule( 5000, setMoveSpeed , 0.5 );
```

## Reaching a Destination

In addition to the four movement methods discussed above, there is an `AIPlayer` movement callback that fires when an `AIPlayer` reaches its current destination. This callback, onReachDestination(), is useful for setting up a variety of goal-oriented responses such as waypoint navigation.

To use this callback, simply define it in the namespace of PlayerData, a parent of PlayerData, or using the name of the AIPlayer's PlayerData datablock.

```
// Using PlayerData namespace
//
function PlayerData::onReachDestination( %DB, %theBot )
{
}

// Using a parent's namespace
//
function GameBaseData::onReachDestination( %DB, %theBot )
{
}

// Using the datablock's name
//
function BlueGuy::onReachDestination( %DB, %theBot )
{
}
```

As you can see (from each of the three samples above), this callback takes two arguments. The first argument is the AIPlayer's datablock ID, and the second is the ID of the AIPlayer object calling this callback.

## Getting Stuck or Blocked

A couple of things can happen to prevent an AIPlayer from reaching its destination.

1. A bot that is blocked by an object will continue to attempt to reach its destination. It will continue to "walk" but may make little or no progress. With luck, it will eventually slide around the blocking object and continue on its way. However, there is no guarantee this will always work.

2. If a bot is blocked by a terrain feature (like a hill that is too steep), it may slide around and eventually pass around it or over it. However, it may walk up and slide back down the hill forever.

In either of these cases, we would hope that the engine might provide a means of sensing the problem. In fact, there is another movement callback, this one called onStuck(), that is supposed to be called when an AIPlayer gets stuck while moving towards a destination. Unfortunately, it doesn't work well.

For the `onStuck()` callback to fire, the bot needs to have an outstanding move destination and be stuck in the exact same place for several ticks.

In the first getting-stuck example above, the bot will move a little every tick. Because of this jitter, the bot will be considered to be making progress, and `onStuck()` will not be called.

In the second case, things are even worse, as the bot may move quite a lot.

## 7.2.4 `AIPlayer` and Weapons (Mounted Images)

Objects made with the `AIPlayer` class are able to hold weapons, to aim them, and to fire them. This is possible because `AIPlayer` inherits all mounting and other `ShapeBaseImageData` related features from `Player` while adding five aiming methods and two line-of-sight callbacks.

### Mounting Weapons

To provide an `AIPlayer` object with a weapon, ammo, and then to mount the weapon, we write code like this.

```
// Add a crossbow and crossbow ammo to the bot's inventory
//
%theBot.setInventory(Crossbow,1);
%theBot.setInventory(CrossbowAmmo,10);

// Mount the crossbow in slot 0
//
%theBot.mountImage(CrossbowImage,0);
```

> Please be aware that the inventory code used in this book is the standard code that is provided with "Starter.FPS", not `SimpleInventory` from GPGT.

### Firing Weapons

The `ShapeBase` class (a grandparent of `AIPlayer`) provides a method for triggering a weapon. We can use this triggering method to make an `AIPlayer` fire a mounted weapon as shown below.

```
// Pull the trigger on slot 0 weapon.
//
%theBot.setImageTrigger( 0 , true );

// Release the trigger on slot 0 weapon.
//
%theBot.setImageTrigger( 0 , false );
```

### Aiming (Looking)

There are five methods associated with aiming. Now, when I say aiming, what I mean is that the `AIPlayer` will look in the direction it is aiming. So, if you want to have a bot look in a specific direction, you can use the aiming methods. The bot doesn't necessarily need to be holding a weapon.

### Aiming at an Object

To cause an `AIPlayer` to aim at any `ShapeBase` derived object, just call the `setAimObject()` method and pass in the ID of the object to look at.

```
// Aim at the player
//
%theBot.setAimObject( localClientConnection.player );
```

In this sample, we have instructed our bot to aim at the player object whose ID is stored in `localClientConnection.player`.

If you were to do this in an actual game, you might notice something a little odd. What is odd is that the bot looks at the player's feet. This happens because when an `AIPlayer` looks at an object, it looks at that object's position, and the `Player` class modifies its position to be a point directly underneath itself. That is, `Player` position is its foot position.

Of course, if an `AIPlayer` is aiming at a player's feet and fires a weapon, the shot will probably miss the player and hit the ground. Fortunately, `setAimObject()` takes an aim offset as an optional second argument.

To provide an aiming offset, simply call `setAimObject()` like this.

```
// Aim at the player with offset
//
%theBot.setAimObject( localClientConnection.player , "0 0 2" );
```

> **Don't forget!** `setAimObject()` ignores non-`ShapeBase` objects. Therefore, you cannot tell a bot to aim at a `TSStatic` object.

This call will aim at a point two world units above the player's foot position.

It is probably obvious, but I would like to mention that once a bot is aiming at an object, it will continue to do so and will rotate its body to look in that object's direction regardless of the motion of the bot or the object.

### Aiming at a Location

Instead of aiming at an object, one could decide to aim at a fixed location (position), using the `setAimLocation()` method.

```
// Aim at world position "10 10 20"
//
%theBot.setAimLocation( "10 10 20" );
```

If this method is called, it will aim at position "10 10 20" and override any prior aim setting. In fact, any new call to an aim method overrides the last aim setting.

As with objects, the bot will continue to look at the last set aim location until it is told to stop or until it is assigned a new aim object or location.

## Getting Aim Position and Object

Torque provides two methods for getting an `AIPlayer`'s current aim, one for the object it may be aiming at and one for the location.

```
// Get bot's current aim object
//
%aimObject = %theBot.getAimObject();

// Get bot's current aim location
//
%aimLocation = %theBot.getAimLocation();
```

The above code will capture the bot's current aim object and aim location. However, if we have not told the bot to aim at an object, `%aimObject` will contain –1, indicating no current aim object is assigned. On the other hand, `getAimLocation()` will always return a value.

## Stop Aiming

There are several ways to make an `AIPlayer` stop aiming at an object or a location.

If we tell a bot to aim at an invalid (non-existent) object, it effectively clears the bot's aim.

```
%myBot.setAimObject( 0 );
```

Alternately, we can delete the object that an `AIPlayer` is aiming at to clear its aim.

```
%targetObject = %theBot.getAimObject();

%targetObject.delete();
```

Lastly, we can simply use the provided `clearAim()` method.

```
%myBot.clearAim()
```

## AIPlayer **Line of Sight**

The final interesting feature we need to discuss is the concept of line of sight as it applies to an `AIPlayer`.

When we tell an `AIPlayer` to aim at an object, it will attempt to keep that object in sight at all times by rotating to look at it. However, if at any time the bot's view of that object is blocked by any other object with a normal collision mesh and/or a line-of-sight collision mesh, the target object is considered out of line of sight. When this happens, we may want to modify our bot's behavior accordingly.

If you are not familiar with the terms "collision mesh" or "line of sight," see Chapter 8.

To tell us when an `AIPlayer`'s current target object goes in or out of line of sight, Torque will call one of two different callbacks named `onTargetEnterLOS()` and `onTargetExitLOS()`, respectively. The first callback is called when an aim object becomes visible to the bot, and the second callback is called when the bot loses sight of the aim object.

If you wish to use these callbacks, simply define them in the namespace of `PlayerData`, a parent of `PlayerData`, or using the name of the `AIPlayer`'s `PlayerData` datablock.

```
// Implement LOS callbacks using datablock name as namespace
//
function BlueGuy::onTargetEnterLOS( %DB, %theBot )
{
}

function BlueGuy::onTargetExitLOS( %DB, %theBot )
{
}
```

Here, we have chosen to implement bot callbacks in the namespace created by the `PlayerData` datablock's name.

## 7.3 `AIWheeledVehicle`

The second class provided by Torque to implement AI behaviors is the `AIWheeledVehicle` class. This derivative of the `WheeledVehicle` class is designed to implement autonomous wheeled vehicle players and opponents (I will sometimes refer to this simply as a wheeled bot). Instances of `AIWheeledVehicle` can be programmed to move to specific destinations and follow paths.

This class has very similar features to those provided by `AIPlayer`, so we can keep this discussion fairly short.

### 7.3.1 `AIWheeledVehicle` Datablock Creation

The `AIWheeledVehicle` class does not have its own datablock type. Instead, we use a `WheeledVehicleData` datablock to initialize instances of `AIWheeledVehicle`.

```
datablock WheeledVehicleData(DefaultCar)
{
  category = "Vehicles";
```

```
    shapeFile = "~/data/shapes/buggy/buggy.dts";

    //...
};
```

## 7.3.2 AIWheeledVehicle Object Creation

Once we have a datablock to initialize our new AIWheeledVehicle(s) with, creating one is simple.

```
%mywheeldBot = new AIWheeledVehicle( Zippy )
{
  dataBlock = DefaultCar;
  //...
};
```

Here, we have created a new instance of AIWheeledVehicle named Zippy. Zippy is initialized using the datablock we created above (DefaultCar).

## 7.3.3 AIWheeledVehicle Movement Methods

AIWheeledVehicle movement methods work almost exactly the same as the AIPlayer movement methods do. In fact, AIWheeledVehicle has all of the methods provided by AIPlayer and adds one more.

➢ **setMoveSpeed( speed )**. Set the overall speed for this vehicle between 0% (0.0) and 100% (1.0) of maximum speed.

➢ **setMoveDestination( position , [ slowdown ] )**. Set the movement destination to some position and optionally slowdown when within five world units of destination.

➢ **getMoveDestination()**. Get the current move destination.

➢ **stop()**. Stop moving.

➢ **setMoveTolerance( tolerance )**. A new method that allows us to set a destination-reached movement tolerance.

### Movement Tolerance

Because wheeled vehicles can move at a significant rate, Torque implements a movement-tolerance feature. This affects when the onReachDestination() is called. Whereas AIPlayer has to actually reach its destination, an AIWheeledVehicle utilizing a move tolerance greater than zero only needs to be within tolerance world units of the destination in order to trigger the onReachDestination() callback.

   For example, if we wrote the following code, our wheeled bot would call its onReachDestination() callback as soon as it got within 15.0 world units of the programmed destination "100 100 0".

**109**

```
%mywheeldBot.setMoveTolerance( 15.0 );

%mywheeldBot.setMoveDestination( "100 100 0" );
```

As you may have noticed, tolerances are specified as floating-point values, and they can be in the range zero to infinity.

## 7.3.4 AIWheeledVehicle Movement Callbacks

AIWheeledVehicle also has both movement callbacks found in AIPlayer.

➤ **onReachDestination( %DB , %wheeledBot )**. This callback is called when the wheeled bot gets to its destination or within tolerance world units of that destination.

➤ **onStuck()**. This callback should be called when the wheeled bot gets stuck, but as is the case with AIPlayer, this feature is too sensitive to jitter to work in most cases.

## 7.3.5 AIWheeledVehicle Tips

We covered AIWheeledVehicle pretty quickly, so I would like to take a little time to share some advice that will make your life easier when you design and use your own wheeled bots.

Section B.4 lists useful datablock movement parameters that can be modified to change an AIWheeledVehicle's speed and other properties.

### Remember WheeledVehicleData Features

Remember that AIWheeledVehicle is derived from the WheeledVehicle class and that it uses the WheeledVehicleData datablock. This means you can take advantage of all of the WheeledVehicle features, including the various movement-force settings, movement limits, physical parameters (mass, density, etc.), special effects, and so forth.

### Solve for Best Move Target

In addition to using sufficiently large move tolerances to hit a destination, you sometimes need to solve for alternate move targets. If you are making a racing game, it would be worthwhile to investigate a more elaborate means of selecting the next move destination than a simple waypoint. You factor in such details as current velocity, upcoming turns, and the narrowness of a driving area when setting a new destination. Ultimately, you will want to calculate destinations instead of selecting them statically.

### Slow Down!

Lastly, remember that you don't always have to drive at full speed. If you know a corner is coming up, slow down. It is perfectly valid to reduce the move speed (or to increase it) as needed.

# 7.4 `AIConnection`

The last AI class we will discuss in this chapter is a child of the `GameConnection` class and is named `AIConnection`.

Unlike the last two classes we discussed, which were designed to create server-controlled objects, this class is used to create scripted client connections.

This class is rarely used, but to be thorough I wanted to at least introduce you to it. So let's take a look.

## 7.4.1 Derived from `GameConnection`

As I said, `AIConnection` is derived from the `GameConnection` class and thus inherits all `GameConnection` features. In addition to those features inherited from the `GameConnection` class, `AIConnection` adds the ability to set movement and looking inputs as well as to set and clear triggers via script.

## 7.4.2 `AIConnection` Creation

To create a server connection using the `AIConnection` class, we write a small piece of code like this.

```
%conn = new AIConnection( ServerConnection );
```

If you have looked at the sample scripts, you will see that this almost exactly like the examples provided with Torque except that we swapped `AIConnection` for `GameConnection`.

```
%conn = new GameConnection( ServerConnection );
```

## 7.4.2 `AIConnection` Movement

`AIConnection` movement is controlled by two methods, `setFreeLook()` and `setMove()`. `setFreeLook()` tells the client whether subsequent calls to `setMove()` should be considered head-movement inputs or body-movement inputs.

### Setting Input Mode

For example, if we pass `false` to `setFreeLook()`, we are telling the client that future inputs should be applied as movement inputs.

```
ServerConnection.setFreeLook( false );
```

I like to think of this as setting the input mode for `AIConnection`.

**Table 7.1**
`setMove()` axis/angle strings and ranges.

It is a good idea to pass all axis/angle setting values as tags, i.e. `'x'` instead of `x` or `"x"`.

| Axis/Angle Setting | Description | Valid Range |
|:---:|:---:|:---:|
| x | Translation input in *x*-plane. | [ -1.0 , 1.0 ] |
| y | Translation input in *y*-plane. | [ -1.0 , 1.0 ] |
| z | Translation input in *z*-plane. | [ -1.0 , 1.0 ] |
| yaw | Rotation input about *z*-axis. | [ -pi , pi ] |
| pitch | Rotation input about *x*-axis. | [ -pi , pi ] |
| roll | Rotation input about *y*-axis. | [ -pi , pi ] |

## Translation and Rotation Inputs

Once we have set the input mode, we need to supply translation and rotation inputs. We do this with the `setMove()` method.

```
ServerConnection.setMove( 'y' , 1.0 );
```

In this example, we have instructed the engine to apply a translation input along the *y*-axis with a value of positive 1.0. This is the equivalent of a forward movement command.

In total, there are six axis/angle settings that can be passed in as the first argument to `setMove()`. These settings are listed in Table 7.1 with their descriptions and the range of values that they can assume (second argument to `setMove()`).

## Determining Current Movement Parameters

At any time, we can use the `getMove()` method to query the translation and rotation parameters.

```
echo( "Current y == " , ServerConnection.getMove( y ) );
```

## 7.4.3 AIConnection Looking

If we wish to apply inputs as looking (head-turning/aiming) inputs, we simply need to switch to free-look mode.

```
ServerConnection.setFreeLook( true );
```

After we call this line of code, any inputs applied to the client will be interpreted as looking inputs.

## 7.4.4 Checking Free-Look (Input) Mode

We can check whether `AIConnection` is currently treating inputs as movement or looking inputs by calling the `getFreeLook()` method.

```
%isFreeLookMode = ServerConnection.getFreeLook( );

if( true == %isFreeLookMode )
{
  echo("Connection is in free-look mode");
}
else
{
  echo("Connection is in movement mode");
}
```

## 7.4.5 Combining Free-Look and Movement

It is possible (within limits) to make an `AIConnection`-controlled player move and free-look simultaneously. To do this, simply place the connection in movement mode.

```
ServerConnection.setFreeLook( false );
```

Set the movement parameters you need.

```
// Running forward ONLY
ServerConnection.setMove( 'x'   , 1 );
ServerConnection.setMove( 'y'   , 0 );
ServerConnection.setMove( 'z'   , 0 );
```

Switch into free-look mode.

```
ServerConnection.setFreeLook( true );
```

And, as a last step, set your free-look value(s).

```
ServerConnection.setMove( 'yaw'   , 1.57 );
```

> Combined movement and looking works well for `Player` control but may not work so well for vehicles, since vehicles use yaw, pitch, and roll as movement inputs.

## 7.4.5 `AIConnection` Triggers

If you recall, the `Player` and `Vehicle` classes have up to six numbered triggers (0, ..., 5), and these triggers do different things depending on the class.

For example, triggers 0 and 1 cause the `Player` class to fire weapons mounted at mount points `mount0` and `mount1`. Also, trigger 2 causes the `Player` class to jump, whereas it causes the `Vehicle` classes to jet.

**Advanced Scripting**

`AIConnection` allows us to set these triggers by calling the `setTrigger()` method.

```
ServerConnection.setTrigger( 2 , true ); // Set trigger 2 to true
```

`AIConnection` also allows us to check the value of a trigger with the `getTrigger()` method.

```
%triggerValue = ServerConnection.getTrigger( 2 );
```

**Table 7.2.**
AI exercises.

| Exercise Summary | Location on Disk |
|---|---|
| `AIPlayer`: Basic creation. | /exercises/ch7_001.pdf |
| `AIPlayer`: Point-to-point navigation. | /exercises/ch7_002.pdf |
| `AIPlayer`: Looping path following. | /exercises/ch7_003.pdf |
| `AIPlayer`: Random path following. | /exercises/ch7_004.pdf |
| `AIPlayer`: Stopping and resuming. | /exercises/ch7_005.pdf |
| `AIPlayer`: Variable speed #1. | /exercises/ch7_006.pdf |
| `AIPlayer`: Variable speed #2. | /exercises/ch7_007.pdf |
| `AIPlayer`: Static speed settings. | /exercises/ch7_008.pdf |
| `AIPlayer`: Look-at position. | /exercises/ch7_009.pdf |
| `AIPlayer`: Looking at an object. | /exercises/ch7_010.pdf |
| `AIPlayer`: LOS callbacks. | /exercises/ch7_011.pdf |
| `AIWheeledVehicle`: Basic creation. | /exercises/ch7_101.pdf |
| `AIWheeledVehicle`: Looping path following. | /exercises/ch7_102.pdf |
| `AIWheeledVehicle`: Random path following. | /exercises/ch7_103.pdf |
| `AIWheeledVehicle`: Stopping and resuming. | /exercises/ch7_104.pdf |
| `AIWheeledVehicle`: Variable speed. | /exercises/ch7_105.pdf |
| `AIWheeledVehicle`: Static speed settings. | /exercises/ch7_106.pdf |
| `AIWheeledVehicle`: Move tolerances. | /exercises/ch7_107.pdf |

## 7.5 Exercises

I realize that this was probably a pretty fast chapter, but at the end of the day, working with the AI classes is pretty simple. However, because the first two classes are frequently used, we will do a bunch of exercises to be sure you know how to use them. Table 7.2 lists all of the exercises.

Have fun!

# Chapter 8
## Collision Detection and Response

## 8.1 Introduction

In a video game, collision detection is the process of determining whether a collision has occurred between two objects in the game world. Collision response is the process of acting upon these occurrences appropriately. Together, these processes determine how a player can interact with a game world.

In practice, the implementation of collision detection and response algorithms is an arduous task requiring significant knowledge, skill, and effort in order to produce. Fortunately for us, we need only make use of these features as they are provided by Torque.

## 8.2 Active versus Passive Colliders

To simplify subsequent discussions, we will refer to all objects as either active or passive colliders. An *active collider* is a moving object that causes a collision. A *passive collider* is always the object that was collided with. Passive colliders may be stationary or in motion.

## 8.3 Collision Meshes

### 8.3.1 Collision Mesh Types

In Torque, all shapes require a render mesh. On top of this requirement, if we wish to test a shape for collisions, a second mesh is required. This second mesh is called a collision mesh. Collision meshes are (generally) not rendered and are usually far simpler (in terms of polygon count) than a render mesh. Most collision meshes only approximate the shape of a model's render mesh.

Torque operates on two implementations of collision mesh, oriented bounding boxes and custom collision meshes.

An *oriented bounding box* (OBB) is a cube or cuboid that encloses all points on a shape. An OBB is a minimal bounding box and reorients when the shape does.

Torque automatically generates an OBB for `Player` and `Item` objects.

**Figure 8.1**
Oriented bounding box.

**Figure 8.2**
Custom collision mesh.

A *custom collision mesh* is a mesh provided by the model designer as part of a shape's design. That is, in addition to creating the (render) geometry of a model, we can also create a custom collision mesh. A custom mesh, like an OBB mesh, rotates with the shape it is attached to. It is possible to use custom collision meshes with any class.

## 8.3.2 Collision Mesh Categories

In addition to operating on two implementations of the collision mesh, Torque separates collision meshes into the following two categories.

➢ **Normal meshes**. A normal (collision) mesh is one used for standard convex-to-convex collision testing.

➤ **Line-of-sight (LOS) meshes**. An LOS (collision) mesh is used strictly for ray casting. Therefore, this type of collision mesh can be used for projectile collisions and for scripted ray-cast tests (we will learn about ray casting in Chapter 9).

> If you want a ray cast to hit an `Item` object, you must design an LOS mesh for that shape. The engine automatically disables ray casts against the `Item` OBB.

### Ray Casts versus Normal Meshes

Although it would be reasonable to assume that an LOS collision mesh is required for ray casting and other line-of-sight operations, this is not true. Ray casts and other line-of-sight operations will hit all normal collision meshes, excluding the OBB generated for `Item` objects.

## 8.3.3 Generated Collision Meshes

As I noted above, the Torque engine automatically generates an OBB for the `Item` and `Player` classes, so you do not need to create a custom collision mesh for `Items` and `Players`. However, if you want to, you can still create custom LOS meshes for each.

## 8.3.4 Custom-Designed Collision Meshes

Creating an efficient custom collision mesh is a nontrivial task. To simplify the procedure of making your own meshes, I supply a simple set of rules of thumb for you to follow. Additionally, I provide you with details on how the mesh-naming system works so you can keep your mesh names straight.

### Custom Collision-Mesh Design Rules

The rules for creating collision meshes are simple.

➤ **Rule #1**. Use only convex collision meshes.
➤ **Rule #2**. Create only as many collision/LOS meshes as are strictly necessary.
➤ **Rule #3**. Design each collision mesh using 20 or fewer vertices if at all possible.
➤ **Rule #4**. Follow the collision-mesh naming guidelines (provided below).

### Custom Collision-Mesh Naming Guidelines

TGE (versions 1.4 and beyond) supports an infinite number of custom collision meshes per shape. In naming these meshes, TGE follows a strict nomenclature based on a set of calculations that take into account the number of meshes a shape has.

#### Naming Normal Collision Meshes

Each normal collision mesh must be given a name of the form Col-*N*, where *N* is 1 for the first collision mesh, 2 for the second, and so forth. The meshes must be numbered consecutively.

## Naming LOS Collision Meshes

Each LOS collision mesh must be give a name of the form LOS-$M$, where $M$ is calculated using the following equations.

- $N$ is the number of normal collision meshes your model has.
- If $N <= 8$
  - The first LOS mesh is $M = 9$.
  - The second LOS mesh is $M = 10$.
  - . . .
- If $N > 8$
  - The first LOS mesh is $M = N + 1$.
  - The second LOS mesh is $M = N + 2$
  - . . .

**Figure 8.5**
DTS Plus naming.

## MilkShape and DTS Plus Exporter Mesh-Naming Exception

If you are using the MilkShape modeling tool and the DTS Plus exporter (and I strongly suggest you do), you must name the meshes as follows.

- **Normal meshes.** Collision-$N$.
- **LOS meshes.** LOSCollision-$M$.

### Rendering Custom Collision and LOS Meshes

The hyphen (-) in a mesh name tells TGE not to render the mesh. Switching this to a plus (+) and re-exporting is a quick way to visually check the behavior of a custom mesh during a game.

### Animating Custom Collision Meshes

The vertices of a shape's custom collision mesh can be attached to bones, meaning they can be rotated, translated, and otherwise morphed by shape animations. A moving mesh won't act as an active collider, but it will act as a passive one.

## 8.4 Collision Callbacks (Responses)

The following two classes in TGE provide collision-response callbacks.

- **ShapeBase.** ShapeBase objects can collide with other ShapeBase objects, InteriorInstances, and the Terrain.
- **Projectile.** Projectile objects can collide with ShapeBase objects, InteriorInstances, and the Terrain.

## 8.4.1 Shape-Collision Callbacks

When one ShapeBase object collides with another, an InteriorInstance, or the Terrain, the engine automatically executes at least one and possibly two different callbacks.

> ➤ **onCollision()**. This callback is used to catch standard collisions. It may be called for both the active and the passive collider.

> ➤ **onImpact()**. This callback is available only to a small subset of ShapeBase objects and requires activation before it can be called. It will be called only for the active collider.

All shape-collision callbacks are scoped to the datablock that was used to create the colliding shape.

### Why Two Kinds of ShapeBase Collision Callbacks?

You may wonder why the ShapeBase class provides two kinds of collision response callbacks.

This design choice was made because it allowed the Torque designers to easily separate out collisions with the ground from the normal collision-response code.

The onCollision() callback does not detect ground collisions, but onImpact() does. Since ground collisions are often ignored, this saves us from writing extra processing code.

As an additional bonus, the ShapeBaseData::onImpact() callback will also register collisions with TSStatic shapes, but ShapeBaseData::onCollision() does not.

## 8.4.2 Using ShapeBaseData::onCollision()

To use the ShapeBaseData::onCollision() callback, simply do the following.

1. Create a custom collision mesh for your model (not necessary for Items and Players).
2. Write your datablock and use the shape you just created as the model.
3. Write an onCollision() callback in the namespace of the datablock you just created.

For example, if we created the following playerdata datablock.

```
datablock PlayerData( BasePlayer )
{
  shapeFile = "~/data/BlueGuy/player.dts";
};
```

We would then specify the `onCollision()` callback for `BasePlayer` as follows.

```
function BasePlayer::onCollision( %colliderDB , %colliderObj ,
                                  %collideeObj , %collisionPos ,
                                  %speed
                                )
{
  // Do something about it ...
}
```

Now any collision detected by the shape created using the `BasePlayer` datablock will call the above callback.

## 8.4.3 Using `ShapeBaseData::onImpact()`

To use the `ShapeBaseData::onImpact()` callback, simply do the following.

1. Create a custom collision mesh for your model (not necessary for `Items` and `Players`).
2. Write your datablock and use the shape you just created as the model. You must also enable impacts during this step; see the `minImpactSpeed` and `groundImpactMinSpeed` discussions below.
3. Write an `onImpact()` callback in the namespace of the datablock you just created.

For example, if we created the following player datablock.

```
datablock PlayerData( BasePlayer )
{
  shapeFile = "~/data/BlueGuy/player.dts";

};
```

We would then specify the `onCollision()` callback for `BasePlayer` as.

```
function BasePlayer::onImpact( %colliderDB , %colliderObj ,
                               %collideeObj , %collisionPos ,
                               %speed
                             )
{
  // Do something about it ...
}
```

Impacts must be enabled, and they can be enabled only for these datablocks and their associated shape classes: `PlayerData`, `WheeledVehicleData`, `HoverVehicleData`, and `FlyingVehicleData`.

## minImpactSpeed

For players, AI players, and vehicles, impacts are enabled by specifying the field `minImpactSpeed` in the datablock definition. For example, we might enable impacts for a wheeled vehicle (traveling at a velocity greater than or equal to 25 m/s) as follows.

```
datablock WheeledVehicleData( TestVehicle )
{
  minImpactSpeed = 25;
  // Collisions >= 25 m/s are registered as impacts
};
```

## groundImpactMinSpeed

For players and AI players, ground impacts may also be enabled. To do this, specify the field `groundImpactMinSpeed` in the datablock definition. For example, we might enable ground impacts for a player (traveling at a velocity greater than or equal to 35 m/s) as follows.

```
datablock PlayerData( BasePlayer )
{
  groundImpactMinSpeed = 35;
  // Ground Collisions must be >= 35 m/s to register
};
```

## Ground Impacts

Ground impacts are gated by the general `minImpactSpeed` datablock parameter. This means that if `minImpactSpeed` is greater than `groundImpactMinSpeed`, ground impacts will not register until a collision occurs at a velocity greater than or equal to `minImpactSpeed`.

## 8.4.4 Callback-Writing Rules

When writing your callbacks, remember the following rules.

- ➢ **Rule #1**. Write callbacks only for active colliders that are required to respond to a collision.
- ➢ **Rule #2**. Write callbacks in the namespace of the shape's datablock.
- ➢ **Rule #3**. Account for cases in which both `onCollision()` and `onImpact()` may be called.

## 8.4.5 Using `ProjectileData::onCollision()`

The `ProjectileData` datablock class also implements an `onCollision()` callback. It is similar in behavior and signature to the `ShapeBaseData` version, with some important differences in the data that is passed to this callback. Additionally, any collision generated by a projectile calls only the `ProjectileData::onCollision()` callback. The passive collider never receives a callback.

## 8.5 Collision Tables and Rules

When you start using Torque, it can be a little confusing trying to remember which collision callback will be called and when. Therefore, I am supplying three collision tables and simple rules.

### 8.5.1 `ShapeBaseData::onCollision()` Table and Rules

When testing for `ShapeBaseData::onCollision()` calls, we need to test both objects, regardless of whether or not they are moving. We do this by taking turns checking the objects against Table 8.1.

**Table 8.1**
`ShapeBaseData::onCollision().`

| Object A | Object B |
|----------|----------|
| AIPlayer | AIPlayer<br>Item<br>Player<br>StaticShape<br>Vehicle |
| Item | AIPlayer<br>Player<br>StaticShape<br>Vehicle |
| Player | AIPlayer<br>Item<br>Player<br>StaticShape<br>Terrain<br>Vehicle |
| StaticShape | AIPlayer<br>Item<br>Player<br>Vehicle |
| Vehicle | AIPlayer<br>InteriorInstance<br>Item<br>Player<br>StaticShape<br>Terrain<br>Vehicle |

## Test Step #1

We always start our testing by selecting one object as Object A and one as Object B (as in Table 8.1). The onCollision() callback will be called for Object A if

➤ Object A's class is under the Object A column, and

➤ Object B's class is under the Object B column in the same row as Object A's class name.

## Test Step #2

The next step is to swap Objects A and B and redo the test. So the object we called Object A is now Object B, and vice versa. Again, the onCollision() callback will be called for Object A if

➤ Object A's class is under the Object A column, and

➤ Object B's class is under the Object B column in the same row as Object A's class name.

## Example `ShapeBaseData::onCollision()` Scenarios

### `ShapeBaseData::onCollision()` Called for Both Colliders

Let's say we have an AIPlayer and a StaticShape.

First, we treat AIPlayer as Object A and StaticShape as Object B. A quick look-up in Table 8.1 will show that AIPlayer is in the first row under the Object A column. And in the same row under the Object B column, we find StaticShape. Therefore, the ShapeBaseData::onCollision() callback will be called for the AIPlayer object.

Now we swap A for B and redo the test. Another quick look-up in Table 8.1 shows that StaticShape is in the fourth row under the Object A column, and we find AIPlayer in the same row under the Object B column. Therefore, the ShapeBaseData::onCollision() callback will be also called for the StaticShape object.

### `ShapeBaseData::onCollision()` Not Called for Either Collider

Now let's suppose we have two shapes, both of which are Items. Knowing the rules, we look up the Item class under the Object A column and then try to find it in the same row under the Object B column. We don't find it, meaning that the ShapeBaseData::onCollision() callback will not be called for either object.

Of course, this example is a bit silly since items can't collide with items.

**123**

**Table 8.2**
**ShapeBaseData::**
**onImpact().**

| Active Collider | Passive Collider |
|---|---|
| AIPlayer | InteriorInstance<br>StaticShape<br>Terrain<br>TSStatic<br>Vehicle |
| Player | InteriorInstance<br>StaticShape<br>Terrain<br>TSStatic<br>Vehicle |
| Vehicle | Terrain |

## 8.5.2 The `ShapeBaseData::onImpact()` Table and Rules

Testing for `ShapeBaseData::onImpact()` calls is the next test. This callback is *only* called for active colliders: an object has to be moving for `onImpact()` to be called.

### The Test

The active collider's `onCollision()` callback will be called if

➤ the active collider's class is in the Active Collider column of Table 8.2, and

➤ the passive collider's class is under the Passive Collider column of Table 8.2 in the same row as the active collider's class.

## 8.5.3 The `ProjectileData::onCollision()` Table and Rules

Testing for calls to `ProjectileData::onCollision()` is the simplest of all three tests. Projectiles register only collisions against the objects listed in Table 8.3.

**Table 8.3**
**ProjectileData::**
**onImpact().**

| Object Classes Projectiles Can Collide With |
|---|
| AIPlayer |
| Projectile |
| TSStatic |
| InteriorInstance |
| StaticShape |
| Vehicle |
| Player |
| Terrain |

## 8.5.4 Special Cases

### Item Deletion and Callbacks

You may be surprised to find that items often will not call their `onCollision()` callback. At first this may seem rather mysterious, but if you investigate, you will find that the item is being deleted before the callback can be called. This happens if you implement an inventory system and the item is deleted during pickup.

### Tires Do Not Call `onCollision()`

It is important to remember that tires do not call the `onCollision()` callback. Only the chassis (body) of a vehicle can do this.

### Only Vehicles Call `onCollision()` Against `InteriorInstances`

It is also useful to know that only the `vehicle` classes call `onCollision()` for collisions with `InteriorInstances`. All other shapes ignore these collisions.

### Catching Collisions with `TSStatic` Objects

The `onCollision()` callback does not catch collisions with `TSStatic` objects at all, but if you check, you will see that `Player` objects (and `AIPlayer` objects) can register a collision with a `TSStatic` object using the `onImpact()` callback.

### Ballistic Arming Delays and Collisions

Don't forget that ballistic projectiles with a nonzero arming delay will not collide with anything until the delay time has elapsed. This means no `onCollision()` callbacks will be issued until that time is up.

| Exercise Summary | Location on Disk |
|---|---|
| Use ShowTool Pro to examine collision meshes. | /exercises/ch8_001.pdf |
| Because the images in this chapter benefit from the use of color and the images in this book are printed in grayscale, I am including color images in this PDF file. | /exercises/colorimages.pdf |

Table 8.4.
Collision detection and response exercises.

## 8.6 Exercises

We won't actually do any exercises involving collision detection and response until the next chapter, but I did want to take the opportunity to examine a few collision meshes, so one exercise has been supplied for folks who use the ShowTool Pro.

# Chapter 9
# Containers and Ray Casting

## 9.1 Introduction

### 9.1.1 Containers

In Torque, a container is specified as any polygon enclosing a world volume. For the purpose of this chapter, we are interested in non-rendered, mathematically defined containers that are used for searching a world volume. These containers come in two basic forms, a sphere and a rectangular prism. Torque provides a few ways to search/test the volume of these two container types for the presences or absence of objects.

### 9.1.2 Rays and Ray Casting

A traditional ray is a mathematical construct defined as a point and a directional vector (see Figure 9.1). It is possible to extend a ray so that its tail is at a specified starting position and its head is at a specified ending position. Furthermore, using collision-detection algorithms, it is possible to see if this ray intersects (collides with) any objects between its starting and ending points (see Figure 9.2).

This concept of determining intersection takes us to the heart of what we use ray casting for. When we cast a ray in games, we are checking to see if there are objects in a direct line between a starting point and an ending point. This tells us if we can see to the end of the ray, whether objects cast along the ray will hit anything, etc.

**Figure 9.1**
A ray.

**Figure 9.2**
A ray intersecting objects.

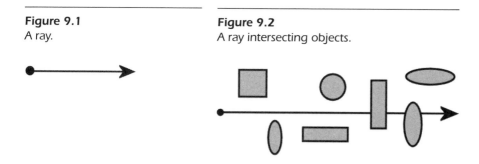

127

## 9.1.3 Type Masks

TGE defines 29 bitmasks that it uses internally and in scripts to differentiate object types. 24 of these bitmasks are exposed to the console in the form of global variables that use names of the form $TypeMasks::XYZ, where XYZ is an object class name followed by ObjectType. For example, $TypeMasks::CameraObjectType is the type bitmask for a Camera object.

When working with ray casts and container searches, we may wish to filter objects based on their type. To do this, we use type masks.

**Figure 9.3**
**TypeMasks** hierarchy.

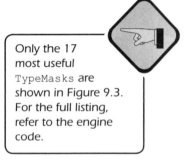

Only the 17 most useful TypeMasks are shown in Figure 9.3. For the full listing, refer to the engine code.

$TypeMasks::GameBaseObjectType

➤ $TypeMasks::EnvironmentObjectType

➤ $TypeMasks::ExplosionObjectType

➤ $TypeMasks::ProjectileObjectType

➤ $TypeMasks::ShapeBaseObjectType

　➤ $TypeMasks::CameraObjectType

　➤ $TypeMasks::ItemObjectType

　➤ $TypeMasks::MarkerObjectType

　➤ $TypeMasks::PlayerObjectType

　➤ $TypeMasks::StaticShapeObjectType

　➤ $TypeMasks::VehicleObjectType

➤ $TypeMasks::TriggerObjectType

$TypeMasks::InteriorObjectType

$TypeMasks::StaticObjectType

$TypeMasks::TerrainObjectType

$TypeMasks::VehicleBlockerObjectType

$TypeMasks::WaterObjectType

## Mask All Is –1

When doing a ray cast or container search, if you which to find any and all objects without filtering any out, simply set the type mask to –1.

This works because (in two's-complement notation) setting all the bits in an integer to 1 (on) is the equivalent of the decimal value –1.

# 9.2 Finding Objects via Ray Cast

Torque provides a single function, `containerRayCast()`, for finding objects along a ray. Using the `containerRayCast()` function is simple. If, for example, we have a player object named Bob and we want to cast a ray in front of Bob for 100 world units to check for a ray collision with any and all object types, we can write the following code.

```
// 1
%startPosition = Bob.getWorldBoxCenter();

// 2
%forwardVector = Bob.getForwardVector();

// 3
%endPosition  = VectorScale( %forwardVector , 100 );
%endPosition  = VectorAdd( %startPosition, %endPosition );

// 4
%hitObject = containerRayCast( %startPosition ,
%endPosition, -1 , Bob );
```

Breaking down the steps we took above, we see the following.

1. We determined Bob's starting position (using an object's center is usually best.)
2. We determined Bob's forward-pointing vector (be aware that this vector is automatically normalized by TGE).
3. We scaled Bob's forward vector by 100 and then added in his starting position to get the end position for our ray.
4. We used `containerRayCast()` to cast a ray from Bob's position to the ending position we calculated. Furthermore, we told the function to look for all object types (a mask of –1), and to exclude Bob from the list of hit candidates.

When we execute this code, the variable `%hitObject` will be assigned a value. If that value is zero, no objects were hit. If the value is nonzero, the value is equivalent to the nearest collided object along our ray (starting at the tail).

## 9.3  Finding Objects in a Cube or Cuboid

Torque provides two functions for finding objects inside a user-specified cube or cuboid, `containerFindFirst()` and `containerFindNext()`.

We use `containerFindFirst()` to initiate a new search, and we use `containerFindNext()` to iterate through the results of our search.

Let's look at an example to see how this is done.

In our example, we want to search for all objects of class type `Item` in a 10 × 20 × 15 world-unit cuboid centered at position < 10 15 20 >.

```
// 1
%obj = containerFindFirst(
            $TypeMasks::ItemObjectType , // Type mask
            "10 15 20" ,             // Cuboid center
            5 , 10 , 7.5             // Cuboid radii
            );

// 2
while( isObject( %obj ) )
{

  // 3
  echo("Found object ID: ", %obj );

  // 4
  %obj = containerFindNext();
}
```

Breaking the above code down, we note the following.

1. We initialized a search for all objects with a type mask matching `$TypeMasks::ItemObjectType`, where the object must be within the bounds of a cuboid centered at < 10 15 20 > and having radial dimensions of < 5 10 7.5 >.

2. We started a while loop that will exit once `%obj` contains a value that is not equal to an object ID.

3. We printed a message showing the ID of the current search object.

4. We requested the next object in the search-results list.

> Every call to `containerFindFirst()` starts a new search and destroys the results from the last search, so be careful when using nested calls to this function unless that is your goal.

When executed, the above code will iterate until the list of found `Item` objects is exhausted. Note that the search results are static, so if an `Item` moves into the cuboid bounds after the search is initialized with `containerFindFirst()`, that `Item` will not show up in our list unless we reinitialize.

## 9.4 Finding Objects within a Sphere (Radius)

Torque provides two functions for finding objects inside a user-specified sphere, `initContainerRadiusSearch()` and `containerSearchNext()`.

We search a sphere in much the same way that we search a cube or cuboid, except the function that initializes the search does not return a value. Let's look at an example.

```
// 1
initContainerRadiusSearch( "10 15 20" , 10 , $TypeMasks::ItemObjectType );

// 2
%obj = containerSearchNext();

// 3
while( isObject( %obj ) )
{
  // 4
  echo("Found object ID: ", %obj );

  // 5
  %obj = containerSearchNext();
}
```

If we examine this example we will see the following.

1. We initialized a search for all objects with a type mask matching `$TypeMasks::ItemObjectType`, where the object must be within the bounds of a sphere centered at < 10 15 20 > with a radius of 10 world units.
2. We retrieved the first search result outside of a loop using `containerSearchNext()` and assigned it to the local variable `%obj`.
3. We then started a while loop that fails as soon as `%obj` contains a value that is not equal to an object ID.
4. We printed a message showing the ID of the current search object.
5. We requested the next object in the search-results list using the function `containerSearchNext()`.

It is worth noting that the sphere search sorts the results list so that objects that are closest to the sphere center are returned first.

## 9.5 Calculating Container Search Distances

Torque provides two interesting functions, `containerSearchCurrDist()` and `containerSearchCurrRadiusDist()`, that go along with the two preceding (cube or cuboid and sphere) container searches.

Both of these functions give us information about the last object retrieved from a cube or cuboid or sphere search list.

**131**

Admittedly, both of these functions are a bit esoteric, but they might be useful in certain circumstances, so you should learn about them.

### 9.5.1 Distance to Search Center

The first function, `containerSearchCurrDist()`, allows us to get the distance between the last retrieved search object's center and the center of the search area.

For example, if we initiated a search at position < 0 0 0 > and retrieved an object whose world box center was at < 0 10 0 >, the following code would print the message "Distance to center is 10 world units."

```
%distance = %obj.containerSearchCurrDist();

echo("Distance to center is ", %distance , " world units.");
```

### 9.5.2 Nearest Point on Hull to Search Center

The second function, `containerSearchCurrRadiusDist()`, allows us to get the distance between the search center and a point on the last retrieved search object's collision mesh, where that point represents the closest point on the collision mesh to the search area center.

For example, if we initiated another search at position < 0 0 0 > and retrieved an object whose collision mesh had a vertex at < 0 0 5 >, the following code would print the message "Nearest hull distance 5 world units."

```
%distance = %obj.containerSearchCurrRadiusDist();

echo("Nearest hull distance is ", %distance , " world units.");
```

## 9.6 Box-Empty Testing

Torque provides a last function that allows us to test whether a user-defined cube or cuboid is empty (of object matching a specified typemask), `containerBoxEmpty()`. This function allows us to check if an arbitrarily sized box encloses (contains) any objects and is, like the other functions, easy to use.

For example, if we wanted to test an area having a world-unit dimension of < 100 200 50 > at position < 30 60 50 > to see if it contains any `Player` or `Vehicle` objects, we would write code like this.

```
%isEmpty = containerBoxEmpty(
            ($TypeMasks::PlayerObjectType | // Typemask
            $TypeMasks::VehicleObjectType),
            "30 60 50",                       // Box center
            50 , 100 , 25                     // Box radii
            );
```

Let's break down the arguments passed into `containerBoxEmpty()`.

➤ **$TypeMasks::PlayerObjectType | $TypeMasks::VehicleObjectType**. In argument one, we ORed together the two bitmasks we need to check for.

➤ **"30 60 50"**. In argument two, we passed the center position for our box test.

➤ **"50 100 25"**. In arguments three, four, and five, we passed the radius values for *x*, *y*, and *z*. It is important to note that these values are half the width of the box we want to test (they are radii, not widths). This may be a little confusing at first (since most people associate the word radius with a circle), but be clear on this point. The values need to be half the width you wish to achieve in the three dimensions.

If we run the above code, and if there are no `Player`, `AIPlayer`, `FlyingVehicle`, `HoverVehicle`, `WheeledVehicle`, or `AIWheeledVehicle` objects in the specified box area, the function will return `true`. Otherwise, it will return `false`.

Simple.

| Exercise Summary | Location on Disk |
|---|---|
| Basic ray cast. | /exercises/ch9_001.pdf |
| Ray cast versus collision and LOS mesh variations. | /exercises/ch9_002.pdf |
| Cuboid search. | /exercises/ch9_101.pdf |
| Sphere search. | /exercises/ch9_102.pdf |
| Box-empty test. | /exercises/ch9_103.pdf |

**Table 9.1.**
Containers and ray-casting exercises.

## 9.7 Exercises

Yet another small chapter has flown by, and now it is time to do some exercises to help this information cement. Note that these exercises use information from this chapter and Chapter 8, so be sure to read both chapters before doing the exercises in Table 9.1.

# Engine Coding

Part IV

# Chapter 10
## Introduction to Engine Coding

### 10.1 Introduction

All Torque owners have access to the full source code of the Torque Game Engine. This gives them the ability, in theory, to fix bugs, modify features, and enhance the engine behavior by adding new code. I say "in theory" because approaching any of these tasks can be difficult without proper experience and/or guidance.

TGE version 1.5.2 has 828 source files and about 230,000 lines of source code, not including comments. Add to this the fact that the engine utilizes higher-order mathematics, advanced graphics techniques, physics calculation, etc. to implement its functionality, and you've got quite a challenge in front of you if you do want to make any changes.

Fortunately, working with the source isn't as bad as it sounds, for two reasons. First, there are vast parts of the engine you will never have to touch. You can make the majority of changes you need by restricting yourself to specific areas and features. Second, you have this guide. In this chapter and the next, I will take you on a tour of those features and details that you are most likely going to use and need.

So, let's start our examination of the engine now, by talking about how it is organized.

### 10.2 Organization Of The Engine

### 10.2.1 The Simple View

If you have ever run the TGE demo, you have have seen the feature tour provided therein. In that feature tour you will come across an image describing the parts of the engine (Figure 10.1). This image is nice because it is simple and because it conveys the basic organization of the engine. In this representation, the engine has the following parts.

➤ The bottom layer is commonly referred to as the platform layer. It provides transparent and interchangeable support for the Windows, OSX, and Linux operating systems.

➤ Above the platform layer is the Torque porting layer. This layer consists of a set of system libraries, graphics toolkits, and math libraries that

**Figure 10.1**
The simple view of TGE.

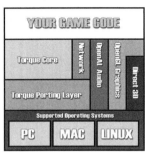

supplement and/or replace several standard ANSI C libraries. One must use these libraries instead of standard libraries to ensure consistent game behavior regardless of the platform on which your game is run. We will learn about much of this layer in this chapter.

➤ Above the Torque porting layer is the Torque core layer. This layer contains all of the game classes, interior classes, simulation classes, the scripting console, and the other code which provide the bulk of the engine's features. Although this block is shown as relatively small, it contains a significant amount of source code. We will be spending a good deal of time talking about this block in the next chapter.

➤ To the right of the Torque core layer and the Torque porting layers, one sees these blocks: Network, OpenAL Audio, OpenGL Graphics, and Direct3D. Of these we will mainly restrict our discussion to the networking code and then only in certain contexts.

➤ Lastly, there is a big block titled "YOUR GAME CODE" at the top of the image. This is for the most part scripts, models, sound files, and perhaps some engine changes. In other words, it is the content you add and modify to make your game on top of the engine itself.

## 10.2.2 The Directory View

Of course, it would be nice if the engine were as simple as Figure 10.1, but it is actually a little bit more complex than that. Table 10.1 lists the engine's major directories and describes the kinds of code you will find within them.

## 10.3 TGE Naming Conventions

Now, we are almost ready to start talking about actual engine code, but before we do, I'd like to take a short amount of time to discuss everybody's favorite topic, naming conventions.

If you are an experienced programmer, then you will already know that coding standards and naming conventions vary from organization to organization and even from project to project. In fact, you may already be familiar with more than one convention and may very likely have your own preferences.

The purpose of our discussion over the next few pages is not to convince you that the Torque conventions are the best and that you should use them. Instead, I wish to familiarize you with them so that you won't be confused and so that, if you should choose, you may follow them when making your own engine modifications.

| Engine Component | Purpose |
|---|---|
| **\engine\audio** | |
| OpenAL API | The Open Audio Library API is a LGPL'd cross-platform library. It can supply multi-channel 3D audio output and supports a wide variety of target platforms, including the three default Torque platforms (Win32, OS X, Linux). |
| Ogg Vorbis codec | Ogg Vorbis is an open-source audio-compression compressor-decompressor library. |
| **\engine\collision** | |
| GJK convex COLDET library | GJK (Gilbert-Johnson-Keerthi) is a real-time convex collision-detection algorithm. This directory contains an implementation of said algorithm, using Torque convex geometry storage structures. |
| **\engine\console** | |
| Scripting console | This is the scripting engine that by now you should be familiar with. It is tightly integrated with the engine core. |
| `ConsoleObject` base class `SimObject` base class | These are the base classes in the console object hierarchy. We will discuss them again later in this chapter and in Chapter 11. |
| `Sim` dictionary | This is a data structure used to track all registered `SimObject` derived objects. It provides mechanisms for quickly finding said objects using IDs and names. |
| `SimSet` and `SimGroup` classes | These are the base simulation container classes. You will find them used throughout the engine source and in scripts. Additionally, `SimGroup` is the parent to `GuiControl`. |
| **\engine\core** | |
| `Stream` classes | These classes provide a generic means for transmitting homogenized data streams between various sources and destinations. Some streams provide data compression. |
| Object ID utilities | The code for generating unique IDs lives in this directory (see "idGenerator.[cc,h]"). |
| `ResManager` | `ResManager` is a file resource-management class. It is responsible for providing read and/or write access to all file resources such as sound files, texture and model files, etc. It also reduces the game's memory footprint by guaranteeing that only one instance of any specific resource will ever be loaded at once, i.e., the resource may be in use by several game objects, but only one copy of the resource will be loaded. |
| `StringTable` | `StringTable` is a global string hashing and tracking class. It is designed to allow for the unique storage of strings and to provide short-hand (ID) references to the strings, thereby reducing storage requirements and comparison costs. We will take another look at this class shortly. |
| `FrameAllocator` | `FrameAllocator` is a fast memory allocation class used to provide temporary memory that can be used for memory operations in any single frame. It provides mechanisms for quick allocation and deallocation of small chunks of memory. |

**Table 10.1**
Engine directories content.

**139**

**Table 10.1
(continued)**
Engine directories
content.

| Engine Component | Purpose |
|---|---|
| `iTickable` base class | `iTickable` is a special class that allows one to create a lightweight non-`GameBase` tickable class (by derivation). Tickable objects provide per-tick processing, tick interpolation, and time-advancing methods. It is suggested that you use this class to derive new simulation classes that need to execute operations on some regular time basis. This bypasses the need to use the less-accurate and higher-overhead scheduling system. |
| **\engine\dgl** | |
| DGL | Dynamix Graphics Library (DGL) is a portable graphics utility library that extends OpenGL to support higher-level primitives and resources, as well as performing texture management |
| **\engine\editor** | |
| World editor tools | This is where you will find the source code for all of the world editor tools that are built into Torque. |
| **\engine\game** | |
| `GameBase` and children | Here, you will find `GameBase` and all of its child classes. These classes are used to represent and render all of the 3D content in your games, excluding interior and terrain type meshes (see \engine\interior and \engine\terrain). |
| `SimDataBlock` and children | Here, you will find `SimDataBlock` and all of its child classes. |
| `GameConnection` and children | Here, you will find `GameConnection` and its child class `AIConnection`. |
| **\engine\gui** | |
| `GuiControl` and children | Here, you will find `GuiControl` and all of its child classes. These classes are used to render all of the 2D output for your game. |
| GUI editor tool | This directory also includes all of the code for Torque's built-in GUI editor. |
| **\engine\interior** | |
| Interiors library | This directory contains the declaration/definition of `InteriorInstance`, as well as utility code for managing lightmaps, mirrors, the portalized subdivision of interior meshes, etc. |
| **\engine\math** | |
| Torque Math Library | This directory contains many portable math functions and classes, which are used throughout the engine. It also contains the code required to identify and take advantage of various math-related CPU extensions. |

| Engine Component | Purpose |
|---|---|
| **\engine\platform** | |
| Generic platform layer | This code is the foundation of Torque. Running at the lowest level, it provides a common cross-platform, cross-architecture interface to the system for the game. This code handles the details of file and network I/O, graphics and device initialization, device I/O, and time events. |
| Torque Standard Library | Standard library calls are proxied through the platform layer, so that the game code can be safe from platform-specific idiosyncrasies. |
| **\engine\platformMacCarb (Mac OS X)** **\engine\platformWin32 (Microsoft Windows)** **\engine\platformX86UNIX (x86 UNIX/Linux)** | |
| OS-specific platform layers | Each of these directories includes OS/platform-specific implementations of platform code that is then used by the generic platform layer. |
| **\engine\sceneGraph** | |
| Scene-graph library Zone classes and utilities | All of the code for the `SceneGraph` class and supporting scene graph utilities are included in this directory. The scene graph is designed to manage all objects in the game world, ensuring that they get processed at the right time and that the correct objects are ghosted to the proper clients (we will talk about this more later). |
| **\engine\sim** | |
| `ActionMap` | The `ActionMap` class is maintained here. |
| Decal manager | The implementation for the `DecalManager` and `DecalData` classes can also be found here. |
| `NetConnection` | The basic networking class is also implemented in this directory. It is responsible for streaming data between server and clients. |
| **\engine\terrain** | |
| Terrain, water, sky, sun, and all other "outdoor" object classes | All of the code for objects that make up the outdoor part of the world are located in this directory. This includes the following classes: `Sky`, `terrData`, `WaterBlock`, and `Sun`. |
| **\engine\ts** | |
| (Dynamix) Three Space Library | This special library implements the code required to read and use DTS shape files. It also provide all of the code for animating and rendering their meshes. This code is subsequently used by many of the game classes. |
| **\engine\util** | |
| Miscellaneous utility code | As the name implies, this is a dumping ground for various bits of utility code. Most of these utilities are related to rendering and collision calculations. |

**Table 10.1 (continued)**
Engine directories content.

## 10.3.1 Variable Naming Conventions

While examining the Torque source, you will see the following rules applied to variables.

➤ Global variable names are prefixed with a lowercase g.

```
gConsole->printf();
gManager = NULL;
```

➤ Member variable names of non-data classes are prefixed with a lowercase m.

- Data classes are those classes designed to be used in computations. For example, Box3D is a data class, while ShapeBaseData is not.

```
// A non-data class
//
class ShapeBase : public GameBase
{
 // ...

private:
 ShapeBaseData* mDataBlock;
 ShapeBase* mControllingObject;
 bool mTrigger[MaxTriggerKeys];
 // ...
};
// A data-class
//
class Point3F
{
 // ...
 F32 x,y,z;

 // ...
};
```

➤ Static member variables are prefixed with a lowercase sm. (This rule is not well followed in the engine at this time.)

```
static S32 SomeClass::smSomeVariable;
```

➤ All non-constant variables use lowerCamelCase.

```
S32 mMemberVariable; // good member variable
F32 volumeLevel; // good local variable
```

➤ All constant variables use uppercase and words are separated by under-scores.

➤ const is preferred over the use of #define, because the compiler will catch incorrectly typed const definitions, whereas #define statements are ambiguous.

```
#define MAX_FILE_SIZE 256 // good
const S32 MAX_FILE_SIZE = 256; // better
```

➤ Inline functions are (generally) preferred over #define macros.

```
#define IS_EQUAL( a , b ) ( a == b ) // bad
```

```
inline bool IsEqual(F32 a, F32 b) { return a == b; } // good
```

➢ Pointers have the asterisk next to the variable name, not the type name. This is to prevent confusion.

```
char* myFirstPointer, mySecondPointer; // Unclear
char *myFirstPointer, *mySecondPointer; // Very Clear
```

## 10.3.2 Function, Class, and Method Naming Conventions

While examining the Torque source, you will see the following rules applied to functions, classes, and methods.

➢ Function names should use lowerCamelCase.

```
S32 thisIsAGoodFunctionName( )
{
}
```

➢ Class names should use UpperCamelCase.

```
class ShapeBaseData
{
 // ...
};
```

➢ Method names (excluding constructors and destructors) should use lower-CamelCase

```
class Container
{
 Container();

 ~Container();

 // ...

 void findObjects( ... );
};
```

## 10.4 Torque Data Types

The C and C++ languages have built-in (intrinsic) types. A list of these types includes `int`, `char`, `float`, and other type names. For general computing, these types and type names are sufficient, but in a multi-platform game engine, these types suddenly becoming lacking.

To solve this problem, Torque supplies its own set of data types, which are frequently used instead of the intrinsic types. These types are part of the Torque porting layer we discussed above. Table 10.2 lists these types and their intrinsic matches. TGE was designed with portability and future compatibility in mind. Also, much attention was given to reducing ambiguity. Lastly,

**Engine Coding**

**Table 10.2**

Intrinsic versus Torque
data types.

| Intrinsic Type | Torque Type | Description |
|:---:|:---:|:---|
| signed char | S8 | 8-bit signed integer. |
| signed short | S16 | 16-bit signed integer. |
| signed int | S32 | 32-bit signed integer. |
| unsigned char | U8 | 8-bit unsigned integer. |
| unsigned short | U16 | 16-bit unsigned integer. |
| unsigned int | U32 | 32-bit unsigned integer. |
| float | F32 | 32-bit floating-point. |
| double | F64 | 64-bit floating-point. |
| char | UTF8 | 8-bit Unicode character. |
| unsigned short | UTF16 | 16-bit Unicode character. |
| unsigned int | UTF32 | 32-bit Unicode character. |

because data is often sent across networks, it is crucial to know the exact bit widths of that data. The Torque data types were designed to enable and provide these features.

As you examine the engine code, you will see that both Torque data types and intrinsic data types are used. This raises the question, "When should I use a Torque data type?" The answer is, "You should always use Torque data types when writing engine code that will be transmitted over a network or exposed to the console." Alternatively, simply using Torque data types all of the time is also valid.

For the most part, the engine header files will already sub-include the header file that defines these types. So, you can use these types just like you use intrinsic types.

```
// Code using intrinsic type
//
int i = -10;

// Code using Torque data type
//
S32 j = -10;
```

However, if you do find yourself in a situation where your code won't compile because of a Torque type, be sure to include the file "platform/types.h".

## 10.4.1 Torque Data Type Constants

To assist with the initialization and (loop) bounding of Torque data types, the engine supplies a short list of Torque data type constants (also defined in "platform/types.h") for your use.

- ➤ **Float_One**. 1.0f
- ➤ **Float_Half**. 0.5f
- ➤ **Float_Zero**. 0.0f
- ➤ **Float_Pi**. (float) pi
- ➤ **Float_2Pi**. (float) (2 * pi)
- ➤ *TYPE_MIN* / *TYPE_MAX*. Minimum and maximum values for variables of the specified *TYPE* (F32, S8, S16, S32, U16, U32). (Actually, U8_MIN, U16_MIN, and U32_MIN are not defined. As unsigned values, the min for each of these is simply 0.)
  - For example, S8_MIN is -128, while S8_MAX is 128.

## 10.4.2 Torque Data Type Utility Functions

Lastly, Torque supplies a small set of functions for doing common (utility) work with the Torque types.

- ➤ **U32 getNextPow2(U32 io_num )**. Returns a U32 value which is the next power-of-two greater than the passed value io_num.
- ➤ **U32 getBinLog2(U32 io_num )**. Returns a U32 value equal to LOG2( io_num ). (io_num must be a power of two for this to work.)
- ➤ **bool isPow2(U32 in_num )**. Returns true if in_num is a power of two.
- ➤ *TYPE* **getMin( *TYPE* a , *TYPE* b )**. Returns a or b, depending upon which is the smallest. This is defined for each *TYPE* (F32, S8, S16, S32, U16, U32).
- ➤ *TYPE* **getMax( *TYPE* a , *TYPE* b )**. Returns a or b, depending upon which is the largest. This is defined for each *TYPE* (F32, S8, S16, S32, U16, U32).
- ➤ **BIT(x)**. This is actually a macro and returns the bit-mask equivalent to (1 << x).

## 10.5 The Torque Standard Library

Torque provides a full set of substitute functions designed to replace the functionality normally provided by the ANSI C standard library. This library of functions is referred to as the Torque Standard Library. These libraries are part of the Torque porting layer.

## 10.5.1 Why Is the Torque Standard Library Needed?

"Why is this necessary and what does it do for me?", you may ask.

Let me try to answer this question for you.

**Engine Coding**

As you may be aware, not all computer hardware is equivalent. In today's computing world, we have all of the following issues to deal with.

➢ CPU-dependent variable bit-width buses, registers, and instruction sets.

➢ Big-endian and little-endian instruction sets.

➢ RISC and CISC architectures.

➢ Numerous instruction-set extensions (MMX, 3DNow!, AltiVec, KNI, SSE2, SSE3, etc.).

➢ Non-traditional computing devices such as,

• Consoles: Xbox, Xbox 360, PS2, PS3, ...

• Hand-held devices (currently not directly supported by Torque).

• Arcade machines.

"So what," you might say, "doesn't the ANSI C standard library deal with all of this?"

Yes and no.

Yes, it deals with and is sufficient for generalized computing. No, it does not guarantee explicit implementation details in some instances that may affect the outcome of the specialized computing operations which are exercised in a game engine.

To resolve this problem, the developers of the Torque Game Engine decided to implement their own version of several standard library functions instead of relying upon the ANSI C standard versions provided by individual compiler makers and their associated libraries.

In the end, this protects you, the game programmer, from having to resolve weird hardware-specific computing dilemmas, and it enables forward compatibility with future hardware.

## 10.5.2 How Do I Use the Library?

The essential references in Appendix B list all of the Torque Standard Library functions and their reciprocal standard C functions. With that information and a standard C reference, you can look up any functions you are not familiar with.

If you are an experienced programmer, you will already be familiar with most of the ANSI C standard functions. Therefore, to use the Torque equivalent, simply do the following.

➢ Be sure that the "platform/platform.h" header is included in your file.

➢ Use Torque data types instead of intrinsics (this is optional, but strongly suggested).

➢ Choose the ANSI C standard function you wish to use and modify the name using these simple steps.

1. Add a lowercase `d` to the front.
2. Change the second letter (what was the first letter) to uppercase.
3. Use the function as you normally would.

### `sprintf()` -> `dSprintf()` **Example**

Let's do an example to show how easy it is to use the Torque Standard Library functions. In this example, we will convert code that uses `sprintf()` to the equivalent Torque version.

Originally, we would write the following code in ANSI C.

```
#include <stdio.h>

char buffer[256];

sprintf( buffer , "Hello %s!", "world" );

// buffer now contains: "Hello world!"
```

We would convert this code as follows for Torque.

```
#include "platform/platform.h"

S8 buffer[256];

dSprintf( buffer , "Hello %s!", "world" );

// buffer now contains: "Hello world!"
```

Notice that the only changes made here were the following.

1. Instead of including `<stdio.h>`, we included `"platform/platform.h"`.
2. Instead of `char`, we used `S8`.
3. We prepended a `d` to `sprintf()` and raised the case of the first letter of the original function name (which follows the lowerCamelCase rule for functions).

That is it!

## 10.6 Torque Rendering and DGL

The Torque Game Engine does not implement its own graphics rasterization layer. Instead, OpenGL was chosen as the graphics API. This is fortunate because OpenGL is a mature, community-supported graphics API that provides simplified cross-platform support and ease of use.

In addition to using OpenGL, Torque includes a utility library called the Dynamix Graphics Library (DGL), which extends OpenGL to support higher-level primitives and resources, as well as to perform texture management. These features can be accessed by including the "dgl/dgl.h" header in your code.

## 10.6.1 Torque Rendering versus OpenGL Rendering

A full discussion of OpenGL and the DGL features are beyond the scope of this guide. However, I do want you to be aware that, if you do write your own render code, you need to account for two major differences between OpenGL rendering and Torque (DGL) rendering.

### Major Difference #1—Coordinate Systems

In OpenGL, the forward vector (the vector the eye normally looks down) is –z. In Torque, the forward vector is +y. This effects the frustum calculation. To compensate for this, DGL replaces the OpenGL function setFrustum() with dglSetFrustum().

If you forget this and use the setFrustum() function, your objects will be incorrectly oriented in the world.

### Major Difference #2—Matrix Organization

Also different in Torque is the way matrices are organized.

OpenGL uses column-major ordering, whereas Torque uses row-major ordering. I will elaborate on this difference a bit later when we talk about the MatrixF class, but for now just remember that you need to use DGL functions (and MatrixF methods) instead of OpenGL functions when working with matrices.

➢ Use dglLoadMatrix() instead of glLoadMatrix().
➢ Use dglMultMatrix() instead of glMultMatrix().
➢ etc.

## 10.6.2 What about DirectX?

Torque offers the ability to use DirectX as the rendering interface on machines that support it. It does this via a DLL that converts OpenGL calls into Direct3D calls. As long as you do not intend to use any DirectX-specific optimizations in your render code, you can safely use the OpenGL and DGL libraries. Subsequently, users can select DirectX as the render methodology, and the engine will handle it automatically.

## 10.7 The Torque Math Library and Math Classes

TGE provides a large set portable math functions and mathematically oriented classes. These are all part of the Torque porting layer.

### 10.7.1 The Math Functions

As with the Torque Standard Library, Torque supplies replacement functions for a large number of ANSI C standard math functions. The full list of Torque versus ANSI C math functions is listed in the essential references in Appendix B.

To access the Torque equivalent of an ANSI C math function, simply do the following.

1. Check Appendix B to see if there is a Torque equivalent for the ANSI C function.
2. If there is, simply include "math/mMath.h" in your code and use the Torque function.

You will notice that the Torque math functions all use a (ANSI C) name-modification scheme similar to that used by the Torque standard libraries, except in this case the rules work as follows.

1. Add a lowercase `m` to the front of the function name (as defined in ANSI C).
2. Change the second letter (what was the first letter) to uppercase.
3. Use the function as you normally would.

For example, the `abs()` function in ANSI C is replaced with the Torque Math Library `mAbs()` function.

### 10.7.2 The Math Constants

When you include the "math/mMath.h" header, the file "math/mConstants.h" is automatically included. This file defines a small set of (eight) math constants.

➢ **M_PI, M_2PI**. pi and 2 * pi.
➢ **M_SQRT2**. Square root of 2.
➢ **M_SQRTHALF**. Square root of 2 over 2.
➢ **M_*_F**. Same as each value above, but using (x)f notation, forcing the value to be typed as a `float`.

### 10.7.3 The Torque Math Classes

Games are very math-intensive, usually requiring the use of vector math, matrix math, and some calculus. Additionally, writing code to solve these kinds of problems can be tedious and difficult. Fortunately, the makers of the Torque Game

Engine realized this and chose to provide ready-made classes for representing and operating on the most commonly used (in games) math quantities.

All of the following math classes are provided by Torque.

- ➢ **Point\***. Several point classes, sharing a common set of features and addressing 2D, 3D, and 4D integer and floating-point point representation needs.
- ➢ **RectI**, **RectF**, and **RectD**. Three classes defining rectangular spaces used for GUI and game-world calculations.
- ➢ **PlaneF**. A class that uses a Point3F and a direction to represent a plane.
- ➢ **AngAxisF**. A class uses a Point3F and a floating-point angle to represent arbitrary rotations about an axis.
- ➢ **QuatF**. A quaternion class. (The quaternion is an advanced mathematical extension of complex numbers and is used to solve traditionally difficult problems such as three-dimensional rotation while avoiding common issues like gimbal lock.)
- ➢ **SphereF**. A class used to represent spheres and implement basic sphere tests.
- ➢ **Box3F** and **Box3D**. Two box classes with several useful features as applied to three-dimensional cubic spaces.
- ➢ **MatrixF**. A 4 × 4 row-major ordered matrix class, implemented using F32 values.

In this chapter, we will be discussing the Point\*, Box\*, and MatrixF classes.

The QuatF class (used for quaternion calculations) is too advanced to discuss here.

The remaining classes, Rect\*, Plane\*, AngAxisF, and SphereF all use the Point3F class to embody a simple concept. Therefore, I will leave future investigation of these classes as an exercise for the reader.

## Which Header File?

The simplest way to get access to any and all of the Torque math libraries is to include the "math/mMath.h" header file. This file will, in turn, include all of the necessary headers to properly declare the Torque math classes.

## The Point\* Classes

The point classes are a nice place to start our discussion.

These classes are designed to contain and to operate on two-dimensional, three-dimensional, and four-dimensional point information.

The two-dimensional classes are used primarily for GUI work, whereas the three- and four-dimensional classes are primarily used for 3D rendering and higher-order mathematical calculations.

| Class Name | Description |
|------------|-------------|
| Point2I | A two-dimensional integer (S32) point class. < X Y > |
| Point2F | A two-dimensional floating-point (F32) point class. < X Y > |
| Point2D | A two-dimensional double floating-point (F64) point class. < X Y> |
| Point3I | A three-dimensional integer (S32) point class. < X Y Z > |
| Point3F | A three-dimensional floating-point (F32) point class. < X Y Z > |
| Point3D | A three-dimensional double floating-point (F64) point class. < X Y Z > |
| Point4F | A four-dimensional floating-point (F32) point class. < X Y Z W > |

**Table 10.3**
The point classes.

In total, there are seven base point classes in use throughout the engine (see Table 10.3).

## Important Point* Methods

Excluding constructors and destructors, these classes share a small set of common methods, each tailored to the individual class. Table 10.4 lists and describes these methods.

### Point* Methods By Class

Note that not all of the point classes support every one of the methods in Table 10.4. In fact, the only class that supports all of these methods is Point3F (this is not that surprising since Point3F is used more than any other point class). Table 10.5 shows which classes do and do not support the methods from Table 10.4.

**Convolving points.** When I first saw this method, I thought that it was designed for convolution, but a closer inspection showed that it merely does multiplication. For example, we can take two Point2I instances and convolve.

```
Point2I A( 1 , 2 );

Point2I B( 3 , 4 );

A.convolve( B );
```

This results in the following operation.

$$< Ax * Bx , Ay * By > \ = \ < 1 * 3 , 2 * 4 > \ = \ < 3 , 8 >$$

The result will be stored in A (the calling instance).

**Checking Point3F equality.** Because Point3F is implemented using floating-point (F32) values, we need to be cautious when operating on the

**Table 10.4**
Common point methods.

| Method Name | Description |
|---|---|
| convolve() | This method multiplies the individual components of one point against the corresponding components of another point. <br><br> See the "Convolving points" discussion below. |
| convolveInverse() | This method divides the individual components of one point by the corresponding components of another point. |
| equal() | This method (only used by Point3F) checks to see if the elements of two points match to within POINT_EPSILON, where POINT_EPSILON is set to 1E-4. <br><br> See the "Checking Point3F equality" discussion below. |
| interpolate() | This method interpolates between two given points (A and B) by a specified factor, producing a point. This point exists somewhere along the line specified by A and B. <br><br> See the "Interpolating points" discussion below. |
| isZero() | This method tests whether all elements of the point are set to zero. |
| len() | This method treats the point as a vector and returns the length of this vector. <br><br> See the "Point lengths" discussion below. |
| lenSquared() | This method is the same as len() except the squared length is return instead. <br><br> See the "Point lengths" discussion below. |
| magnitudeSafe() | This does the same thing as len() but checks to see if the point isZero() first. In this case, it returns zero instead of a length. |
| neg() | This method inverts the sign of each element in the point. |
| normalize() | This method treats the point as a vector and normalizes its elements. After calling this method, the point (vector) will have a unit length of one. <br><br> **Note:** Most classes provide a second variant of this method that can be passed a value. In this case, the point is normalized and then each element of the point is multiplied by the passed value, effectively normalizing and scaling the point in one step. |
| normalizeSafe() | This method does the same thing as normalize() except that it first checks to see that the point (vector) has a minimal len() of POINT_EPSILON and then calculates the normalized values. <br><br> **Warning:** If this point (vector) does not have a minimum len() of POINT_EPSILON (1E-4), the operation will silently fail, making no changes to the point. |
| set() | This method sets the individual elements of this point. <br><br> **Note:** Some classes have more than one variant of set(), taking different arguments. |
| setMax() | This method compares one point to another point and sets each element of the current point to the highest value of the two. <br><br> See the "Setting min and max" discussion below. |
| setMin() | This method compares one point to another point and sets each element of the current point to the lowest value of the two. <br><br> See the "Setting min and max" discussion below. |
| zero() | This method (only used by Point3F) sets all elements of the point to zero. |

**Table 10.5**
Point methods by class.

| Method Name | Point2I | Point2F | Point2D | Point3I | Point3F | Point3D | Point4F |
|:---:|:---:|:---:|:---:|:---:|:---:|:---:|:---:|
| convolve() | × | × | × | × | × | × | |
| convolveInverse() | | | × | | × | × | |
| equal() | | | | | × | | |
| interpolate() | | × | | | × | | × |
| isZero() | × | × | × | × | × | × | |
| len() | × | × | × | × | × | × | |
| lenSquared() | | × | × | | × | × | |
| magnitudeSafe() | | | | | × | | |
| neg() | × | × | × | × | × | × | |
| normalize() | | × | × | | × | × | |
| normalizeSafe() | | | | | × | | |
| set() | × | × | × | × | × | × | × |
| setMax() | × | × | × | × | × | × | |
| setMin() | × | × | × | × | × | × | |
| zero() | | | | | × | | |

individual elements. Additionally, we should decide upon a suitable precision level. That is, we need to decide how many digits after the decimal point are important to us. TGE does this when checking for equality of two Point3F points by setting the minimum difference equal to POINT_EPSILON, where POINT_EPSILON is equal to 1E-4 (0.0001).

Therefore, equal() will return true in the following example.

```
Point3F A( 10.00009 , 20.0 , 30.0 );

Point3F B( 10.0 , 20.0 , 30.0 );

Con::printf( "Equal ?= %d" , A.equal( B ) ); // Will print: Equal ?= 1
```

**Interpolating points.** All of the floating-point (F32) point classes (Point2F, Point3F, and Point4F) provide an interpolation method. This method allows us to calculate the position of a new point, anywhere along the line between two other points.

```
Point3F A( 0.0 , 0.0 , 0.0 );

Point3F B( 10.0 , 10.0 , 10.0 );
```

**153**

```
Point3F C;

C.interpolate( A , B , 0.5 );
```

After executing the above code, the point C will have the position < 5.0 , 5.0 , 5.0 >. This is because we asked the engine to interpolate a point 50% of the way between the points < 0.0 , 0.0 , 0.0 > and < 10.0 , 10.0 , 10.0 >. Alternately, if we wrote this code.

```
C.interpolate( A , B , 0.25 );
```

The position of C would be < 2.5 , 2.5 , 2.5 >.

The third argument, `factor`, can be any value between 0.0 and 1.0 and is equivalent to a percentage. It specifies how far along the line to interpolate.

**Point lengths.** There are two methods provided for getting the length of a point (vector), namely `len()` and `lenSquared()`. The former method is equivalent to this operation (using `Point2F`):

$$< \text{mSqrt}( X * X ) , \text{mSqrt}( Y * Y ) >$$

The latter method is equivalent to this operation (again for a `Point2F`):

$$< X * X , Y * Y >$$

As you can see, these are quite different, so be sure to use the proper method.

**Setting min and max.** The last two point methods we will discuss are `setMin()` and `setMax()`. These have the opposite effect of each other, where `setMin()` will choose the lowest individual elements between two points and `setMax()` will choose the highest.

```
Point2I A( 2 , 7 );

Point2I B( 3 , 4 );

Point2I C( 5 , 3 );

B.setMin( A ); // Now B contains < 2 , 4 >

B.setMax( C ); // Now B contains < 5 , 4 >
```

### `Point*` Operators

In addition to the list of methods supplied in Table 10.4, the point classes support a number of operators, including ==, !=, +, -, +=, -=, *, /, *=, /=, -, and [].

With the exception of the `*`, `*=`, `/`, `/=`, and `[]` operators, all of these operators act on two instances of the specific class and return either a boolean value or another instance of the class.

```
Point3F A( 10.00009 , 20.0 , 30.0 );

Point3F B( 10.0 , 20.0 , 30.0 );

Con::printf( "Equal ?= %d" , A == B );

Con::printf( "A.y + B.y = %g" , (A + B).y );
```

When we run the above example, we will see this in the console.

```
Equal ?= 0
A.y + B.y = 40.0
```

In the case of the operators `*`, `*=`, `/`, and `/=`, the operand on the right side must be of the same type as the individual elements in the point. For example, since `Point2I` is comprised of two elements, each of which is an `S32`, we would write a multiplication like this.

```
Point2I A( 1 , 2 );

A = A * 5;

Con::printf( "A = < %d , %d >" , A.x , A.y );
```

> The data members containing the vertex values for the `Point3F` class are public `F32` values named x, y, and z. You can access any of these values directly using standard dot notation.
>
> ```
> Point3F myPoint;
> myPoint.x =   10.0f;
> myPoint.y =    0.0f;
> myPoint.z =  -15.0f;
> ```

Then, when we run the above example, we will see this in the console.

```
A = < 5 , 10 >
```

Finally, there is the funny operator `[]`. It is not an array operator in the normal sense but rather provides an indexed access to the three elements of this point. That is, we use this operator to get at the $x$ (0), $y$ (1), $z$ (2), and $w$ (3) elements of a point, assuming of course that the `Point*` class in question has that element.

In this example, we will print the $x$, $y$, and $z$ elements of a `Point3F` class.

```
Point3F A( 1.0 , 2.0 , 3.0 );

Con::printf( "A = < %g , %g , %g >" , A[0] , A[1] , A[2] );
```

When we run the above example, we will see this in the console.

```
A = < 1.0 , 2.0 , 3.0 >
```

## The `Box3F` and `Box3D` **Classes**

The next classes I would like to discuss are the `Box3F` and `Box3D` classes. These two classes are used to represent cubic and cuboid spaces. These boxes are specified by two values, `min` and `max`, where the points for a `Box3F` use `Point3F` points, and the points for `Box3D` use `Point3D` points.

Of these two box classes, `Box3F` is the most interesting and provides the most features, so we will discuss it first.

### Creating a Box

```
Point3F min( 0.0 , 0.0 , 0.0 );

Point3F max( 10.0 , 10.0 , 10.0 );

Box3F A( min , max );

Box3F B( 0.0 , 0.0 , 0.0 , 10.0 , 10.0 , 10.0 );
```

In the above example, we created two identical boxes with one corner at < 0.0 , 0.0 , 0.0 > and another corner at < 10.0 , 10.0 , 10.0 > .

Box A was created using two instances of `Point3F` for initialization purposes. Box B was created using six `F32` values for initialization purposes.

It is worth noting that when we created Box A, we could have passed a third boolean value specifying whether to override the min/max check. By default, when we create a `Box3F` instance using two `Point3F` instances to initialize it, the constructor will check to be sure that min is smaller than max. That is, we could have generated the same box using the following code.

```
Box3F A( max , min );
```

In this case, the constructor will notice that min is smaller than max and vice versa. It will then automatically swap the values. Although you can override this behavior by passing `true` as the third argument, I strongly suggest that you do not. If you create a bad box, it can mess up any subsequent calculations you use this for.

Lastly, it is possible to create a null box and to initialize it later.

```
Box3F C; // Warning: min and max are not initialized yet!!!
```

### `Box3F` Tests

`Box3F` provides us with several useful tests and operations as listed in Table 10.6.

| Method Name | Description |
|---|---|
| collideLine() | This method (two variants) is used to test whether a line specified by two Point3F points collides with this box. See the"Colliding Lines" discussion below. |
| collideOrientedBox() | This method is used to check for a collision between this box and a calculated oriented box. See the "Colliding Boxes" discussion below. |
| getCenter() | This method sets a (passed) Point3F to the center coordinates of this box. Used in the "Finding the Nearest Point" discussion below. |
| getClosestPoint() | This method returns a Point3F equivalent to the nearest point on this box to a second (passed) Point3F. In other words, this locates a point on this box nearest to the point which is passed as an argument. Used in the "Finding the Nearest Point" discussion below. |
| intersect() | This method should calculate the intersection of two boxes, but it is currently broken. Do not use this unless you fix it. |
| isContained() | This method (two variants) is used to test whether a point or another box is contained within the bounds of this box. See the "Checking for Containment and Overlap" discussion below. |
| isOverlapped() | This method is used to test whether another box is overlapping the bounds of this box. See the "Checking for Containment and Overlap" discussion below. |
| isValidBox() | This method is used to check if the current box is valid. That is, it tests that min is less than max. You should always use this method and check the result. If the test fails, you can simply swap min and max and then proceed. See the "Fixing Invalid Boxes" discussion below. |
| len_x() len_y() len_z() | These methods return the length, width, and height of your box, respectively. |

**Table 10.6**
Useful **Box3F** tests and operations.

## Colliding Lines

The line-box collision is probably one of the operations you will use most often when dealing with Box3F, so I will provide you functional code for the two variants here.

In the first variant, we only need to check for a collision and don't care about the position or the normal of the collision itself.

```
Box3F D( 0.0 , 0.0 , 0.0 , 10.0 , 10.0 , 10.0 );

Point3F start( 5.0 , 20.0 , 5.0 );
```

```
Point3F end( 5.0 , 0.0 , 5.0 );

if( D.collideLine( start , end ) )
{
  // Do something about collision
}
```

In the above code, we created a new box D with min and max bounds on the points < 0.0 , 0.0 , 0.0 > and < 10.0 , 10.0 , 10.0 >, respectively.

Next, we set up two points for drawing our line, where the starting point is at < 5.0 , 20.0 , 5.0 > and the ending point is at < 5.0 , 0.0 , 5.0 >.

Last, we called `collideLine()` and tested for a collision. Simple!

So, what if we need the position and/or the normal at the collision point? This is also easy. We just use the second variant of the `collideLine()` method to capture the position (along the line) of the collision as well as the collision normal. Then, we can calculate the collision point using interpolation.

```
Box3F D( 0.0 , 0.0 , 0.0 , 10.0 , 10.0 , 10.0 );

Point3F start( 5.0 , 20.0 , 5.0 );

Point3F end( 5.0 , 0.0 , 5.0 );

F32 collisionPos;

Point3F collisionPoint;

Point3F collisionNormal;

if( D.collideLine( start , end , & collisionPos ,
                   & collisionNormal ) )
{
  collisionPoint.interpolate( start , end , collisionPos );
}
```

In the above code, we created a new box D with min and max bounds of < 0.0 , 0.0 , 0.0 > and < 10.0 , 10.0 , 10.0 >, respectively.

Next, we set up two points for drawing our line, where the starting point is at < 5.0 , 20.0 , 5.0 > and the ending point is at < 5.0 , 0.0 , 5.0 >.

Then, we a created three blank variables, an F32 for the collision position (along the line) and two points, one for the collision point (which we will calculate) and one for the normal.

After setting up, we call `collideLine()`, passing in the addresses of our two new arguments, `collisionPos` and `collisionNormal`.

Last, if a collision is detected, we calculate the position of the hit by interpolating along our line segment from `start` to `end` by a factor of `collisionPos`.

## Colliding Boxes

In addition to line-box collisions, TGE provides another useful collision test, namely oriented-box–current-box.

```
MatrixF toUsMatrix;

Point3F boxRadii( 1.2 , 1.2 , 2.3 );

if( A.collideOrientedBox( boxRadii , toUsMatrix )
{
 // Do something about collision
}
```

In the above example, we are checking to see if a box with dimensions < 1.2 , 1.2 , 2.3 > and transformed by the matrix `toUsMatrix`, will collide with the box we created at the beginning of our box discussion. `collideOrientedBox` returns a boolean value of `true` if a collision occurred and `false` otherwise.

The real trick to using this method is the proper creation of a transform matrix. Unfortunately, we need to defer any discussion of matrices for just a little bit longer.

## Finding the Nearest Point

It is often useful to take a box and to find the point on that box closest to some other point. TGE provides us with a simple means of accomplishing this task in the form of the `getClosestPoint()` method.

```
Point3F sourcePoint( 15.0 , 25.0 , 5.0 );

Point3F closestPoint;

closestPoint = A.getClosestPoint( sourcePoint );
```

For example, after we execute the above code, which uses our box from above which was specified as [ min , max ] = [ < 0.0 , 0.0 , 0.0 > , < 10.0 , 10.0 , 10.0 > ], the point `closestPoint` will contain the value < 10.0 , 10.0 , 5.0 >. This may or may not seem correct to you at first, but remember we are looking for the nearest point on the box. This is not the same as a collision point between the source point and the box's center.

```
Point3F sourcePoint( 15.0 , 25.0 , 5.0 );

Point3F boxCenter;

F32 collisionPos;
Point3F normal;

A.getCenter( & boxCenter );
A.collideLine( sourcePoint , boxCenter , & collisionPos , & normal);
```

**159**

In the above example, we found the center of our box using the `getCenter()` method and then calculated a line collision from `sourcePoint` to `boxCenter`. This value was then stored in `collisionPos`.

## Checking for Containment and Overlap

As was stated previously, there are two containment testing methods, one for points and one for boxes. Additionally, there is one method for testing whether one box is overlapping a second box.

The first containment method, `isContained()`, is designed to check if a single `Point3F` point is contained within the bounds of our box.

```
Box3F containedTestBox( 0.0 , 0.0 , 0.0 , 10.0 , 10.0 , 10.0 );

Point3F containedTestPoint( 5.0 , 5.0 , 5.0 );

if( containedTestBox.isContained( containedTestPoint ) )
{
 // Do something about point being contained in this box
}
```

In the above example, we created a simple 10 × 10 × 10 box (`containedTestBox`). Then, we created a single point (`containedTextPoint`) which just happens to be in the middle of our box. Finally, we tested to see if the point is in fact contained in our box by calling the `Point3F` variant of `isContained()`, which returns `true` if the point is contained in the box and `false` otherwise.

The second version of `isContained()` works exactly the same way as the first version except that it checks to see if a box is entirely contained in the box that is calling the method.

```
  Box3F boxA( 0.0 , 0.0 , 0.0 , 10.0 , 10.0 , 10.0 );

  Box3F boxB( 2.0 , 2.0 , 2.0 , 8.0 , 8.0 , 8.0 );

  if( boxA.isContained( boxB ) )
  {
   // Do something about boxB being contained in boxA
  }
```

In the above example, we created two boxes, a 10 x 10 x 10 box centered at < 5 , 5 , 5 > and a 6 x 6 x 6 box, also centered at < 5 , 5 , 5 >. Then, we checked to see if the second box was contained within the first. That is, we checked to see if `boxB` was contained in `boxA`.

Note that if you read from left to right, the statement implies we are testing for `boxA` in `boxB`, but this is incorrect. Just remember that the passed box is tested for containment within the calling box.

The third test we need to discuss here is overlap testing. Fortunately, this test is no harder to write than the box version of `isContained()`.

```
Box3F boxA( 0.0 , 0.0 , 0.0 , 10.0 , 10.0 , 10.0 );

Box3F boxB( 5.0 , 5.0 , 5.0 , 15.0 , 15.0 , 15.0 );

if( boxA.isOverlapped( boxB ) )
{
 // Do something about the overlap
}
```

In the above example, we created two boxes that clearly overlap and tested for this overlap using the `isOverlapped()` method. Of course, this example pretty clear, but what about the case where only the edges are the same, or just a point is the same?

If even a single point on the edge of one box overlaps another, the boxes are considered to be overlapping

```
// These boxes overlap at point < 5.0 , 5.0 , 5.0 >
//
Box3F boxA( 0.0 , 0.0 , 0.0 , 5.0 , 5.0 , 5.0 );

Box3F boxB( 5.0 , 5.0 , 5.0 , 15.0 , 15.0 , 15.0 );
```

## Fixing Invalid Boxes

Above, I said that a poorly created box can mess up your calculations. Regardless of how you create your box, there is the possibility of creating a bad box. Therefore, I suggest that when you are using boxes in a critical calculation that you test it, try to fix it if it is wrong, and then test it again.

```
Box3F boxA( 10.0 , 10.0 , 10.0 , 0.0 , 0.0 , 0.0 );

Point3F temp;

if( false == boxA.isValidBox() ) // This box is bad!
{
 // Try swapping min and max to fix it
 temp = boxA.min;

 boxA.min = boxA.max;

 boxA.max = temp;
}

if( true == boxA.isValidBox() ) // This is a good box
{
 // Do your box operations here.
```

```
  }
  else
  {
    // Do something about this bad box!
  }
```

Note that the above code is not elegant and is only intended to show you how to check for a valid box. It also shows how to get and set the `min` and `max` points in a box.

> The concept of a bad box may sound funny, but you should understand that the constructors for `Box3F` are fairly simple. They take either two points or a series of `F32` values that can be treated as two points. Furthermore, they require that all of the elements <X Y Z> in the second point be greater than the elements in the first point. In other words, if `point2` minus `point1` results in a vector where X, Y, or Z is zero or less, the box is bad.

## What About `Box3D`?

We talked a lot about `Box3F`, but what about `Box3D`? Well, this box class might be considered the lesser cousin of `Box3F`. It doesn't support nearly as many features as `Box3F`. In fact, it only supports these methods:

> **getCenter()**. Get the center point of this box as a `Point3D` value.

> **intersect()**. Generate a box that is the equivalent to the intersection of two `Box3D` instances, but this is broken.

> **isContained()**. Only supports checking for `Point3D` contained in this box.

> **isOverlapped()**. Checks to see if another `Box3D` box is overlapping this box.

> **len_x() / len_y() / len_z()**. Returns the length, width, and height, respectively, of the box edges as `F64` values.

You might ask, "With this limited set of features? Why would I want to use this box type?" The answer is, "When range and precision counts." This box uses `F64` values for all point information and thus has a much higher range and precision than `Box3F`. This is important for calculations involving really large and really small numbers.

So, unless you need to deal with very large and/or very small box vertexes, I suggest that you use `Box3F`.

## What About Rectangles?

In addition to the `Box*` classes, TGE provides three rectangle classes, `RectD`, `RectF`, and `RectI`, for those times when you only need to work in two dimensions. Each of these provides a similar set of features to those found in the `Box*` classes. Thus, having run through the above discussion, I feel confident that you can quickly learn to use and understand the rectangle classes without supplementary discussion.

**Figure 10.2**
*Row-major versus column-major.*

**Figure 10.3**
*An identity matrix.*

Row Major

$$\begin{pmatrix} A & B & C & D \\ E & F & G & H \\ I & J & K & L \\ M & N & O & P \end{pmatrix}$$

Column Major

$$\begin{pmatrix} A & E & I & M \\ B & F & J & N \\ C & G & K & O \\ D & H & L & P \end{pmatrix}$$

$$\begin{pmatrix} 1 & 0 & 0 & 0 \\ 0 & 1 & 0 & 0 \\ 0 & 0 & 1 & 0 \\ 0 & 0 & 0 & 1 \end{pmatrix}$$ Identity Matrix

Torque
DirectX

Mathematics
OpenGL

## The MatrixF Class

This class represents a 4 × 4 row-major ordered matrix, where each element is an F32 value. These matrices are used throughout Torque for a variety of purposes. Although a full discussion of matrix math is beyond the scope of this guide, I do want to mention some key features.

### Row-Major, Not Column-Major

This class has the potential for causing you endless headaches if you do not understand how the data within it are organized.

This matrix class is organized in row-major order. This organization is different from what one might expect. By default, in mathematics and OpenGL, matrices are organized in column-major order. Figure 10.2 shows the difference between the two matrix orders.

Fortunately, if you do find yourself in a situation where you need to import some OpenGL into a TGE matrix, you can simply use the provided transpose() method.

### The Different Matrices

Although I strongly suggest that one use the built-in operations, there may be times when you need to create your own matrices for translation, rotation, scaling, etc. In order to do this, you need to initialize your matrices properly.

**Identity matrix.** An identity matrix (see Figure 10.3) should be used as the starting point for all calculations. Unmodified, it is the equivalent of "no operation" when used in multiplication. We must modify specific parts of the matrix in order to actually make the matrix do something for us.

```
// Get the MODELVIEW matrix from OpenGL and convert
// to Torque matrix.
MatrixF *m;
```

**Engine Coding**

---

**Figure 10.4**
*An Affine Matrix*

$$\begin{pmatrix} X & X & X & T \\ X & X & X & T \\ X & X & X & T \\ 0 & 0 & 0 & 1 \end{pmatrix} \quad \text{Affine} \\ \text{Matrix}$$

**Figure 10.5**
*Arbitrary translation.*

$$\begin{pmatrix} 1 & 0 & 0 & X \\ 0 & 1 & 0 & Y \\ 0 & 0 & 1 & Z \\ 0 & 0 & 0 & 1 \end{pmatrix} \quad \text{Translation} \\ \text{Matrix}$$

```
glGetFloatv( GL_MODELVIEW_MATRIX , *m );

m->transpose();
```

**Affine matrices.** An affine matrix (see Figure 10.4) is used for applying various kinds of transforms, including translation, rotation, scaling, and shearing. In order to do this properly, the matrix must follow a specific form. Figure 10.4 shows this form. Notice that the lower row in our affine matrix must always be set to $< 0\ 0\ 0\ 1 >$. Then, if we wish to produce some kind of arbitrary translation, we can modify the first three elements of column 3 (the Ts). Alternately, or in addition, we may wish to produce a rotation, a scaling, or a shear. To do this, we would modify the $3 \times 3$ sub-matrix, starting at row 0, column 0 and ending at row 2, column 2 (the X's).

## Basic Transforms

Although you can find this information in any good book on mathematics, I thought it would be handy to have it here. So, let's take a quick tour of some basic affine transforms.

All of these transforms are used by multiplying the supplied transform by another $4 \times 4$ matrix, containing an object's transform.

**Arbitrary translation.** As I noted above in the affine matrix discussion, the first three elements of column 3 are used for producing a translation. Specifically, one uses a matrix like that shown in Figure 10.5 to produce an arbitrary translation $< X\ Y\ Z >$.

**Arbitrary scaling.** In order to use a $4 \times 4$ matrix for scaling, we start with the identity matrix and then set the scale value ($< X\ Y\ Z >$) we want along the first three diagonal elements as shown in Figure 10.6. This will produce an arbitrary scaling matrix.

**Arbitrary rotation.** You can produce an arbitrary rotation about the center of an object by creating a matrix of the form shown in Figure 10.7. Note that the

**Figure 10.6**
*Arbitrary scaling.*

$$\begin{pmatrix} X & 0 & 0 & 0 \\ 0 & Y & 0 & 0 \\ 0 & 0 & Z & 0 \\ 0 & 0 & 0 & 1 \end{pmatrix}$$  `Scaling Matrix`

**Figure 10.7**
*Arbitrary rotation.*

$$\begin{pmatrix} A & B & C & 0 \\ D & E & F & 0 \\ G & H & I & 0 \\ 0 & 0 & 0 & 1 \end{pmatrix}$$  `Rotation Matrix`

**Table 10.7**
Arbitrary rotation (t = rotation angle in radians).

| Rotation about... | Use these values | | |
|---|---|---|---|
| x-axis | A = 1<br>D = 0<br>G = 0 | B = 0<br>E = cos( t )<br>H = −sin( t ) | C = 0<br>F = sin( t )<br>I = cos( t ) |
| y-axis | A = cos( t )<br>D = 0<br>G = sin( t ) | B = 0<br>E = 1<br>H = 0 | C = −sin( t )<br>F = 0<br>I = cos( t ) |
| z-axis | A = cos( t )<br>D = −sin( t )<br>G = 0 | D = sin( t )<br>E = cos( t )<br>H = 0 | C = 0<br>F = 0<br>I = 1 |

rotation is defined by the 3 × 3 sub-matrix whose elements are shown as the values A through I in Figure 10.7. To set up a proper rotation, use the values shown in Table 10.7.

I know, you might be thinking, "Gee that looks like a lot of work, and it's error-prone, too!" You are right on both counts. Fortunately, TGE provides helper methods to create some useful matrices. Let's look at them next.

## Useful `MatrixF` Operations

**Identity methods.** First, TGE provides a method for initializing our matrices to the identity matrix.

```
MatrixF matrixA;

matrixA.identity(); // Start with the identity matrix.
```

Although it might seem superfluous, we can subsequently test a matrix to see if it is in fact an identity matrix.

```
if ( matrixA.isIdentity() )
{
 // Do something ...
}
```

165

**Checking for affine.** More important than this, we can test if a matrix is affine. That is, if we should choose to construct our own matrices, we should always check that they are in fact affine before using them in calculations.

```
if ( matrixA.isAffine() )
{
 // Proceed with calculations
}
else
{
 Con::errorf( "This matrix is not affine!" );
}
```

**Arbitrary rotation.** Once we have initialized the matrix and tested to find out if it is affine, we can use it for our transforms. One oft needed and painful to set up (manually) transform is the rotation transform. TGE provides a nice method for setting up a rotation, using standard Euler notation.

```
// Rotate the current object 45 degrees about its z-axis
//
MatrixF matrixA;

MatrixF matrixB( object->getTransform() );

matrixA.identity();

Point3F eulerRot( 0.0 , 0.0 , mDegToRad(45.0) );

matrixA.set( eulerRot ); // Set up transform

matrixB.mul( matrixA ); // Apply it
```

We haven't discussed all of the methods used in the above example, but the important part is highlighted. In the highlighted section, we create an instance of `Point3F` containing the value < 0.0 0.0 0.785398 >, which is equivalent to a 45-degree rotation about the *z*-axis in Euler notation. We then used the `set()` method to modify our affine matrix, producing a rotation matrix.

**Rotation about a point.** After arbitrary rotation, the next hardest transform to calculate is the rotation about an arbitrary point. Fortunately, TGE again comes to the rescue.

```
// Rotate the current object 45 degrees about the world origin
//
MatrixF matrixA;

MatrixF matrixB( object->getTransform() );
```

```
matrixA.identity();

Point3F eulerRot( 0.0 , 0.0 , mDegToRad(45.0) );

Point3F worldOrigin( 0.0 , 0.0 , 0.0 );

matrixA.set( eulerRot , worldOrigin ); // Set up transform

matrixB.mul( matrixA ); // Apply it
```

In this example, we modified our prior code slightly to create a rotation about some external point (the origin, in this case). TGE did the rest of the work for us.

**Translation and scaling.** Setting up a translation or a scaling transform is as simple as starting with an identity matrix and then modifying the requisite column or diagonal elements (as shown in Figures 10.5 and 10.6). This is accomplished using the access methods that we will cover next.

## MatrixF Access Methods

`MatrixF` offers a variety of access methods. Some of these are fairly straightforward to use, while others are slightly less clear.

**get*() / set*().** The simplest of the `MatrixF` access methods are the get and set methods. These come in a variety of forms, including the following.

➢ **getColumn( col , dest )**. Get column `col` and store the result in `dest`.
➢ **setColumn( col , src )**. Set column `col` to the value passed in `src`.
➢ **getRow( row , dest )**. Get column `row` and store the result in `dest`.
➢ **setRow( row , src )**. Set column `row` to the value passed in `src`.
➢ **getPosition( )**. Return position part of this matrix as a `Point3F`.
➢ **setPosition( pos )**. Set position part of this matrix to the value passed in `pos`.

For each of the row and column `get*()`/`set*()` methods, the arguments can be any of the following types.

➢ **col and row**. Any `S32` in the range 0..3.
➢ **dest and src**. A pointer to a `Point3F` or a `Point4F` object.

In the case of `setPosition()`, `pos` can only be a pointer to a `Point3F` object.

As an example, let us write the code to translate an object by < 10.0 0.0 0.0 >.

```
// Translate this object by 10 world units
//
MatrixF matrixA;

MatrixF matrixB( object->getTransform() );

matrixA.identity();

Point3F simpleTranslation( 10.0 , 0.0 , 0.0 );

matrixA.setColumn( 3 , simpleTranslation ); // Set up transform

matrixB.mul( matrixA ); // Apply it
```

We haven't discussed all of the methods used in the above example, but the important part is highlighted. In the highlighted section, we create an instance of Point3F containing the value < 10.0 0.0 0.0 >. Then, we use this value to set the first three elements of the third column in our matrix, creating a simple translation matrix.

Alternately, we could have used the setPos() method.

```
matrixA.setPos( simpleTranslation );
```

**Array accesses and idx().** In addition to the get and set methods, we are allowed to access MatrixF directly using array notation and a special array-like notation.

```
F32 a, b, c;

MatrixF m( object->getTransform() );

// Get entry at row 1, column 3

a = m( 1 , 3 ); // 1

b = m[ MatrixF::idx( 3 , 1 ) ]; // 2

c = m[ 7 ]; // 3
```

In the above example, we created a MatrixF instance containing the transform of some object. Then, we retrieved the value at row 1 / column 3 (an F32) in three different ways.

1. **m( row , column )**. The first way uses a specially provided access method that takes two arguments, row and column.

2. **m[ Matrix::idx( column , row ) ]**. The second way treats the instance of MatrixF as an array where the index is the result of a call to

the special `MatrixF` method `idx()`. `idx()` takes two arguments, `column` and `row`, which are then used to calculate an array index.

- Note: It is important to remember that `idx()` takes the column as the first, not the second, argument.

3. **`M[ 7 ]`**. The third and final way we retrieved row 1 / column 3 from our instances of `MatrixF` was by using the array notation (again) and by calculating the index ourselves, based on what we know about the topology of an instance of `MatrixF`.

- Note: I suggest that you *never* use this methodology. Use one of the other two means of accessing a `MatrixF` instance instead.

As an example, let us write the code to scale an object by < 0.5 2.0 1.5 >.

```
// Translate this object by 10 world units
//
MatrixF matrixA;

MatrixF matrixB( object->getTransform() );

matrixA.identity();

matrixA( 0 , 0 ) = 0.5; // Set up X scale transform

matrixA[ MatrixF::idx( 1 , 1) ] = 2.0; // Set up Y scale transform

matrixA[ 10 ] = 1.5; // Set up Z scale transform

matrixB.mul( matrixA ); // Apply it
```

We haven't discussed all of the methods used in the above example, but the important part is highlighted. In the highlighted section, we use each of the three ways available to us to modify a single element of the matrix.

## `MatrixF` *Standard Operations*

The `MatrixF` class supports several standard operations, including multiplication, scaling, and rotation.

**`MatrixF` by `MatrixF` multiplication.** `MatrixF` supplies two `MatrixF` by `MatrixF` multiplication methods (see Figure 10.8).

➢ **`mA.mul( mB )`**. `MatrixF` mA is multiplied by `MatrixF` mB, with the result both returned and `stored` in mA.

➢ **`mA.mul( mB , mC )`**. `MatrixF` mB is multiplied by `MatrixF` mC, with the result both returned and stored in `MatrixF` mA.

**Figure 10.8**
**`MatrixF`** by **`MatrixF`** multiplication.

$$\begin{pmatrix} A & B & C & D \\ E & F & G & H \\ I & J & K & L \\ M & N & O & P \end{pmatrix} * \begin{pmatrix} A & B & C & D \\ E & F & G & H \\ I & J & K & L \\ M & N & O & P \end{pmatrix}$$

**Figure 10.9**
**MatrixF** by **F32** multiplication.

$$\begin{pmatrix} A & B & C & D \\ E & F & G & H \\ I & J & K & L \\ M & N & O & P \end{pmatrix} * X$$

**Figure 10.10**
**MatrixF** by **Point4F** multiplication.

$$\begin{pmatrix} A & B & C & D \\ E & F & G & H \\ I & J & K & L \\ M & N & O & P \end{pmatrix} * \begin{pmatrix} X & Y & Z & W \end{pmatrix}$$

**MatrixF by F32 multiplication.** MatrixF supplies two MatrixF by F32 multiplication methods (see Figure 10.9).

➢ **mA.mul( X )**. MatrixF mA is multiplied by F32 X, with the result both returned and stored in MatrixF mA.

➢ **mA.mul( mB , X )**. MatrixF mB is multiplied by F32 X, with the result both returned and stored in MatrixF mA.

**MatrixF by Point4F multiplication.** MatrixF supplies one MatrixF by Point4F multiplication method (see Figure 10.10).

➢ **mA.mul( pA )**. MatrixF mA is multiplied by Point4F pA, and the result is stored in pA.

**MatrixF by Point3F multiplication.** MatrixF supplies four MatrixF by Point3F multiplication methods.

➢ **mA.mulP( pA )**. MatrixF mA is multiplied against Point3F pA, where pA is treated as a Point4F vector with the last value set to 1 (see Figure 10.11).

➢ **mA.mulP( pA , & pB )**. Same as the previous method except that the result is stored at the Point3F address specified by & pB (see Figure 10.11).

➢ **mA.mulV( pA )**. MatrixF mA is multiplied by Point3F pA, where pA is treated as a Point4F vector with the last value set to 0 (see Figure 10.12).

➢ **mA.mulV( pA , & pB )**. Same as the previous method except that the result is stored at the Point3F address specified by & pB (see Figure 10.12).

**MatrixF by Box3F multiplication.** MatrixF supplies one MatrixF vs. Box3F multiplication method (Figure 10.13).

➢ **mA.mul( bA )**. MatrixF mA is multiplied by Box3F bA, and the result is stored in bA.

**Figure 10.11**
**MatrixF** by **Point3F** multiplication.

$$\begin{pmatrix} A & B & C & D \\ E & F & G & H \\ I & J & K & L \\ M & N & O & P \end{pmatrix} * \begin{pmatrix} X & Y & Z & 1 \end{pmatrix}$$

**Figure 10.12**
**MatrixF** by **Point3F** multiplication.

$$\begin{pmatrix} A & B & C & D \\ E & F & G & H \\ I & J & K & L \\ M & N & O & P \end{pmatrix} * \begin{pmatrix} X & Y & Z & 0 \end{pmatrix}$$

**Figure 10.13**

**MatrixF** by **Box3F** multiplication.

$$\begin{pmatrix} A & B & C & D \\ E & F & G & H \\ I & J & K & L \\ M & N & O & P \end{pmatrix} * \begin{pmatrix} L & M & N \\ O & P & Q \end{pmatrix}$$

***Scaling and rotation.*** With the above multiplication methods, you can apply a number of multiplication-based transforms to matrices, including scaling and rotation. However, before you write your own code to do this, be aware that you can scale MatrixF instances directly using the scale() method.

```
Point3F myScale( 1.0 , 2.0 , 1.5 );

MatrixF myMatrix;

// do various set-up work on the matrix ...

// scale the matrix directly
myMatrix.scale( myScale );
```

Additionally, if you need a rotation matrix, you can create one directly using a special MatrixF constructor.

```
// Euler rotation of 45-degrees about z-axis
Point3F rotationVector( 0.0, 0.0 , 0.7 );

MatrixF myRotationMatrix( rotationVector );
```

When executed, the above code will create an instance of MatrixF that can be used to rotate objects by 45 degrees about their *z*-axis.

Alternately, if you need to create a matrix that will be used for rotating an object about an arbitrary point, you can use yet another specialized constructor.

```
// Point to rotate about
Point3F rotationPoint( 10.0, 10.0 , 10.0 );

// Euler rotation of 45-degrees about z-axis
Point3F rotationVector( 0.0, 0.0 , 0.7 );

MatrixF myRotationMatrix( rotationVector , rotationPoint );
```

When executed, the above code will create an instance of `MatrixF` that can be used to rotate objects by 45 degrees about a *z*-axis located at the world position < 10.0 , 10.0 , 10.0 >.

## `MatrixF` Inversion, Transposition, and Normalization

So, what do we have left? Well, in addition to those operations discussed above, TGE provides three different methods for inverting a matrix, two means of transposing a matrix, and one way to normalize a matrix.

**Which invert should I use?** You may find it confusing that TGE provides three different means of inverting a matrix, but there is a reason for this. Each of the inversion methods operates differently. However, before we take this discussion any further, you should know that as long as your matrix is affine (see Figure 10.4), all three methods produce exactly the same result.

The three `MatrixF` inversion methods provided by TGE are:

➢ `inverse()`. This method does a full inversion using Cramer's rule. This method should be the fastest of the three, and I suggest that you use it for general matrix inversions.

  • Note that if you have not followed my suggestions regarding the construction of your matrix, you may find that this method does not work. Technically, Cramer's rule cannot be used if the matrix has more than (or fewer than) one solution.

➢ `fullInverse()`. This method does a full inversion of the matrix, using the long-hand (brute-force) methodology you will find in all standard mathematics textbooks. This is probably the slowest of the three (depending on various factors), but you will need to use it if your matrix is not affine or if you find that `inverse()` doesn't work for you all of the time.

➢ `affineInverse()`. This last method is designed to work with affine matrices only. It takes advantage of the properties of an affine matrix to shortcut part of the inversion operation. That is, it merely transposes the rotation matrix and then calculates the new translation matrix (contrary to what the doxygen documentation says). Because the bottom row of an affine matrix is always $< 0\ 0\ 0\ 1 >$, it can be ignored, significantly short-ening the calculation time.

- Note that this method may sometimes be faster than using `inverse()`, but you should investigate this fact by writing your own test cases and checking both methods.

**Transposition.** We already discussed one of the transposition methods at the beginning of our `MatrixF` discussion, when I mentioned that you can convert an OpenGL matrix to a Torque matrix (and vice versa ) using `transpose()`.

```
// Get the MODELVIEW matrix from OpenGL and convert to Torque matrix.
//
MatrixF *m;

glGetFloatv( GL_MODELVIEW_MATRIX , *m );

m->transpose();
```

This operation simply trades rows for columns and stores the result in the same `MatrixF` instance that was used to call the method (see Figure 10.14).

So, what if we want to store the result elsewhere? Easy: use the `transposeTo()` method.

**Figure 10.14**
**MatrixF** transposition.

$$\begin{pmatrix} A & B & C & D \\ E & F & G & H \\ I & J & K & L \\ M & N & O & P \end{pmatrix} \rightarrow \begin{pmatrix} A & E & I & M \\ B & F & J & N \\ C & G & K & O \\ D & H & L & P \end{pmatrix}$$

```
// Convert an OpenGL matrix to
// a TGE compatible matrix
//
MatrixF *m;
MatrixF n;

glGetFloatv( GL_MODELVIEW_MATRIX , *m );

m->transposeTo( (F32*) & N );
```

It is also worth mentioning that the same method can be used to transpose a TGE matrix to an OpenGL-usable floating-point array.

```
// Convert a TGE matrix to an OpenGL compatible matrix
// and load it as the model view matrix.
//
MatrixF *m;
F32 n[16];

m->transposeTo( N );

glMatrixMode(GL_MODELVIEW);

glLoadMatrixF( n );
```

**173**

**Matrix normalization: How, why, and when?** The last operation we will discuss is matrix normalization, which is accomplished using the `normalize()` method. Generally, you won't need to use this method if you have constructed an affine matrix and checked that it is in fact affine; however, if you use the same matrix over and over, each time modifying it with some calculation, there is the possibility that you will start to accumulate floating-point round-off errors. You can fix this by simply renormalizing the matrix as often as you feel it is needed. Honestly, I never feel the need, but TGE is a fully featured engine and provides for this rare need nonetheless.

## 10.8 The Console Class Hierarchy

The console classes are those classes from which (nearly) all other interesting game interfaces and scripting classes are derived. We will be spending almost all of the next chapter learning how to use them and to derive from them, but I want to at least introduce them to you before we talk about any other topics in this chapter.

The console classes (see Figure 10.15) include:

➤ **ConsoleObject**. This is the virtual parent to all console classes, that is, all classes that can be instantiated from scripts.

➤ **SimObject**. This child of `ConsoleObject` is the first derivable class that will allow classes to be exposed to the the console (scripting engine).

➤ **NetObject**. This child of `SimObject` adds the ability to ghost objects across the network.

➤ **SceneObject**. This child of `NetObject` is the parent of all objects that can be added to the scene graph. It adds a large set of rendering-related features. It also adds physics- and collision-related features.

**Figure 10.15**

Console class hierarchy.

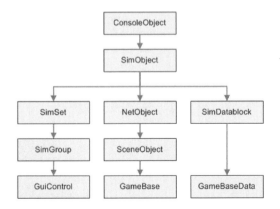

➤ **GameBase**. This child of `SceneObject` introduces the concept of pairing a scene-graph object with a datablock. This powerful concept enables a significant set of features in TorqueScript and provides a lightweight solution to the networking problem that is created by large sets of data-heavy objects that are similar and/or frequently created.

➤ **SimDataBlock**. This child of `SimObject` is the parent of all datablock classes.

➤ **GameBaseData**. This child of `SimDataBlock` is the mate to `GameBase`.

➤ **SimSet and SimGroup**. These children of `ConsoleObject` are both container classes, used for storing instances of `SimObject` and its children.

➤ **GuiControl**. This great-grandchild of `SimObject` is the root class to all rendered GUI classes.

## 10.9 The String Table

When making games with the Torque Game Engine, you will find that you use a large number of strings. This fact improves the usability of the engine, since it means we can use meaningful names (strings) instead of numbers in our scripts and elsewhere. However, unaccounted for, this prevalent use of string data could cause significant performance issues. Fortunately, the TGE designers were aware of both the benefits and the drawbacks of working with strings and have provided a class that resolves some of the major string issues, including wasted storage space and slow comparisons.

The Torque Game Engine provides a very useful class, `_StringTable`. This class has the following jobs:

➤ **Store unique strings**. When a string is inserted into the table, the class will check to see if that string is already present, in which case the insert operation will be ignored.

➤ **Provide unique references to each stored string**. In other words, when working with an entry from the table, we are guaranteed to always receive the same pointer for the same string (based on rules we'll discuss later).

➤ **Enable simple comparisons using the comparison operator (==)**. In C/C++ we normally use the `strcmp()` and `stricmp()` (`dStrcmp()` and `dStricmp()` in the Torque Standard Library) functions to compare strings. As you know, these operations are fairly slow. However, since any single string is guaranteed to have the same pointer value (in the string table), we can simply use these pointers for comparison instead. In other words, what used to be a long and slow operation has been reduced to a single look-up (per string) followed by an integer comparison(s).

## 10.9.1 There Can Be Only One

The `StringTable` class has been declared using (a variant of) the single-ton design pattern, meaning that only one instance of this class can ever be instantiated. This is done so that we are guaranteed to store all string data in one place. Additionally, since the engine is responsible for instantiating this class, you can simply use it and forget about the specific implementation details.

However, just for your reference, you should be aware that the string table pointer is declared at the top of " ~ \engine\core\stringTable.h".

```
_StringTable *StringTable = NULL;
```

Meanwhile, the class is instantiated in " ~ \engine\game\main.cc".

```
static bool initLibraries()
{
 // ...

 _StringTable::create();
 TextureManager::create();
 ResManager::create();
```

## 10.9.2 New Strings

Before we can do anything with the table, we need to create a string table entry pointer to work with.

```
StringTableEntry myString;
StringTableEntry myString2;
StringTableEntry myString3;
```

As can be seen, this code is very simple. We merely used the (provided) typedef `StringTableEntry` to declare three string table entry pointers `myString`, `myString2` and `myString3`. For now, we'll leave them uninitialized.

## 10.9.3 Insertions

In order to use the string table, it is necessary to populate it. To enable this, the class provides two methods, `insert()` and `insertn()`.

➢ **insert( string [ , caseSens == false ] )**. This method is used to insert a new string into the string table, where the string is enclosed in double quotes, just like any other string. Additionally, we can specify whether case should be ignored or not. By default, the case of the string is ignored (not case-sensitive).

```
myString = StringTable->insert( "Hello World!" , true );
```

At the end of this operation, "Hello World!" will be stored in the string table, and our string table entry pointer (myString) will contain a pointer to that entry.

➤ **insertn( string , len [ , caseSens == false ] )**. This method is similar to insert(), with the additional ability to truncate the string to a specified maximum length.

```
myString2 = StringTable->insertn( "hello world! not added" , 12 );
```

In this operation, we are attempting to add the string "hello world! not added" to our string table, but if you read the code closely, you will see that we have requested that the entry be truncated at 12 characters long, and that we have used the default case-insensitive insertion. In other words, this is like trying to add "hello world!", and since the insert is case-insensitive, it will not add a new string but will instead find the string "Hello World!" that we added above.

At the end of this operation, "Hello World!" will still be stored in the string table and our string table entry pointer (myString2) will contain a pointer to that entry.

## 10.9.4 Look-ups

Once the table is populated, when we want to do string comparisons, it will be necessary for us to look up entries. In order to facilitate this operation, TGE provides two methods.

➤ **lookup( string [ , caseSens == false ] )**. This method is used to search the string table for an entry matching that passed in string. As with insert(), this method defaults to using a case-insensitive look-up. If a match is found, the pointer for that entry is returned, otherwise this method returns NULL.

```
myString3 = StringTable->lookup( "Hello world!" );
```

At the end of this operation, the variable myString3 will contain a pointer to the location of "Hello World!", which we added previously.

➤ **lookupn( string , len [ , caseSens == false ] )**. This is the length-constrained version of lookup().

## 10.9.5 Comparisons

Assuming that you have done an insert and/or a look-up, and that you have stored the resulting pointers in some string table entry pointers, it is very simple to compare these strings.

```
if( ( myString == myString2 ) && ( myString2 == myString3 ) )
{
 // Do something
}
```

If you have followed along, looking at both the insertion and look-up code snippets, you should see that the if statement above will test true and enter the code braces to "do something." That is, `myString` contains the same pointer value as `myString2`, which contains the same pointer value as `myString3`.

## 10.9.6 Hashing

The `StringTable` class offers us the ability to generate a numeric hash value from any string. If two strings are different (even if only in capitalization), their hashes are guaranteed to be different.

Because numeric comparisons are much faster than string comparisons (especially for long strings), we can gain a significant performance boost by using hashes instead of strings in cases where the same string(s) is compared against other strings repeatedly.

To create a hash, we can do something like the following.

```
U32 myHash = StringTable->hashString( "Hello World!" );
```

**// OR**

```
U32 myHash = StringTable->hashStringn( "Hello World!IGNORED" , 12 );
```

## 10.10 Torque Pointers

The last of the useful classes I want to discuss in this chapter is the smart pointer class, `SimObjectPtr`. This class is used to store and to safely reference an instance of `SimObject` (or one of its children).

## 10.10.1 (Dumb) Pointers

There are basically two type of pointers, dumb pointers and smart pointers.

As C++ programmers, we are all aware of dumb pointers, which we generally refer to simply as pointers.

```
someClass *myDumbPtr = NULL;
```

The above code snippet shows a standard pointer. It is used to store the address of an instance of `someClass` (or its children) and is currently initialized to `NULL`. This pointer has no smarts whatsoever. That is, if we delete the object it is pointing to, the pointer will be completely unaware of this and will still contain the address of the deleted object.

## 10.10.2 What Is a Smart Pointer?

If you are new to C++, then you may never have heard the term smart pointer before, or you may not know exactly what it is.

Basically, a smart pointer is a pointer that is able to detect whether the object instance that it is pointing to is still valid. That is, if a smart pointer is assigned the address of an object and that object is subsequently deleted, the smart pointer knows this and can reflect that fact when queried. We'll see an example of this shortly, but first let me drive home the reason this is important.

## 10.10.3 Safety First

One of the biggest challenges we face as C++ programmers is pointer safety. That is, we must always be careful when writing code not to get into a situation where we are attempting to access a pointer that references an invalid (deleted) object. For example, imagine if we had the following code.

```
someClass *myClassPtr = new someClass;

myClassPtr->doSomething();

// ...

delete( myClassPtr );

// ...

myClassPtr->doSomething();
```

As you can see, the last statement will be (at the very least) problematic. We are attempting to access an object (using a pointer) that was previously deleted.

If we are lucky, this code will execute and do something unexpected but non-fatal.

If we are not lucky, we will get a segmentation violation (or some other loathsome error), and the program will crash.

"Ah!" you say, "We could always improve the code as follows."

```
// ...
delete( myClassPtr );

myClassPtr = NULL;
```

**Engine Coding**

```
// ...
if( NULL != myClassPtr )
{
 myClassPtr->doSomething();
}
```

In this "fixed" version of the code, we set our pointer to NULL after deleting the object, and then we checked for NULL before manipulating the pointer.

Bravo! This is a valid and safe solution.

Unfortunately, it is cumbersome and prone to error. In fact, the first time we forget to set a pointer to NULL, we are in big trouble.

What we need is a way to do this automatically.

## 10.10.4 Let Me Do That for You

The SimObjectPtr class comes to the rescue in this instance. It has been designed such that it will automatically set itself to NULL once the object it is pointing to is deleted.

Using this class is very easy, as the following code demonstrates.

```
// 1
SimObjectPtr<GameBase> mOrbitObject = NULL;

// 2
GameBase * pOtherPointer = NULL;

// 3
mOrbitObject = pOtherPointer = Sim::findObject("theCamera");

// 4
while( NULL != mOrbitObject )
{

  // 5
  pOtherPointer->deleteObject();

}
```

The above code follows these steps:

1. Using the SimObjectPtr template, we create a smart pointer capable of storing a reference to GameBase (or any child of GameBase).

2. For demonstration purposes, we also create a dumb pointer.

3. Now, we assign a value to both the smart pointer and to the dumb pointer, referencing the location of some object named "theCamera".
   - Note that we will discuss the use of Sim::findObject() and other useful functions later.

4. Next, we start a loop, controlled by a simple `NULL` pointer test. We continue to loop as long as `mOrbitObject` is not equal to `NULL`.

5. Because this is a simple example, the very first thing we do in this loop is tell the object to delete itself using the special method `deleteObject()`.

   - Note: If you do not use the `deleteObject()` method, the smart pointer system will not work. However, using `deleteObject()` is required anyway (as we will learn in Chapter 11), so this is a no-brainer.

It is important to understand that when this code executes, even though we have used the dumb pointer to delete the object, the smart pointer still gets notified (is aware) that the object has been deleted.

## 10.11 Printing Messages to the Console

Let me start off by saying that this is really a debugging topic, but since the use of message printing as a means for getting feedback (from code) is so prevalent and so fundamental, I will introduce the topic here instead of waiting for the debugging chapter.

### 10.11.1 Normal Messages

A normal message is one that is designed to provide non-warning and non-error information. That is, it is a simple print statement of some type. In Torque, all messages (normal or otherwise) are printed to the console.
In order to print a message to the console from withing C++, we simply write some code like this.

```
Con::printf("Hello World!");
```

Alternately, if we need to print more than just a string, we can format our print statement just like the standard ANSI C `printf()` function.

```
Con::printf( "Print a string %s, integer %d, float %g, etc..."
             "Hello!" , 10 , 3.14159f );
```

If you need more details on formatting, see the description for `printf()` in any standard C reference.

### 10.11.2 Warnings and Errors

TGE also provides two functions for printing warnings and errors (one for each) to the console. These functions work identically to `Con::printf()`, with the exception that when viewed in the console, warnings are generally printed in yellow and errors are generally printed in red. I say generally because you can modify these colors if you wish by updating the console profiles.

```
Con::warnf("This is a warning!");

Con::errorf("This is an error!");
```

## 10.12 Main Loop

Often, the first serious coding discussion with a new user goes something like the following.

"Hi. I'm ready to make a cool game with Torque, but I'm having trouble finding the main loop. I mean, I found several different copies of `main()`, and I'm not sure which one I need to modify."

"You don't need to modify the main loop. You can just ignore it for now."

"Huh? No, really, where is it? I mean how can I get started if I don't know where to put my new code?"

"You're misunderstanding how this works. You don't need to modify `main()`."

(I always pause here because I hate absolute statements.)

"What I mean is that just starting out, you probably won't need to make any changes to `main()`. It does everything you need it to do. In fact, modifying `main()` is a bit of an advanced topic."

"`main()`, an advanced topic? Now I know you're yanking my chain. Hey, if you're too busy, that's cool. I'll ask someone else."

"No, I'm not too busy it's just, ... it's just, ... Sigh.... Here, let's look at the main loop."

## 10.12.1 The Entry Point

Before we can look at the main loop, we have to find the engine's entry point.

The entry point is the code that executes first when you run an executable. Traditionally, the entry point in a C/C++ program is the function `main()`.

```
void main( int argc, char** argv)
{
}
```

The good news is that for the OS X and the Linux versions of TGE, `main()` is still the entry point. The bad news is that for Windows, it is not.

## Windows Entry Point

Since about Windows 95 or so, the entry point for a Windows application, which is started from a menu or icon (by clicking), has changed to WinMain().

```
S32 PASCAL WinMain( HINSTANCE hInstance,
 HINSTANCE hPrevInstance,
 LPSTR lpszCmdLine,
 S32 nCmdShow
 )
{

}
```

For those folks building Windows versions of the engine, you can find WinMain() in the file " ~ /platformWin32/winWindow.cc".

Note that if you search, you will also find the function main() defined in this file. Feel free to ignore it.

### Starting the Main Loop under Windows

When started, the Windows executable will get to the main loop by following these steps:

1. Windows loads the executable and does some initialization.
2. Windows executes the function WinMain().
3. WinMain() calls the function run().
4. run() calls the method main().

```
S32 ret = Game->main(argc, argv);
```

We will talk more about the call to Game->main() shortly, but first let's finish our talk about entry points.

## The OS X and Linux Entry Points

As I said above, the entry point for both OS X and Linux variants of TGE is still main().

### Starting the Main Loop under OS X

For those building OS X versions of the engine, you can find the definition of main() in the file " ~ /platformMacCarb/macCarbMain.cc".

When started, the OS X executable will get to the main loop by following these steps.

1. OS X loads the executable and does some initialization.

**Engine Coding**

2. OS X executes the function `main()`.

3. An event fires and calls the function `_MacCarbRAELCallback()`.

4. `_MacCarbRAELCallback()` calls the function `_MacCarbRunTorqueMain()`.

5. `_MacCarbRunTorqueMain()` calls the method `main()`.

```
platState.appReturn = Game->main(platState.argc,
                                 platState.argv);
```

### Starting the Main Loop under Linux

For those building Linux versions of the engine, you can find the definition of `main()` in the file " ~ /platformX86UNIX/x86UNIXWindow.cc".

When started, the Linux executable will get to the main loop by following these steps.

1. Linux loads the executable and does some initialization.

2. Linux executes the function `main()`.

3. `main()` calls the method `main()`.

```
returnVal = Game->main( newCommandLine.size(),
const_cast<const char**>
(newCommandLine.address())
);
```

## 10.12.2 DemoGame Main Loop

The main loop for all version of the engine can be found in the file " ~ /engine/game/main.cc". Within this file, you will find a class definition for the class `DemoGame`. `DemoGame` is in turn derived from the class `GameInterface`, which can be found in the files "engine/platform/gameInterface.[h,cc]".

If we look closely at the implementation of the method `DemoGame::main()`, we will see it is pretty simple (this is a simplified version).

```
int DemoGame::main(int argc, const char **argv)
{
// 1
initLibraries();
initGame();

// 2

while ( Game->isRunning() )
{
Game->journalProcess();
Net::process();
```

```
Platform::process();
TelConsole->process();
TelDebugger->process();
TimeManager::process();
Game->processEvents();
}

// 3
shutdownGame();
shutdownLibraries();
}
```

In short, it does the following.

1. Do some one-time initialization.
2. Loop while the game is "running," and on each loop execute these steps:
   - Play back next part of recorded journal if in playback mode.
   - Read in all events.
   - Processes mouse, keyboard, etc. input.
   - Processes telnet commands (if a session is active).
   - Processes debugger commands (if a session is active).
   - Advance time.
   - Process all non-sim posted events.
3. Do some one-time cleanup.
4. Exit.

That is it! Of course, the code behind these steps is complicated, but the loop itself is quite simple.

## More about `Game` and the `GameInterface` Class

The observant reader will still be wondering where the `Game` pointer got initialized.

First, `Game` is a pointer of type `GameInterface`.

Second, `Game` points to an instance of `DemoGame`, which is a child class of `GameInterface`.

Third, the instance of `DemoGame` is created when the executable is loaded, that is, during that initialization I talked about above when we were discussing entry points.

### Singleton, but Not a Singleton?

Reading my three statements above, you might automatically jump to the conclusion that `GameInterface` is a singleton class, but this isn't exactly

**185**

correct. The code is written to enforce singleton behavior, but it doesn't use the traditional singleton design pattern to do so.

Regardless, like a singleton, there will only ever be one instance of the DemoGame (a child of GameInterface) class created when you run TGE. Let's talk about how that happens next.

## The Initialization Flow

1. The GameInterface class is declared in "~/platform/gameInterface.h" and implemented in "~/platform/gameInterface.cc". The declaration starts like this.

   ```
   class GameInterface
   {
   ```

2. The global variable GameInterface* Game is declared and initialized (to NULL) in "~/platform/gameInterface.cc".

   ```
   GameInterface *Game = NULL;
   ```

3. Looking at the constructor GameInterface::GameInterface(), one will see that the pointer Game is initialized to the special variable this. That is, when the constructor is called, the global pointer is initialized.

   ```
   GameInterface::GameInterface()
   {
    AssertFatal(Game == NULL, "ERROR: Multiple games declared.");
    Game = this;
   ```

4. In an unmodified version of TGE, a new class, DemoGame, is declared, which inherits from GameInterface. This class is declared in "~/plat-form/demoGame.h" and implemented in "~/platform/demoGame.cc". The declaration starts like this.

   ```
   class DemoGame : public GameInterface
   {
   ```

5. Looking closely at the file "~/platform/demoGame.cc", one will see that an instance of DemoGame is implemented with this code.

   ```
   DemoGame GameObject;
   ```

6. When the (above) instance of DemoGame is created in "demoGame.cc", it will automatically call the constructor of GameInterface, which will in turn assign this (the address of the the newly created instance of Demo-Game) to Game. Voila! Now, we have a global pointer to an instance of DemoGame. This instance is created and the pointer is initialized as soon as the engine executable is loaded.

| Exercise Summary | Location on Disk |
|---|---|
| Compiling Torque in Windows. | /exercises/ch10_001.pdf |
| Compiling Torque in OS X. | /exercises/ch10_002.pdf |
| Engine organization. | /exercises/ch10_003.pdf |
| Printing messages. | /exercises/ch10_004.pdf |
| Using Torque data types. | /exercises/ch10_005.pdf |
| Using The Torque Standard Library. | /exercises/ch10_006.pdf |
| Torque Math #1: Points. | /exercises/ch10_007.pdf |
| Torque Math #2: Boxes. | /exercises/ch10_008.pdf |
| Torque Math #3: Matrices. | /exercises/ch10_009.pdf |
| Strings (the string table). | /exercises/ch10_010.pdf |

**Table 10.8.**
Introduction to engine
coding exercises.

## 10.13 Exercises

I know that this chapter included a lot of varied and somewhat difficult topics and you may have had some trouble digesting them. So, to assist you, I have included a number of step-by-step exercises to get you started with individual topics. Table 10.8 lists these exercises.

# Chapter 11

# Creating and Using New Game Classes

## 11.1 Introduction

This chapter provides a discussion of the major game classes and is ordered to match the `ConsoleObject` classes hierarchy. In this chapter, we will learn about the individual game classes and how to derive from of them, and we will examine some class-derivation examples.

### 11.1.1 Templates Provided

To simplify the task of creating new game classes, several templates are provided on the accompanying CD. The location of each template is listed below.

> **ConsoleObject template.** "templates\ConsoleObject\t_ConsoleObject.[cc,h]".

> **SimObject template.** "templates\SimObject\t_SimObject.[cc,h]".

> **SceneObject template.** "templates\SceneObject\t_SceneObject.[cc,h]".

> **GameBase(Data) template.** "templates\GameBase\t_GameBase.[cc,h]".

> **GuiControl template.** "templates\GuiControl\t_GuiControl.[cc,h]".

### 11.1.2 Feature Discussions

The feature discussions that follow are conversational in nature and are intended to provide an introduction to individual features. By no means are these discussions meant to be definitive references. Instead, each section is supplemented by a quick reference in Appendix B pertaining to the class under discussion and the features it provides.

### 11.1.3 Derivation Recipes

All of the derivation recipes are short lists designed as a reminder for experienced users. You can gain this experience by examining the derivation examples and practicing with your own classes.

### 11.1.4 Derivation Examples and Exercises

There are three derivation examples in this book and many exercises on the accompanying CD where you can expand your experience in deriving new classes and using features of these game classes.

We are not discussing the derivation of new `GuiControl` children classes in this chapter. This is partly because `GuiControl` is a simple class to derive from but mostly because there just wasn't space for a full discussion of GUI creation.

I know this may be a bit of a disappointment, so I have provided a template for creating new `GuiControl` children, and I have provided two examples creating new GUIs. I think this will set you well on the path to creating your own GUIs in the future.

## 11.2 The Con **Namespace**

Torque provides a large set of features for interfacing C++ engine code with the TorqueScript console. Several of these features are provided by the Con namespace.

In this section, we will examine the Con namespace features without applying them. Instead, we will begin to apply these features (later in this chapter) as we discuss subsequent classes that use them.

### 11.2.1 Including Con **Namespace Features**

To use any of the Con namespace features, you must include the "console.h" header file in your code as shown below.

```
#include "console/console.h"
```

### 11.2.2 **Printing Messages From C++ to the Console**

In Chapter 10, we discussed the Con::printf(), Con::warnf(), and Con::errorf() functions. As you can see (by the prefix), each of these functions is provided by the Con namespace. Each of these functions prints a colorized message to the console window. These colors will match the current color scheme used by the corresponding TorqueScript functions echo(), warn(), and error().

For example, this C++ statement

```
Con::errorf("Bad value! => %d", 10 );
```

will produce the same result as this TorqueScript statement

```
error("Bad value! => ", 10 );
```

### 11.2.3 **Registering C++ Globals as Console Globals**

The Con namespace provides the capability to register (expose) C++ global variables with the console. Subsequently, changes made to these exposed variables will be visible from both C++ and TorqueScript. In other words, if an exposed variable is changed in C++, that change will be reflected in the TorqueScript version of this global and vice versa.

The task of exposing C++ globals is handled by a single function, `Con::addVariable()`. For example, the C++ `S32` global `myCPPGlobal` could be exposed as a TorqueScript global `$myTSGlobal` with the following code.

```
S32 myCPPGlobal;


void myClass::consoleInit()
{
   Con::addVariable( "$myTSGlobal",   TypeS32,   &myCPPGlobal
);
}
```

This function works equally well for exposing static class members (which are considered global by the rules of C++). Just remember to use the namespace when exposing this type of global variable.

```
class sgRelightFilter
{
public:
 static bool sgFilterRelight;

...


void sgRelightFilter::sgInit()
{
 Con::addVariable( "SceneLighting::sgFilterRelight",
                   TypeBool,
                   &sgRelightFilter::sgFilterRelight);
...
```

> You may have noticed, but calls to `Con::addVariable()` do not require that the $ symbol be added to the TorqueScript global name specification. If it is not provided, the engine adds one for you.

The above call to `Con::addVariable()` registers the static member `sgFilterRelight` of the class `sgRelightFilter` with the console as `$SceneLighting::sgFilterRelight`.

## Removing Previously Registered Global Variables

There is a reciprocal function for `Con::addVariable()` named `Con::removeVariable()`. If it is called after a call to `Con::addVariable()`, and if it is passed the same TorqueScript variable name as was used for the `Con::addVariable()` call, that TorqueScript global will be unregistered.

```
void mySecondClass::consoleInit()
{
   Con::removeVariable( "$myTSGlobal" );
}
```

## 11.2.4  Manipulating Console Variables from C++

The Con namespace provides the ability to access console variables from C++ in various ways. Specifically, it offers the functions in Table 11.1. Some simple examples follow.

```
// Get, modify, and then re-set the console floating-point global
// $pref::precipitationDensity
//
F32 precipDensity = Con::getFloatVariable("$pref::precipitationDensity");

precipDensity = 2 * precipDensity;

Con::setFloatVariable("$pref::precipitationDensity", precipDensity);

// Get, modify, and then re-set the console boolean global
// $pref::Video::fullScreen
//
boolean fullScreen =  Con::getBoolVariable("$pref::Video::fullScreen");

fullScreen = !fullScreen;

Con::setBoolVariable( "$pref::Video::fullScreen", fullScreen );

// Get and then set the console string global
// $pref::Video::resolution
//
const char* resString = Con::getVariable( "$pref::Video::resolution" );
```

**Table 11.1**

*Functions for accessing console variables from C++.*

| Function | Purpose |
|---|---|
| Con::getBoolVariable()<br>Con::setBoolVariable() | These functions allow us to get and set the value of a global boolean console variable from within the engine using C++ code. |
| Con::getFloatVariable()<br>Con::setFloatVariable() | These functions allow us to get and set the value of a global floating-point console variable from within the engine using C++ code. |
| Con::getLocalVariable()<br>Con::setLocalVariable() | These functions allow us to get and set the value of a local TorqueScript variable from within the engine using C++ code. The context of any local variable is entirely dependent upon the scripting context in which either of these functions is called. |
| Con::getVariable()<br>Con::setVariable() | These functions allow us to get and set the value of any type of console variable from within the engine using C++ code. The get function returns a pointer to a string, and the set function takes one. |

```
char tempBuf[15];

dSprintf( tempBuf, sizeof( tempBuf ), "%d %d %d", 1024, 768, 32 );

Con::setVariable( "$pref::Video::resolution", tempBuf );
```

## 11.2.5 Creating Console Functions and Methods from C++

The `ConsoleObject` class (see Section 11.3) provides the capability to register a C++ console class with the console. Once a class is registered, we can create and manipulate instances of that class in the console using TorqueScript.

There are three macros (see Table 11.2) found in the "console.h" header file that allow us to create console functions and methods from within the engine using C++ code.

Each of the macros takes a similar set of arguments.

> **className** (only for method macros). The class that the new console method should be associated with.

> **name**. A string containing the name to use for the new console function/method.

> **returnType**. An intrinsic or Torque-specific type identifier.

> **minArgs**. An integer specifying the minimum number of arguments that can be passed to the new console function/method.

> **maxArgs**. An integer specifying the maximum number of arguments that can be passed to the new console function/method.

> **usage1**. A string containing usage instructions for the new console function/method.

As with calls to `Con::addVariable()`, it is not necessary to provide the preceding $ or % symbol (for TorqueScript variable names) when calling any of the get and set methods listed in Table 11.1.

### Using the Console Function/Method Creation Macros

The beauty of the function/method creation macros is that using them is effectively the same as writing a normal C++ function or method. To clarify this statement, let's look at a simple example to see how the `ConsoleFunction()` macro is used.

**Table 11.2**

C++ Macros for creating console functions and methods.

| Macro |
|---|
| ConsoleFunction(name, returnType, minArgs, maxArgs, usage1) |
| ConsoleMethod(className, name, returnType, minArgs, maxArgs, usage1) |
| ConsoleStaticMethod(className, name, returnType, minArgs, maxArgs, usage1) |

```
ConsoleFunction( strcmp, S32, 3, 3, "strcmp(string one, string two)"
                " - Case sensitive string compare." )
{
   return dStrcmp( argv[1], argv[2] );
}
```

The above code creates a new console function named strcmp. This new console function returns an S32 value, takes a minimum and a maximum of 3 arguments and has the usage (help) string "strcmp(string one, string two) - Case sensitive string compare.". The body of this function simply calls the Torque Standard Library function dStrcmp(), passing it two automatic argv variables, and then returns the result. (We will discuss automatic variables in a moment.)

The ConsoleMethod() and ConsoleStaticMethod() macros are equally simple and elegant as can be seen by examining the following code.

```
ConsoleMethod(SimObject, setName, void, 3, 3, "obj.setName(newName)")
{
   object->assignName(argv[2]);
}
```

The above call to the ConsoleMethod() macro creates a new console method in the SimObject namespace that allows the user to set the name (set-Name()) of any SimObject using TorqueScript.

### Automatic Variables

The above macros generate C++ code at compile time. This code in turn is placed before the bodies that we add after the macro calls. To clarify, in the strcmp() example, the body we added after the macro call was this code.

```
{
    return dStrcmp( argv[1], argv[2] );
}
```

The generated code above these bodies will contain up to three useful variables.

➢ **char \*\* argv**. This variable is an array of strings passed from the console when this function or method is called. All three macros provide this to the body code.

➢ **S32 argc**. This variable is an integer (S32) value containing a count of the argv strings passed to this function or method. All three macros provide this to the body code.

➢ *className* **\*Object**. This variable is a pointer to the object that this method was called on in the console. Only the macros for generating console methods provide this to the body code.

**argv values and `ConsoleFunction()`.** With the `ConsoleFunction()` macro, the `argv` variable is populated as follows.

➤ `argv[0]`. The name of the console function as it was called in the console.

➤ `argv[1]` .. `argv[n]`. Any arguments passed in the call to this method.

For example, the following call to `strcmp()` will produce three (`argc == 3`) `argv` values.

```
strcmp( bob , bill );
```

The strings passed in `argv` are as follows.

➤ `argv[0]` contains `"strcmp"`.
➤ `argv[1]` contains `"bob"`.
➤ `argv[2]` contains `"bill"`.

**argv values and `ConsoleMethod()`/`ConsoleStaticMethod()`.** With the `ConsoleMethod()` and `ConsoleStaticMethod()` macros, the `argv` variable is populated as follows.

➤ `argv[0]`. The name of the console function as it was called in the console.

➤ `argv[1]`. The console ID of the object that this method was called on.

➤ `argv[2]` .. `argv[n]`. Any arguments passed in the call to this method.

For example, the following call to `strcmp()` will produce three (`argc == 3`) `argv` values.

```
1725.setName( "Bob" );
```

The strings passed in `argv` are as follows.

➤ `argv[0]` contains `"setName"`.
➤ `argv[1]` contains `"1725"`.
➤ `argv[2]` contains `"Bob"`.

Additionally, the body following the macro will be passed a `SimObject` pointer named `object`.

## The `minArgs` / `maxArgs` Settings

In the list of values provided to the console function and method macros are the `minArgs` and `maxArgs` values. As was noted above, these values are integers specifying the minimum and maximum number of arguments that the resultant console function or macro expects to receive. If the wrong number of

**Engine Coding**

| Macro | Rules |
|---|---|
| `ConsoleFunction()` | minArgs = 1 + arguments needed for function.<br>maxArgs = 0 or minArgs + optional arguments. |
| `ConsoleMethod()` | minArgs = 2 + arguments needed for method.<br>maxArgs = 0 or minArgs + optional arguments. |
| `ConsoleStaticMethod()` | minArgs = 1 + arguments needed for method.<br>maxArgs = 0 or minArgs + optional arguments. |

**Table 11.3**

**minArgs/maxArgs** rules.

arguments are used later, the engine will automatically print the value passed in the `usage1` argument.

When calculating the value for `minArgs`, be sure to account for the argument the engine passes automatically. For `ConsoleFunction()`, the minimum value for `minArgs` is one, while the minimum value for `minArgs` is two for `ConsoleMethod()` and `ConsoleStaticMethod()`.

When calculating `maxArgs`, be sure to set it to at least the value of `minArgs` and then add any additional optional values. When `maxArgs` is higher than `minArgs`, it means that the function or method requires at least a certain number of arguments but can handle more. Also, if there is no limit to the maximum arguments the function or method can handle, simply set `maxArgs` to 0.

To simply your life, the rules for calculating the correct values for `minArgs` and `maxArgs` are listed in Table 11.3.

## Returning Values

There are rules for how data is returned by a function or method created using the above macros.

➤ Any constant string may be returned directly.

- `return "";`
- `return "hello";`

➤ Any value returned directly from an engine function or method may be returned directly. In the following example, the return value from the `getName()` method is returned directly.

```
ConsoleMethod(SimObject, getName, const char *, 2, 2, "obj.getName()")
{
    const char *ret = object->getName();

    return ret ? ret : "";
}
```

➤ If the value to be returned is generated in the function or method body, then you need to allocate space for that return value using the `Con::`

`getReturnBuffer()` method. In the following example, a 256-byte buffer is generated using `Con::getReturnBuffer()`. Then, it is populated with a string value containing three floating-point values. Finally, it is returned.

```
ConsoleMethod( SceneObject, getScale, const char*, 2, 2, "" )
{
    char *returnBuffer = Con::getReturnBuffer(256);

    const VectorF & scale = object->getScale();

    dSprintf(returnBuffer, 256, "%g %g %g", scale.x, scale.y, scale.z );

    return(returnBuffer);
}
```

## 11.2.6 Registering C++ Functions and Methods with the Console

There is another way to add console functions and console methods to the console from C++. There are two `Con` namespace functions, `Con::addFunction()` and `Con::addCommand()`, used to register existing C++ functions or methods directly with the console.

These functions are used primarily by the macros we just discussed and also by the newly added lighting system. However, for general use, these functions are deprecated, meaning it is not suggested that you use them. The macros do all you need and in a consistent way. Using the functions requires a higher level of engine skill and is error prone. However, if you do want to use them, try examining the lighting system usages as found in "volLight.cc".

## 11.2.7 Executing Console Functions and Methods from C++

A critical feature that the `Con` namespace provides is the ability to execute console (script) functions and methods from within the engine code.

This functionality is provided by four overloaded functions.

➢ **Con::execute()**. This overloaded function is used to execute a script function or method from C++ and takes a fixed number of arguments.

➢ **Con::executef()**. This overloaded function is used to execute a script function or method from C++ and takes a variable number of arguments.

### Executing a Script Function with `Con::execute()`

The script function variant of `Con::execute()` has the following signature.

```
const char *execute(S32 argc, const char* argv[]);
```

**Engine Coding**

This function takes two arguments, an integer argument count and an array of strings. A simple example of this function in use would look as follows.

```
void addItUp()
{
    static const char *argv[3];

    argv[0] = "echo";
    argv[1] = "10 + 10 == ";
    argv[2] = "20";

    Con::execute(3, argv);
}
```

Here, we have an engine function called `addItUp()`. It defines a `static const char` array and then populates it with three strings. The first string is the name of the script function to execute, while the second and third are values to be passed to that script function. When called, the engine will execute code equivalent to the following script.

```
echo( "10 + 10 == ", "20" );
```

## Executing a Script Function with `Con::executef()`

The script function variant of `Con::executef()` has the following signature.

```
const char *executef(S32 argc, ...);
```

This function takes one integer argument and an unspecified number of additional arguments. Using this variant, we could re-write `addItUp()` as follows.

```
void addItUp()
{
    Con::executef(3, "echo" , "10 + 10 == ", "20" );
}
```

As can be seen, this form is simpler, making it the preferred form.

## Executing a Script Method with `Con::execute()`

The script method variant of `Con::execute()` has the following signature.

```
const char *execute(SimObject * object, S32 argc, const char* argv[]);
```

This function takes two arguments, an integer argument count and an array of strings. A simple example of this function in use would look as follows.

```
void dumpIt( SimObject * someObject )
{
```

```
    static const char *argv[1];

    argv[0] = "dump";

    Con::execute(someObject , 2, argv);
}
```

Here, we have an engine function called `dumpIt()`. It defines a `static const char` array and then populates it with one string. That string is the name of the script function ("`dump`") to execute on the object (`someObject`) that was passed to our function. When called, the engine will execute code equivalent to the following script (assuming the ID of `someObject` is 123).

```
    123.dump();
```

## Executing a Script Method with `Con::executef()`

The script method variant of `Con::executef()` has the following signature.

```
    const char *executef(SimObject * object, S32 argc, ...);
```

This function takes a `SimObject` pointer and one integer argument (`argc`) specifying the number of variable (`...`) arguments that will be passed in. Using this variant, we could rewrite `dumpIt()` as follows.

```
    void dumpIt( SimObject * someObject )
    {
        Con::executef(someObject , 1, "dump");
    }
```

> Both `execute()` and `executef()` require us to pass a `const char **`, but sometimes you may find yourself wanting to pass a non `const` array of pointers. To accomplish this, simply use the C++ `const_cast<const char**>` casting mechanism. (Search the engine source code to see this in action.)

Again, this form is simpler, making it the preferred form.

## Passing Data

Sometimes, you will find yourself in a situation where you need to pass some kind of variable-sized data to one of the `Con::executef()` functions.

In a situation like this, you can use one of three different method depending upon your needs.

> ➤ **char \* getFloatArg( F64 arg )**. This `Con` namespace function takes a 64-bit floating-point value and returns a string that can then be passed directly to `Con::executef()`.

> ➤ **char \* getIntArg( S32 arg )**. This `Con` namespace function takes a 32-bit integer value and returns a string that can then be passed directly to `Con::executef()`.

> ➤ **char \* getArgBuffer( U32 buffersize )**. This `Con` namespace function takes a 32-bit integer buffer size and returns an empty `char *`

buffer of that length (in bytes). You can then populate this buffer using `dSprintf()` and then pass it directly to `Con::executef()`.

All three of these methods produce data that is stored on a data stack and cleaned up automatically by the engine.

## 11.2.8 Evaluating Console Scripts in C++

In addition to the ability to execute script functions and methods from C++, we can evaluate strings of TorqueScript directly in C++. There are two `Con` namespace functions provided to do this.

The first function has the following signature.

```
const char *evaluate( const char* string, bool echo = false,
                      const char *fileName = NULL);
```

The arguments this function takes are as follows.

➢ **string**. A string containing the script to evaluate.
➢ **echo**. A boolean value specifying whether to echo string to the console. (This is mainly to enable easy debugging of your scripts.)
➢ **fileName**. A string containing the name and path of a file in which to store the compiled script. Subsequently, if this function is called again with exactly the same arguments, the compiled version of `string` will be executed instead of recompiling and then executing it. This feature is only useful if you expect `string` to be both large and executed multiple times without changing. In such a case, you may benefit from the saved time associated with executing the precompiled script.

In a simple example, we could evaluate a one-line script.

```
Con::evaluate("echo(\"Torque Rocks!\");", true );
```

This example call will print the following to the console when executed.

```
echo("Torque Rocks!");
Torque Rocks!
```

The second function has the following signature.

```
const char *evaluatef(const char* string, ...);
```

The arguments this function takes are as follows.

➢ **string**. A string containing the script to evaluate.
➢ **....** A variable number of additional arguments.

This function is a bit more flexible regarding arguments but does not have the nice features of printing the pre-evaluated script to the console and of saving the compiled script to file. Nonetheless, it is useful because the variable arguments can be used like those found in `printf()`, `sprintf()`, and other functions taking variable arguments.

Here is the `Con::evaluatef()` variant of our last example.

```
Con::evaluatef("echo(\"Torque Rocks!\");");
```

Here is a more elaborate example.

```
Con::evaluatef("echo(\"10 + 10 == \", %d + %d );", 10, 10 );
```

The above code will produce the following script and then evaluate it.

```
echo( "10 + 10 == ", 10 + 10 );
```

## 11.3 The `ConsoleObject` Class

The `ConsoleObject` class provides the remaining (base) functionality for interfacing C++ engine code with the TorqueScript console.

To use any of these features, you must include the "consoleObject.h" header file in your code.

```
// Use features of the ConsoleObject class
//
#include "console/consoleObject.h"
```

In the following pages, we will examine the `ConsoleObject` class features.

## 11.3.1 Registering C++ Classes with the Console

The `ConsoleObject` class provides the capability to register a C++ console class with the console. Once a class is registered with the console, we can create and manipulate instances of the registered class in TorqueScript.

To register a new console class with the console, it is necessary to write a sequence of specialized registration code that allows the new class to be integrated with the console. This code is somewhat complicated and relies on some interesting programming tricks. Fortunately, because this code always has the same form, the engine developers have provided a set of macros to do the work. In short, we don't need to know how it works; we just need to use the macros. In total, `ConsoleObject` provides four macros for handling

If you choose to write code using the `evaluate()` or `evaluatef()` functions from within a console function or console method implementation (in C++), be aware that they corrupt the console function's/method's argument list. So, before calling either of these functions in a console function/method, be sure to extract that function's/method's arguments from `argv[]` first, storing them in temporary variables for safety.

class registration. Collectively, these macros are referred to as the ConObject macros.

## DECLARE_CONOBJECT()

This macro is used universally to register all console class declarations. To use this macro, simply include it in a public area of your class declaration and pass in the name of the class.

```
class myConsoleObject : public ConsoleObject
{
public:
    DECLARE_CONOBJECT( myConsoleObject );

    ...
```

> All implementation macros must be called after the DECLARE_CONOBJECT() macro. If your new class only has a source file (often true of new GuiControl classes), be sure to call DECLARE_CONOBJECT() first, then call the necessary implementation macro.

## IMPLEMENT_CONOBJECT()

This macro is used to implement the registration code for all new classes derived from ConsoleObject. Primarily, you will use this when writing new GuiControl classes.

To use this macro, simply include it in a source file with your new class and pass in the name of the class.

```
IMPLEMENT_CONOBJECT( myConsoleObject );
```

## IMPLEMENT_CO_NETOBJECT_V1()

This macro is used to implement the registration code for all new classes derived from NetObject and children of NetObject. Primarily, you will use this when writing new GameBase classes.

To use this macro, simply include it in a source file with your new class and pass in the name of the class.

```
IMPLEMENT_CO_NETOBJECT_V1( myNetObject );
```

## IMPLEMENT_CO_DATABLOCK_V1()

This macro is used to implement the registration code for all new classes derived from SimDatablock and children of SimDatablock. Primarily, you will use this when writing new GameBaseData classes, but it is possible to create new classes from SimDatablock, too.

To use this macro, simply include it in a source file with your new class and pass in the name of the class.

```
IMPLEMENT_CO_DATABLOCK_V1( mySimDatablock );
```

# 11.3.2  Registering C++ Class Members as Persistent Console Fields

When we implement and register a new console class, it is possible to make any `public` member of that class available as a persistent field in the console. This is called registering and is also referred to as exposing.

To register a class's `public` member(s) as persistent fields in the console, we use one of several built-in `ConsoleObject` methods. These methods are referred to collectively as the `addField()` methods. Table 11.4 lists the available `addField()` methods and their uses. In addition to the four methods mentioned in Table 11.4, `ConsoleObject` also provides two macros for registering members. Table 11.5 lists these macros.

## The `Offset()` Macro

In order to register a public C++ class member as a persistent field, the engine needs to calculate the exact location and size of the variable as it resides in memory. We pass this offset to the `addField()` methods.

This kind of calculation is OS-implementation-specific and requires some know-how. Fortunately, TGE implements a cross-platform macro called `Offset()` that does all the work for us.

| Method | Used to... |
|---|---|
| addField() | ... register a single `public` member or member array as a persistent field(s). |
| addFieldV() | ... register a single `public` member as a persistent field and to attach a validating function to that field. The validating function is used to ensure that users set only legal values (defined by you) while using the inspector to modify the persistent field. |
| addDepricatedField() | ... register a single `public` member as a persistent field and to write-protect that field. Any class member registered using this method will create a persistent field in the console, but writes to that persistent field will not change the value of the class member. This effectively write-protects a field in the console. (Yes, the word deprecated is misspelled as depricated, that is not a typo.) |
| removeField() | ... unregister a previously registered field. |

Table 11.4
**addField()** methods.

| Method | Used to... |
|---|---|
| addNamedField() | ... register a single `public` member. The persistent field is given the same name as the member. |
| addNamedFieldV() | ... register a single `public` member using validation. The persistent field is given the same name as the member. |

Table 11.5
**addField()** macros.

The `Offset()` macro takes two arguments, class member name and class name. Given these two arguments, it returns an integer value equal to the byte offset of the class member within an instance of that class.

```
int offsetInBytes = Offset( memberName , className );
```

We will use this macro below while discussing example `addField()` cases. Now, let's discuss the rules for registering class members.

### Class Member Registration Rules

The rules for registering a class member as a persistent field are as follows.

1. The member has to be declared as `public`. (Members declared as `protected` and `private` cannot be exposed to the console.)
2. The member to be exposed cannot be an arbitrary pointer, although it may be a pointer to a registered datablock class. (See Section 11.7.4.)
3. The member to be exposed must be non-static. (A static member is globally visible and is registered differently. See Section 11.2.3.)
4. `addField()` methods and macros must only be called in the new class's `initPersistFields()` method.

### Using `addField()`

In reality, there are two variants of the `addField()` method, one designed for registering single members and one designed for registering arrays.
The first variant takes four arguments.

1. **Field name**. A string containing the name for the new persistent field.
2. **Field type**. An enumerated value specifying the type of this class member. (You can find the full list of registrable types and their enumerated constants in Section B.6.1.)
3. **Field offset**. A byte value calculated using the `Offset()` macro.
4. **Description**. An optional pointer to a string containing a description of the new field.

The following snippet shows this variant of `addField()` in use.

```
addField( "materialList",
        TypeFilename ,
        Offset( mMaterialListName , Sky ) ,
        ""
    );
```

This code will register a persistent field named "`materialList`" for instances of the `Sky` console class. This field will point to a variable containing a file name and stored at the offset calculated for the `mMaterialListName` class member. No description has been supplied.

The second variant (used for arrays) takes six arguments.

1. **Field name**. A string containing the name for the new persistent field.

2. **Field type**. An enumerated value specifying the type of this class member. (You can find the full list of registrable types and their enumerated constants in Section B.6.1.)

3. **Field offset**. A byte value calculated using the `Offset()` macro.

4. **Element count**. An optional integer value specifying the number of elements in this array. This count defaults to 1 if not specified, meaning that this method can be used to expose non-array class members, too.

5. **Enumerated-table pointer**. An optional pointer to an instance of structure `EnumTable`. (This is used for registering enumerated types. See "Registering an Enumerated Class Member with `addField()`" below to see how this works.)

6. **Description**. An optional pointer to a string containing a description of the new field.

The following snippet shows this variant of `addField()` in use.

```
addField( "cloudHeightPer" ,
         TypeF32 ,
         Offset( mCloudHeight , Sky ) ,
         3,
         NULL,
         "The cloud layer height parameters"
        );
```

This code will register a persistent field array named "`cloudHeightPer`" for instances of the `Sky` class. This field will point to a member array with three elements, where the first element is located at the `Offset()`-calculated byte position of `mCloudHeight`. Since this is not an enumerated type, we just pass a `NULL` for the enumerated-table pointer. In this example, we have provided a simple description of `"The cloud layer height parameters"`.

Once this is compiled into the engine, we will be able to edit this field in the inspector, where it will show up as three new fields: `cloudHeightPer0`, `cloudHeightPer1`, and `cloudHeightPer2`.

Alternately, we could print the value of these fields using the following script.

```
// Assume %sky contains an instance of the Sky console class

for( %i = 0; %i < 3; %i++)
{
    echo( "mCloudHeight[", %i , "] == ", %sky.mCloudHeight[%i] );
}
```

### Registering an Enumerated Class Member with `addField()`

The second variant of the `addField()` method is capable of registering enumerated class members and enumerated arrays. In either case, we can supply an instance of the special structure `EnumTable`. This special structure allows us to use named values instead of integer values in the inspector and in our scripts. Enabling this feature is a four-step process.

### Step #1: Define an Enumerated Type

First, we need an enumerated type (defined in the public area of a class declaration). The following snippet lists a real engine enumerated type called `horizSizingOptions` (used by children of `GuiControl`).

```
public:
   enum horizSizingOptions
   {
      horizResizeRight = 0 ,
      horizResizeWidth ,
      horizResizeLeft ,
      horizResizeCenter ,
      horizResizeRelative
   };
```

The above enumerated type contains five entries whose numeric values range from 0 to 4.

> An instance of `EnumTable` must be created in the source file of the class that will be using it.

### Step #2: Create an Instance of `EnumTable`

Second, we need to create an instance of `EnumTable`.

```
static EnumTable::Enums horzEnums[] =
{
   { GuiControl::horizResizeRight,      "right"     },
   { GuiControl::horizResizeWidth,      "width"     },
   { GuiControl::horizResizeLeft,       "left"      },
   { GuiControl::horizResizeCenter,     "center"    },
   { GuiControl::horizResizeRelative,   "relative"  }
};

static EnumTable gHorizSizingTable( 5 , & horzEnums[0] );
```

In this example, we have used the `EnumTable` structure to correlate strings containing names to enumerated values. For example, if we implement the next step properly, `"center"` can be used instead of the integer value 3 (in our scripts).

## Step #3: Create Variable(s) using the `enum`

Third, we create one or more public variables in the class using our enumerated type (from Step #1). (If we don't create at least one variable, then we have nothing to expose.)

```
public:
    enum horizSizingOptions mHorizSizing;
```

## Step #4: Register the Class Member using `addField()`

Fourth, we register the enumerated field using our newly created `EnumTable` instance.

```
addField( "HorizSizing" ,
          TypeEnum ,
          Offset( mHorizSizing , GuiControl ) ,
          1 ,
          &gHorizSizingTable
        );
```

This code will register a persistent field array named "HorizSizing" for instances of the `GuiControl` class. This field will point to an enumerated class member named `mHorizSizing`. Because this is a single field, we pass 1 as the element count. Last, we pass in the address of `gHorizSizingTable`, the `EnumTable` structure we made.

> If you create an `enum` type and later want to expose it, you can expose it as an `S32`. Alternately, you can create an `S32` variable and assign `enum` values to it. In fact, as long as the variable is 32 bits wide, you are OK using it to store `enum` values.

## Using `addFieldV()`

In addition to the last two methods for registering C++ class member as a field, TGE provides a third method covering a special case. That special case occurs when you need to limit the values that can be assigned to a field. This limiting is called field validation.

To handle this need, we use the `addFieldV()` method and pass in the address of a validator class instance. Now, when the field is modified via the inspector, the engine will call the validator function to ensure that the new value is legal. If it is not, the validator will change it to a legal value.

## The Field Validator Classes

TGE provides classes for the two most commonly encountered validation cases.

➤ **IRangeValidator**. This class can be used to limit a field's range to some value between a low and a high integer value.

➤ **FRangeValidator**. This class can be used to limit a field's range to some value between a low and a high (32-bit) floating-point value.

To use these classes, you must include the "typeValidators.h" header file in your code.

```
// Include predefined validator classes
//
#include "console/typeValidators.h"
```

Alternately, you may create a custom validator using these validators as examples.

### Exposing a Validated Variable

The addFieldV() method is not used in the engine, so I can't show an actual example using engine code here. So, instead, I will borrow a line of code from the engine and rewrite it to use the addFieldV() method.

```
addFieldV( "lightRadius" ,
        TypeF32 ,
        Offset( lightRadius , ProjectileData ) ,
        new FRangeValidator(1.0f, 20.0f)
      );
```

This code will register a new field named "lightRadius" with the console. It specifies that this field points to a variable of type F32 and provides an Offset()-calculated for the lightRadius public member of class ProjectileData. Last, it uses the new keyword to create an instance of the FRangeValidator class, specifying that the range for this validator is between 1.0f and 20.0f.

### Using addDepricatedField()

Occasionally, we may want to retain a previously exposed field but ensure that changes to the field don't do anything. To accomplish this, we use the method addDepricatedField().

```
addDepricatedField("SetFirstResponder");
```

### Using the addNamedField() Macro

To complement the addField() methods, there are two macros. These macros simply wrap calls to the methods and require that we name our field the same as the actual member.

For example, in a previous example, we used the addField() method to add a persistent field named "materialList" to the Sky class.

```
addField( "materialList" ,
        TypeFilename ,
        Offset( mMaterialListName , Sky ) ,
        ""
          );
```

While this code is certainly not complicated, we might wish to further simplify our life and use the following call to the `AddNamedField()` macro instead.

```
addNamedField(  mMaterialListName , TypeFilename , Sky );
```

This would effectively do the same thing as our last example, except in this case, the field will be named "`mMaterialListName`" instead. This is the lazy person's `addField()`.

In another example, we could re-implement the code using the `addFieldv()` method that added the validated field "`lightRadius`" to the class `ProjectileData`.

```
addNamedFieldV( lightRadius ,
                TypeF32 ,
                ProjectileData ,
                new FRangeValidator( 1.0f , 20.0f ) );
```

This example produces exactly the same result as our last implementation. Why? Because in this case, the member name really is `lightRadius`.

### Unregistering Fields

If you derive from a class and find that you need to unregister a class member registered in that parent class (or a grandparent class), you can do so by calling the `removeField()` method.

```
removeField("position");
```

### Grouping Fields (for Inspector)

It is possible to organize fields so that they show up in nice groups in the inspector. To do this, we simply use the `addGroup()` method before a set of fields we wish to group, and then we close the group by calling the `endGroup()` method.

```
addGroup( "Debugging" );

addField( "UseDepthMask", TypeBool, Offset( mUseDepthMap,
WaterBlock ) );

endGroup( "Debugging" );
```

## 11.3.3 Modifying Persistent Fields from C++

Like with registered variables, if we modify the value of a class's class member and if that member has been exposed to the console, the reciprocal persistent field will be set to the same (new) value in the console. However, if we want to modify the member/field value of another class we are referencing, it is better to use the `setField()` access method instead of using direct manipulation.

```
mBrowseButton->setField( "text", "..." );
```

> The fact that the engine provides the `setField()` method prevents us from having to write access methods for every registered public member we want to access in other classes. Nice.

## 11.3.4 Getting Class ID and Name

The last of the interesting features are fairly trivial but can be used for important debugging work. The `ConsoleObject` class provides the following methods for learning how your new class was registered.

➢ **getClassId()**. This method returns the integer ID this class was registered with in the net class group.

➢ **getClassName()**. This method returns the name of this class as it was registered with the engine

## 11.3.5 The `ConsoleObject` Derivation Recipe

### Step #1: Prepare the Template Files

1. Select a name for your new class.
   - Example: `"myConsoleObject"`
2. Copy the `ConsoleObject` template files to an engine directory of your choice.
3. Rename the copied files.
   - Example: "t_ConsoleObject.h" becomes "myConsoleObject.h"
   - Example: "t_ConsoleObject.cc" becomes "myConsoleObject.cc"
4. Open both files using a C++ editor of your choice.
5. Replace all instances of the string `"t_ConsoleObject"` with the name of your class.
   - Example: All instances of `"t_ConsoleObject"` become `"myConsoleObject"`

You may place new engine files anywhere in the "~\engine\..." tree that you wish; however, most new console classes are placed under the "~\engine\game\" directory.

6. Save both files.

7. Add these files to your current project and run a test compile to be sure there are no syntax errors.

## Step #2: Override `ConsoleObject` Methods

`ConsoleObject` provides a small set of methods that should be overridden when creating a new class.

➤ `initPersistFields()`. This method is used to register (or unregister) class members as persistent fields in the console.

➤ `consoleInit()`. This static method is called once per class when the engine is started. Use this method to register (and unregister) global variables in the console. You may also use this method to do any other one-time initialization tasks that affect the global space. To learn more about the mechanics of registering and unregistering globals, see Section 11.2.3.

## Step #3: Add New Features and Functionality

Once you have modified the template files, you should add any new code and features that are necessary for your new class. This part is up to you and depends upon your needs.

## 11.4 The `SimObject` Class

`SimObject` is the base class for all objects involved in a (game) simulation. To use any of its features, you must include the "simBase.h" header file in your code.

```
// Use features of the SimObject class
//
#include "console/simBase.h"
```

This class can (reasonably) be considered the ubiquitous class, not because you will find it everywhere in the engine, but rather because many of the classes you will work with while coding new classes and modifying existing code are derived from `SimObject`. We will often find ourselves working with `SimObject` pointers and instances of classes derived from `SimObject`. So, being familiar with the information in this section is critical to your general success writing engine code.

In the following pages, we will examine the `SimObject` class features and learn how to work with pointers and instances of this class.

## 11.4.1 Creating and Deleting SimObject

As you make your first, second, third, fourth, and so on game or prototype, there will eventually come a time when you need to instantiate a SimObject.

Traditionally, when we want to create an instance of a class in C++, we simply use the new keyword to do the work.

```
myClass * mObj = new myClass();
```

This is fine, but in Torque, when working with SimObjects, it is necessary to register the new class instance, too. Until the object is registered with the engine, it will not be tracked by the simulator and will not be updated.

To register a class we simply do the following.

```
AIPlayer *mObj = new AIPlayer();

mObj->registerObject();
```

In the above example, we have created a new instance of AIPlayer and registered it. As soon as this is done, our new class instance will start being processed by the engine.

Instead of using the above method, we can alternately register our object and assign it a name as follows.

```
ActionMap* globalMap = new ActionMap;

globalMap->registerObject( "GlobalActionMap" );
```

Here, we created a new instance of ActionMap, registered it, and gave it the name "GlobalActionMap".

### Manually Assigned IDs

In TGE, there is one more way we can create and register a new SimObject, but it is a bit advanced so I will only give you a peek at how it works.

Normally, when you register a SimObject, the engine automatically assigns that object an ID. However, you may find yourself in a situation where you wish to control the assignment of IDs instead (perhaps you want your object to have a specific ID).

You may assign specific IDs as long as you know exactly what you are doing. There are two steps to the process.

### Setting Aside IDs

First, IDs are tracked by the global variable Sim::gNextObjectId. If you so choose, you may increment this variable a few times yourself and set these IDs aside for your own use.

## Assigning an ID

Second, having set aside your pool of IDs, you simply create and register your new objects as follows.

```
AIPlayer *mObj = new SimObject();

mObj->registerObject( id ); // Pass in a known ID

// OR

mObj->registerObject( "SomeName" , id ); // Name it and pass in a known ID
```

In the above code, we created a `SimObject` and stored its ID in the variable `mObj`. Then, using one of our stored IDs, we registered the object and passed the ID in. (The example also shows that we could have registered the object using a name and ID.)

The `onAdd()` callback will not be called until a `SimObject` is registered.

## 11.4.2 Destroying `SimObject` Instances

Having created a `SimObject`, we will eventually want to destroy it. However, before we can delete a `SimObject`, we must unregister it. Unregistering can be done in one of two ways.

```
mObj->unregisterObject()

delete mObj;
```

The `deleteObject()` method really deletes the object, so don't use the C++ keyword `delete` on the pointer to this object afterwards.

In this example, we manually unregister the object and delete it immediately.

Alternately, we could simply unregister and delete the object in one step.

```
mObj->deleteObject(); // Automatically calls unregisterObject()
```

### Unregister without Deleting

There is no rule that says we must delete a `SimObject` after unregistering it. In fact, if we wanted to, we could unregister a `SimObject`, and reregister it at a later time with no ill effect.

Why would we want to unregister but not delete?

The answer is simple. It is entirely possible that we'd like to step an object through the normal "I am being deleted" steps and then reuse the object.

When an object is unregistered, the following actions occur in the listed order.

1. The `onRemove()` callback is executed.
2. All pending notifications to this object are cleared.

**213**

3. The object is removed from the name and ID dictionaries (we'll talk about them soon).

4. The object is removed from any `SimGroup` it may be in.

5. All actions scheduled on the object are canceled.

### Remember to Clear `mID`

There is one thing you need to do on your own if you intend to reregister a previously registered object at a later time. You must set the object's `mID` member to 0 after you unregister it. `mID` is the place where the object's ID is stored, and it must be cleared before the engine will allow the object to be registered again. Also, the engine frees IDs when objects are unregistered, so you can't use the same ID anyway.

## 11.4.3 Manipulating Static and Dynamic Fields in C++

In the console, instances of `SimObject` may have dynamic fields added to them. To round out the picture (we can already access persistent fields in C++), the `SimObject` class provides a set of methods to help access both static (persistent) and dynamic (script-only) fields.

To begin the discussion, let's assume that we created an object (in the console) and later added a dynamic field named `billy`. We did this by assigning a value to `billy`, which told the engine to create the field for us.

```
%obj.billy = "Hi!";
```

### getDataField()

Now, in order to get the value stored in `billy`, we can do the following in C++.

```
StringTableEntry fieldName = StringTable->insert( "billy" );

Con::printf("billy == %s ", myObject->getDataField( fieldName , NULL )
```

In the above example, we first created a string table entry containing the name "billy". Then, we printed out the value of `billy` by calling the method `getDataField()` and passing in the `StringTableEntry` fieldName and `NULL` as the second argument (tells engine that `billy` not an array).

### setDataField()

Later, we could change the value of `billy` in C++ like this.

```
myObject->setDataField( fieldName , NULL , "Bye!" );
```

Here, we called `setDataField()`, passing in `fieldName` (reused from last call), a `NULL` (`billy` is not an array), and the new value for `billy` ("`Bye!`").

## Working with Arrays

The first time around, especially without a reference like this, you may be puzzled by that pesky `array` argument that both `getDataField()` and `setDataField()` take. In the examples above, we passed in `NULL`. This indicated, in both instances, that `billy` was a single field and not an array.

So, what do we do if we need to manipulate an array?

In the following example, we will create a new dynamic field named `joe` from within C++ by assigning it a set of values. `joe` is an array.

```
StringTableEntry fieldName = StringTable->insert( "joe" );

myObject->setDataField( fieldName , "0" , "100" );

myObject->setDataField( fieldName , "2" , "Testing!" );
```

Later, if we wanted to, we could access our new array from TorqueScript like this.

```
echo( "joe[0] == ", %obj.joe[0] );

echo( "joe[1] == ", %obj.joe[1] );

echo( "joe[2] == ", %obj.joe[2] );
```

As you will have guessed, we will get the following for our output.

```
joe[0] == 100
joe[1] ==
joe[2] == Testing!
```

Likewise, we could print out these same messages from C++ as follows.

```
Con::printf("joe[0] == %s ", myObject->getDataField( fieldName , "0" ) );

Con::printf("joe[1] == %s ", myObject->getDataField( fieldName , "1" ) );

Con::printf("joe[2] == %s ", myObject->getDataField( fieldName , "2" ) );
```

Although TorqueScript allows us to use any string as an index, the `getDataField()` and `setDataField()` methods only accept array indexes containing integer values ("0", "1", "2", etc.). Passing a non-integer value in the index string will cause the `getDataField()` method to ignore the request, and it will return `NULL`.

# 11.4.4 Working with the Field Dictionary

Above, we talked about how to access persistent and dynamic fields using a pointer to the object and the name of the field we wished to access. For the most part, you will get along fine using that methodology; however, there will be circumstances when you only wish to access dynamic fields and when you will want a more regular method of accessing them. To that end, let us discuss the (dynamic) field dictionary.

## Already Included

If you are working with `SimObject` or any child of `SimObject`, the necessary header file for working with field dictionaries is already included.

```
#include "console/simDictionary.h"
```

## Getting the Field Dictionary

In order to find only the dynamic fields in an object instance, we can look in that object's field dictionary (`mFieldDictionary`). The dictionary, which contains references to all dynamic fields for an object, is private, but an access method allows us to access it.

```
// Get a copy of the field dictionary for the current class

SimFieldDictionary * fieldDictionary = object->getFieldDictionary();
```

## Examining All Dynamic Fields

Once we have the dictionary, we can iterate over the dynamic field entries by using the ++ operator.

```
// Dump name and (string) value of all dynamic fields in this object

for( SimFieldDictionaryIterator ditr( fieldDictionary ) ; *ditr ; ++ditr )
{
    SimFieldDictionary::Entry * entry = (*ditr);

    Con::printf( "Dynamic Field: %s == %s",
                 entry->slotName , entry->value );
}
```

If you are familiar with STL, then the above code should be clear, but if you are not, let me explain.

Previously, we retrieved an object's field dictionary and stored it in the pointer variable `fieldDictionary`. Using a for loop, we loop over the dictionary through an iterator (`ditr`). On each iteration, we assign the value of the iterator to a temporary field dictionary entry (`entry`). This variable is

| Method | Used to... |
|---|---|
| `assignFrom()` | ... assign the contents of another dictionary to this dictionary. |
| `getFieldValue()` | ... get the current value of a named field in this dictionary. |
| `printFields()` | ... print all of the field dictionary entries for a specified `SimObject` object. |
| `setFieldValue()` | ... set the current value of a named field to a new value. |
| `writeFieldValues()` | ... write the names and values of all dictionary entries for the current `SimObject` object to the specified stream. |

**Table 11.6**
*Field dictionary methods.*

actually a structure containing two fields, `slotName` and `value`, representing the current field's name (in the console) and the value of that field.

## Dictionary Access Methods

We can use a dictionary iterator and entry in order to examine each field in the dictionary, but if we want to modify or otherwise manipulate the dictionary (and its contents), we need to use the methods listed in Table 11.6. See Section B.7.8 to get additional details on the field dictionary methods.

# 11.4.5 Finding Instances of `SimObject`

The `SimObject` class does not provide a means of searching for instances of `SimObject`, but four easy-to-use functions in the `Sim` namespace do.

## Already Included

If you are working with `SimObject` or any child of `SimObject`, then you are already including the "simBase.h" header file. In addition to declaring the `SimObject` class and methods, this header file includes the `Sim` namespace declarations.

## `findObject()`

Thanks to the power of C++ (overloading), all four functions have the same name, `findObject()`, so there isn't much to remember except for their signatures.

First, we can find a `SimObject` by its console ID.

```
// Find object with ID of 10

SimObjectId toFind = 10;

SimObject* ptr = Sim::findObject( toFind );
```

In this example, we are searching for a `SimObject` with a console ID of 10. If no matching object is not found, `ptr` will contain `NULL`; otherwise, it will contain a valid `SimObject` pointer.

Second, we can repeat our search using a string containing the object name.

```
// Find first instances of SimObject named "rocky"

SimObject* ptr = Sim::findObject( "rocky" );
```

This code will function in nearly the same way as the ID variant except that this version will return the first instance of a `SimObject` with this name, or `NULL` if none was found.

The third and fourth variants are very similar except that instead of returning a `SimObject` pointer, these functions take a `SimObject` pointer as an argument and then assign the address (or `NULL` if no object found) of the located object to that pointer.

```
ShapeBase* obj;

SimObjectId toFind = 10;

Sim::findObject( toFind , obj );

// OR

Sim::findObject( "rocky" , obj );
```

Both of these functions will assign an valid pointer or `NULL` to `obj` depending on the results, and they will also return a boolean value indicating success or failure.

## Handling Pointers to Children of `SimObject`

It is important to remember that the `Sim::findObject()` functions both return `SimObject` pointers. If you are searching for an instance of a `SimObject` child class, and if you need to store the resulting pointer in a pointer of that type, then be sure to use the C++ dynamic-casting feature.

```
Camera * ptr = dynamic_cast< Camera* >( Sim::findObject( "mainCamera" ) );
```

In this example, we searched for a `Camera` object named `"mainCamera"`, and because we wanted to store the resultant pointer in a Camera pointer, we needed to use the dynamic-cast mechanism.

Of course, to save work, we could have written the above code like this instead.

```
Camera * ptr = NULL;

Sim::findObject( "mainCamera" , ptr )
```

# 11.4.6 Access Methods

The SimObject class introduces a few access methods that will be useful to us when coding and working with SimObject and its children.

## Getting and Setting ID

There are three methods for getting and setting the ID of a SimObject. We can request a SimObject's ID as follows (in each example, obj is a pointer to a SimObject instance).

```
SimObjectId myID = obj->getID();
```

Alternately, we can get the ID as a const char*.

```
const char* myStringID = obj->getIDString();
```

Last, we can change the ID of our object at any time.

```
SimObjectId myNewID = Sim::gNextObjectId++;

obj->setID( myNewID );
```

## Getting and Setting Name

There are two methods, one each, for getting and setting the name of a SimObject. They operate as you might imagine.

```
const char * oldName = obj-> getName();

obj->assignName( "Buddy" );
```

## What Type Is It?

All SimObjects have a bitmask value designating their type. This bitmask is declared as a protected U32 member named mTypeMask. We can get this value and test its type as follows.

```
U32 myType = obj->getType();

if( GameBaseObjectType & mType )
{
    // This is a GameBase object, or a child of GameBase.
}
```

> The two-variable variants of Sim::findObject() are actually templated, meaning that the second variable can be a SimObject or a child-class pointer and the engine will automatically generate code for a proper assignment.

> SimObjectId is merely a typedef U32. This type was added in "simBase.h" for the express purpose of clarifying instances where we are working with simulation object IDs.

> If you pass 0 to setID(), the engine will grab the next available ID from the global Sim::gNextObjectId, thus allowing you to skip the manual step shown above.

**Table 11.7**
**SimObject** type bitmasks.

| Type Bitmasks | | |
|---|---|---|
| AIObjectType | InteriorMapObjectType | StaticRenderedObjectType |
| AtlasObjectType | InteriorObjectType | StaticShapeObjectType |
| CameraObjectType | ItemObjectType | StaticTSObjectType |
| CorpseObjectType | MarkerObjectType | TerrainObjectType |
| DamagableItemObjectType | PhysicalZoneObjectType | TriggerObjectType |
| DebrisObjectType | PlayerObjectType | VehicleBlockerObjectType |
| DecalManagerObjectType | ProjectileObjectType | VehicleObjectType |
| EnvironmentObjectType | ShadowCasterObjectType | WaterObjectType |
| ExplosionObjectType | ShapeBaseObjectType | |
| GameBaseObjectType | StaticObjectType | |

The SimObject type bitmasks in Table 11.7 are defined in the file "engine/game/objectTypes.h". If you need to add new masks, follow the examples you will find there.

This example checks to see if the object `obj` is of type `GameBase`.

As of version 1.5.2, TGE contains 28 bitmask values (listed alphabetically in Table 11.7). This means that only four types remain to be used out of the full 32 bits that the mask can store.

## 11.4.7 Important Callbacks

Once a `SimObject` class has been created and registered with the engine, it will begin to receive callbacks. Callbacks are methods that are called on an object by the engine in response to some specific event. We must implement some of these callbacks when creating a new class, but most of them are optional. However, all of them are useful, so I will list them for you (see Table 11.8) and tell you when they are called. Then, you may choose to implement them or not, depending on your needs.

## 11.4.8 Internal Names

A relatively new feature in TGE is the internal name. Previously, all objects could be assigned names, and these names would provide a second namespace for those objects (in addition to the namespace provided by their class name).

| Callbacks | Called when ... |
|---|---|
| onAdd() | ... the object is registered with the simulator. |
| onRemove() | ... the object is unregistered with the simulator. |
| onGroupAdd() | ... the object is added to a SimGroup. |
| onGroupRemove() | ... the object is removed from a SimGroup. |
| onNameChange() | ... the object's name is changed. |
| onStaticModified() | ... a static field is modified. |
| inspectPreApply() | ... (before) any property of the object is changed in the world editor inspector tool. |
| inspectPostApply() | ... (after) any property of the object is changed in the world editor inspector tool. |
| onDeleteNotify() | ... a SimObject is deleted. |
| onEditorEnable() | ... the world editor is activated. |
| onEditorDisable() | ... the world editor is deactivated. |

**Table 11.8**
SimObject callbacks.

| Method | Used to ... |
|---|---|
| getInternalName() | ... retrieve the internal name of a SimObject. |
| setInternalName() | ... assign an internal name to a SimObject. |
| findObjectByInternalName() | ... find a SimObject within a SimGroup, using the object's internal name. |

**Table 11.9**
Internal name methods.

Internal names are especially useful when working with GuiControls. With them, we can uniquely name controls and search for them using the methods listed in Table 11.9.

For this very reason, the programmers at GarageGames found that using names was not always the most efficient way to track and find objects. So, the internal name was born. An internal name is similar to a standard name except that it does not add a new namespace to the object.

The methods in Table 11.9 are provided for the express purpose of working with internal names.

## 11.4.9 The SimObject Derivation Recipe

### Step #1: Prepare the Template Files

1. Select a name for your new class.
   - Example: "mySimObject"
2. Copy the SimObject template files to an engine directory of your choice.

3. Rename the copied files.
   - Example: "t_SimObject.h" becomes "mySimObject.h"
   - Example: "t_SimObject.cc" becomes "mySimObject.cc"

4. Open both files using a C++ editor of your choice.

5. Replace all instances of the string "t_SimObject" with the name of your class.
   - Example: All instances of "t_SimObject" become "mySimObject"

6. Save both files.

7. Add these files to your current project and run a test compile to be sure there are no syntax errors.

### Step #2: Override Inherited Methods

SimObject inherits all of the features found in ConsoleObject. At the very least, we should override initPersistFields() and consoleInit().

### Step #3: Override Needed SimObject Methods

SimObject provides a small set of methods that may optionally be overridden when creating a new class. See Table 11.8 for a listing of these callbacks.

### Step #4: Add Needed Console Functions and/or Console Methods

At the end of the source file, you should add any console methods or console functions you will need to work with this class in the console. To accomplish this, use the ConsoleFunction() and ConsoleMethod() macros.

### Step #5: Add New Features and Functionality

Once you have modified the template files, you should add any new code and features that are necessary for your new class. This part is up to you and depends upon your needs.

## 11.4.10 A SimObject Derivation Example

In this derivation example, we will do the following.

1. Create a new SimObject child class named "mySimObject".
2. Add a single new class member and expose it to the console.
3. Add a global variable and expose it to the console.

4. Create a console function that can print the contents of a named field for any `SimObject`.

5. Create a console method that dumps out the value of our new class member (to the console).

## Step #1: Prepare the Template Files

The first step in creating a new class is to use the supplied template files. In this example, we will do the following.

1. Select a name for our class.
   - Our selection is `"mySimObject"`.
2. Copy the template files to an engine directory of our choice.
   - Create this directory: "engine/game/examples"
3. Rename the files.
   - Header file: "engine/game/examples/mySimObject.h"
   - Source file: "engine/game/examples/mySimObject.cc"
4. Open the source files in favorite editor.
5. Replace all instances `"t_SimObject"` with `"mySimObject"`.
6. Save both files.
7. Add the files to current project and test compile.

## Steps #2 and #3: Skip for Now

The `SimObject` recipe instructions #2 and #3 tell us to override inherited methods and to override needed `SimObject` methods, respectively. At this time, we really don't know which of these methods we want, and the ones provided by the template are just fine, so we can skip these two steps for now.

## Steps #4 and #5

The next two steps in the recipe involve adding new content. The content list for our example class includes all of the following.

➢ **Console-registered class member**. In this example, we will add a new `S32` variable named `mTestVal` and expose it to the console as the field `testVal`.

➢ **Console-registered Global**. In this example, we will add a new boolean global variable named `testGlobal` and expose it to the console as `$testGlobal`.

➢ **Console function**. In this example, we will add a new console function named `printField()`. When executed, this function will attempt to locate a specified SimObject and then print out the contents of a single named field in that object. This console function will take up to three arguments.

- obj. A SimObject.
- fieldName. The name of a field in the object
- idx. An optional index for the field (for arrays.)

➤ **Console method**. In this example, we will add a console method named printTestVal(). It will simply print the value of mTestVal to the Console.

## Add New Class Member

To add a new class member, we simply add it to the class declaration.

```
public:
    mySimObject();
    S32 mTestVal;
```

I also suggest initializing it in the constructor.

```
mySimObject::mySimObject()
{
    mTestVal = 0;
}
```

## Expose Class Member to Console

After adding our new class member, exposing it is as easy as opening the source file and locating the initPersistFields() method.

```
void mySimObject::initPersistFields()
{
```

Then, not forgetting to call the Parent version of initPersistFields() first, we add code to register mTestVal as a console field named testVal.

```
void mySimObject::initPersistFields()
{
    Parent::initPersistFields();

    addField("testVal" , TypeS32 , Offset( mTestVal,
            mySimObject) );
}
```

Notice that we used the addField() method and passed it the following arguments.

➤ **Field name**. We selected "testVal" as the name for our field in the console.

➢ **Field type**. The class member is an S32, meaning we need to use the TypeS32 type to register it.

➢ **Field offset**. We called the Offset() macro and passed in the member name (mTestVal) and the class name (mySimObject).

➢ **Description**. In this example, we chose not to add a description.

## Add and Expose Global to Console

Adding and registering a global is quite similar to adding and registering a class member. First, we add the global (in our source file).

```
#include "console/consoleTypes.h"
#include "console/console.h"
#include "core/bitStream.h"

#include "mySimObject.h"

bool testGlobal = true;
```

Second, we expose it. However, remember that when we expose a global, we need to do this in the class's consoleInit() method, not in initPersistFields().

```
void mySimObject::consoleInit()
{
    Con::addVariable("$testGlobal", TypeBool, &testGlobal);
}
```

Here, we used the Con::addVariable() function and passed it the following arguments.

➢ **Field name**. We selected "$testGlobal" as the name for our new console global. Note that we could also have chosen "testGlobal". The engine would automatically added the $ symbol for us.

➢ **Field type**. The C++ global is a bool, so we need to register it using the TypeBool type.

➢ **Global address**. As a last argument, we pass in the address of our global (&testGlobal) so that the engine can link this address to the new console global.

## Add Console Function

So far, everything has been pretty easy. Now we're going to do the first hard part. We're going to make a console function that is capable of looking up any instance of SimObject and then printing the value of a single named field in that object. As we discussed above, this console function has the following parameters.

**Engine Coding**

> ➤ **Console-function name.** `"printField"`
> ➤ **Arguments.**
>   - **obj.** Required field containing the name or ID of a `SimObject`.
>   - **fieldName.** Required field containing the name of the field whose value we want to print.
>   - **idx.** Optional field containing an index. We only pass a value here if the field we are looking up is an array.
> ➤ **Return value.** Before this point, we didn't specify whether the function would return a value, but I'd like to return `true` if it is able to print the field and `false` otherwise.

**Empty declaration.** To create a function with the above listed parameters, we first write an empty declaration like this.

```
ConsoleFunction( printField, bool , 3 , 4 ,
                "printField( Obj , fieldName [, idx ])"
                )
{
    return true;
}
```

Because `idx` is optional, this function will take a minimum of three arguments and a maximum of four. All the other arguments should be pretty clear.

**Logic outline.** Next, let's outline our logic. We need to locate an object by name, and then we need to locate a named field. If either of these steps fails, we return `false`; otherwise, we print the field value and return `true`. With this in mind, we could outline our logic like this.

```
{
    //// Try to find the object
    //
    if( true /* not found */ )
    {
        return false;
    };

    //// Try to find the field
    //
    if( true /* not found */ )
    {
        return false;
    };

    //// Print the field and return true.
    //
```

```
        return true;
    }
```

**Finding the object.** Now, with a logic outline, we can fill in the pieces. The first piece is finding an object using either a name or an ID. To do this, we need to have a place to store the resultant object address, and we need to call the `Sim::findObject()` function to get that address.

```
{
    //// Try to find the object
    //
    SimObject* obj;

    if( !Sim::findObject( argv[1] , obj ) )
    {
        return false;
    };
```

In the above code we have done the following.

➤ Created a `SimObject` pointer named `obj`.

➤ Called `Sim::findObject()`, passing in two arguments.

  • **argv[1]**. Remember that the first argument to any console function (declared in C++) is always the name of the function. All additional arguments are passed after that. So, since `obj` is the first argument to our console function, it will be passed as the second entry in `argv[]`.

  • **obj**. This is the pointer storage we just created. After this call, if the object is found, obj will contain the address.

Don't forget that calls to `Sim::findSimObject()` return either a pointer or a boolean value, depending upon the variant you call. In this case, we called a templated variant that returns a `bool`. In either case, both would be suitable for use in our if statement.

    If our function gets beyond this code, we know that the object we wanted was located. Now, we need to field the field.

**Finding the field.** As we learned above, the SimObject class supplies a handy method for locating named fields, `getDataField()`. As you may recall, this method takes two arguments, a string table entry containing the field name, and an optional pointer to a string containing a numeric index. So, using this information and the logic outline we already prepared, we could write the following code.

```
    //// Try to find the field
    //
```

**Engine Coding**

```
const char * curIndex = (4 == argc) ? argv[3] : NULL;
if( !obj->getDataField( StringTable->insert(argv[2], false ),
                         curIndex )
    )
{
    return false;
};
```

In the above code we have done the following.

➢ Copied the optionally passed index into a `const char *` variable named `curIndex`.

- This code may look elaborate, but it is actually very simple. Basically, it is checking if the `argc` value is 4 (indicating an index was passed in) and if so, assigning that string directly to our pointer (`curIndex`); if `argc` is only 3, `NULL` is assigned to our pointer instead. (This line of code uses what is called a conditional operator.)

➢ Called `getDataField()`, passing in two arguments.

- `StringTable->insert( argv[2], false )`. Here, we use the globally visible `StringTable` pointer and call `insert()`, passing in the field name (`argv[2]`) and `false` (indicating we don't want to use case-sensitive storage). If this entry doesn't exist in the string table already, it will be created. Either way, it will return a pointer to this entry, and that pointer will then get passed to `getDataField()`.

- `curIndex`. This is the pointer we created above to hold the numeric index of our field.

If our function gets beyond this code, we know that the object we wanted was located and that the field was located, too. Please notice that we didn't store the field value anywhere. We simply checked if it was found. This isn't very efficient, but for this example it's fine.

**Printing the field's value.** Now, all we have left to do is to add code for printing the value of the field, and we are done. To do this, we use the `Con::printf()` function.

```
Con::printf( "%s.%s == %s", argv[1], argv[2],
        obj->getDataField( StringTable->insert(argv[2], false),
                           NULL )
        );
return true;
}
```

This code should look pretty familiar. As you can see, we print out a message containing the object name (or ID), the field name, and its value. The first two strings are pulled right out of the `argv[]` variable, and the last value is returned from a call to `getDataField()`, which is specified exactly as it was when we looked up the field above.

We will test this code later, but for now, we need to move on to the console method.

## Add Console Method

After writing the console function above, you will probably find this step to be refreshingly simple. Here, we will be creating a new console method for our class having the following parameters.

➢ **Console-method name.** `"printTestVal"`

➢ **Arguments.** None. This console method has one job, to print the value of `mTestVal`.

➢ **Return value.** None. Alternately, we could choose to return the value of `mTestVal`, but I've decided to leave that as an exercise for you.

**Empty declaration.** To create a console method with the above listed parameters, we first write an empty declaration like this.

```
ConsoleMethod( mySimObject , printTestVal , void, 2, 2,
               "Prints the current value of the field testVal"
             )
{
}
```

It should come as no surprise that this call to the `ConsoleMethod` macro takes these arguments.

➢ **className**. Our class's name is `mySimObject` (no quotes).

➢ **name**. The name for our new console method is `printTestVal` (again no quotes).

➢ **returnType**. Since no value is returned, we select `void`.

➢ **minArgs/maxArgs**. This console method only takes the default arguments so the minimum and maximum argument counts are both 2.

➢ **usage1**. Unlike our last example, we chose to add a help string: `"Prints the current value of the field testVal"`.

**Printing the field's value.** Now, the only thing left to do is to add the code for printing out our class member. Again, we use the `Con::printf()` function.

```
ConsoleMethod( mySimObject , printTestVal , void, 2, 2,
               "Prints the current value of the field testVal"
             )
{
   Con::printf("testVal == %d", object->mTestVal);
}
```

**Engine Coding**

At this point, we are done coding. Now, we need to test our new class and all of its new features.

## Test New Class

### Compile the Code

To test our new class, we first need to compile the code. Please do so now.

If you don't want to type this code in, or if you ran into problems, feel free to use the answers I have provided for you. This example can be located on the accompanying CD in the directory "C++Samples(Finished)/".

### Copy the Executable

To test run this code, locate the executable we just generated by compiling and copy it into the "Kit/" directory you created in Chapter 1. It is OK to overwrite the executable in that directory.

### Run and Test the Executable

Now, run the kit as we learned in the Chapter 1 exercise, "Using the Kit." When you have the Chapter 1 mission running, open the console and type this.

```
new mySimObject( test );
```

This should execute with no errors and create a new instance of `mySimObject` named `test`.

**testVal**. Now, manipulate the `testVal` field.

```
echo( test.testVal);
test.testVal = 10;
echo( test.testVal);
```

This should result in the following being printed to the console.

```
0
10
```

**printTestVal()**. Now, test our console method.

```
testval.printTestVal();
test.testVal = 10;
echo( test.testVal);
```

This should result in the following being printed to the console.

```
testVal == 10
```

**printField()**. Last, test our console function.

```
printField( test , testVal );
```

This should result in the following being printed to the console.

```
test.testVal == 10
```

## 11.5 The `NetObject` **Class**

`NetObject` is the super-class for all ghostable networked objects. It is not often derived from (only four classes derive from it in TGE), but it is a base class to `SceneObject`, and it introduces some critical features.

We will not discuss derivation of this class; instead, we will examine the new features it provides and use those features in the derivation examples of the `SceneObject` and `GameBase` classes later in this chapter.

## 11.5.1 Ghosting and Scope Settings

### `mNetFlags`

Server object instances of `NetObject` and its children can be transmitted over a network to clients as ghosts. To control the mechanics of ghosting, `NetObject` maintains a `protected` member called `mNetFlags`. In all classes deriving from `NetObject`, this flag (really a mask of flags) must be given an initial value in the constructor. Subsequently, the class may modify the flag directly and can test its value using the handy flag-testing methods discussed below.

### Assigning Flags

In the case of a constructor assignment, we might use a statement like this.

```
mNetFlags.set( Ghostable );
```

Here, the flag has been set to `Ghostable`, meaning that the engine can ghost this object if it is in scope for a client.

In total, there are four bit masks that can be assigned to this flag in up to five different (legal) ways. Table 11.10 lists all five of these legal settings and their meaning.

| Setting | Result |
|---|---|
| `mNetFlags.set(0);` | Not ghosted. |
| `mNetFlags.set(Ghostable);` | Ghosted. |
| `mNetFlags.set(Ghostable \| ScopeAlways);` | Ghosted and always rendered, i.e., always in scope. |
| `mNetFlags.set(Ghostable \| ScopeLocal);` | Ghosted and only rendered on the client that owns the object. |
| `mNetFlags.set(Ghostable \| ScopeAlways \| ScopeLocal );` | Ghosted, always rendered, but only rendered on the client that owns the object. (The owner client is equivalent to the client that caused an object to be created on the server. ) |

**Table 11.10**
Legal `mNetFlags` settings.

**231**

| Testing Method | Test Performed |
|---|---|
| isScopeLocal() | mNetFlags & ScopeLocal |
| isGhostable() | mNetFlags & Ghostable |
| isScopeable() | (mNetFlags & Ghostable) && !(mNetFlags & ScopeAlways) |
| isGhostAlways() | (mNetFlags & Ghostable) && (mNetFlags & ScopeAlways) |

**Table 11.11**
**mNetFlags** testing methods.

| Testing Method | Returns true if ... |
|---|---|
| isClientObject() | ... this object is on a client (it may or may not be a ghost). |
| isGhost() | ... this object is on a client and is a ghost of a server object. |
| isServerObject() | ... this object is on the server. |

**Table 11.12**
Scope testing methods.

### Flag-Testing Methods

To avoid messy logical comparisons, NetObject provides four flag-testing methods. These methods and the settings they test are listed in Table 11.11.

### Object Scope

When one works with a NetObject, it is often necessary to test if the current object is a server object or a client object, and/or whether a client object is a ghost or not.

To help with this task, NetObject supplies three scope-testing methods to help us determine where an object is and if it is associated with a server object (see Table 11.12).

## 11.5.2 Packing and Unpacking Data

To enable ghost updates, NetObject provides two methods, packUpdate() and unpackUpdate(), that pack server data prior to ghosting this data and unpack the data when it is received by a ghost.

### packUpdate()

This method has the job of packing data from a server object so that this data can be sent across a network to a ghost(s). This is the first half of the mechanism that allows us to ghost an object.

All implementations of packUpdate() follow a basic recipe. To clarify this, let's examine a simple example.

```
U32 mySampleClass::packUpdate( NetConnection * con,
                               U32 mask,
                               BitStream * stream)
```

```
{
    // 1
    U32 retMask = Parent::packUpdate(con, mask, stream);

    // 2
    stream->write(mSomeData);

    // 3
    return(retMask);
}
```

This example implementation of a `packUpdate()` method does three things.

1. It calls the `Parent` version of `packUpdate()` and stores the return mask for later use. The order of this call is critical. If you pack data on a `BitStream` before calling the `Parent` version of this method, your code will fail later during the unpack, and the failure will be very hard to debug. Be sure to always do this step first.

2. It packs some data (from the server object) onto the `BitStream`. Don't worry about what this data is for now. We'll talk about `BitStream`s and how to send specific data on them in just a moment.

3. It returns the results we stored in Step 1.

Now, of course, this code can be a lot longer and much more complex, but all implementations of `packUpdate()` will do these three basic steps.

## unpackUpdate()

This method has the job of unpacking data from a network `BitStream` and applying this data as updates to the current ghost. As with `packUpdate()`, all implementations of `unpackUpdate()` follow a basic recipe. Let's look at an example that would unpack the data we put on the `BitStream` in our `packUpdate()` example above.

```
void mySampleClass::unpackUpdate(NetConnection * con, BitStream * stream)
{
    // 1. Call parent's version of this method FIRST.
    Parent::unpackUpdate(con, stream);

    // 2. Retrieve and apply object transform.
    stream->read(&mSomeData);

    // 3. NEW CODE HERE
}
```

This example implementation of an `unPackUpdate()` method does three things.

1. It calls the `Parent` version of `unPackUpdate()`. Again, this ordering is critical. If you don't get it right, your game may experience a variety of issues, up to and including crashing.

2. It unpacks some data from the `BitStream`.

As you can see, this method is even simpler since it doesn't need to pass on any status from prior calls to `unPackUpdate()`.

However, I'm sure that by now you're probably wondering about `BitStream`s. So, let's talk about them next.

### BitStream

Torque's `BitStream` class is a data-streaming class specifically used to store data in an efficient manner for transmission over a network. This class (and its parent class `Stream`) provides a large number of methods for placing data on and removing data from a data stream. The beauty of this class is that with all of these data-stream writing and reading methods, we can very efficiently pack just the data we want onto a stream (using only the space necessary) and later remove that data safely.

The real question is, "Given any particular data that I want to pack or unpack, how do I know which stream method to use?" The answer is, "See the references in Appendix B." I have listed all of the packing and unpacking methods there, according to data and class type.

Let's make up a hypothetical example. In this example, our class has a member of type `MatrixF` named `myMatrix`.

```
class myClass : public NetObject
{
   public:
      MatrixF myMatrix;

   // ...
```

If I wanted to pack the data in this matrix, I could go to Appendix B and look for a data-packing (write) method that handles matrices. Finding the `writeAffineTransform()` method, I would use it like this in my class's `packUpdate()` method.

```
stream->writeAffineTransform( &myMatrix );
```

Later, to unpack this data, I could use the reciprocal unpacking (read) method `readAffineTransform()` and use it like this in my class's `unpackUpdate()` method.

```
stream->readAffineTransform( &myMatrix );
```

## Dirty Masks (`mask`)

As you work on your classes, you may come to the realization that it isn't very efficient to send all of your updates every cycle. In fact, doing so would be a huge waste of network bandwidth. Fortunately, the folks who designed Torque considered this.

While examining the implementation of `packUpdate()`, you may have noticed that this method receives an argument called `mask`. This mask is a 32-bit value used to track an object's dirty state. Let's learn how this works.

### Create Dirty Bitmasks

First, in our class declaration, we decide how many bits we need for tracking dirty data. In this example, we will track two different class members with one bit each.

```
class myClass : public NetObject
{
   public:
       U32 mFirstData;

       U32 mSecondData;

   protected:
       enum { firstDataDirty = BIT(0),
              seconDataDirty = BIT(1) };

   // ...
```

In this code, you will see that we declared two `U32` members, `mFirstData` and `mSecondData`. These are the data members we will track in this example. Additionally, we used the `enum` keyword to declare two masks, `firstDataDirty` and `secondDataDirty`. The values of these two masks are respectively `BIT(0)`, which is `0x1`, and `BIT(1)`, which is `0x2`. (The `BIT()` macro was discussed in Section 10.4.2).

### Set a Bit As Dirty

Second, some place in our code we will make the decision that our data is dirty and needs to be sent to the ghost. Where we make this decision will vary, but how we mark the data as dirty does not. To set a dirty mask, we write code like this.

```
// Mark mFirstData as dirty
//
setMaskBits( firstDataDirty );

// elsewhere ...
```

> In the context of this discussion, clean data is data that doesn't need to be sent to clients for ghost updates. Dirty data is data that should be sent. Ideally, we would only send dirty data. By using the technique we are discussing here, we can achieve that ideal.

**235**

**Engine Coding**

```
// Mark mSecondData as dirty
//
setMaskBits( secondDataDirty );
```

## Send Dirty Data

Third, in our `packUpdate()` implementation, we check for dirty bits and only send data if it is dirty.

```
U32 mySampleClass::packUpdate( NetConnection * con,
                               U32 mask,
                               BitStream * stream)
{

  U32 retMask = Parent::packUpdate(con, mask, stream);


  // Only send mFirstData if it is dirty
  //
  if (stream->writeFlag(mask & firstDataDirty))
  {
    stream->write( mFirstData );
  }


  // Only send mSecondData if it is dirty
  //
  if (stream->writeFlag(mask & secondDataDirty))
  {
    stream->write( mSecondData );
  }


  return(retMask);
}
```

In this code, we use the data-streaming method `writeFlag()` to pack a single bit on the `BitStream`. This single bit is set to `true` if the mask operation is nonzero; that is, if the specified bit is set, we pack a `1` on the `BitStream`, otherwise we pack a `0` on the `BitStream`. In addition to packing a bit on the `BitStream`, this method will return `true` or `false` depending on whether the bit was set to `1` or `0`. With this information, we can decide whether to send the data or not.

## Get Dirty Data

Fourth and last, in our `unpackUpdate()` implementation, we check for dirty bits and only take data off the stream if the dirty flag is set.

```
void mySampleClass::unpackUpdate(NetConnection * con, BitStream * stream)
{
   Parent::unpackUpdate(con, stream);

   //// Get mFirstData if it was dirty
   //
   if(stream->readFlag())
   {
      stream->read( &mFirstData );
   }

   //// Get mSecondData if it was dirty
   //
   if(stream->readFlag())
   {
      stream->read( &mSecondData );
   }

}
```

In this code, we use the data-streaming method `readFlag()` to unpack the single bit of data we put on the `BitStream` in our `packUpdate()` method. If this bit is set to `1`, `readFlag()` will return `true`, and we will read more data. If this bit is set to `0`, `readFlag()` will return `false`, and we will skip on to the next dirty data section of our method.

Be aware that the example we just walked through is a bit silly. In real code, we would group several related pieces of data together using one bitmask.

As always, order is critical. You must unpack data in the same order you packed it or your code will not work properly.

### What Are the Savings?

If our data is clean, we only send a single bit of data for any data controlled by that dirty bit. If it is dirty, we send enough bits to represent our data, plus one extra bit. So, as long as your data is more frequently clean than dirty, this will save networking bandwidth.

### How Many Dirty Bits?

Don't forget that the mask that is passed to `packUpdate()` is only 32 bits wide. This means that you can have a maximum of 32 dirty bits. Additionally, a parent class may use some of those bits, so you need to be conservative and efficient in your use of this technique. (We will talk more about parent classes using these dirty bits when we discuss the `GameBase` class in Section 11.8.)

## 11.6 The `SceneObject` Class

`SceneObject` is the superclass for all 3D game objects. As such, it introduces a wealth of features, including the concept of a scene graph (used to organize and store all entities in a game world), physical attributes (position, velocity, mass, etc.), collision and detection response, lighting, the ability to manipulate other SceneObjects, and object rendering.

It is this last feature that we will primarily be focusing on. The remaining features are either advanced topics, worthy of their own dedicated guides, or so simple that the supplied reference in Appendix B should be enough for you to use them.

To use any features of the SceneObject class, you must include the "sceneObject.h" header file in your code.

```
// Use features of the SceneObject
//
#include "sim/sceneObject.h"
```

In the following pages, we will learn a little bit about scene management and then examine the rendering features of the SceneObject class.

## 11.6.1 Scene Management

Although the engine is responsible for managing the scene graph, it is the responsibility of all classes derived from SceneObject to handle their own addition to and removal from the scene graph.

Because an object cannot be managed by the scene graph until it is registered with the simulator, we must not add a new SceneObject instance to the scene graph until registration is completed. As we learned in Section 11.4.7, the onAdd() callback is called after an object has been registered with the simulator.

### Add Objects to Scene Graph in onAdd()

Because the onAdd() callback is called after an object is registered, and because we can't add objects to the scene graph until they are registered with the simulator, it is the ideal place to add our new SceneObject to the scene graph.

```
bool myObject::onAdd()
{
   addToScene();

}
```

### Remove Objects from Scene Graph in onRemove()

Reciprocally, the onRemove() callback is the ideal place to remove a SceneObject from the scene graph.

```
bool myObject::onRemove()
{
```

```
    removeFromScene();

}
```

## 11.6.2 `SceneObject` Rendering

There are two primary methods involved in rendering a `SceneObject`, `prepRenderImage()` and `renderObject()`.

### `prepRenderImage()`

It is this method's job to prepare an object for rendering. This method is called for any object that is in scope and should be rendered.

In a nutshell, this method prepares a special data structure called an `image` (of type `SceneRenderImage`.) This `image` contains a pointer to the current `SceneObject`. Additionally, it has a number of attributes that may be modified. These attributes are later used to determine how the current `SceneObject` is rendered.

We will experiment with the image attributes in the `SceneObject` and `GameBase` derivation examples later in this chapter, but let's take some time to talk about them now.

### `image` (`SceneRenderImage`) Attributes

Before we add code to manipulate `image` attributes, we will have some code like the following in our new `SceneObject` class's implementation of `prepRenderImage()`.

```
if (state->isObjectRendered(this))
{
    SceneRenderImage* image = new SceneRenderImage;

    image->obj = this;

    // More code here

    state->insertRenderImage(image);
}
```

As can be seen, this code creates a new instance of `SceneRenderImage`, storing a pointer to that instance in `image`. Then, the first thing we do after assigning `image` is store a pointer to `this SceneObject` in the `obj` member of the `image`. After that, we are free to set any of the following `image` members (attributes).

➤ **isTranslucent**. A boolean value specifying whether this `SceneObject` is translucent (or has translucent parts).

**239**

**Table 11.13**
**sortType** types.

| Type | Description and Rules |
|---|---|
| SceneRenderImage::Sky | Used for the Sky object only. |
| SceneRenderImage::BeginSort | Object is a translucent object that should be rendered before all other translucent objects. |
| SceneRenderImage::Terrain | Used for the Terrain object only. |
| SceneRenderImage::Normal | Standard for all nontranslucent objects. |
| SceneRenderImage::Point | Object is a translucent point object that should use the Point3F value in image->poly[0] for sorting. |
| SceneRenderImage::Plane | Object is a translucent plane object that should use the Point3F value in image->poly[0..3] for sorting (water uses this). |
| SceneRenderImage::EndSort | Object is a translucent object that should be rendered after all other translucent objects. |

> **tieBreaker**. A boolean value specifying that this object should be rendered after any other object having the same render position, i.e., if there are two or more objects that have an equal chance of being rendered next (a tie), this object should be rendered last, thus rendering it before the other objects in the tie.

> **useSmallTextures**. A boolean value specifying that this object should use the low resolution version of its textures (if they exist).

> **sortType**. An enumerated value specifying how this object should be sorted against other objects that will also be rendered (see Table 11.13 for a list sort types).

> **textureSortKey**. A U32 value used to suggest a render order for objects in the same sortType. In the case of a tie between nontranslucent objects of the same sortType, objects with a lower textureSortKey are rendered first while those with higher values are sorted last.

## Multiple Images?

It is possible to add multiple images to the image list when we execute the prepRenderImage() method. The renderObject() method will be called once for each of these images.

## renderObject()

The renderObject() method is responsible for rendering a SceneObject. Just exactly what rendering means is determined by the object itself. However, there are common steps that SceneObjects generally follow while rendering. We will look at those steps below. Then, we will see these steps in action during the SceneObject and GameBase derivation examples.

The subsequent discussion assumes you are familiar with 3D rendering concepts and, more specifically, rendering with OpenGL.

## Checking Canonical State

The first thing we need to do when entering the `renderObject()` method is to check for a canonical state.

The term "canonical" refers to the projection volume. A canonical projection volume is the unit cube. If left unchanged, this will produce an orthographic projection.

To get a proper perspective projection matrix, we must start from a known state. That known state is the canonical projection volume (otherwise known as the canonical state).

If you enter the `renderObject()` method and the projection matrix is not in the canonical state, you're only option is to flag an error and to quit. It is very unlikely that any rendering done after this will work appropriately.

```
AssertFatal( dglIsInCanonicalState(),
             "Error, GL not in canonical state on entry" );
```

## Save Current Projection Matrix and Viewport

If the state is canonical, we move on. The next thing we must do is save the current projection matrix and viewport. We do this so that we can return them to their original state after manipulating them.

```
glMatrixMode(GL_PROJECTION);
glPushMatrix();

RectI viewport;
dglGetViewport( &viewport );
```

## Set Projection Matrix

Now we are ready to set our own projection matrix. TGE provides the code necessary to do this for us. In fact, you should not write your own projection-matrix code unless you absolutely know what you are doing, and perhaps not even then. This function call will set up the projection-matrix and leave us in `ModelView` matrix mode.

```
state->setupObjectProjection(this);
```

## Save `ModelView` Matrix

The next step is to save the `ModelView` matrix. Again, this is so we can restore it when we're done.

```
glPushMatrix();
```

### Transform `ModelView` using Object Transform

Now, we're almost ready to render our object, but before we can do so, we need to transform the view using our object's current transform matrix.

```
dglMultMatrix( & getTransform() );
```

This step translates the `ModelView` to local space for this object, making it simple to render our object and relieving us of the responsibility for translating and rotating every point to match the object's current transform.

### Render the Object

Finally, we get to the part where we render our `SceneObject`. Exactly what goes on here is entirely up to you and depends on what your `SceneObject` is.

> If you are using OpenGL code that you are borrowing (or previously wrote on your own), you may need to call the following code (first) to account for the difference in Torque versus standard OpenGL world orientation.
>
> `glRotatef(90,1,0,0); // Rotate to account for TGE orientation`

### Restore Saved Settings

Once we've finished rendering, we need to restore all of the state information that we saved.

```
glPopMatrix();
glMatrixMode(GL_PROJECTION);
glPopMatrix();
glMatrixMode(GL_MODELVIEW);
dglSetViewport(viewport);
```

### Recheck Canonical State

Lastly, we should recheck the canonical state to ensure that nothing was broken.

```
AssertFatal( dglIsInCanonicalState(),
             "Error, GL not in canonical state on exit" );
```

## Projections

In our `renderObject()` example, we used the `setupObjectProjection()` method to configure the projection matrix prior to rendering our object. However, this method was only one of the three such methods available to us. Table 11.14 lists all three methods and discusses when they should be used.

| Method | Description |
|---|---|
| `setupZoneProjection()` | This method takes a zone number. It is for use by zone-managing objects only. (We don't discuss zones in this book.) |
| `setupObjectProjection()` | This method takes a reference to any `sceneObject` (normally the one doing the render). It will search through the available zones and try to find the most efficient projection that applies to the current view. |
| | Use this for individual and small objects. It does a better job of culling objects but can be costly because it traverses a large (zone) data structure to do its calculations. |
| `setupBaseProjection()` | This is the simplest of the methods and executes the most quickly, but it may produce a less-than-optimal projection matrix. Use it for large objects and when in doubt. |
| | This does a (relatively) poor job of culling. If we use this, some objects may be rendered when they don't really need to be. However, since this doesn't traverse any data structures during calculations, it is very fast. |

**Table 11.14**
Render-projection methods.

## 11.6.3 The `SceneObject` Derivation Recipe

### Step #1: Prepare the Template Files

1. Select a name for your new class.
   - Example: "`mySceneObject`"
2. Copy the `SceneObject` template files to an engine directory of your choice.
3. Rename the copied files.
   - Example: "t_SceneObject.h" becomes "mySceneObject.h".
   - Example: "t_SceneObject.cc" becomes "mySceneObject.cc".
4. Open both files using a C++ editor of your choice.
5. Replace all instances of the string "`t_SceneObject`" with the name of your class.
   - Example: All instances of "`t_SceneObject`" become "`mySceneObject`".
6. Save both files.
7. Add these files to your current project and run a test compile to be sure there are no syntax errors.

### Step #2: Override Inherited Methods

`SceneObject` inherits all of the features found in `NetObject` and its parent classes. At the very least, we should override the following meth-

**243**

ods: `initPersistFields()`, `consoleInit()`, `packUpdate()`, and `unpackUpdate()`.

Additionally, we may optionally override any of these inherited methods: `onAdd()`, `onRemove()`, `onGroupAdd()`, `onGroupRemove()`, `onNameChange()`, `onStaticModified()`, `inspectPreApply()`, and `inspectPostApply()`.

### Step #3: Override Needed `SceneObject` Methods

At the very least, we should override the following methods/callbacks: `prepRenderImage()`, `renderObject()`, `onAdd()`, and `onRemove()`.

We may also optionally override the method `renderShadow()`.

### Step #4: Add Needed Console Functions and/or Console Methods

At the end of the source file, you should add any console methods or console functions you will need to work with this class in the console. To accomplish this, use the `ConsoleFunction()` and `ConsoleMethod()` macros.

### Step #5: Add New Features and Functionality

Once you have modified the template files, you should add any new code and features that are necessary for your new class. This part is up to you and depends upon your needs.

## 11.6.4 A `SceneObject` Derivation Example

This example is designed to introduce you to a complete (if minimal) `SceneObject` derivation and to provide a base for several exercises on the accompanying CD.

In this example, we will do the following.

1. Create a new `SceneObject` child class named "`myFirstSceneObject`".
2. Add the code necessary to render a three-dimensional colored pyramid.
3. Incorporate that code into the `SceneObject` render flow.

Again, we are following the provided (`SceneObject`) recipe. Of course, once you become familiar with the process, you won't need to adhere to it in such strict order, but for now, let's proceed with the steps in order.

### Step #1: Prepare the Template Files

To prepare our template files, we will do the following.

1. Select a name for our class.
   - Our selection is "`myFirstSceneObject`".

2. Copy the template files to an engine directory of our choice.

- Copy them to our directory: "engine/game/examples".

3. Rename the files.

- Header file: "engine/game/examples/myFirstSceneObject.h".
- Source file: "engine/game/examples/myFirstSceneObject.cc".

4. Open the files in your favorite editor.

5. Replace all instances of `"t_SceneObject"` with `"myFirstSceneObject"`.

6. Save both files.

7. Add the files to the current project and test compile.

## Steps #2 and #3

As in the last example (`SimObject`), the recipe instructions #2 and #3 tell us to override inherited methods and to override needed `SimObject` methods, respectively. Again, the templated ones are satisfactory for our purposes. Nonetheless, I would like to take some time to examine a few important methods so that you can see how they work.

### Constructor Definition

Open the source file and examine the constructor definition. Without all the comments, the code looks like this.

```
myFirstSceneObject::myFirstSceneObject()
{
    mNetFlags.set(Ghostable);
}
```

As you can see, the only thing the constructor does is set the `mNetFlags` member. In this case, the class is being marked as ghostable, meaning it will start calling the `packUpdate()` and `unpackUpdate()` methods after it is created.

### onAdd() and onRemove()

For any `SceneObject` class to be added to be properly added to and removed from the scene graph, we need to implement suitable `onAdd()` and `onRemove()` callbacks. Such suitable callbacks are included in the templates. The provided `onAdd()` and `onRemove()` callbacks look something like this.

```
bool myFirstSceneObject::onAdd()
{
  // 1
  if(!Parent::onAdd()) return(false);
```

**Engine Coding**

```
// 2
mObjBox.min.set( -1.0f, -1.0f, -1.0f );
mObjBox.max.set( +1.0f, +1.0f, +1.0f );
resetWorldBox();
setRenderTransform(mObjToWorld);

// 3
addToScene();

return(true);
}

void myFirstSceneObject::onRemove()
{
// 1. Remove this object from the scene graph.
removeFromScene();

// 2. Call parent's version of this method LAST.
Parent::onRemove();
}
```

As you can see, the onAdd() callback does three things.

1. It calls the Parent version of onAdd().
2. It sets up an initial two-by-two-by-two (world unit) bounding box and resets the world box to match it.
3. It adds this object to the scene graph.

The onRemove() callback has two steps.

1. It removes this object from the scene graph.
2. It calls the Parent version of onRemove().

### packUpdate() and unpackUpdate()

As you know, SceneObject is a child of NetObject. Therefore, it inherits the two data-packing methods, packUpdate() and unpackUpdate(). In our recipe, these two methods are listed for overriding. Let me explain why they are required.

As you know, these methods are used to pack changed data found in a server object so that those changes can be sent to any ghosts of the server object. As you also know, data updates are class-implementation-specific. It is one of those implementation details that makes it necessary for us to override these two methods for SceneObject and all children of SceneObject.

In order for a SceneObect to be rendered properly, the engine needs to know where that object is in the world. This information (as it is applied to rendering) is stored in a MatrixF member named mObjToWorld. Having said that, it is our responsibility that this information is transmitted to any ghosts a server object may have.

To enable this, the `SceneObject` template for `packUpdate()` has these parts (after the renaming step in our recipe).

```
U32 myFirstSceneObject::packUpdate( NetConnection * con,
                                    U32 mask,
                                    BitStream * stream
                                  )
{
   // 1
   U32 retMask = Parent::packUpdate(con, mask, stream);

   // 2
   stream->writeAffineTransform(mObjToWorld);

   // 3
   return(retMask);
}
```

This code follows these steps.

1. Calls `Parent` version of `packUpdate()` and stores the return value. (Unchanged from the standard implementation of this method.)
2. Packs this object's `mObjToWorld` transform on `BitStream`.
3. Returns the return value stored in Step 1.

Reciprocally, the `SceneObject` template for `unpackUpdate()` has these parts (after the renaming step in our recipe).

```
void myFirstSceneObject::unpackUpdate( NetConnection * con,
                                       BitStream * stream
                                     )
{
   // 1
   Parent::unpackUpdate(con, stream);

   // 2
   MatrixF         ObjectMatrix;

   stream->readAffineTransform(&ObjectMatrix);

   setTransform(ObjectMatrix);
}
```

This code follows these steps.

1. Calls `Parent` version of `unpackUpdate()`. (Unchanged from the standard implementation of this method.)
2. Retrieves `mObjectToWorld` from `BitStream` and sets this object's current transform using that value.

With these minor changes, we are ensured that ghosts of this object will always be rendered in the proper locations and that they will be updated when the server object is updated.

### prepRenderImage()

Another method that our new class needs to implement is the `prepRenderImage()` method.

```
bool myFirstSceneObject::prepRenderImage( SceneState* state,
                                          const U32 stateKey,
                                          const U32 startZone,
                                          const bool modifyBaseZoneState )
{
    // 1
    if (isLastState(state, stateKey)) return false;
    setLastState(state, stateKey);

    // 2
    if (state->isObjectRendered(this))
    {
        // 3
        SceneRenderImage* image = new SceneRenderImage;

        // 4
        image->obj = this;
        image->isTranslucent = false;
        image->sortType = SceneRenderImage::Normal;
        image->useSmallTextures = false;
        image->tieBreaker = false;
        image->textureSortKey = 0;

        // 5
        state->insertRenderImage(image);
    }

    return false;
}
```

Since we haven't made changes yet, the `prepRenderImage()` method does the following default set-up.

1. Does that (advanced) last state check we talked about above. (Don't worry about this step. Just remember to do it.)

2. Checks if this object will be rendered and enters the set-up code if it will be.

3. Allocates a single render image. Don't forget that you can allocate as many as you need, but this simple example only needs one.

4. Sets the image record up with the following default settings.
   - Sets the object to be rendered as `this` object.
   - Marks object as not being translucent.
   - Specifies that this object uses normal sorting; that is, it gets no special sorting preferences.
   - Tells the engine not to force the use of small textures. This gives the engine the freedom to mipmap any textures this object may use.
   - Marks the tie breaker flag as `false`. So, if this object and another object tie for rendering, and if the other object also has its flag set to `false`, the engine will decide on its own which object to render first. (Recall that if we set this to `true`, this object would be rendered last in the case of a tie.)
   - Initializes the texture sort key to 0. Again, if there is a rendering tie, this setting will affect rendering order. However, this setting has the opposite effect of the tie breaker. By setting this value to 0, we're saying to render this object first. (Recall that objects with a higher value in this variable are rendered last.)
5. Adds the image record into the (current) scene.

## `consoleInit()` and `renderObject()`

There are two more methods listed as required, namely `consoleInit()` and `renderObject()`. In the case of the former, we don't have any work for this method to do in this example, so the empty template version is fine. In the case of the latter, we're going to defer discussing that until we add some new content. Then, we will talk about its implementation for this example.

## Steps #4 and #5

The last two steps in our recipe deal with adding new features. Unlike our last example, we don't have any new console functions or console methods to add. We're only going to add some rendering code and then plug that rendering code into `renderObject()`.

## Render Code

To save time, and because this isn't a test of OpenGL knowledge, I will borrow a code snippet from Neon Helium's (NeHe) Lesson 5. This snippet renders a three-dimensional multicolored pyramid.

> If you want to increase your knowledge of OpenGL coding, then you should visit NeHe's website (http://nehe.gamedev.net/). He has a ton of excellent (progressive stepped) exercises and answers showing how to use many OpenGL features.

**Extract code from NeHe Lesson 5.** The example code in Lesson #5 as provided on NeHe's website does a lot more than we need. So, I have extracted just the portion that renders the pyramid. The extracted code looks something like this.

```
glBegin(GL_TRIANGLES);
    glColor3f(1.0f,0.0f,0.0f);
    glVertex3f( 0.0f, 1.0f, 0.0f);
    glColor3f(0.0f,1.0f,0.0f);
    glVertex3f(-1.0f,-1.0f, 1.0f);

    // many more lines ...

glEnd();
```

As you can see, this is very standard and very simple OpenGL rendering code. I only state this because it is easy to forget that all of the work we do, setting up and creating a rendering environment, comes down to a few lines of code like those shown above.

**Implement new method containing code.** Now that we have some rendering code, we need to create a method to contain that code. In theory, we could put this code right in the body of renderObject(), but because this render code is so long and because I want to reuse this example later, I've decided to put the rendering code in its own method. Then, I will call that method from renderObject().

The render function I've created is called DrawGLScene(). To implement this method, we declare it in the header like this.

```
class myFirstSceneObject : public SceneObject
{
private:
    // ...
  void myFirstSceneObject::DrawGLScene(void);
```

Then, in the source file, we add this definition.

```
void myFirstSceneObject::DrawGLScene(void)
{
 glRotatef(90,1,0,0); // Rotate to account for TGE orientation

 // Render goes code here (not shown from brevity's sake)

}
```

When you look at this method (in your favorite editor), you will notice that it includes the render code from above and one extra line of code.

```
glRotatef(90,1,0,0); // Rotate to account for TGE orientation
```

Remember how I told you (in Chapter 10) that TGE uses a different orientation than standard OpenGL? Well, since I'm borrowing code and because I'm too efficient (lazy) to go back and modify every line to account for the rotation difference, I cheated and simply reoriented my ModelView transform. Now NeHe's code will render properly in Torque in an otherwise unmodified state. This is a real time-saver and a valid trick when using code designed for standard OpenGL.

## renderObject()

The last piece of code we need to add in this example is a call to DrawGLScene(). We will do this in the appropriate spot in the template's renderObject() method.

```
void myFirstSceneObject::renderObject( SceneState* state,
                                       SceneRenderImage* )
{
   // 1
   AssertFatal( dglIsInCanonicalState(),
                "Error, GL not in canonical state on entry" );

   // 2
   glMatrixMode(GL_PROJECTION);
   glPushMatrix(); // Push current Projection Matrix
   RectI viewport;
   dglGetViewport(&viewport);

   // 3
   state->setupObjectProjection(this);

   // 4
   glPushMatrix(); // Push current ModelView Matrix

   // 5
   dglMultMatrix(&getTransform());

   // 6
   DrawGLScene();

   // 7
   glPopMatrix(); // Pop stored ModelView Matrix
   glMatrixMode(GL_PROJECTION);
   glPopMatrix(); // Pop stored Projection Matrix
```

```
glMatrixMode(GL_MODELVIEW);
dglSetViewport(viewport); // Restore Viewport

// 8
AssertFatal( dglIsInCanonicalState(),
             "Error, GL not in canonical state on exit");
}
```

This method does the following.

1. Checks that TGE is in a canonical state. Remember that although this is an optional step, it can save you lots of trouble.

2. Saves the current projection matrix and viewport so we can restore them after we are done rendering.

3. Sets up the projection and `ModelView` matrices.

4. Stores the `ModelView` matrix so we can restore it after rendering.

5. Applies the object's current transform matrix (so we render in the correct world location).

6. Calls our rendering method, `DrawGLScene()`.

7. Restores all the matrices we saved.

8. Rechecks for a canonical state. (Very important!)

### Test New Class

Now, we're ready to test our new class.

#### Compile the Code

To test our new class, we first need to compile the code. Do so now.

#### Copy the Executable

To test run this code, locate the executable we just generated by compiling and copy it into the "Kit/" directory you created in Chapter 1. It is OK to over-write the executable in that directory.

#### Modify World Editor Scripts

In the future, when you create new `SceneObject` classes and if you want to use the World Editor Creator to create and place instances of them in the world, you will have to modify the World Editor scripts to do so. In this case, I have already modified the World Editor scripts in the kit to allow you to place instances of `myFirstSceneObject`.

So, let me show you the changes I made. Then, in the future, you can follow my example.

If you don't want to type this code in, or if you ran into problems, feel free to use the answers I have provided for you. This example can be located on the accompanying CD in the directory "C++Samples(Finished)/".

**Add to list of known Creator objects.** First, I searched for the string
`"%Environment_Item["` in the kit scripts. My search located a file named
"Kit/creator/editor/EditorGui.cs" containing some code like this.

```
%Environment_Item[12] = "sgLightObject";
%Environment_Item[13] = "VolumeLight";
%Environment_Item[14] = "sgMissionLightingFilter";
%Environment_Item[15] = "sgDecalProjector";

%Mission_Item[0] = "MissionArea";
%Mission_Item[1] = "Path";
%Mission_Item[2] = "PathMarker";
%Mission_Item[3] = "Trigger";
%Mission_Item[4] = "PhysicalZone";
%Mission_Item[5] = "Camera";

%System_Item[0] = "SimGroup";
```

Here, I had to make my first decision. Was my new object an environment
object, a mission object, or a system object? I decided that it was a mission
object and decided to add a new mission object entry like this.

```
%Mission_Item[6] = "myFirstSceneObject";
```

**Add object builder script.** Second, after having added our new class to the
list of known object types, I needed to create a builder script. To do this, I
searched for the build script associated with `"Camera"` (the item before my
new item on the object list). From experience, I knew to search for a string like
`"::buildCamera"`. Doing this search turned up the file "Kit/creator/editor/
objectBuilderGui.gui". In this file, after the definition for `buildCamera()`, I
added this new builder function.

```
function ObjectBuilderGui::buildmyFirstSceneObject(%this)
{
    %this.className = "myFirstSceneObject";
    %this.process();
}
```

That's it. Now, we're ready to test the new class and to place instances of it
using the World Editor Creator.

## Run and Test the Executable

Now, run the kit as we learned in the Chapter 1 exercise. When you have
the Chapter 1 mission running, start the World Editor Creator (F11 followed
by F4).

In the Creator tree, locate `myFirstSceneObject` (see Figure 11.1) and
place one in the world (see Figure 11.2.)

**Engine Coding**

---

**Figure 11.1.**
**myFirstSceneObject** in Creator list.

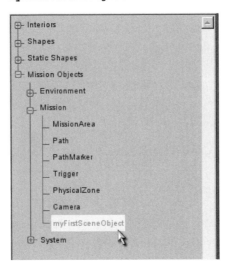

**Figure 11.2.**
**myFirstSceneObject** in world.

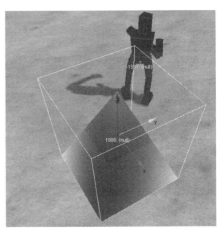

## 11.7 The SimDataBlock **Class**

SimDataBlock is the root datablock class. It provides an entity, transmitted once per mission, that holds static information for use by other objects. To handle the networking requirements of this data, the SimDataBlock class adds a few features that are similar to those found in NetObject. (Remember that SimDataBlock is derived from SimObject, not NetObject.)

To use any of these features, you must include the "simBase.h" header file in your code.

```
// Use features of the SimDataBlock class
//
#include "console/simBase.h"
```

In this section, we will learn about the new features SimDataBlock adds for transmitting and handling data.

## 11.7.1 Packing and Unpacking Data

In the Section 11.5, we were introduced to the packUpdate() and unpackUpdate() methods. These methods allow NetObject instances to transmit data updates from server objects to ghost objects.

SimDatablock instances also need to transmit data from the server to clients, but in this case, the operation is a one-time (per mission) affair. So, instead of inheriting from `NetObject` and modifying the update methods, the TGE programmers determined that it would be more efficient to implement the new data-packing methods `packData()` and `unpackData()`.

## `packData()`/`unpackData()`

The `packData()` and `unpackData()` methods are almost exactly the same as `packUpdate()` and `unpackUpdate()` with the following exceptions.

➢ Generally, the entire datablock is transmitted so dirty masks are not needed, although flags may still be utilized

➢ When transmitting pointers to datablock instances, we will not have the address available yet, so we will substitute an ID instead. Subsequently, on the client, before this datablock can be used, all IDs must be resolved to pointers (addresses).

We can reuse the skill we acquired when learning about `NetObject`. The `packData()` and `unpackData()` methods both use the same data-transmission method used by the NetObject update methods. So, let's talk a little about optimizing datablock transmissions and then move on to some other `SimDataBlock` topics.

### Optimizing Data Packing

Normally, when we send data between objects, we seek to minimize data transmission to just the data that is needed. In the case of a datablock, all the data will be needed. At first, this would seem to leave no room for optimization. However, there is a way if we are smart.

We can use flags to group data that is rarely modified. Then if we find that this data is in fact left at its default value, we can skip it. Both the clients and the server create instances of their datablocks from the same classes, and both will get the same default values. So, if we only send data that is modified, we can optimize.

## 11.7.2 Preloading Data

The `SimDataBlock` class provides a method named `preload()`. This method is used to resolve data dependencies that can and will occur when using datablocks. Consider for a moment. Datablocks create a strange dependency for the classes that use them. When a class uses a datablock, not only does that datablock need to be loaded, but any data in the datablock needs to be loaded. Furthermore, if the datablock references another datablock, the problem becomes worse.

The `preload()` method is called on both the server and the client to resolve different problems. Therefore, every implementation of this method

**Engine Coding**

should have at least two sections, the part for clients and the part for the server.

```
bool myDatablock::preload( bool server, char errorBuffer[256] )
{
   if (Parent::preload(server, errorBuffer) == false)
     return false;

   if (server)
   {
      // Server preload work goes here.
   }
   else
   {
      // Client preload work goes here.
   }
}
```

Of course, this is a simple template, and most implementations are a bit more complex.

### Common Server `preload()` Responsibilities

The server code in most `preload()` implementations will be concerned with the following issues.

➢ Ensuring the presence of meshes.

➢ Calculating CRCs on meshes.

➢ Verifying the presence of required nodes and animations in meshes.

### Common Client `preload()` Responsibilities

The client code in most `preload()` implementations will be concerned with the following issues.

➢ Resolving pointers to other datablocks.

➢ Loading textures.

➢ Loading sound files.

### A Concrete Client Example

Let's look at an example to put this discussion in more concrete terms. In this example, the client needs to ensure that some textures are loaded before this datablock can be used, and the server has no tasks.

```
bool myDataBlockPairData::preload(bool server, char errorBuffer[256])
{
```

```
   // Call parent preload first
   //
   if (Parent::preload(server, errorBuffer) == false)
      return false;

   // Is this the server?  If so, we're done.
   if( server ) return true;

   // Have the client load its texture.
   //

   if( mTextureName != StringTable->insert(this.texture) )
   {
      if (mTextureHandle) delete mTextureHandle;
      mTextureHandle = TextureHandle(mTextureName, BitmapTexture, false);
   }
   else
   {
      if (mTextureHandle) delete mTextureHandle;
      mTextureHandle = TextureHandle();  // Start with a NULL texture
   }

   return true;
}
```

This example is made up, but the pattern should be fairly clear. The method
calls the parent implementation and then gets down to the task of doing either
server or client tasks.

## 11.7.3 More about Resolving Datablock IDs

The following snippet is taken directly from the source code. It is a portion of
the VehicleData datablock definition. At the end of this snippet, we can see
that VehicleData contains an array of AudioProfile datablock pointers.

```
struct VehicleData: public ShapeBaseData
{
   typedef ShapeBaseData Parent;

   struct Body {
      enum Sounds {
         SoftImpactSound,
         HardImpactSound,
         MaxSounds,
      };
      AudioProfile* sound[MaxSounds];
```

Now, if we look at a snippet of the VehicleData packData() method, we
will see that the last statement in the snippet (the for loop) places IDs in the

place of addresses and sends them. (It also uses the ranged optimization technique, but we're not interested in that except to note that it is used.) It does this because the server can't know what the addresses will be on the client. If it sends the IDs (which are the same on both server and clients), the clients can resolve them into IDs.

```
void VehicleData::packData(BitStream* stream)
{
    S32 i;
    Parent::packData(stream);

    stream->write(body.restitution);
    stream->write(body.friction);

    for (i = 0; i < Body::MaxSounds; i++)
        if (stream->writeFlag(body.sound[i]))
            stream->writeRangedU32(packed? SimObjectId(body.sound[i]):
                                    body.sound[i]->getId(),
                                    DataBlockObjectIdFirst,
                                    DataBlockObjectIdLast);
```

Next, we look at a snippet of the `VehicleData unpackData()` method and see that in the last part of the snippet (the for loop), the code only unpacks the IDs and stores them. It does not yet try to resolve them since there is no guarantee at this point that the required datablocks have been received.

```
void VehicleData::unpackData(BitStream* stream)
{
    Parent::unpackData(stream);

    stream->read(&body.restitution);
    stream->read(&body.friction);

    S32 i;
    for (i = 0; i < Body::MaxSounds; i++) {
        body.sound[i] = NULL;
        if (stream->readFlag())
            body.sound[i] =
            (AudioProfile*)stream->readRangedU32( DataBlockObjectIdFirst,
                                                DataBlockObjectIdLast);
    }
```

Finally, if we examine a snippet of the `VehicleData preload()` method, we will see how the clients resolve the IDs into pointers. Here, the client merely looks up the address of the individual datablock IDs using the `Sim` namespace function `Sim::findObject()`.

```
bool VehicleData::preload(bool server, char errorBuffer[256])
{
   if (!Parent::preload(server, errorBuffer))
      return false;

   // Resolve objects transmitted from server
   if (!server) {

      for (S32 i = 0; i < Body::MaxSounds; i++)
         if (body.sound[i])
            Sim::findObject(SimObjectId(body.sound[i]),body.sound[i]);

   }
```

So, as you can see, what may sound like a difficult task is merely a long but simple one instead.

In the `preload()` *snippet, you will see this code:*
`SimObjectId(body.sound[i]).`

This statement is merely casting the `AudioProfile *` into a `SimObjectId` (`U32`) so that the value stored there can be passed to `Sim::findObject()`.

## 11.7.4 Registering New Classes as Console Types For Use with `addField()`

In Section 11.3, we discussed the `addField()` method. At that time, I asserted that general pointers could not be registered as fields but that datablock pointers could. I didn't elaborate further, but in order to register a new `SimDataBlock` class using the `addField()` method, we need a type specifier. I would like to show you how to generate type specifiers for new `SimDataBlock` classes.

In "simBase.h", there are four macros provided that will do all the work of adding new types to the console. To register a class as a new console type, we merely need to call the first of these macros (after the class declaration) in our header file and the remaining three macros (anywhere) in the source file.

```
// Declare our new console type in the header file
//
DECLARE_CONSOLETYPE( className );

// Implement our new console type in the source file
//
IMPLEMENT_CONSOLETYPE( className );
IMPLEMENT_GETDATATYPE( className );
IMPLEMENT_SETDATATYPE( className );
```

**259**

The above code will produce a new console type with a name of the form
`"TypeclassNamePtr"`.

## 11.7.4 The `SimDataBlock` Derivation Recipe

### Step #1: Prepare the Template Files

1. Select a name for your new class.
   - Example: `"mySimDataBlock"`
2. Copy the `GameBase` template files to an engine directory of your choice.
3. Rename the copied files.
   - Example: "t_SimDataBlock.h" becomes "mySimDataBlock.h"
   - Example: "t_SimDataBlock.cc" becomes "mySimDataBlock.cc"
4. Open both files using a C++ editor of your choice.
5. Replace all instances of the string `"t_SimDataBlock"` with the name of your class.
   - Example: All instances of `"t_SimDataBlock"` become `"mySimDataBlock"`
6. Save both files.
7. Add these files to your current project and run a test compile to be sure there are no syntax errors.

### Step #2: Override Inherited Methods

`SimDataBlock` inherits all of the features found in `SimObject` and its parent classes. At the very least, we should override the methods `initPersistFields()` and `consoleInit()`.

Additionally, we may optionally override any of these inherited methods: `onAdd()`, `onRemove()`, `onGroupAdd()`, `onGroupRemove()`, `onNameChange()`, `onStaticModified()`, `inspectPreApply()`, and `inspectPostApply()`.

### Step #3: Override Needed `SimDataBlock` Methods

It is likely that we will want to override all of the following methods: `preload()`, `packData()`, and `unpackData()`.

### Step #4: Add Needed Console Functions and/or Console Methods

At the end of the source file, you should add any console methods or console functions you will need to work with this class in the console. To accomplish this, use the `ConsoleFunction()` and `ConsoleMethod()` macros.

### Step #5: Add New Features and Functionality

Once you have modified the template files, you should add any new code and features that are necessary for your new class. This part is up to you and depends upon your needs.

## 11.7.5 A `SimDataBlock` Derivation Example

Most of the time, when we create a new datablock class, we create it for the purpose of pairing it with some other class. This is where the `GameBase` and `GameBaseData` classes come into play. Because we will be discussing these two classes next, and because the steps for deriving a `GameBaseData` class are similar to those used to derive from `SimDataBlock`, I am not providing a derivation example for `SimDataBlock`.

## 11.8 The `GameBase` and `GameBaseData` Classes

`GameBase` is the base class for game objects that use datablocks and are networked. In addition to the features they inherit from their parent class `SceneObject`, they add the ability to make time-based updates and to send controlling client-specific data updates.

`GameBaseData` is the base class for all scriptable, demoable datablock classes that are paired with children of `GameBase`.

Together, these two classes are the culmination of all that we have learned in this chapter. Of all the previous classes, it is most likely that you will use `GameBase` and `GameBaseData` as the base classes for your new game classes. In fact, one of my favorite quotes (from the engine source code) mirrors that fact and adds some advice, too.

*"For truly it is written: The wise man extends **GameBase** for his purposes, while the fool has the ability to eject shell casings from the belly of his dragon."* —KillerBunny

The point of this statement is that you are better off deriving your new classes from `GameBase` and `GameBaseData` rather than attempting to use one of their child classes. If you use a child class, you will get loads of features you don't need instead of the perfect balance provided by these two.

To use any of the features provided by these two classes, you must include the "gameBase.h" header file in your code.

```
// Use features of the GameBase and GameBaseData classes
//
#include "game/gameBase.h"
```

In this section, we will examine the `GameBase` and `GameBaseData` classes' features.

Recall that ticks are (by default) time slices 32 milliseconds in length.

## 11.8.1 GameBase and Time-Based Updates

The most important feature added by `GameBase` is the ability to make time-based updates. `GameBase` provides three different methods associated with the time-based processing.

## Using `processTick()`

This method is called on every object once per tick. It is passed a single argument, which is a pointer to the controlling client's move manager.

Within the body of this method, both clients and servers execute tasks that need to be done every tick, including things like recharging, taking damage, responding to movement inputs, etc.

## Using `interpolateTick()`

This is called every frame on client objects and allows them to interpolate actions between ticks. A single floating-point value is passed to this method, which represents the amount of time remaining until the next tick occurs.

Remember that we're dealing with tick time (32 milliseconds per tick), so a value of 0.5 would be equal to saying there are 16 milliseconds until the next tick.

This mechanism combined with `processTick()` allows us to provide accurate physics interactions regardless of the frame rate that the client is experiencing.

## Using `advanceTime()`

This is called on client objects so they can execute time-based behavior such as animations or fixed-rate sound emissions. A single floating-point value is passed to this method equivalent to the time in milliseconds since the last `advanceTime()` call.

This mechanism combined with `processTick()` allows us to provide accurate animations regardless of the frame rate that the client is experiencing.

## Enabling and Disabling Ticking

If at any time you wish to enable or disable tick processing, you can simply call the `setProcessTick()` method.

```
// Stop processing ticks
//
setProcessTick(false);

...

// Start processing ticks
//
setProcessTick(true);
```

While disabling ticks will disable `processTick()` and `interpolateTick()`, it will not affect `advanceTime()`.

## Controlling Tick Processing Order

Sometimes, GameBase objects depend upon another object's position, rotation, or other attributes, and ideally, the dependent object will get processed after the object it depends on. However, without forcing the engine to order object processing, you can't depend on this relationship.

To force one GameBase object to process after another GameBase object, simply call the processAfter() method.

```
GameBaseObject * obj1;
GameBaseObject * obj2;

...

// Force obj1 to process after obj2
//
obj1.processAfter( obj2 );
```

To determine what object any GameBase object is processing after, we can write code like this.

```
GameBaseObject * thisObject;
GameBaseObject * afterObject;

...

// Find out what GameBase object thisObject is processing after.
//
afterObject = thisObject.getProcessAfter();

if( NULL == afterObject)
    printf("This is not processing after any other specific object.\n")
else
    printf("This is processing after another specific object.\n")
```

Finally, we can tell a GameBase object to stop processing after another specific GameBase object like this.

```
GameBaseObject * thisObject;

...

// Clear our process after status
//
thisObject.clearProcessAfter();
```

## 11.8.2 New Callback

The GameBase class adds a new (and important) callback, onNewDataBlock(). This callback is called whenever a new datablock is assigned to a GameBase (derived) class. A typical implementation of this callback will have all of the parts shown below.

```
bool myGameBaseExample::onNewDataBlock( GameBaseData* dptr )
{
   // 1
   mDataBlock = dynamic_cast< myGameBaseData* >( dptr );

   // 2
   if( !mDataBlock || !Parent::onNewDataBlock( dptr ) )
   {
      return false;
   }

   // 3
   if ( isClientObject() )
   {
      // Client object does some updates and work
   }
   else
   {
      // Server object does some updates and work

    // 4
    scriptOnNewDataBlock();

    // 5
    setMaskBits(transmitOnNewDatablock);
   }

   // 6
   return true;
}
```

1. Cast the datablock pointer (which is passed into this callback) to the current class type so we can access its members and methods.

2. Double check that we didn't get a NULL pointer. If we did, abort and return false, otherwise call up the Parent chain.

3. Update any datablock-dependent members and features. Notice that in this example, we are checking to see if this callback is being called on a client object or on a server object. In some cases, you may want to do different tasks based on this information.

4. Trigger the script version of onNewDatablock(), if this isn't already done by the class's parent.

5. Mark any datablock-related data as dirty so that the packUpdate() will refresh it.

6. Return true if we have reached the end of this method without encountering errors. What constitutes an error really depends on your code, but

basically an error is anything that will cause the new datablock to not work with this class. Returning `false` effectively blocks this datablock assignment, leaving this class with its old datablock.

Note that all of these steps (except for 2 and 6) are optional and implementation dependent.

## 11.8.3 Controlling Client

During the course of writing your game and while implementing a new `GameBase` class, you may need to get the `GameConnection` object that controls the current instance of your `GameBase` class; that is, you may need a pointer to the controlling client. To get this, we can write the following code.

```
GameConnection * myMaster = NULL;

myMaster = getControllingClient();
```

Alternately, we may want to change the client that controls this object. We can do that using code like this.

```
GameConnection * anotherMaster = NULL;

setControllingClient( anotherMaster );
```

## 11.8.4 Dirty Masks

In our discussion of the `NetConnection` class, we talked about the use of dirty masks to control when `packUpdate()` sends data to a server object's ghost(s). In our discussion, we used a set of bitmasks that were defined like this.

```
protected:
   enum { firstDataDirty = BIT(0),
          seconDataDirty = BIT(1) };
```

When we write code like this, we are making the assumption that all the bits are available; that is, we are assuming that the parent class isn't using any bits in the dirty mask.

This is not a safe assumption, and if we are wrong, we may reuse bits that were in use by the parent class and cause unintended updates in our new class.

Fortunately, the folks who wrote the Torque Game Engine considered this dilemma. To resolve it (for the `GameBase` class and its children), they defined the `GameBase` dirty masks like this.

```
enum GameBaseMasks {
   InitialUpdateMask =        Parent::NextFreeMask,
   DataBlockMask =            InitialUpdateMask << 1,
   ExtendedInfoMask =         DataBlockMask << 1,
   ControlMask =              ExtendedInfoMask << 1,
   NextFreeMask =             ControlMask << 1
};
```

In this implementation, the last `enum` type is called `NextFreeMask` and is equal to the next available bit after the last bit that was used by `GameBase`.

By doing this, the TGE designers have allowed us to derive from `GameBase` and then to subsequently define our own dirty masks like this.

```
enum {transmitOnInspect            = Parent::NextFreeMask << 0,
     transmitOnNewDatablock        = Parent::NextFreeMask << 1,
     NextFreeMask                  = transmitOnNewDatablock << 2
    };
```

Notice that in this code, our first new dirty mask starts at the bit position defined by `Parent::NextFreeMask`. Also notice that we implement a new `NextFreeMask` and set its value to the next free bit in the list.

At first this may look odd, but after a while it should become clear that this entire mechanism is designed to ensure that no children of `GameBase` will accidentally reuse bits that a parent class has already used. It also gives us a simple mechanism for creating our bitmasks.

## 11.8.5 GameBase Packet Updates

The `GameBase` class provides two additional data-update methods on top of the two inherited from `NetObject`. These two specialized methods, `writePacketData()` and `readPacketData()`, operate using the same mechanics as those found in `NetObject`, with the exception that the server will use these methods to update client control objects.

In other words, if a `GameBase` object is the control object from some client, then that client will receive additional data regarding this one object in the form of calls to `writePacketData()` and `readPacketData()`.

These calls are provided to enable client-side prediction and are intended to keep control objects as up-to-date as possible.

## 11.8.6 The GameBase Derivation Recipe

### Step #1: Prepare the Template Files

1. Select a name for your new class.

   - Example: `"myGameBase"`

2. Copy the `GameBase` template files to an engine directory of your choice.

3. Rename the copied files.
   - Example: "t_GameBase.h" becomes "myGameBase.h"
   - Example: "t_GameBase.cc" becomes "myGameBase.cc"

4. Open both files using a C++ editor of your choice.

5. Replace all instances of the string `"t_GameBase"` with the name of your class.
   - Example: All instances of `"t_GameBase"` become `"myGameBase"`

6. Save both files.

7. Add these files to your current project and run a test compile to be sure there are no syntax errors.

## Step #2: Override Inherited Methods

`GameBase` inherits all of the features found in `SceneObject` and its parent classes. At the very least, we should override the following methods: `initPersistFields()`, `consoleInit()`, `packUpdate()`, `unpackUpdate()`, `prepRenderImage()`, and `renderObject()`.

Additionally, we may optionally override any of these inherited methods: `onAdd()`, `onRemove()`, `onGroupAdd()`, `onGroupRemove()`, `onNameChange()`, `onStaticModified()`, `inspectPreApply()`, `inspectPostApply()`, and `renderShadow()`.

## Step #3: Override Needed `SceneObject` Methods

It is likely that we will want to override one or all of the following methods: `processTick()`, `interpolateTick()`, `advanceTime()`, `writePacketData()`, and `readPacketData()`.

We may also, optionally, override the method `onNewDataBlock()`, which is called when this object's datablock is changed.

## Step #4: Add Needed Console Functions and/or Console Methods

At the end of the source file, you should add any console methods or console functions you will need to work with this class in the console. To accomplish this, use the `ConsoleFunction()` and `ConsoleMethod()` macros.

## Step #5: Add New Features and Functionality

Once you have modified the template files you should add any new code and features that are necessary for your new class. This part is up to you and depends upon your needs.

## 11.8.7 The `GameBaseData` Derivation Recipe

### Step #1: Prepare the Template Files

We already prepared these files in Section 11.8.6.

### Step #2: Override Inherited Methods

`GameBaseData` inherits all of the features found in `SimDataBlock` and its parent classes. At the very least, we should override the following methods: `initPersistFields()`, `consoleInit()`, `preload()`, `packData()`, and `unpackData()`.

Additionally, we may optionally override any of these inherited methods: `onAdd()`, `onRemove()`, `onGroupAdd()`, `onGroupRemove()`, `onNameChange()`, `onStaticModified()`, `inspectPreApply()`, and `inspectPostApply()`.

### Step #3: Add Needed Console Functions and/or Console Methods

At the end of the source file, you should add any console methods or console functions you will need to work with this class in the console. To accomplish this, use the `ConsoleFunction()` and `ConsoleMethod()` macros.

### Step #4: Add New Features and Functionality

Once you have modified the template files you should add any new code and features that are necessary for your new class. This part is up to you and depends upon your needs.

## 11.8.8 A `GameBase` and `GameBaseData` Derivation Example

This example is designed to introduce you to a complete (if minimal) `GameBase` and `GameBaseData` derivation and to provide a base for several exercises on the accompanying CD.

In this example, we will do the following.

1. Create a new `GameBase` child class named `myGameBase`.
2. Create a new `GameBaseData` child class named `myGameBaseData`.
3. Add the code necessary to render a three-dimensional colored pyramid and/or a three-dimensional colored cube.

By now, you may be getting tired of rigidly following the recipe, so instead, we will still do the first step, then we'll jump right into the interesting parts of this example.

## Step #1: Prepare the Template Files

One last time, let's walk through template file preparation. Let's do the following.

1. Select a name for our `GameBase` class.
   - Example: Our selection is `"myGameBase"`.
2. Copy the template files to an engine directory of our choice.
   - Copy them to our directory: "engine/game/examples"
3. Rename the files.
   - Header file: "engine/game/examples/myGameBase.h"
   - Source file: "engine/game/examples/myGameBase.cc"
4. Open the source files in your favorite editor.
5. Replace all instances of `"t_GameBase"` with `"myGameBase"`.
6. Save both files.
7. Add the files to current project and test compile.

Remember that Step #1 for `GameBase` automatically handles Step #1 for `GameBaseData`. So, we're now done preparing both new classes and all their methods/callbacks.

## New Render Code

In this example, we're going to use the pyramid and cube rendering code from NeHe's Lesson 5. Then, we will place this code in the following two methods.

```
void myGameBase::DrawGLPyramid(void)
{
   glRotatef(90,1,0,0);
   glBegin(GL_TRIANGLES);
      glColor3f(1.0f,0.0f,0.0f);
      glVertex3f( 0.0f, 1.0f, 0.0f);

      // ...
      glColor3f(0.0f,1.0f,0.0f);
      glVertex3f(-1.0f,-1.0f, 1.0f);
   glEnd();
}

void myGameBase::DrawGLCube(void)
{
   glRotatef(90,1,0,0);
   glTranslatef( 0.0f, 2.0f, 0.0f );  // Render above pyramid.
   glBegin(GL_QUADS);
```

**269**

```
        glColor3f(0.0f,1.0f,0.0f);
        glVertex3f( 1.0f, 1.0f,-1.0f);
        glVertex3f(-1.0f, 1.0f,-1.0f);
        glVertex3f(-1.0f, 1.0f, 1.0f);
        glVertex3f( 1.0f, 1.0f, 1.0f);

        // ...

        glColor3f(1.0f,0.0f,1.0f);
        glVertex3f( 1.0f, 1.0f,-1.0f);
        glVertex3f( 1.0f, 1.0f, 1.0f);
        glVertex3f( 1.0f,-1.0f, 1.0f);
        glVertex3f( 1.0f,-1.0f,-1.0f);
    glEnd();
}
```

Notice that our two methods are named `DrawGLPyramid()` and `DrawGLCube()`. Also notice that both methods implement the rotation trick I mentioned in the `SceneObject` example and that `DrawGLCube()` adds a small translation so that it is always drawn above the pyramid (in the case where both are rendered).

Don't forget that these two methods should be declared like this in the header file.

```
class myGameBase : public GameBase
{
private:
    typedef GameBase Parent;

    myGameBaseData    * mDataBlock;

    void DrawGLPyramid(void);
    void DrawGLCube(void);
```

## New Datablock Members/Fields

In this example, we want the datablock to control whether the `GameBase` child renders a pyramid or a cube or both. To do this, we can simply add two boolean fields to the `GameBaseData` child, expose them as fields, and make sure they are sent to the clients as part of the datablock send during mission load.

This code declares them.

```
struct myGameBaseData : public GameBaseData
{
    typedef GameBaseData Parent;

public:
```

```
    myGameBaseData();
    ~myGameBaseData();

    bool mDrawPyramid;
    bool mDrawCube;
```

This code initializes them.

```
myGameBaseData::myGameBaseData()
{
    mDrawPyramid = true;
    mDrawCube    = true;
}
```

This code registers them with the console.

```
void myGameBaseData::initPersistFields()
{
    Parent::initPersistFields();

    addField("drawPyramid", TypeBool, Offset( mDrawPyramid,
            myGameBaseData) );
    addField("drawCube", TypeBool, Offset( mDrawCube,
            myGameBaseData) );
}
```

This code ensures that they are sent to all clients during datablock uploads.

```
void myGameBaseData::packData(BitStream* stream)
{
    Parent::packData(stream);

    stream->write(mDrawPyramid);
    stream->write(mDrawCube);
}

void myGameBaseData::unpackData(BitStream* stream)
{
    Parent::unpackData(stream);

    stream->read(&mDrawPyramid);
    stream->read(&mDrawCube);
}
```

So far, this should all look very familiar. Now, let's look at some final changes to the predefined template content, and then we can test our new class.

## Adding Render Code and Render Control

We already have the render code, but we need to add it to `renderObject()` in such a way that the datablock files control which methods are called.

**271**

**Engine Coding**

To do this, we can add the following code to the predefined user code area in `renderObject()`.

```
// 6. ADD YOUR RENDER CODE HERE
if( mDataBlock->mDrawPyramid ) DrawGLPyramid();

// Reset the render matrix before drawing again.
glPopMatrix(); // Pop stored ModelView Matrix

glPushMatrix(); // Push current ModelView Matrix

dglMultMatrix(&getTransform());

if( mDataBlock->mDrawCube ) DrawGLCube();
```

Take a close look at this code.

## Datablock-Controlled Rendering

The first thing you should notice is that the `DrawGL*()` calls are both controlled by if statements. Each of these statements inspects the value of boolean flag, `mDrawPyramid` for `DrawGLPyramid()` and `mDrawCube` for `DrawGLCube()`. This makes sense because we do want the datablock to control our rendering code. It's the next thing that might seem a little odd.

## Reseting Render Transforms

The second thing you should notice is the snippet of code between the two `DrawGL*()` calls. You might be wondering what this code does. What it does is reset the render transform.

Why reset the transform? Because if we don't, and if the pyramid and the cube are both rendered, the cube will inherit all the transform modifications made by the pyramid code. Yes, don't forget that the render code is modifying our transform in order to place the pyramid's vertices in the correct places.

Because we want to start with a fresh slate, we simply pop the matrix (which we thoughtfully saved before rendering), push the matrix again (we're getting ready to modify it again), and reapply this object's current transform to the `ModelView` matrix.

Now, we're ready to render again.

### Test New Class

Now, we're ready to test our new class.

## Compile the Code

To test our new class, we first need to compile the code. Do so now.

> If you don't want to type this code in, or if you ran into problems, feel free to use the answers I have provided for you. This example can be located on the accompanying CD in the directory "C++Samples(Finished)/".

## Copy the Executable

To test run this code, locate the executable we just generated by compiling and copy it into the "Kit/" directory you created in Chapter 1. It is OK to over-write the executable in that directory.

## Run and Test the Executable

The kit comes with a run script to test this example. So, instead of running the Chapter 1 exercise mission this time, run the Chapter 11 mission "001_Game-Classes: GameBase/GameBaseData Derivation Example". This will automatically launch the script "Kit/gpgt/server/scripts/gpgt/chapter11/exercise001. cs", and inside this script, you will find the following datablock definitions and test code.

```
datablock myGameBaseData( renderBoth )
{
   category    = "Misc";
   drawPyramid = true;
   drawCube    = true;
};

datablock myGameBaseData( pyramidOnly )
{
   category    = "Misc";
   drawPyramid = true;
   drawCube    = false;
};

datablock myGameBaseData( cubeOnly )
{
   category    = "Misc";
   drawPyramid = false;
   drawCube    = true;
};

package exercisePackage_001
{

function startexercise001()
{
   // 1
   new myGameBase( testMyGameBase )
   {
      position = exerciseCenter.getPosition();
      dataBlock = "renderBoth";
      scale     = "1 1 1";
   };
```

```
        MissionGroup.add( testObj );

    }

    function myGameBaseData::create(%data)
    {
        %obj = new myGameBase()
        {
            dataBlock = %data;
        };
        return %obj;
    }

};
```

Notice that this exercise automatically creates an instance of `myGameBase` named `testMyGameBase` and uses the datablock `renderBoth` to initialize it.

**Figure 11.3.**
Cube and pyramid both rendering.

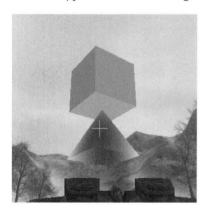

**Figure 11.4.**
Only cube is rendering.

**Figure 11.5.**
Only pyramid is rendering.

### Experiments to Try

Once this mission is running, you will see something like the image in Figure 11.3 when you first start this mission.

Now, open the console and type the following.

```
testMyGameBase.setDatablock( cubeonly );
```

Running this code should produce an image like Figure 11.4.
Now, try this code.

```
testMyGameBase.setDatablock( pyramidonly );
```

Running this code should produce an image like Figure 11.5.

Finally, we can go back to rendering both by typing this code in the console.

```
testMyGameBase.setDatablock( renderboth );
```

| Exercise Summary | Location on Disk |
|---|---|
| Not an exercise. Mission 001 is used to test the `GameBase` and `GameBaseData` derivation example. | None |
| More examples registering and exposing standard variable types. | /exercises/ch11_002.pdf |
| Exposing enumerated types. | /exercises/ch11_003.pdf |
| Using field validators. | /exercises/ch11_004.pdf |
| More examples creating console functions and methods. | /exercises/ch11_005.pdf |
| Using `Con::execute()` and `Con::executef()`. | /exercises/ch11_006.pdf |
| Adding `forEach*()` to `SimSets`. (Hard exercise.) | /exercises/ch11_007.pdf |
| `mySecondSceneObject`: Learning more about `image` sorting. | /exercises/ch11_008.pdf |
| Creating (two) new `GuiControls`. | /exercises/ch11_009.pdf |

**Table 11.15.**
Game class creation and use exercises.

## 11.9 Exercises

Whew! We covered a lot of information in this chapter, and so far we haven't had the opportunity to apply but a mere fraction of it. So, in order for you to get a proper start learning to create and use new game class, we will run through several exercises.

Table 11.5 lists the exercises included on the accompanying CD that supplement this chapter.

# Debugging

## Part V

# Chapter 12

## It's Broken! Debugging Torque

### 12.1 Introduction

This is the first chapter in a series of debugging chapters. In this chapter, we focus on things that you can do if your game is broken or otherwise misbehaving.

Although the majority of the topics we discuss in this chapter are related to scripts or built-in tools, we do discuss some C++ coding techniques, and the concepts we discuss with regard to debuggers can be translated to C++ debugging tools.

It is also worth noting that, although some of the topics in this chapter can be related to performance analysis, the bulk of our (performance) profiling discussions will happen in Chapter 13.

### 12.2 Torque Debuggers (and Editors)

The Torque Game Engine provides internal hooks that allow us to test and debug our games using external debugging tools called debuggers.

Debuggers are, more often than not, editors with the embedded (or plug-in supported) capability to attach to an externally running program (our game).

There are two kinds of debuggers we care about: debuggers that are designed to debug game scripts (TorqueScript) and debuggers that are designed to debug engine source code (C++).

In this chapter, we will only discuss the TorqueScript variety. The primary reason for this is that for the average Torque game, the majority of game logic is implemented in script. Additionally, it would take several tens, if not hundreds, of pages to just scratch the surface of the many different editor/debugger combinations that are available under Windows and OS X, not to mention Linux.

I will briefly introduce you to fundamental debugging concepts and terms. To make the discussion concrete, I will show examples of these topics in action, using the Torsion TorqueScript integrated development environment (IDE).

The Torsion TorqueScript IDE is a feature-rich tool that, among other things, allows us to edit and ebug Torque scripts and Torque games. I use it as my preferred TorqueScript editor and debugging tool in the Windows environment. If you don't already have a personal preference, I strongly suggest that you give this tool a test run. You can find a trial version on the GarageGames website.

### 12.2.1 Torsion Basics

Because I will be using Torsion in these examples and because I encourage you to use it too, I would like to take just a moment to introduce some very basic features of this wonderful tool to you.

**Figure 12.1**
Torsion.

## Two Areas of Interest

First, let's take a look at the Torsion interface, or more specifically at two areas of interest on that interface. In Figure 12.1, the full Torsion interface is shown with two areas highlighted (gray boxes).

The first area (1) is the editor window and shows the current source code we are editing. If you will look closely at the left side of this area, you will see a gray column with numbers in it. This strip is used to display the line number of every line of code in the editor. Additionally, it is used to select and display breakpoints.

The second area (2) is actually a tabbed window containing each of the following tabs.

> **Output.** This pane displays any console output that your game produces as well as warnings/errors when your code doesn't compile properly. (Don't forget that Torque scripts get compiled before execution.) This pane is not related to Torsion's interactive debugging features, so we won't discuss it further.

➢ **Watch.** This pane displays the current list of watch variables and their values. We discuss this in Section 12.2.4.

➢ **Callstack.** This pane displays the call stack for the function we are currently in. We discuss this in Section 12.2.5.

➢ **Find Results.** This pane displays the results for your last code search. This pane is not related to Torsion's debugging features, so we won't discuss it further.

➢ **Breakpoints.** This pane displays the current list of breakpoints and their current status (enabled/disabled/hit count), as well as any conditions they may have associated with them. We discuss this in Section 12.2.2.

### Running and Stopping from Torsion

Assuming we are running Torsion and have a valid project loaded, we can run the game represented by that project by pressing F5. We can later stop this game (from the editor) by pressing SHIFT + F5.

### Torsion Features

This tool has a myriad of nice features that we will not discuss in this book. Fortunately, Torsion has a decent help feature, so you can self-educate to your heart's content. For now, let's get back to talking about debuggers (and editors) and use Torsion to illustrate the discussion.

## 12.2.2 Breakpoints

The first debugging concept we will examine is the breakpoint. Breakpoints are mechanisms designed to allow us to stop a running program (script) at a specified point(s), based on either a static selection or some condition.

### Static Breakpoints

In the Torsion editor, we can statically select breakpoints by clicking next to the line numbers in the code-editing pane.

For example, imagine that we are editing the file "Kit/gpgt/server/scripts/game.cs" and that we want to stop on line 28 in the function `onServerCreated()` (see Figure 12.2). We can do this by first clicking next

```
21
22  ⊟ function onServerCreated()
23    {
24       if($GPGT::MPDebug) echo("\c5 ====> MPNET(mod/server):" SPC "onServerCreated()" );
25
26       // Server::GameType is sent to the master server.
27       // This variable should uniquely identify your game and/or mod.
28       $Server::GameType = "FPS Starter Kit";
29
30       // Server::MissionType sent to the master server.  Clients can
```

**Figure 12.2**
Line 28 in
`onServerCreated()`.

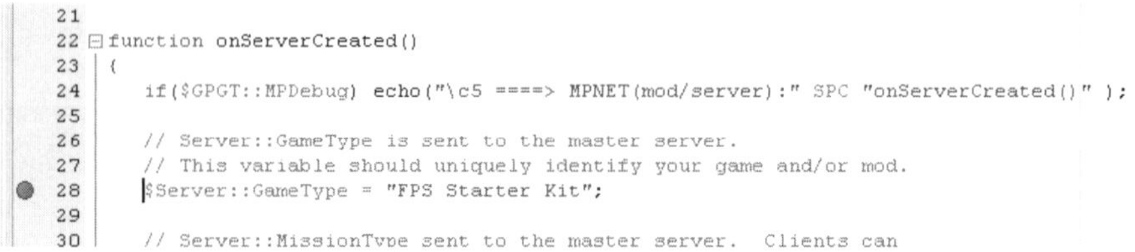

**Figure 12.3**
Breakpoint marker.

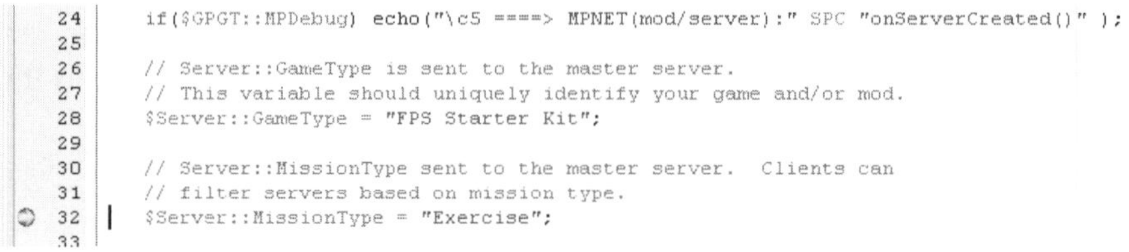

```
   21
   22 ⊟ function onServerCreated()
   23 | {
   24 |     if($GPGT::MPDebug) echo("\c5 ====> MPNET(mod/server):" SPC "onServerCreated()" );
   25
   26 |     // Server::GameType is sent to the master server.
   27 |     // This variable should uniquely identify your game and/or mod.
●  28 |     $Server::GameType = "FPS Starter Kit";
   29
   30 |     // Server::MissionTvpe sent to the master server.  Clients can
```

**Figure 12.4**
Stopped!

```
   24 |     if($GPGT::MPDebug) echo("\c5 ====> MPNET(mod/server):" SPC "onServerCreated()" );
   25
   26 |     // Server::GameType is sent to the master server.
   27 |     // This variable should uniquely identify your game and/or mod.
   28 |     $Server::GameType = "FPS Starter Kit";
   29
   30 |     // Server::MissionType sent to the master server.  Clients can
   31 |     // filter servers based on mission type.
↻  32 |  |  $Server::MissionType = "Exercise";
   33
```

to line 28 in the editor and then running the game (press F5 and then run any mission). As soon as we click next to 28, we will see a red dot (gray in our illustration) appear next to that line (see Figure 12.3). This dot is a breakpoint marker, and the breakpoint we just set is a static breakpoint.

When we run the game and when we start up a mission, eventually the onServerCreated() function will be executed. When this happens, Torsion will allow the function to run until it hits line 28, and then Torsion will break (stop) the script. At this point, Torsion will pop to the front of the screen, and we should see a little yellow arrow on top of our red dot (see Figure 12.4).

As you can probably imagine, this is a very handy feature when you want to stop a game on some code the first time it is executed, but what do you do if you only want to stop at a breakpoint under certain conditions? You use a conditional breakpoint, which just happens to be our next topic.

## Conditional Breakpoints

A conditional breakpoint is a breakpoint that will only stop program execution if certain conditions are met. Torque debuggers support two basic kinds of conditions.

> **Break on pass.** This kind of condition states that the debugger will only stop on this breakpoint on the $n$th pass. For example, a break-on-pass setting of 5 would stop on the breakpoint the fifth time the script attempted to execute that particular line of code (during the current game run).

> **Break on true.** This kind of condition is a general logical statement. Torque allows us to specify a line of script representing a logical condition or test that must be true for this breakpoint to activate.

We will examine both of these conditional breakpoints below, but before we can do so, we need to talk about the breakpoint pane some more.

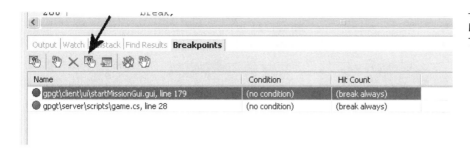

**Figure 12.5**
The breakpoint pane.

## Examining Our Breakpoints

Recall from Section 12.2.1 that there is a pane in the Torsion editor that lists all of our current breakpoints. As you can see in Figure 12.5, there are two breakpoints currently enabled. (I have already selected another breakpoint for our next example, so yours will only show one if you are following along.) Additionally, you will see a number of buttons at the top of the pane. These buttons have the following functions from left to right.

➢ **New Breakpoint.** Add a new breakpoint.
➢ **Disable (Enable).** Disable (or enable) the currently selected breakpoint.
➢ **Delete.** Delete the currently selected breakpoint.
➢ **Properties.** Display this breakpoint's properties (dialog).
➢ **Go to Source.** Open the file this breakpoint is set in and take us to it.
➢ **Delete All Breakpoints.** Delete all breakpoints in the breakpoint list.
➢ **Disable (Enable) All Breakpoints.** Disable (or enable) all breakpoints in the breakpoint list.

## Example Break on Pass

Now, let's talk more about how the conditional break-on-pass breakpoints work. In the editor, I have selected the file "Kit/gpgt/client/ui/startMissionGui.gui" and placed a static breakpoint on line 179 (in method startMissionGui:: onWake()). However, I only want this breakpoint to stop here on the third pass. So I need to do the following.

First, I open the breakpoints pane and select the breakpoint I wish to edit (see Figure 12.5).

Second, I need to edit this breakpoint's properties (by clicking the Properties button).

Third, I need to enable break on pass and set the count to 3. Figure 12.6 shows the properties dialog for my breakpoint with the proper settings.

Now, when I run the kit, and if I click the Chapter 7 button (has more than three missions), the breakpoint will stop the third time it gets to this line.

**Figure 12.6**
Break on third pass.

**Figure 12.7**
Break when `%i == 3`.

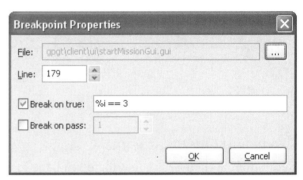

### Example Break on True

Now, let's create a generic condition instead. We will use the same line of code, but instead of break on pass, we will use break on true and set the condition to this snippet (see Figure 12.7).

```
%i == 3
```

Now, when I run the kit, and if I click the Chapter 7 button, the breakpoint will stop at this line as soon as the local variable `%i` is equal to 3. If this condition is never met, the breakpoint will not trigger.

### Combining Conditions

As you may have guessed, it is possible to combine break on pass and break on true. Just enable both and set up the condition. However, be aware that conditional breakpoints using both break criteria will only break when both are true.

## 12.2.3 Code Stepping

Now that we know what breakpoints are and how to make the Torsion debugger use them to stop on a line of code, we should talk about code stepping.

Code stepping is the practice of executing code one line or function at a time. In order to use this functionality (in any debugger), we need to run the program under test (our game) and get it to stop on a breakpoint, or halt it manually (CTRL + ALT + BREAK in Torsion). Then, once the game is stopped (in the debugger), we can start stepping.

The question of course is what kind of stepping do we wish to do? Let's talk about each type.

## Step

The first stepping type we have available to us is called *step* and can be accessed by pressing the F11 key in Torsion. This is the simplest of the stepping types and causes Torsion to execute the current line of code and to stop on the next valid line it finds.

If we step and the current line executes either a script function or a script method, Torsion will open that function/method definition and stop on the first valid line of code it finds.

If we step and the current line contains no script functions or methods, Torsion will execute it and then stop on the next valid line it finds, wherever that may be.

Finally, if we step and execute the last valid line of code in a script function or method, Torsion will leave this function/method and go back to the place this function/methods was called, again stopping on the next valid line of code it finds.

The Torsion TorqueScript IDE has many of the same keyboard shortcuts found in VisualStudio, making these two tools nicely consistent in that respect.

## Step Over

The second stepping type we have available to us is called *step over*. This stepping type functions much like step and can be accessed by pressing the F10 key in Torsion. In fact, it behaves just like step except that when it encounters a script function or method, instead of entering the code, it simply executes the entire function/method (regardless of how many lines of code it has) and then stops on the next valid line after the current line.

## Step Out

The third and last stepping type we have available to us is called *step out*. It executes all code between the current position and the end of the current script function or method. Then, after executing the last line of code in that function/method, Torsion will stop executing the program and go to the location where the function/method was called, stopping on the next valid line of code it finds.

## Continuing (Go)

Although it really isn't stepping, it is also possible to start the game running again (after the engine stops at a breakpoint) by pressing F5. Of course, if Torsion hits another valid breakpoint, the game will be stopped again (at the new breakpoint).

## 12.2.4 Watches

So far, we know how to make the engine stop at breakpoints as well as how to step through the code. Now, let's learn how to inspect the code as we step through it.

> Torsion is context-sensitive and will evaluate all local variables in the context of the current cursor position.

**Figure 12.8**
Three watches.

There is a common debugger feature called *watch* or *watch variable*. Most TorqueScript debuggers (including Torsion) support this feature. In essence, this feature allows us to tag pieces of code and then to have these pieces of code evaluated as we step. The results of this evaluation are usually dumped into a window (in the editor/debugger we are using to tag the watches). In Torsion, that window is the Watch pane we discussed above.

## Example Watches

In Torque, we can watch a variety of script constructs, including the following.

> **Single variables (local or global).** See the first watch line in Figure 12.8.
> **Simple scripts including assignment and comparison operations.** See the second watch line in Figure 12.8.
> **Complex scripts, including calls to functions and methods.** See the third watch line in Figure 12.8.

## Don't Forget Cursor Hover

> Be careful with conditional watches and the cursor-hover feature. Both of these features execute code and can change the state of your game. For example, if you select the (hypothetical) code `$player.delete();` and hover over it, Torsion will execute this code to see what it evaluates to, thereby deleting the object pointed to by `$player`.

While we're talking about watches and Torsion, let me remind you (or tell you) that Torsion supports a feature where it will evaluate any variables or selected scripts that the cursor is currently hovering over. That is, if you have stopped at a breakpoint and you hover your cursor over a variable, Torsion will display the value of that variable after a short delay. Additionally, you can select a piece of script and hover the cursor over it. If Torsion is able to evaluate that selection, it will do so and present the result to you in a bubble next to the cursor. Figure 12.9 shows this feature in action.

**Figure 12.9**
Hover script evaluation.

**Figure 12.10**
Sample call stack.

## 12.2.5 Call Stacks

The last major debugging feature we need to discuss is called a *call stack*. When we are debugging Torque scripts, the engine keeps track of where we are in terms of functions calls. That is, it is possible to call a function (or method) and have the function/method call another function/method, and so on. At any time, we could be very deep in a stack of calls.

A call stack is merely a listing (of some sort) telling us what functions/ methods are currently stacked up and waiting for us to return to them. Torsion displays this information in the Callstack pane (see Figure 12.10).

If you examine Figure 12.10, you will see that we the call stack is telling us that we are currently at line 48 in the function/method `loadMission()`. This function/method was called by `createServer()` at line 52, which in turn was called by `SM_StartMission` at line 159.

## 12.2.6 Other Debuggers?

To be fair to folks who don't have Torsion or don't work in the Windows environment, let me point out that there are other editor/debugger solutions out there. A short list of these includes the following two editors/debuggers.

> **TribalIDE.** This is another Windows-based editor/debugger, originally designed for editing *Tribes* scripts. It is pretty old and kind of hard to find now, but it is free and works OK with Torque.

> **JEdit + TIDE.** JEdit is a very portable editor (written in Java) that runs on several operating systems, including OS X and Linux. With the TIDE (Torque IDE) plug-in, you can use JEdit to edit and debug Torque scripts.

## 12.3 Script Debugging Tips and Techniques

Debuggers are great tools, and I recommend that you use them regularly. However, there will be times when a simpler approach is needed. One simple approach to debugging a problem is the use of custom debug code. By custom debug code, I mean any code that is inserted into a script that will produce an output (to the console or perhaps to a GUI control).

"Yeah, I am familiar with that. I have been doing it since Programming 101. Why do you even bring it up?", you might ask. I bring it up because not all readers are experienced programmers and even experienced programmers might benefit from the following tips.

## 12.3.1 TorqueScript Debug Messages

As you should know, there are three script functions for printing messages to the console.

➤ **echo( arg0, arg1, ..., argN )**. This is the standard method for producing non-error messages in a script. Messages produced in this fashion are (normally) printed using black in the drop-down console.

➤ **warn( arg0, arg1, ..., argN )**. This is the less sever of two error-message types for scripts. Messages produced in this fashion are (normally) printed using yellow/orange in the drop-down console.

➤ **error( arg0, arg1, ..., argN )**. This is the more sever of two error message types for scripts. Messages produced in this fashion are (normally) printed using red in the drop-down console.

It is entirely up to you which of these functions you use. Personally, I like to always use echo() except when I write temporary debug code. Then, I use error() to make the output easy to find in the console. I rarely use warn().

## 12.3.2 Colorized Messages

Before you even start to add extra echo() statements in your scripts, consider using colorized console messages. This will make them much easier to find while examining the drop-down console content. You could use the warn() and error() functions, but I suggest reserving them for debug code that is left in. For temporary debug code, you can use echo() and prefix any statements with a color escape sequence. Remember that the color escape sequences are \c0 to \c9.

If you're not familiar with color escape sequences, or if you have forgotten exactly what they do, try the following lines of code in the console.

```
echo("Normal text same as \\c0");
warn("Warning text same as \\c1");
error("Error text same as \\c2");
echo("\c0Text using escape sequence \\c0");
echo("\c1Text using escape sequence \\c1");
echo("\c2Text using escape sequence \\c2");
echo("\c3Text using escape sequence \\c3");
echo("\c4Text using escape sequence \\c4");
echo("\c5Text using escape sequence \\c5");
echo("\c6Text using escape sequence \\c6");
```

```
echo("\c7Text using escape sequence \\c7");
echo("\c8Text using escape sequence \\c8");
echo("\c9Text using escape sequence \\c9");
```

## 12.3.3 Regularize Messages

Because we will be stripping out our custom messages later, it is a *very* good idea to make debug messages and statements easy to identify. It would be bad to strip out messages that should be retained and likewise bad to leave in debug messages that should be removed.

So, if a message will be later stripped out, I suggest adding a common tag to the message. I like to use my initials (EFM) for this purpose.

```
echo("EFM: Sample debug message");
```

Later, when I get ready to release my code, I simply search for any instances of my initials and remove the debug statements I find.

## 12.3.4 Echo Major Branches

When I start debugging a script problem, I almost always add `echo()` statements at major branches in my code.. This allows me to verify that my scripts have executed in the correct order. My definition of a major branch is any point where scripts will be loaded or executed conditionally.

## 12.3.5 Entry and Exit Points

Another technique I like to use is the addition of `echo()` statements at the entry point of major functions/methods, as well as any points where those functions/methods can return from. This way, I can easily trace the path my scripts are taking while executing script functions/methods.

```
function ABC()
{
   echo("EFM: ABC() => Entry");

   if( true )
   {
      echo("EFM: ABC() => Exit A");
      return;
   }

   // ...

   if( true )
   {
      echo("EFM: ABC() => Exit B");
```

```
        return;
    }

    // ...

    echo("EFM: ABC() => Exit C");
}
```

## 12.3.6 Echo Key Variables

In addition to showing entry and exit points, it is often useful to get a snapshot of the contents of current key variables. By "key," I mean variables that affect the execution of the current script or the actions of some object in the game. If a function/method modifies values, it might even be useful to dump these values upon entry and exit from that routine.

## 12.3.7 Echo Control Evaluation Results

If a particular function looks as if it should be working but it continually makes an inappropriate exit or follows an incorrect execution path, consider breaking down the condition that makes this decision and/or dumping the individual contributors. Often, I find that when a conditional statement looks good but exits incorrectly or is skipped, I have made a fundamental syntactical error or assumed something about one of the contributors that is, in fact, not actually true. You can never be too skeptical when debugging.

## 12.3.8 Reloaders

I encourage you to be disciplined in your planning and to think about the code you're writing before you write it, but at the same time, I understand that it is often quicker to tweak-and-test. Thus, my next suggestion is to add reloaders to script files that you'll be editing so you don't need to restart the game too frequently.

A reloader is nothing more than a function that, when called, will reload and `exec()` the file that function is defined in. By reloading a file, we effectively load any changes that were made to that file since it was last loaded.

```
// Utility function used while making the guide to reload
// this file.
function rdwds() {

    exec("./DebuggingWorkflow_DebugSample0.cs");

}
```

The function `rdwds()` will reload and `exec()` the file "./DebuggingWorkflow_ DebugSample0.cs" when it is called.

## Reloaders Don't Always Work

Note that this technique is not guaranteed to work for all cases. Most notably, if you are editing datablock definitions *and* if you are running a multiplayer game, this method will not work correctly. Why? Because once a client has connected, the server does not normally retransmit datablock definitions to it.

## Beware of Object Pollution

When using reloaders, be aware of what the scripts you are reloading do. If they add new objects, modify globals, or call various server methods, you may encounter problems.

# 12.3.9  Tracing and Backtracing

## `trace()`

TGE provides a function called `trace()`. This function takes a single boolean argument that enables or disables tracing, depending on whether we pass `true` or `false`. When tracing is turned on, TGE will start to echo a stack-ordered list of entries to and exits from all functions and console methods. Additionally, TGE will print the arguments that were passed in to these routine calls, as well as any return values.

```
==>trace(true);
      Console trace is on.
    Entering updateConsoleErrorWindow()
    Leaving updateConsoleErrorWindow() - return
Leaving ConsoleEntry::eval() - return
Entering ToggleConsole(1)
    Entering [CanvasCursor]GuiCanvas::popDialog(Canvas, ConsoleDlg)
        Entering ConsoleDlg::onSleep()
        Leaving ConsoleDlg::onSleep() - return 692 477
        Entering [CanvasCursor]GuiCanvas::checkCursor(Canvas)
        Leaving [CanvasCursor]GuiCanvas::checkCursor() - return 1232
    Leaving [CanvasCursor]GuiCanvas::popDialog() - return 1232
Leaving ToggleConsole() - return 1232
```

As you can see from this (very) small example, the output is great (and informative) but can easily become overwhelming.

To minimize output, I suggest adding the `trace()` enabling and disabling statements around the trouble areas in code. This way, it is only turned on for as long as you need it.

## `backtrace()`

There is another tracing function that can be used in scripts to see the current call stack. This function is called `backtrace()`.

**Debugging**

When we dump the current call stack, we are showing the current list of open calls to routines. An open routine call is one that has not yet exited.

For an example of how `backtrace()` works, let's look at the following code.

```
function tbt0() {
    echo("Entering TBT0\n");
    tbt1();
    backtrace();
    echo("\nExitting TBT0");
}

function tbt1() {
    echo("-Entering TBT1\n");
    tbt2();
    backtrace();
    echo("\n-Exitting TBT1");
}

function tbt2() {
    echo("--Entering TBT2\n");
    backtrace();
    echo("\n--Exitting TBT2");
}
```

If we load this script and then run the `tb0()` function, the console will display the following messages.

```
Entering TBT0

-Entering TBT1

--Entering TBT2

BackTrace: ->ConsoleEntry::eval->tbt0->tbt1->tbt2

--Exitting TBT2

BackTrace: ->ConsoleEntry::eval->tbt0->tbt1

-Exitting TBT1

BackTrace: ->ConsoleEntry::eval->tbt0

Exitting TBT0
```

Basically, by using `backtrace()`, we can determine the sequence of function calls that got us to the place where we are calling `backtrace()`. This can be very useful for debugging control structures (switch, if-then-else, etc.) in our scripts.

## 12.3.10 Journaling

While debugging a problem in scripts or in the engine, you may find yourself needing to rerun the same code over and over and over and ... well, you get the idea. Alternately, you may need to demonstrate an issue to someone who is working with you remotely. So, what do you do? Read on.

TGE provides a built-in means of recreating game sequences. It is called journaling. By using this features, it is possible to run a game in journal-recording mode and then later to recreate the exact sequence of events by playing back the journal.

In order to reproduce a sequence, the following items are required.

> **Functionally identical executable and scripts.** If you try to run a journal with a different executable or different scripts than those used while recording the journal, there is no guarantee that your journal will play properly. This doesn't mean that you can't add debug code to scripts while playing a journal; it just means thatyou shouldn't change the logical flow.

> **A journal file.** Of course, to play a journal you'll need a journal file.

So, how do we use this feature?

### Record a Journal

To record a journal, run your game with this argument added on the command line.

```
torque.exe -jSave journal.jrn
```

The name "journal.jrn" can be any value you choose as long as the file name ends in ".jrn".

As an alternate to using command-line arguments, you can call the saveJournal() function in your scripts.

```
saveJournal("./journal.jrn");
```

### Play a Journal

To play a previously recorded journal, place the journal file in the same directory as the game executable and run the game using command-line arguments like this.

```
torque.exe -jPlay journal.jrn
```

In this case, the name "journal.jrn" should be the name of the journal file you wish to play.

**Debugging**

As an alternate to using command-line arguments, you can call the `playJournal()` function in your scripts.

```
playJournal( "./journal.jrn" );
```

## 12.4 C++ Debugging Tips and Techniques

Now that we have discussed TorqueScript debugging techniques, it is time to turn our attention to C++ debugging.

### 12.4.1 Console Messages

If you have read Chapters 10 and 11, then you will already know this, but the engine supplies three functions for printing messages to the console from within our C++ code.

```
Con::printf(const char *_format, ...);

Con::warnf(const char *_format, ...);

Con::errorf(const char *_format, ...);
```

These functions operate just like the ANSI C `printf()` function except that the output from these functions goes to the console and is colorized like the `echo()`, `warn()`, and `error()` script functions.

### 12.4.2 Torque Memory Manager

TGE comes with its own memory manager, Torque Memory Manager (TMM). The TMM overrides the standard `new()` keyword and replaces this functionality with its own code.

Using the TMM, allocations are done in 8 MB chunks. Subsequently, smaller chunks of this 8 MB chunk are doled out as requested, until the chunk is gone or too fragmented to use. At that time, the TMM acquires a new 8 MB chunk.

The advantages of this methodology are as follows.

➤ It enables tracking of allocated/deallocated memory, making it easier to locate leaks.

➤ It may increase memory-allocation performance.

Unfortunately, there are also disadvantages.

➤ It may cause external libraries, such as the Standard Template Library (STL), to fail.

➤ It may reduce memory-allocation performance.

I know that this may be confusing, since I said that TMM can increase and decrease memory-allocation performance, but allow me to talk more about the purpose of TMM first, then I'll come back and explain these conflicting statements.

## Memory Leaks

The TMM provides a relatively painless method of tracking down memory leaks. The question is, "Without TMM, how can you detect that there may be leaks?" Easy. If you see any of the following symptoms while running your game, you may have a memory leak(s).

➢ You observe reduced performance as time progresses. That is, the longer the game runs, the worse the performance gets.

➢ The memory footprint of the game continues to increase over time. This may become extremely obvious if the OS starts to swap memory to disk, at which time your game may practically halt while waiting for the swaps to finish.

➢ The game crashes mysteriously.

### Identifying Leaks

Once you suspect memory leaks, you can can easily identify them by following these simple steps.

> TORQUE_DEBUG_GUARD is defined in the file "torqueConfig.h".

1. Enable the memory manager by recompiling the engine with the `TORQUE_DEBUG_GUARD` macro defined.
2. Run your game to the point *before* where you think there may be a problem (more on this below).
3. Type: `flagCurrentAllocs();`
4. Type: `dumpUnflaggedAllocs("./baseLineTMMDump.txt");`
5. Run the suspect code/script, cause the suspect interaction, or allow the game to run for a bit, depending on the type of memory leak detected.
6. Type: `dumpUnflaggedAllocs("./debugTMMDump.txt");`

Starting at Step #3, exactly what are we doing?

First (Step #3), the call to `flagCurrentAllocs()` tags all current allocations so they will be ignored when we request a dump. This is part of setting a baseline. We are looking for changes that occur after a known baseline.

Second (Step #4), we finish setting up a baseline by dumping the most current list of unflagged allocations (first call to `dumpUnflaggedAllocs()`). This file shows where we were before trying to cause a leak.

Third (Step #5), we run the suspect code (hoping to get a leak).

Fourth (Step #6), we call `dumpUnflaggedAllocs()` again to get the full list of unflagged allocations. After following Step #6, we are ready to check for leaks.

### The Unflagged-Allocation Files

If we look at our baseline file "baseLineTMMDump.txt", we will see something like this.

```
h:\example\console\compiler.cc           610    20      56347
h:\example\console\consoleinternal.cc 395      48      56352
h:\example\console\console.cc            777    56      56354
Undetermined                       0    8064    56353
h:\example\console\compiler.cc           510    40      56358
h:\example\console\consoleinternal.cc 280      60      56350
h:\example\console\compiler.cc           610    36      56357
h:\example\console\compiler.cc           510    28      56348
h:\example\console\consoleinternal.cc 249      32      56351
h:\example\console\console.cc            777    56      56344
h:\example\console\consoleinternal.cc 442      32      56349
```

The first question that may arise is, "Why are there any lines at all in this file?"

The reason is that although we set a baseline with our call to `flagCurrentAllocs()`, the engine was still running, meaning that current processes could and did still allocate data.

The second question that may arise is, "How do I read this?"

Each line has the following format.

```
filename line_num alloc_size alloc_num
```

> **filename.** File allocation was made from this file. Displays `Undetermined` if the allocation source trace failed.

> **line_num.** Line from which allocation was made. Zero for `Undetermined`.

> **alloc_size.** Allocation size in bytes.

> **alloc_num.** Unique ID for this allocation. Every allocation gets a unique ID.

Now, to see what has changed, look at the file "debugTMMDump.txt" and compare it to our first (baseline) file "baseLineTMMDump.txt". Any differences between these files may indicate a leak.

## Leaks in Our Code?

If you've been adding new engine code or modifying existing engine code, and you suspect a memory leak, you should look for lines in the debug file associated with that new code. Confirming this kind of leak is relatively straightforward.

As the author of the code, you should have a pretty good idea when the code is called and when memory allocated in the code should be deallocated. Thus, if memory allocated in this code is being flagged as still allocated, you probably missed a delete somewhere.

## Leaks in Engine Code?

What about leaks in the pre-existing engine code? You may run your test and dump the debug allocation file only to find that it is filled with all kinds of allocated entries from code you've never touched. Consider the following possibilities.

➢ Our choice of a baseline was not very good. Try running the test again and then doing a second debug dump (to a new file). Did the second dump accumulate new mysterious allocations from the same files? You may have a leak.

➢ Consider that our scripts may be doing allocations via the creation of new objects that never get deleted.

• This can happen if you create an object in a mission without placing it in the `MissionGroup` (or another `SimGroup` that is automatically emptied at the end of the mission).

• This can happen if you create GUI controls dynamically and do not delete them. In this case, dynamically can mean: 1) created by a script, or 2) created on file exec, where the same file is re-exec'd at some point without deleting old controls first.

• This can happen if you create GUI `ControlProfiles` dynamically and do not delete them. (Same definition for dynamic.)

The lessons here are the following.

➢ Always make sure that objects that are created have a way to to get deleted automatically (regardless of your intention to delete them manually).

➢ Check for instances of named objects such as GUI `Controls` and `ControlProfiles`. If they exist, delete them prior to creating the new instance.

➢ Consider that your new code may be calling engine code with the assumption that this code will take responsibility for deleting new allocations, when the called code does not in fact guarantee this.

In the end, you'll have to break out an editor and inspect these mysterious allocations in order to track them down.

## Poor TMM Performance

I said above that the TMM may improve allocation performance or it may reduce performance. You may be wondering, "What kind of nonsense is this?"

It isn't nonsense. Historically, the performance of the XYZ (any name will do) memory allocation routines have varied; thus, being smart guys, the team that developed TGE created their own allocation manager so that they could, to some degree, take control of this performance. "More nonsense!" you say.

**Debugging**

The point is that if you're developing for Windows, OS X, or Linux, the memory manager provided by these operating systems may in fact be superior to the one in TGE, but if you're developing for some new console, the performance of its memory manager may lag compared to that of TGE's. You have the freedom to select which you will use, and you can tune the TMM itself since you have the code.

So, if you are especially interested in tweaking performance, you should experiment with the TMM. You should test your applications with and without the TMM (on your target platform(s)) to determine the best configuration.

## 12.5 Other Debugging Techniques

The last set of debugging topics we need to cover in this chapter are not realted to scripts or C++ but are really related to special debug features provided by individual game classes.

### 12.5.1 Bounding Boxes

When debugging shapes, it is sometimes useful to see the bounding box associated with a shape. In TGE, all bounding boxes for all shapes can be made visible by setting a single global variable:

```
$GameBase::boundingBox = 1; // Show all shape bounding boxes
```

This is especially useful for vehicles, as it shows visual representations of mass center and the wheels' bounding boxes.

### 12.5.2 Visible Collision Meshes

In addition to bounding boxes, it is occasionally nice to see the collision mesh(es) of a shape. As we discussed in Chapter 8, you can render collision meshes by changing the "-" symbols in the collision mesh names to "+" symbols and re-exporting the model containing that mesh.

### 12.5.3 Interior Debug Render Modes

The `InteriorInstance` class supplies a number of debug render modes. These render modes can be accessed using the `setInteriorRenderMode()` method, which takes one numeric (mode number) argument specifying the debug render mode to use. Table 12.1 lists the various modes and their purpose.

| Mode Number | Mode Name | Mode Purpose |
|---|---|---|
| 0 | Normal | Normal. |
| 1 | Render Lines | Render interior brush outlines only. |
| 2 | Detail | Render interior brushes with flat coloration. White colored blocks indicate brushes that do not change with level-of-detail (LOD) changes. Red colored blocks will change. |
| 3 | Ambiguous | Shows ambiguous polygons. (Good models have none.) |
| 4 | Orphan | Shows orphaned polygons. (Good models have none.) |
| 5 | Light Map | Shows light maps on flat (white) shaded model. |
| 6 | Textures Only | Shows textures without light maps. |
| 7 | Portal Zones | Colorizes portalized zones to make them distinct and easily identifiable. |
| 8 | Outside Visible | Marks insides of interiors as white and outsides as red. Tip: An interior with no portals is marked as all red. |
| 9 | Collision Fans | Displays calculated (by exporter) collision fans with axes showing face directions. |
| 10 | Strips | Shows surfaces divided into colorized triangular strips. Each strip has a distinct color from adjacent strips. Tip: Large strips generally give the best performance, but don't overdo it. |
| 11 | Null Surfaces | Renders all faces with null texture applied as red. Tip: Excluding portals, no red surfaces should be visible without taking the camera into walls, or you will have a hole/gap in your surface. |
| 12 | Large Textures | All large textures will be rendered with a colorized shading. Blue – width or height equal to 256 pixels. Green – width or height equal to 512 pixels. Red – width or height greater than or equal to 1024 pixels |
| 13 | Hull Surfaces | Renders hull surfaces with distinct flat colors. |
| 14 | Vehicle Hull Surfaces | Renders specialized vehicle hull surfaces with distinct flat colors. |
| 15 | Vertex Colors | -- Currently Unavailable -- |
| 16 | Detail Levels | Renders entire interior at current LOD coloration (see Table 12.2). |

**Table 12.1.** `InteriorInstance` render mode.

**Table 12.2.** `InteriorInstance` LOD colors.

| Level of Detail (LOD) | Render Color |
|---|---|
| 0 | white |
| 1 | blue |
| 2 | green |
| 3 | red |
| 4 | yellow |
| ... | See source code. |

## 12.5.4 Tree

Using the inspector should be a natural part of the debug process if you suspect that an object has been wrongly configured and has some bad data in its fields. Unfortunately, not all objects show up in the inspector.

If you find yourself needing to inspect objects that do not show up in the inspector, you can start the `tree()` utility. This utility will display a tree starting at the base `SimGroup RootGroup`. All currently created objects are listed in this tree.

### `inspect(obj)`

The `tree()` utility is great, but searching through the tree may be a bit painful, especially if you already know the ID or name of the object you want to inspect. Fortunately, by using the `inspect()` command, it is possible to open the `tree()` utility to a specific object. Simply type the following.

```
inspect( obj );
```

This will open the `tree()` utility and select the specified object it it exists.

## 12.5.5  Make Inspector Act Like `tree()`

For folks who use the `tree()` utility frequently, it may be easier to modify the World Editor Inspector to act like `tree()`.

To do this, simply search for this string in your scripts.

```
EditorTree.open(MissionGroup,true);
```

Then, replace it with this.

```
EditorTree.open(RootGroup,true);
```

## 12.5.6 Dumping

Using the World Editor Inspector or the `tree()` utility, it is possible to check the values of fields for any particular object, but sometimes this is not enough. At times, we need to know more about an object or a datablock.

In order to obtain this information, simply use the `dump()` command.

```
%obj.dump();
```

The `dump()` command will produce a rather long list containing the following.

➤ **Member fields.** These are nondynamic fields.

➤ **Tagged fields.** These are dynamic fields.

➤ **Methods.** These are methods associated (either directly or by inheritance) with this object.

A sample dump might look like this.

```
==>1507.dump();
Member Fields:
```

```
    dataBlock = "PlayerBody"
    position = "212.452 340.104 240.94"
    rotation = "0 0 -1 40.6736"
    scale = "1 1 1"
Tagged Fields:
    client = "1452"
    invCrossbow = "1"
    invCrossbowAmmo = "10"
    mountVehicle = "1"
Methods:
    applyDamage() - (float amt)
    applyImpulse() - (Point3F Pos, VectorF vel)
    applyRepair() - (float amt)

// etc.
```

As with the `tree()` utility, `dump()` can be used at any time and for any object.

| Exercise Summary | Location on Disk |
|---|---|
| Using debuggers. (This exercise is designed for Torsion users but can be followed using other debuggers, too.) | /exercises/ch12_001.pdf |
| Writing and using reloaders. | /exercises/ch12_002.pdf |
| Journaling. | /exercises/ch12_003.pdf |
| Test run the TMM. | /exercises/ch12_004.pdf |
| Interior render modes. | /exercises/ch12_005.pdf |

**Table 12.3.**
Debugging exercises.

## 12.6 Exercises

Because debugging is part art and part science, and because everyone can benefit from learning more about this skill, let's do a few exercises to cement the debug topics we just discussed.

# Chapter 13
# It's Slow! Performance Profiling

## 13.1 Introduction

Debugging suspiciously slow code can be at best painful, and at worst infuriating. The problem with slow code is that technically, the code may not be incorrect, just poorly written. In this chapter, we will first focus on slow engine code and then come back to slow scripts.

## 13.2 The TGE Profiler

TGE provides a built-in profiler. However, before we can jump into learning about this profiler, you need to know some things about profilers in general to avoid making profiling errors.

By definition, a profiler is a program used to track the performance of another program. It does so by sampling such information as:

➢ Number of times a piece of code is visited.
➢ Time spent in a piece of code.
➢ Individual times relative to total loop time.

Additionally, there are various types of profilers. The two major categories of profilers are sampling and instrumenting. TGE implements an instrumenting profiler.

An instrumenting profiler collects its data by embedding code (hooks) within the flow of the program under test (PUT).

Invariably, instrumenting affects the execution time of the PUT, and if done poorly, the instrumentation code itself can bias the results. This is true because the instrumenting code incurs its own execution penalty. If this penalty outweighs the cost of the section under test (SUT), the results may be unreliable.

TGE's instrumentation is a hybrid of assembly code and C++. It takes advantage of various precision and optimization techniques. Nonetheless, it has weight. So, use caution when profiling small pieces of code.

### 13.2.1 Instrumenting the Engine

When profiling the PUT, individual SUTs are delineated with markers. This is done using two macros.

> ➤ **PROFILE_START( markerName )**. This starts the profiler and indexes these results using the string markerName. markerName can be any unique (not previously used) string. Quotes are not required.

> ➤ **PROFILE_END()**. This stops the profiler for the last started marker. It is important to remember to place this macro at each exit point for the current SUT (see example below).

Currently, the engine has several predefined markers, which can be located by searching for the PROFILE_START() macro.

In addition to these predefined markers, you may add as many additional markers as you need. For example, we could add a marker TorqueRocks (although, in practice, meaningfully named markers are better) to some code as follows.

```
void DoSomething(void) {
    // ... Some preceding code

    PROFILE_START( TorqueRocks );

    // ... Code were profiling

    // An if-then-else check that may exit
    if( SomeCondition ) {

        // Do something

    } else {

        // Do something else, then exit.

        PROFILE_END(); // Closes prior open

        return;
    }

    PROFILE_END(); // Closes prior open
}
```

Notice how there are two calls to PROFILE_END() in the above sample. This is because the code can exit at two points. Just remember that for every exit there must be a closing PROFILE_END() to match the PROFILE_START(). Thought of another way, for each PROFILE_START() we have to be sure to call PROFILE_END().

## 13.2.2 Enabling the Profiler

After markers have been added, the profiler itself is enabled and used from script.

In order to enable the profiler, start your game, get to the area you wish to profile (menus, mission, etc.), and type this in the console.

```
profilerEnable( true );
```

Later, you can turn off the profiler like this.

```
profilerEnable( false );
```

## 13.2.3 Resetting the Profiler

In older versions of TGE, the function `profilerReset();` was supplied to reset the profiler. In version 1.5.2, if you want to reset the profiler, simply disable it then re-enable it using the `profilerEnable();` function.

Resetting the profiler starts data acquisition from scratch.

## 13.2.4 Dumping Profile Data

To dump the results that have been captured since the last call to `profilerReset()`, use the following code.

```
profilerDump();
```

Calling this function will produce output similar to this.

```
profilerDump();
Profiler Data Dump:
Ordered by non-sub total time -
%NSTime   % Time   Invoke #   Name
 11.770   85.961        647 CanvasRenderControls
  8.429    8.429        647 glFinish
  2.322    2.322        647 SwapBuffers
  1.932  100.000        647 MainLoop
  0.461    0.461        647 CanvasPreRender
  0.382    0.445        647 ClientProcess
  0.122   98.023        647 ProcessTimeEvent
  0.102   97.274        647 RenderFrame
  0.087    0.087        332 AdvanceObjects
  0.061    0.122        647 AdvanceServerTime
  0.044    0.045         62 ProcessInputEvent
  0.036    0.063        647 AdvanceClientTime
  0.022    0.144        647 ServerProcess
  0.017    0.017        647 ServerNetProcess
  0.014    0.014        647 SimAdvanceTime
  0.007    0.007        647 ClientNetProcess
  0.001    0.001         14 MemoryAlloc
```

**305**

```
     0.000   0.000        14 MemoryFree
     0.000   0.000         0 MemoryRealloc
    73.202  74.191     36789 DrawText

Ordered by stack trace total time -
% Time  % NSTime  Invoke #  Name
 15.912 -84.088         0 ROOT
100.000   1.932       647  MainLoop
 98.023   0.122       647   ProcessTimeEvent
 97.274   0.102       647    RenderFrame
 85.961  11.770       647     CanvasRenderControls
 74.191  73.202     36789      DrawText
  8.429   8.429       647     glFinish
  2.322   2.322       647     SwapBuffers
  0.461   0.461       647     CanvasPreRender
  0.445   0.382       647   ClientProcess
  0.063   0.036       647    AdvanceClientTime
  0.026   0.026       166     AdvanceObjects
  0.144   0.022       647   ServerProcess
  0.122   0.061       647    AdvanceServerTime
  0.061   0.061       166     AdvanceObjects
  0.017   0.017       647   ServerNetProcess
  0.014   0.014       647   SimAdvanceTime
  0.007   0.007       647   ClientNetProcess
  0.045   0.044        62  ProcessInputEvent
  0.001   0.001        14   MemoryAlloc
  0.000   0.000        14   MemoryFree
```

The first part of the dump is a listing of SUTs ordered by percentage of time consumed. The columns are as follows.

➢ **%NSTime.** This is the percentage of the total profiling time consumed by this function, not including the time spent in subroutines that were being measured. That is, if this function calls another function that is being measured, the time spent in the called function is not included. However, if a function is called from this SUT and that function is not being measured, time spent in that function will be counted towards the total for this SUT. Huh? See the example below for a replay on that dazzling discussion.

➢ **%Time.** This is the total time spent in the SUT, relative to total time measured. This measure includes the time for all subroutines regardless of whether those subroutines are being measured or not.

➢ **Invoke #.** This is the number of times this section of code was invoked in the period of testing.

➢ **Name.** This is the marker name.

The second listing is the same data ordered by stack trace, so the hierarchy of calls is more apparent.

## More about `%NSTime`

Now, let's revisit that business about `%NSTime`.

```
void Foo(void) {
    PROFILE_START( SampleFoo ); // Begin SUT

    Bar();

    Super();

    PROFILE_END(); // End SUT
}

void Bar(void) {
    PROFILE_START( SampleBar ); // Begin SUT

    Duper();

    PROFILE_END(); // End SUT
}

void Super(void) {
  // Some code
}

void Duper(void) {
  // Some code
}
```

If we were to profile the above code, we would get a listing including lines for SampleFoo and SampleBar. The apportioning of time measured would be this:

➤ **SampleFoo**
  - **%NSTime.** Total time spent executing code between the open and close of marker SampleFoo includes time spent in Super() and excludes time spent in Bar() and Duper().
  - **%Time.** Total time spent executing code between the open and close of marker SampleFoo includes time spent in Super(), Bar(), and Duper().

➤ **SampleBar**
  - **%NSTime.** Total time spent executing code between the open and close of marker SampleBar includes time spent in Duper().
  - **%Time.** Same as %NSTime.

In addition to the console dump, we can dump our results to file using the following command.

```
profileDumpToFile( filename );
```

**Debugging**

In the above call, `filename` is any valid filename, and the file will be created if it doesn't exist or overwritten if it does.

## 13.2.5 Adding Profile Markers (Zooming In #1)

Once you've identified an area as having a heavy cost, you'll probably want to zoom in on any possible problems. The first way to do this is by adding more markers and thus further refining your profile. It is perfectly legal to open multiple markers before closing them. That is, markers can be embedded within markers. Just be cautious of the exiting semantics.

## 13.2.6 Disabling Profile Markers (Zooming In #2)

After optimizing trouble code, or when you know you cannot optimize a piece of code, you may wish to take that code out of the measurement. To do this, simply disable the marker. For example, we might decide that there is no point in measuring the time spent in `DrawText` and would prefer to focus on the remaining SUTs. We could disable `DrawText` measurements like this.

```
profilerMarkerEnable( "DrawText", false );
```

This code instructs the profiler to ignore the marker `DrawText` and not include it in the final results.

## 13.3 Other Performance-Measuring Tools

In addition to the Torque profiler, Torque provides a couple of other features for checking performance.

## 13.3.1 Metrics

The standard examples provide a set of metric measurement scripts that can be used for gleaning various performance metrics. These metrics are accessed via the `metrics()` function, which takes a single argument.

```
metrics( fps );
```

In this sample class, we have asked that the metrics GUI enable itself (shows up in the upper-left corner of the game window) and display frames-per-second information.

Table 13.1 lists all of the valid `metrics()` arguments and the measurements they provide.

| `metrics()` argument | Measures |
|---|---|
| audio | fps metrics as well as:<br>• OH: open handles<br>• OLH: open looping handles<br>• AS: active streams<br>• NAS: null active streams<br>• LAS: active looping streams<br>• LS: total looping streams<br>• ILS: inactive looping streams<br>• CLS: culled looping streams |
| debug | fps metrics as well as:<br>• NTL: texels loaded<br>• TRP: percentage of resident memory (on card) used by textures<br>• NP: number of primitives being rendered<br>• NT: number of textures in use<br>• NO: number of objects being rendered |
| interior | fps metrics as well as:<br>• NTL: texels loaded<br>• TRP: percentage of resident memory (on card) used by textures<br>• INP: number of primitives being rendered, for interiors only<br>• INT: number of textures in use, for interiors only.<br>• INO: number of objects being rendered, for interiors only |
| fps | • FPS: frames per second<br>• mspf: milliseconds per frame |
| time | fps metrics as well as:<br>• Sim Time: sim time to date; time since engine started<br>• Mod: ticks since engine started. |
| terrain | fps metrics as well as:<br>• L0: number of terrain blocks rendering at level zero<br>• FMC: full mipmap count<br>• DTC: dynamic texture count<br>• UNU: unused texture count<br>• STC: static texture count<br>• DTSU: dynamic texture space used<br>• STSU: static texture space used<br>• FRB: terrain blocks not rendered due to full fogging. |
| texture<br>Requires:<br>  `GLEnableMetrics(true);` | fps metrics as well as:<br>• NTL: number of texels loaded.<br>• TRP: percentage of resident memory (on card) used by textures<br>• TCM: texture cache misses |

**Table 13.1.**
**`metrics()`**
measurements.

**Table 13.1 (continued).**
`metrics()`
measurements.

| `metrics()` argument | Measures |
|---|---|
| `video`<br>Requires:<br>  `GLEnableMetrics(true);` | fps metrics +<br>• TC: total triangle count<br>• PC: total primitive count<br>• T_T: terrain triangle count<br>• T_P: terrain primitive count<br>• I_T: interiors triangle count<br>• I_P: interiors primitive count<br>• TS_T: shape (DTS) triangle count<br>• TS_P: shape (DTS) primitive count<br>• ?_T: uncategorized triangle count<br>• ?_P: uncategorized primitive count |
| vehicle | fps metrics as well as:<br>• R: integration retry count<br>• C: search count<br>• P: polygon count for vehicles<br>• V: vertex count for vehicles |
| water | fps metrics as well as:<br>• Tri#: water triangle count<br>• Pnt#: water point (vertex) count<br>• Hz#: water haze point count |

## 13.3.2 Network Monitor (`NetGraph`)

The standard examples provide a special GUI called the `NetGraph`. `NetGraph` functions as a textual and graphical network monitor.

This monitor can be turned on during game play to collect networking statistics.

To run the monitor, simply press the letter "N" and you should see something like Figure 13.1 in the upper-right corner of the game screen.

`NetGraph` provides the following information.

> **Ghosts Active.** The number of ghosts active on the local client.

> **Bits Sent.** The number of bits sent in the last `packUpdate()`.

> **Latency.** Ping time between this client and the server.

> **Ghost Updates.** Number of ghost updates received in the last update delivery.

**Figure 13.1**
The network monitor.

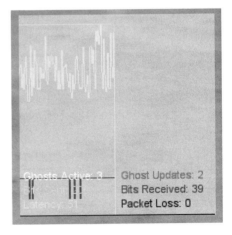

> ➢ **Bits Received.** Number of bits received in the last `unpackUpdate()`.

> ➢ **Packet Loss.** A ratio of packets sent to packets lost.

> ➢ **Graphs.** You can't see it in Figure 13.1, but each of the graphs is a different color, and each color matches one of the above metric strings (Bits Sent, Latency, and Bits Received).

# Chapter 14
# I'm Stuck! Getting Help

There are different kinds of stuck.

There is the, "I am stuck because, like I know what I want to do, but I don't know like how to do it."

Then there is the stuck, "I have been working on this @#$%! thing for the past fourteen hours and it should work, I know it should because it's right, I wrote it, I know what I am doing, but it just...won't...work!"

Because I don't want anyone to completely lose it and go on a rampage, we will discuss the latter kind of stuck first, then we will segue into a discussion that applies to both kinds of stuck.

## 14.1 Get Your House in Order

Before asking for help, we must be sure we have done some basic checks and prepared ourselves properly. I call this "getting your house in order."

### 14.1.1 Clean Up Those DSOs

A common problem, experienced at least once by everyone who has worked with TorqueScript, is stale script files. Remember that the CS files get compiled into DSO files. Remember also that TGE will try to load the DSO file instead of the CS file if it thinks that the DSO file is newer, or if you've been reloading the same script over and over without quitting so many times that TGE has lost its mind and can't tell anymore. I have seen this happen, and it is very frustrating.

Stop! Exit the game entirely. Remove all your DSO files. Start up the game and check to see if your problem still exists.

If so, continue...

### 14.1.2 Use Both Consoles

Next, let us be sure we're not missing something obvious. Now that you've reloaded your game, with all newly compiled scripts, open the console and scroll all the way back to the beginning. Look for bugs.

➢ First, look for the glaring red statements.
➢ Second, look for warnings about missing files, textures, unloadable resources, etc. These problems may not all be color highlighted, so take your time.

➤ Third, look for your debug output and check to see if you are getting what you expect in the way of values. What, you don't have any debug output? If not, go back to Chapter 12 and learn how to add debug output to your code.

So, you've looked in the main console but didn't see anything. Now we need to turn on the external console.

```
TorqueDemo.exe -console
```

This console gets pretty much the same output as the built-in console, but by looking here, we have the opportunity to look at our log with "fresh eyes." Maybe now we will see something to lead us to the source of the problem we're having.

To assist in this process, try reducing the amount of debug output in your scripts. Turn off traces.

By reducing our script output, we can reduce clutter, making it easier to spot real error messages.

Still can't find the problem? Let's continue...

## 14.1.3 Logging and Log Modes

OK, we're getting ready to get help now, but before we do, we need to gather data. Exit the game again. Now, turn up the logging mode.

```
TorqueDemo.exe -log N
```

In the above code, the value N can be 1, 2, 4, or any of these values bitwise OR'd together. Table 14.1 lists what each mode bit does.

Now, you've got the log going. Repeat the steps that cause your issue to occur and then quit the game.

**Table 14.1.**
Logging mode bits and their function.

| Mode Bit | Purpose |
|---|---|
| 1 | Open file and append. Close file on each log write. This allows us to edit the file in a separate editor without having to quit and without getting a file-lock conflict. |
| 2 | Open file and leave it open. This is more efficient for lots of logging, but we may not be able to view the file till we exit the game. (Note: *NIX users can just tail the file: `tail -fn 100 filename`) |
| 4 | Dump anything that has been printed to the console so far. This is needed because the console doesn't get turned on right away, and some output would otherwise be missed. |

Open the log file and check it out one more time.

If you still can't find the source of your troubles, continue reading...

## 14.2 Do Your Homework

Alright, so you've gotten your house in order and you still don't have it licked. Let us talk about getting help.

I have done it, and I am sure you've done it. You get frustrated and jump on IRC or otherwise track someone down and ask for help. This is all well and good, if you've already done your homework and are prepared to ask a meaningful question, but it can also have the effect of getting you labeled as a time-waster or a slacker if you haven't done your homework first. So, we will do our homework, then we will ask for help if we are still stuck.

### 14.2.1 Use the Forums, Luke

The first place to stop when looking for help on a Torque subject is the Garage-Games Forums. Those of us who have been here for a while recall the days when searching the forums was an iffy thing. At one time, only the titles of posts were searched. Today, however, the GarageGames site uses a Google Box to cross-reference and search all of the resource. I am sure you're familiar with using Google. So, searching the GarageGames site should not be too hard. Just click on the Search link and search away.

### 14.2.2 STW and RTM

Now, others may spell these acronyms slightly differently than I do, but STW means "Search the Web," and RTM means "Read the Manual." You're reading the manual already, so all you have left to do is to search the Web.

Why search the Web? Because TGE shares lineage with Tribes and Tribes 2, because Google indexes parts of the GarageGames site, and because there are many Torque-oriented user sites on the Web, you have at least a small possibility of finding an answer to your woes by searching the Web.

## 14.3 Asking for Help

Finally, the time has come to ask for help.

You have two primary avenues available to you.

1. **The forums.** This is the best place to go for a broad audience. In other words, you are most likely to get an answer to your question if you place it in the forums.

2. **IRC.** There are two servers dedicated to hosting GarageGames chats. They can be accessed from the GarageGames website using the Java-based IRC client you will find there, or externally using a standalone client like Trillian. The addresses can be found on the website, but as of this writing they were:

```
IRC Server1: irc.maxgaming.net
IRC Server2: irc.homelan.com
   IRC Port: 6667
    Channel: #GarageGames
```

## 14.3.1 Asking in the Forums

There is no one way to ask questions, but there are better ways and worse ways. Because I want you to get the help you need, I suggest the following when using the GarageGames forums.

> **Select the proper forum.** There are many specialized forums at Garage-Games. Be sure that the question you have is posted in the right one. This is especially true if you intend to post (or receive posts of) engine source code. In this case, be sure you post in the private forums for the correct engine (TGE, TGEA, TGB, or TorqueX).

> **Ask properly.** A clearly stated question that shows a proper investment of effort on your part will glean many more (useful) answers than otherwise. Thus, when asking the question you should include the following.

- **Title.** The title of a post should contain the essence of the problem you are trying to solve. Many people will not even read a post if the title doesn't ask a specific question.

- **Description.** When describing your problem, you should consider having a section for each of the following.

  - **Want to do.** A short description stating what you want to do in general terms. This sets the context for the subsequent description.

  - **Tried to do.** A list of the steps you took in order to achieve your goal.

  - **Expected to see.** A specific description of what you expected to see or have occur.

  - **Saw.** A concise description of what you got instead.

- **My homework.** After the description, you should make a list of the things you tried to do in order to debug the problem on your own, including resources you looked at, code you modified, debugging steps you took, etc.

> **Be patient.** The forums are not an instantaneous medium. Often a thread can go for half a day or longer before getting an answer. Other times it can get an answer in just a few minutes. It all depends on who is watching at the time. Give posts at least one day if not two before pinging the thread.

➢ **Be polite.** The drawback of using forums is the fact that there are no visual or auditory cues. Unlike a face-to-face or phone conversation, with forums (and IRC) you cannot be sure what the tone of a response is. Thus, it best to assume the tone was neutral to friendly. Even if someone does answer like a jerk, you don't get any points by being a jerk back.

➢ **Pay the community back.** The community works because members are willing to spend their time (at some cost to themselves) helping others achieve success. So, when you can, be sure to turn that favor around and help someone with a question you know the answer to.

## 14.3.2 Asking in IRC

The approach used with IRC is a bit different. If you want to get help in IRC, I suggest following these rules in addition to those above.

➢ **No claim jumping.** In addition to the politeness rule above, be sure not to jump in over someone else's conversation. If a topic is under discussion, you should wait. It's hard to tell sometimes, but jumping in over someone else's discussion can get you on people's ignore list really fast.

➢ **Don't spam.** When you do ask your question, be as concise as possible. Nobody wants their screen to suddenly fill with a huge dump. This can get you kicked rather quickly. Don't worry; there will be time to add details as your discussion progresses.

➢ **Stay on topic.** Remember that the IRC is not a place to discuss general topics. It is provided for users like you to get answers to questions related to game creation.

➢ **Take it offline.** Once you've got a discussion going, if it looks like it will go on for a bit, invite folks to discuss it offline. In IRC, you can open private channels to talk outside of the main room.

# Appendices

# Appendix A
# Glossary of Terms

| Term | Definition |
|---|---|
| **access method** | A method designed to allow access (read and/or modify) class members in an abstracted and controlled fashion, versus direct access. |
| **active collider** | A moving object that causes a collision. |
| **address** (C++) | A value that specifies the location of data in memory. |
| **affine matrix** | A matrix that can be used to perform a linear transformation followed by a translation. |
| **ANSI** | American National Standards Institute. |
| **architecture** (computing) | Conceptual design and operation of a structure or system. |
| **big-endian** (byte order) | High-order bytes are first. |
| **bitmask** (TorqueScript/C++) | A value designed to extract bits from another value. For example, a bitmask of 0111b (0x7) can be used to extract bit 3 from the value 0xC.<br><br>`0X7 & 0xC == 0x8 == 1000b` |
| **bus** | Bidirectional universal switch. |
| **callback** (in Torque) | A function or method that is registered with the engine (or scripts) and can later be called asynchronously in response to an event. |
| **CISC** | Complex instruction set computer. |
| **clamp** | To restrict a value to a range between and including some other high and low value.<br><br>For example, 10.5 clamped to [0.0, 10.0] produces the value 10.0. |
| **class** | A programming construct designed to group data (class members) and functionality (class methods). |
| **client** (game architecture) | A participant in a client-server architecture. This object cannot directly control the game state and relies on the server for updates to that state. |
| **client connection** | A general `GameConnection` instance connected to a client. |
| **client-server architecture** (game engine) | A game-engine architecture in which one object (the server) acts as the game controller (controls game state) while other objects (clients) are merely participants that receive game state updates from the client. |
| **COLDET** | See *collision detection*. |

| Term | Definition |
|---|---|
| **collision detection (COLDET)** | A system of algorithms designed to detect collisions between two game objects. |
| **compile** (C++) | To translate from source code into an executable (machine code). |
| **compile** (TorqueScript) | To translate from source code into a byte-code that can then be fed to the Torque scripting engine. |
| **console** | The torque scripting interface. Also a name for the GUI interface to that scripting engine. |
| **console class** | A C++ class that has been registered with and is therefore accessible from the console. Alternately, a TorqueScript-only class. |
| **console field** | A class member accessible from the console. |
| **console function** | A C++ function that has been registered with and is therefore accessible from the console. Alternately, a TorqueScript-only function. |
| **console global** | A C++ global (or static class member) that has been registered with and is therefore accessible from the console. Alternately, a TorqueScript-only global. |
| **console local** | A variable in TorqueScript that has a temporary scope. |
| **console method** | A C++ method that has been registered with and is therefore accessible from the console. Alternately, a TorqueScript-only method. |
| **console variable** | A console global or local. |
| **control object** | A Torque object that has responsibility for scoping a set of game objects on the server, where this scoping determines which objects need to be scoped to the client that owns the control object. |
| **datablock** | A data construct designed to hold data and to be transmitted (to clients) only once per mission load. |
| **debugger** | A program used to test and debug other programs. |
| **dedicated server** | A game instance that controls a game and does not allow local (same game instance) participation in that game by a game player. |
| **degree** | 1/360th of a full angular revolution around a circle. |
| **dirty** | Modified since the last update. |
| **DNS** | See domain name system. |
| **domain name system (DNS)** | An Internet lookup system for converting human readable addresses to numeric IP addresses. |
| **double-precision floating-point number** | A floating-point value that occupies twice the number of data locations as a normal floating-point. |
| **dynamic field** | A class member created from within the console. |

| Term | Definition |
|---|---|
| **editor** | A program designed to edit (source) code. |
| **enumerated type** (C++) | An abstract data type using names to reference numbers. |
| **expose** | See *register*. |
| **function** | A routine not associated with a class. |
| **game** (with regards to Torque organization) | A directory in a Torque game structure containing the primary files that define a game. |
| **ghost** | A game object that is copied to, resides upon, and is updated from the server to the client. |
| **ghost resolution** | The operations of converting a ghost ID into a server object ID or vice versa. |
| **global** | A variable that is visible regardless of scope. |
| **GUI** | Graphical user interface. |
| **hash** | A value that was generated as the result of some computational combination of the elements in another value or set of values. |
| **hosting** | The act of running a game server that supports client connections, which in turn allows external copies of the same game to participate in a multiplayer game. |
| **HTTP** | See *hypertext transfer protocol*. |
| **hypertext transfer protocol (HTTP)** | A communications protocol for transferring data across the World Wide Web. |
| **ID** | A number value uniquely identifying an object. |
| **inherit** (C++) | To take on the behavior(s) of a parent class, getting both members and methods from that parent. |
| **inherit** (TorqueScript) | To copy the fields from another source object (of the same base type as the new type) while creating a new type derived from the base type. |
| **instruction set** [architecture] | A generalized term referring to all the parts that go into making a computing architecture. |
| **Internet protocol (IP)** | A data protocol designed to send data across a packet-switched network. |
| **interpolation** | The act of calculating a new value from two or more known values. When applied to points, interpolation refers to the act of calculating a new point between two other points. When referring to a vector, it is the calculation of a point on a vector based on the original vector (tail) and a provided interpolation distance. |
| **IP** | See *Internet protocol*. |
| **LAN** | See *local-area network*. |
| **LAN party** | A game-hosting scenario where one player hosts a game on his or her computer and all other players access it on a local-area network. |

| Term | Definition |
|------|-----------|
| latency | The time it takes for data to get from a source node to a destination node on a network. |
| level of detail (LOD) | The practice of reducing the rendering complexity of a 3D object as it moves farther away from the observer. |
| line of sight (LOS) | The act of viewing along a line (vector). Usually paired with the phrases "move into" or "move out of," meaning that the object became visible after coming out from behind a visibility-blocking item or went behind a visibility-blocking item, respectively. |
| listen server | A game instance controls the game, while allowing one local (same game instance) participant (player). |
| little-endian (byte order) | Low-order bytes are first. |
| local | A variable that only exists (or is visible) in the current scope. |
| local-area network (LAN) | A single small network, connected within a limited geographic area, usually a home or office. |
| `localClientConnection` | A named `GameConnection` object that connects to the single-player client. |
| `localhost` | A name meaning "this computer" and usually converted to the address 127.0.0.1, which is the loop-back address on standard TCP/IP networks. |
| LOD | See *level of detail*. |
| loop-back address | The address that points back to this machine, usually 127.0.0.1. |
| LOS | See *line of sight*. |
| master server (in Torque) | A server whose job it is to collect/receive data about game servers and to distribute that data to game clients. |
| member | A variable associated with a class in C++ or TorqueScript (member field). |
| memory leak | An error, usually in the design of a program, that results in the loss of memory space to allocations that are never released. |
| method | A routine associated with a class in C++ or TorqueScript (console member). |
| mod (with regards to Torque organization) | A directory in a Torque game structure containing supplemental files for defining a game. |
| multiplayer | A game in which two or more players are allowed to play simultaneously in real-time or to play using a turn-based approach. |

| Term | Definition |
|------|-----------|
| **named address** (Internet protocol) | An IP address utilizing human-readable names instead of numbers that must be sent to a DNS for translation into a numeric address. |
| **normalize** (a vector) | To convert a vector into a unit vector while retaining its pointing direction. |
| **NULL** | A C/C++ keyword used in relation to addresses to mean "this address does not exist." For example, a NULL pointer points to an address that does not exist. It is invalid. |
| **null string** (TorqueScript) | A zero-length string in TorqueScript, represented by two double quotes with nothing between them ("″). |
| **opaque** | Completely blocking. Objects behind an opaque object cannot be seen at all through the opaque object. |
| **OpenGL** | Open Graphics Library. |
| **oriented bounding box** | A bounding box whose vertices rotate with the object that the bounding box encloses. |
| **override** | To replace the functionality/behavior of a function or method while maintaining the signature of that function or method. |
| **packet** | A formatted block of data, usually containing some kind of header (that describes the data and its destination) as well as a payload (the actual data that is being sent in the packet). |
| **packet switching** | A system in which data is broken into packets, transmitted across a network to various nodes, and eventually coalesced and re-ordered at an end node. |
| **passive collider** | A stationary object that receives a collision. |
| **path manager** | A class in Torque that is responsible for managing a client's path information. |
| **peer-to-peer** (game engine) | A game engine supporting multiplayer gameplay where individual game copies are connected to each other and share responsibility for maintenance of the game state. |
| **persistent field** | A console class member representing a C++ class member that was registered with the console. |
| **persistent server** | A type of Web server designed to store data relating to a game world. This allows the game world to grow and maintain its state, regardless of whether players who own that data are currently logged in. |
| **pi** | The mathematical constant whose value begins as 3.1415926... etc. |
| **pitch** | Rotation about the $x$-axis (in Torque). |

| Term | Definition |
|------|------------|
| pointer | A variable that points to the value contained in it. |
| port | A numeric value in the range [0, 65536] used to sub-divide an address such that data for specific purposes come in on the same port.<br><br>In Torque, the engine uses port values between 1000 and 65536 to establish game connections (GameConnection) and TCP connections (TCPObject). |
| profiler | A programming tool designed to track the performance of another program. |
| proxy | An object that helps to do, or does entirely, the work for another object. |
| radian | 180.0/pi degrees. |
| register | To make a C++ global, function, class, class member, or class method visible and/or accessible from within the Torque scripting console. |
| render | To display (as in graphics) or to play (as in sounds). |
| RISC | Reduced instruction set computer. |
| roll | Rotation about the *y*-axis (in Torque). |
| rotation | Movement in a circular motion. |
| scene graph | A data structure used to organize a three-dimensional space in such a way to make that space accessible to and manipulatable by visibility and/or collision algorithms. |
| server | The controller in a client-server architecture. This object controls the game state and sends updates regarding that state to clients. |
| server connection | A general GameConnection instance connected to the server. |
| server object | A game object that resides on the server and controls the state of all copies of itself (ghosts). |
| ServerConnection | A named instance of GameConnection connected to the server. |
| single-player | A game in which only one player at a time may participate. |
| singleton | A design pattern referring to design objects of which there is guaranteed to exist only a single copy. |
| StringTable | A singleton-like class in Torque designed to contain string data. |
| TANSTAAFL! | There ain't no such thing as a free lunch! |
| TCP | See *transmission control protocol*. |
| template | A generic programming construct used to generate type-specific code from a type-unspecific framework. |
| tick | A standard measure of time in Torque equal to 1/32 of a second. |

| Term | Definition |
|------|-----------|
| **TorqueScript** | The Torque scripting language. |
| **translation** | Movement in a linear motion. |
| **translucent** | Partially opaque. Objects behind a translucent object are partially visible through the translucent object. |
| **transmission control protocol (TCP)** | A core Internet protocol designed to provide reliable in-order transmission of data. |
| **transparent** | The opposite of opaque. Objects behind a transparent object can be seen entirely through the transparent object. |
| **transpose** | With respect to matrices, to swap rows for columns (or vice versa). |
| **triangle strip** | A rendering technique that strings connected triangles together when sending them to the rendering pipeline. This saves two vertexes for every triangle in the strip that is sent after the first triangle. |
| **UDP** | See *user datagram protocol*. |
| **unit vector** | A vector of length 1.0. |
| **user datagram protocol (UDP)** | A core Internet protocol that does not guarantee reliable transmission of data and is designed for small messages. |
| **yaw** | Rotation about the *z*-axis (in Torque). |

# Appendix B
# Essential References

# B.1 Game Connections

## B.1.1 GameConnection Globals

| Global | Description |
| --- | --- |
| $pref::Net::LagThreshold | The number of milliseconds a server connection may be quiet before it is considered to be lagging. (Default = 400 milliseconds.) |
| $pref::Net::PacketRateToClient | Limits the packet rate from server to client. |
| $pref::Net::PacketRateToServer | Limits the packet rate from client to server. |
| $pref::Net::PacketSize | Limits the size of any one packet. |
| $stats::netBitsReceived | Bytes in most recently received net packet. |
| $stats::netBitsSent | Bytes in most recently sent net packet. |
| $stats::netGhostUpdates | Cumulative ghost updates transmitted since mission was loaded. |

## B.1.2 GameConnection Methods

| Method | Description |
| --- | --- |
| activateGhosting | Instructs server to start updating ghosts for the current client connection. |
| chaseCam | Delays third-person camera translation and rotation responses (to movement) for the current client connection. |
| checkMaxRate | Verifies packet rate settings and resets them to legal values if necessary. |
| clearCameraObject | Clears the current camera. |
| clearPaths * | Clears any paths previously sent to the current client connection. |
| connect * | A method used by clients to request a connection to a remote server. |
| connectLocal * | A method used by clients to request a connection to a local server. |
| delete | Disconnects and destroys connection object. |
| getAddress * | Returns address and port of machine on other end of connection. |
| getCameraObject | Returns camera object ID for client connection. |
| getControlCameraFov | Returns field-of-view for client connection. |
| getControlObject | Returns control object ID for client connection. |
| getGhostID * | Translates server ID into ghost index (on server). |
| getGhostsActive * | Returns current ghost count for client connection. |
| getPacketLoss * | Returns cumulative packet loss count for a connection. |
| getPing * | Pings machine on other end of connection and returns the result. |
| getServerConnection | Returns ID of the server connection attached to a client connection. |

| Method | Description |
| --- | --- |
| isAIControlled | Returns true if client is using AIConnection or derived connection class to connect to server. |
| isDemoPlaying | Returns true if a connection is currently playing a recorded demo stream. |
| isDemoRecording | Returns true if a connection is currently recording a demo stream. |
| isFirstPerson | Returns true if a connection is currently using 1st point-of-view camera settings. |
| listClassIDs | Lists all class names and IDs a connection is aware of. |
| play2D | Plays a 2D sound on a client. |
| play3D | Plays a 3D sound on a client. |
| playDemo | Starts playback of a demo recording on a server connection. |
| resetGhosting | Stops ghost updates and clears ghost list for a client connection. |
| resolveGhostID * | Translates a ghost index (on server) into a (ghost) object ID on a client. |
| resolveObjectFromGhostIndex * | Translates a ghost index (on server) into a server object ID. |
| setBlackOut | Blacks out (or fades in from black) the client's screen when called on the server connection object. |
| setCameraObject | Sets camera object ID for client connection. |
| setConnectArgs | Sets name and optional 14 additional connection arguments for server connection. |
| setControlCameraFov | Attempts to set field-of-view for a client connection. |
| setControlObject | Sets control object ID for client connection. |
| setFirstPerson | Attempts to change client connection's point-of-view (POV) mode to 1st POV or to 3rd POV. |
| setJoinPassword | Sets the connection password for incoming (joining) connections on the server. |
| setLogging * | Tells connection to print special debug regarding incoming and outgoing traffic. (Engine must be compiled with TORQUE_DEBUG_NET macro enabled.) |
| setMissionCRC | Sets the CRC value for the current mission's lighting file on client connection. |
| setSimulatedNetParams * | A debug feature for setting simulated traffic error rates and delays. |
| startRecording | Starts recording of a demo recording on a server connection. |
| stopRecording | Stops recording of a demo recording on a server connection. |
| transmitDatablocks | Sends all known datablocks across a client connection. |
| transmitPaths * | Transmits all known path manager data across a client connection. |

* This method is actually from the parent class NetConnection.

## activateGhosting

### Purpose
Use the activateGhosting method to start sending ghost updates to a client. This method is called by the server on client connections.

### Syntax
```
con.activateGhosting();
```
con        A client connection.

**Example Call**
```
// Start ghosting objects to the client
%client.activateGhosting();
```

**Notes**
1. The method `trasmitPaths` must be called *before* calling this method, or the client's engine may crash.

**See Also**
`getGhostsActive`, `resetGhosting`, `transmitPaths`

---

## chaseCam

**Purpose**
Use the `chaseCam` method to set the third-person camera response delay. If the client is viewing the world in 3rd POV, camera responses will lag movement inputs by `delay_ms` milliseconds.

**Syntax**
```
con.chaseCam( delay_ms );
```
`con`        A client connection.

`delay_ms`    An integer value specifying a delay ( > = 0) in milliseconds.

**Example Call**
```
// Delay 3rd POV camera response by 100ms
%client.chaseCam( 100 );
```

**See Also**
`isFirstPerson`

---

## checkMaxRate

**Purpose**
Use the `checkMaxRate` method to optionally verify the packet rate settings (see Table B.1.1). If these rates are set incorrectly, the engine will set them to the nearest legal value. This method can be called on both client and server connections.

**Syntax**
```
con.checkMaxRate();
```
`con`      A client or server connection.

**Notes**
1. The engine automatically calls this method when a new GameConnection object is created.
This method is inherited from the parent class NetConnection.

---

**Table B.1.1**
*Packet rate ranges.*

| Packet Rate | Legal Range |
| --- | --- |
| `$pref::Net::PacketRateToClient` | [ 1 , 32 ] |
| `$pref::Net::PacketRateToServer` | [ 8 , 32 ] |
| `$pref::Net::PacketSize` | [ 100 , 450 ] |

---

## clearCameraObject

---

### Purpose
Use the `clearCameraObject` method to clear the current camera object. If you are currently using one object as a control object and a second (camera) object as the scoping object, this will cause the engine to use the control object as the new scoping object.

### Syntax
`con.clearCameraObject();`

  `con`      A client connection.

---

## clearPaths

---

### Purpose
Use the `clearPaths` method to clear this connection's path manager.

### Syntax
`con.clearPaths();`

  `con`      A client connection.

### Notes
1. This method should not be called until after the method `resetGhosting` has been called, or the client's engine may crash.
2. This method is inherited from the parent class NetConnection.

### See Also
`resetGhosting, transmitPaths`

---

## connect

---

### Purpose
Use the `connect` method to request a connection to a remote server at the specified *address*. Valid addresses contain both an IP address (A.B.C.D) and a port number (P): "A.B.C.D:P". The elements of an IP address may each be between 0 and 255, while ports can be between 1000 and 65536.

### Syntax
`con.connect( address );`

  `con`         A server connection.
  `address`     A string containing an IP address and a port number.

### Example Call
```
%address = "192.168.123.101";
%port = "28002";
%serverConnection.connect( %address @ ":" @ %port );
```

### Notes
1. This method is inherited from the parent class NetConnection.

### See Also
`connectLocal, getAddress`

---

## connectLocal

**Purpose**
Use the `connectLocal` method to request an internal client-server connection.

**Syntax**
`error = con.connectLocal();`

`con`        A server connection.

`error`      A string containing the result of the connection attempt. If this string is set to "", the connection succeeded; otherwise it failed.

**Example Call**
```
%error = %conn.connectLocal();
if( "" !$= %error )
{
   error( "Local connection request failed for reason: " , %error );
}
```

**Notes**
1. This method is inherited from the parent class NetConnection.

**See Also**
`connect, getAddress`

---

## delete

**Purpose**
Use the `delete` method to destroy and disconnect the current connection, optionally providing the *reason* for the disconnect. If a reason is specified, it will be transmitted to the client/server on the other end of the connection.

**Syntax**
`con.delete( [ reason ] );`

`con`        A client or server connection.

`reason`    An optional string explaining why the connection is being severed.

**Example Call**
```
%client.delete( "You have been kicked from this server" );
```

---

## getAddress

**Purpose**
Use the `getAddress` method to get the address and port that this connection is currently attached to.

**Syntax**
`address = con.getAddress();`

`con`        A client or server connection.

address    An string containing the address of the machine this connection is attached to. Addresses come in three forms:

1. "" — A null-string address indicates that this connection is not attached to any other GameConnection object.

2. "local" — This string means the connection is internal (single player connection type.)

3. "A.B.C.D:Port" — An address of this form indicates that the connection is external. In this variety, A..D are values in the range [0,255], and Port is a value in the range [1000,65536].

**Example Call**
```
echo( "CADD: " @ %client @ " " @ %client.getAddress() );
```

**Notes**
1. This method is inherited from the parent class NetConnection.

**See Also**
connect, connectLocal

---

## getCameraObject

**Purpose**
Use the getCameraObject method to determine the ID of the camera object currently assigned to this client.

**Syntax**
```
objID = con.getCameraObject();
```
con        A client connection.
objID      The numeric ID of the camera assigned to this client.

**Example Call**
```
%objID = %client.getCameraObject();
echo( "Client " , %client , " using camera " , %objID );
```

**See Also**
clearCameraObject, setCameraObject

---

## getControlCameraFov

**Purpose**
Use the getControlCameraFov method to retrieve the current field-of-view (FOV) settings for a client.

**Syntax**
```
fov = con.getControlCameraFov();
```
con        A client connection.
fov        A floating-point value in the range of 0.0 to 180.0 representing the client's current FOV in degrees.

**Example Call**
```
%fov = %client.getControlCameraFov();
echo( "Client " , %client , " field-of-view is " , %fov , " degrees." );
```

**See Also**
getCameraObject, setControlCameraFov

## getControlObject

### Purpose
Use the `getControlObject` method to determine the ID of the current control object for this connection.

If this method is called by the server on its client connection, the ID that is returned will be a server object.

If this method is called by a client on its server connection, the ID that is returned will be a ghost object (present only on this client.)

### Syntax
```
objID = con.getControlObject();
```

con                      A client or server connection.

objID                    The numeric ID of the client's current control object.

### Example Call
```
// This call would be executed on the client
// Get the ghost object acting as this client's control object
%controlGhost = serverConnection.getControlObject();

// This code would be executed on the server
// Get the server object acting as this client's control object
%control = %client.getControlObject();
```

### See Also
```
setControlObject
```

## getGhostID

### Purpose
Use the `getGhostID` method to translate a server object ID into a client index for that object's ghost.

### Syntax
```
index = con.getGhostID( serverObj );
```

con                      A client connection.

index                    An integer value representing the index number for the ghost corresponding to the server object on this client.

serverObj                A server object which has been ghosted to the specified client.

### Example Call
```
%ghostIndex = %client.getGhostID( %obj );
if( -1 == %ghostIndex)
{
   echo( "Server object " , %obj , " not ghosted to client " , %client );
}
else
{
   echo( "Server object " , %obj , " ghosted to client " , %client ,
         ", and has index " , %ghostIndex );
}
```

### Notes
1. Calling `getGhostID` on a server connection may crash the engine.
2. This method is inherited from the parent class `NetConnection`.

**See Also**
getGhostsActive, resolveGhostID, resolveObjectFromGhostIndex, NetObject::getGhostID

---

## getGhostsActive

**Purpose**
Use the getGhostsActive method to determine how many ghosts are active on the current client.

**Syntax**
count = con.getGhostsActive();

con                     A server connection.
count                   An integer value equal to the number of server objects currently being
                        ghosted on a client connection.

**Example Call**
%count = %client.getGhostsActive();
echo( %count , " server objects are currently being ghosted to client " ,
      %client );

**Notes**
1. This method can only be called on server connections.
2. This method is inherited from the parent class NetConnection.

**See Also**
activateGhosting, getGhostID, resetGhosting, resolveGhostID, resolveObjectFromGhostIndex

---

## getPacketLoss

**Purpose**
Use the getPacketLoss method to determine the cumulative packet loss count for a connection.

**Syntax**
count = con.getPacketLoss();

con                     A client or server connection.
count                   Total packets lost since this connection was established.

**Example Call**
%count = %client.getPacketLoss();
echo( %count ,
      " packets have been lost since this connection was established." );

**Notes**
1. This method is inherited from the parent class NetConnection.

**See Also**
getPing, setSimulatedNetParams

---

## getPing

**Purpose**
Use the getPing method to determine the round-trip packet travel time for this connection.

**Syntax**

```
delay = con.getPing();
```

con　　　　　　　A client or server connection.

delay　　　　　　The round-trip packet travel time for this connection measured in milliseconds.

**Example Call**

```
%delay = serverConnection.getPing();
echo( "One-way packet travel time to the server is approximately " ,
      %delay / 2 ,  " milliseconds." );
```

**Notes**

1. This method is inherited from the parent class NetConnection.

**See Also**

getPacketLoss, setSimulatedNetParams

---

## getServerConnection

**Purpose**

Use the getServerConnection method to get the ID of a client's server connection.

**Syntax**

```
conID = con.getServerConnection();
```

con　　　　　A client or server connection.

conID　　　　ID of the server connection object in a client-server connection. (See notes.)

**Example Call**

```
// List all client connections and the server connections attached to them
echo( "# - Client number." );
echo( "S - Server-side GameConnection object." );
echo( "C - Client-side GameConnection object.\n" );
echo( " #" TAB " S" TAB " C");
echo( "--" TAB "--" TAB "--");

for( %cl = 0 ; %cl < %count ; %cl++ )
{
   %client = ClientGroup.getObject(%cl);
   %conID  = %client.getServerConnection();

   echo( %cl TAB %client TAB conID );
}
```

**Notes**

1. This method can be called on a client connection or a server connection. However, calling it on a server connection will simply return the ID of that connection object.

---

## isAIControlled

**Purpose**

Use the isAIControlled method to determine whether a client is using AIConnection (or a child) to connect to this server.

**Syntax**
```
result = con.isAIControlled();
```
con     A client connection.

result    A boolean value specifying whether the client is attaching to this server with an instance of `AIConnection` (or a child of that class).

**Example Call**
```
%isAI = %client.isAIControlled();
if( %isAI )
{
   echo( %client , " is controlled by (AI) scripts." );
}
else
{
   echo( %client , " is controlled by a person." );
}
```

## isDemoPlaying

**Purpose**

Use the `isDemoPlaying` method to see whether this server connection is playing a previously recorded demo stream.

**Syntax**
```
result = con.isDemoPlaying();
```
con     A server connection.

result    A boolean value set to `true` if the server connection is currently streaming a previously recorded demo to this client.

**Example Call**
```
if( serverConnection.isDemoPlaying() )
{
   echo( "Currently playing a demo stream." );
}
else
{
   echo( "Not currently playing a demo stream." );
}
```

**See Also**

`isDemoRecording, playDemo, startRecording, stopRecording`

## isDemoRecording

**Purpose**

Use the `isDemoRecording` method to see whether this server connection is recording a demo stream.

**Syntax**
```
result = con.isDemoRecording();
```
con     A server connection.

result    A boolean value set to `true` if the server connection is currently recording a demo stream.

**Example Call**
```
if( serverConnection.isDemoRecording() )
{
   echo( "Currently recording a demo stream." );
}
echo
{
   echo( "Not currently recording a demo stream." );
}
```

**See Also**
```
isDemoPlaying, playDemo, startRecording, stopRecording
```

---

## isFirstPerson

**Purpose**
Use the `isFirstPerson` method to see whether a client is currently using 1st person point-of-view (POV) or 3rd POV.

**Syntax**
```
result = con.isFirstPerson();
```
con        A client or server connection.

result     A boolean value set to `true` if the client is viewing the world in 1st POV, and `false` if it is using 3rd POV.

**Example Call**
```
// Client checks current POV
%firstPOV = serverConnection.isFirstPOV();
if( %firstPOV )
{
   echo( "Viewing the world in first POV." );
}
else
{
   echo( "Viewing the world in third POV." );
}
```

**Notes**
1. This method works equally well on both client and server connections.

**See Also**
```
setFirstPerson
```

---

## listClassIDs

**Purpose**
Use the `listClassIDs` method to dump a list of all class IDs and the corresponding class names that the connection knows about.

**Syntax**
```
con.listClassIDs();
```
con     A client or server connection.

**Notes**

1. This is a debug feature. In any client-server connection pair, the client and the server connection objects should both produce the same list of class IDs and names.

## play2D

**Purpose**

Use the `play2D` method to play a 2D sound on a client.

**Syntax**

error = con.play2D( profile );

| | |
|---|---|
| con | A client connection. |
| error | A boolean value specifying whether the play succeeded or not. |
| profile | An `AudioProfile` datablock. |

**Example Call**

```
function ServerPlay2D( %profile )
{
   // Play the given sound profile on every client.
   // The sounds will be transmitted as an event, not attached to any object.
   For( %idx = 0 ; %idx < ClientGroup.getCount() ; %idx++ )
      ClientGroup.getObject( %idx ).play2D( %profile );
}
```

**Notes**

1. Be sure to use only AudioProfiles created using the datablock keyword.

**See Also**

play3D

## play3D

**Purpose**

Use the `play3D` method to play a 3D sound on a client.

**Syntax**

error = con.play3D( profile , transform );

| | |
|---|---|
| con | A client connection. |
| error | A boolean value specifying whether the play succeeded or not. |
| profile | An `AudioProfile` datablock. |
| transform | A string containing the seven-element transform representing the sound position and facing vector. |

**Example Call**

```
function ServerPlay3D(%profile,%transform)
{
   // Play the given sound profile at the given position on every client
   // The sound will be transmitted as an event, not attached to any object.
   for(%idx = 0; %idx < ClientGroup.getCount(); %idx++)
      ClientGroup.getObject(%idx).play3D(%profile,%transform);
}
```

**See Also**
play2D

---

## playDemo

**Purpose**
Use the playDemo method to play a previously recorded demo on the specified server connection.

**Syntax**
result = con.playDemo( demoFile );

con                A server connection.

result            A boolean value equal to true if the demo can be played and false otherwise.

demoFile         A string containing the full path and filename of a previously recorded demo stream.

**Example Call**
ServerConnection.playDemo( %file );

**See Also**
isDemoPlaying, isDemoRecording, startRecording, stopRecording

---

## resetGhosting

**Purpose**
Use the resetGhosting method to stop ghosting on a client connection and to clear all ghosts on that client.

**Syntax**
con.resetGhosting();

con                A client connection.

**Notes**
1. This should be done before calling the clearPaths method, or the client's engine may crash.

**See Also**
activateGhosting, clearPaths

---

## resolveGhostID

**Purpose**
Use the resolveGhostID method to translate a ghost index into a ghost object ID on a server connection.

**Syntax**
ghostID = con.resolveGhostID( index );

con                A server connection.

ghostID            An object ID (on a client).

index              A ghost index.

**Example Call**
```
// Get the Ghost ID of the control object in a single-player game
//
%controlObject = localClientConnection.getControlObject();
```

```
%index = localClientConnection.getGhostID( %controlObject )

%controlGhost  = serverConnection.resolveGhostID( %index );

echo( "The server ID for the client's control object is: " , %controlObject );
echo( " The ghost ID for the client's control object is: " , %controlGhost );
```

**Notes**

1. Calling `resolveGhostID` on a client connection may crash the engine.

**See Also**

`activateGhosting, getGhostID, NetObject::getGhostID, resolveObjectFromGhostIndex`

---

## `resolveObjectFromGhostIndex`

**Purpose**

Use the `resolveObjectFromGhostIndex` method to get the server object ID corresponding to a client connection's ghost index.

**Syntax**

```
objID = con.resolveObjectFromGhostIndex( index );
```

| | |
|---|---|
| con | A client connection. |
| objID | A server object ID. |
| index | A ghost index. |

**Example Call**

```
// Get the server object IDs for all objects ghosted to localConnection
%ghostCount = localConnection.getActiveGhosts();

for( %count = 0 ; %count < %ghostCount ; %count ++ )
{
    %objID = localClientConnection.resolveObjectFromGhostIndex( count );

    echo( "Object " , %objID , " was ghosted to localConnection at index " ,
        %count );
}
```

**Notes**

1. Calling `resolveObjectFromGhostIndex` on a server connection may crash the engine.

**See Also**

`activateGhosting, getActiveGhosts, getGhostID, NetObject::getGhostID, resolveGhostID`

---

## `setBlackOut`

**Purpose**

Use the `setBlackOut` method to fade out to black and back in again (from black).

**Syntax**

```
con.setBlackout( doFade , timeMS );
```

| | |
|---|---|
| con | A server connection. |

doFade                  A boolean value. If this value is `true`, the screen will fade out to black. If this value is `false`, the
                        screen will fade in from black.

timeMS                  An integer value specifying the fade time in milliseconds.

**Example Call**
```
// Fade to a blacked-out screen over 5 seconds
serverConnection.setBlackout( true , 5000 );

// Start with the screen blacked-out and fade back in over 8.5 seconds
serverConnection.setBlackout( false , 8500 );
```

**Notes**
1. This method will only work if it is called on a server connection. Calling it on a client connection does nothing.
   That is, client scripts control the blackout, not the server.

## setCameraObject

**Purpose**
Use the `setCameraObject` method to change the object that a client is using for scoping. This allows you to use one
object as the control object while assigning a second object as the scoping object.

**Syntax**
```
result = con.setCameraObject( newCamera );
```

con                     A client connection.

result                  A boolean value specifying whether the call worked (`true`), or failed (`false`).

newCamera               The ID of any ShapeBase object on the server.

**Notes**
1. Any ShapeBase object can be used as a camera object, not just camera-derived objects.

**See Also**
`clearCameraObject`, `getCameraObject`

## setConnectArgs

**Purpose**
Use the `setConnectArgs` method to set the connection arguments for a server connection object before attempting
to connect to a server.

**Syntax**
```
con.setConnectArgs( name [ , arg1 , ... , arg14 ] );
```

con                     A server connection.

name                    A required string containing the name for this player.

arg1                    Up to 14 optional arguments containing any values.

...

arg14

**Example Call**
```
%conn = new GameConnection( ServerConnection );
RootGroup.add( ServerConnection );
%conn.setConnectArgs( $pref::Player::Name );
```

**Notes**

1. When a client successfully connects to a server, the server will call the onConnect callback on its client connection. The name and extra arguments specified using the setConnectArgs method are passed to that callback.

**See Also**

setJoinPassword, onConnect

---

## setControlCameraFOV

**Purpose**

Use the setControlCameraFOV method to change the field-of-view (FOV) for a client.

**Syntax**

con.setControlCameraFOV( newFOV );

con             A client connection.

newFOV          A floating-point value between 0.0 and 180.0 specifying the new FOV angle for the client.

**Example Call**

%client.setControlCameraFOV( 120.0 );

**Notes**

1. This setting is sticky. If the camera/control object is changed, this value will be retained.

2. These values are constrained by the current camera/control object's associated datablock settings as follows:

```
        if( newFOV < datablock.cameraMinFOV )
                currentFOV = datablock.cameraMinFOV;
        else if( newFOV > datablock.cameraMaxFOV )
                currentFOV = datablock.cameraMaxFOV;
```

**See Also**

getControlCameraFov

---

## setControlObject

**Purpose**

Use the setControlObject method to change the client's control object.

**Syntax**

result = con.setControlObject( object );

con             A client connection.

result          A boolean value specifying success (true) or failure (false).

object          Any ShapeBase object.

**Example Call**

```
%control = %client.player;
%client.setControlObject( %control );
```

**Notes**

1. All clients must use unique control objects.

**See Also**

getControlObject

## setFirstPerson

**Purpose**

Use the `setFirstPerson` method to change a client's current point-of-view (POV) to first-person or third-person.

**Syntax**

con.setFirstPerson( isFirstPerson );

| | |
|---|---|
| con | A client or server connection. |
| isFirstPerson | A boolean value. If set to `true`, the POV for this client is set to 1st person POV; otherwise it is set to 3rd person POV. |

**Example Call**

`%client.setFirstPerson( false );`

**Notes**

1. This method works equally well for client and server connections.
2. This will not override value specified in the control-object/camera datablocks enabling or disabling a particular POV.

**See Also**

`isFirstPerson`

## setJoinPassword

**Purpose**

Use the `setJoinPassword` method to set or clear a server connection password before attempting to connect to a server.

**Syntax**

con.setJoinPassword( password );

| | |
|---|---|
| con | A server connection. |
| password | A string containing the password to send to a server while attempting to connect, or a NULL-string for no password. |

**Example Call**

```
%conn = new GameConnection( ServerConnection );
RootGroup.add( ServerConnection );
%conn.setConnectArgs( $pref::Player::Name );
%conn.setJoinPassword( $Client::Password );
```

**See Also**

`setConnectArgs`

## setLogging

**Purpose**

Use the `setLogging` method to enable or disable `GameConnection` debug output on client or server connection.

**Syntax**

con.setLogging( enable );

| | |
|---|---|
| con | A client or server connection. |
| enable | A boolean value enabling (`true`) or disabling (`false`) logging. |

**Notes**
1. Only works if the engine was compiled with the TORQUE_DEBUG_NET macro enabled.

---

## setMissionCRC

**Purpose**
Use the setMissionCRC method to set the cyclic-redundancy-check (CRC) value for the current mission file. This value has two purposes.
1. This value will be passed the client. Subsequently, the client can use this value to search for a previously generated mission lighting file. If one is found, and if lighting calculations are not forced, the client may skip the lighting calculations and load the lighting file instead.
2. If the client's mission file has a different CRC, the mission load will fail. This means the client's mission file doesn't match the server's.

**Syntax**
```
con.setMissionCRC( CRC );
```
con       A client connection.

CRC       An integervalue in the range [ 0x0 , 0xFFFFFFFF ].

**Example Call**
```
%client.setMissionCRC( $missionCRC );
```

---

## setSimulatedNetParams

**Purpose**
Use the setSimulatedNetParams method to force a connection to experience a certain degree of packet-loss and/or latency.

This is a debug feature that allows us to see how a distributed game will behave in the face of poor connection quality.

**Syntax**
```
con.setSimulatedNetParams( packetLoss , delay );
```
con          A client connection.
packetLoss   A floating-point value in the range [0.0 , 1.0] specifying the percentage of packets to artificially lose.
delay        An integer value specifying the number of milliseconds to insert into transmission latencies.

**Example Call**
```
// Force this client to experience 50% packet loss and
// 500 millisecond packet latency
%client.setSimulatedNetParams( 0.5 , 500 );
```

**Notes**
1. This method is inherited from the parent class NetConnection.

**See Also**
getPacketLoss, getPing

---

## startRecording

**Purpose**
Use the startRecording method to start recording a demo stream from a server connection.

**Syntax**

```
con.startRecording( fileName );
```

con            A server connection.

filename       A string containing the path and filename in which to store the demo stream.

**Example Call**

```
ServerConnection.startRecording( $DemoFileName );
```

**See Also**

isDemoPlaying, isDemoRecording, playDemo, stopRecording

---

## stopRecording

**Purpose**

Use the stopRecording method to stop recording a demo stream from a server connection.

**Syntax**

```
con.stopRecording();
```

con            A server connection.

**Example Call**

```
if(ServerConnection.isDemoRecording())
{
    ServerConnection.stopRecording();
}
```

**See Also**

isDemoPlaying, isDemoRecording, playDemo, startRecording

---

## transmitDataBlocks

**Purpose**

Use the transmitDataBlocks method to start sending datablocks to a client.

**Syntax**

```
con.transmitDatablocks( sequence );
```

con            A client connection.

sequence       A magic number used by standard TGE scripts to ensure that a client doesn't receive or accept stale datablocks.

**Example Call**

```
%client.transmitDataBlocks($missionSequence);
```

**See Also**

onDataBlocksDone, onDataBlockObjectReceived

---

## transmitPaths

**Purpose**

Use the transmitPaths method to send path information to a client.

**Syntax**

```
con.transmitPaths();
```

con          A client connection.

**Notes**

1. This method must be called before calling the activateGhosting method, or the client's engine may crash.
2. This method is inherited from the parent class NetConnection.

**See Also**

activateGhosting, clearPaths

# B.1.3 GameConnection Callbacks

| Callback | Description |
|----------|-------------|
| initialControlSet | Called by client on a server connection, indicating the server has set initial control object for this client. |
| onConnect | Called by server on a client connection, indicating a client has successfully connected to this server. |
| onConnectionAccepted | Called by client on a server connection, indicating this client successfully connected to a server. |
| onConnectionDropped | Called by client on a server connection, indicating this client was disconnected (dropped) by the server. |
| onConnectionError | Called by client on a server connection, indicating this client has seen some type of fatal connection error. |
| onConnectionTimedOut | Called by client on a server connection, indicating the connection to the server has timed out (disconnection without notice). |
| onConnectRequest | Called by server on a client connection, indicating a client is trying to connect to this server. |
| onConnectRequestRejected | Called by client on a server connection, indicating this client's connection request to a server was rejected, and providing the reason for that rejection. |
| onConnectRequestTimedOut | Called by client on a server connection, indicating this client's connection request to a server timed out without a response. |
| onDataBlocksDone | Called by server on a client connection, indicating that all datablocks have been successfully sent to this client. |
| onDataBlockObjectReceived | Called on client, indicating that this client has received a new datablock. |
| onDrop | Called by the server on a client connection, indicating that the client was disconnected and why. |
| setLagIcon | Called by the client on a server connection, indicating no traffic has been received from the server in $Pref::Net::LagThreshold milliseconds. |

## GameConnection::initialControlSet

**Purpose**

The initialControlSet callback is called by the *engine* on the client side and serviced by *script* on the client side (servicing meaning defining what happens during the callback). When this callback is called, this indicates that the server has set this client's initial control object. This indicates that the client may safely display the game interface (PlayGui) and that the player may begin interacting with the game world.

**Syntax**

initialControlSet( con );

con        A server connection.

## Appendices

### Example Implementation

```
function GameConnection::initialControlSet( %this )
{
   if (!Editor::checkActiveLoadDone())
   {
      if (Canvas.getContent() != PlayGui.getId())
         Canvas.setContent(PlayGui);
   }
}
```

### Notes

1. You may add or remove additional features to/from the standard callback definition as you see fit. The important thing to remember is not to do any work that requires scoping until this callback is called.

---

## GameConnection::onConnect

### Purpose

The `onConnect` callback is called by the *engine* on the client side and serviced by *script* on the client side (servicing meaning defining what happens during the callback) when that client has successfully attached to the server. This callback provides the client's (player's) name and up to 14 optional arguments if these arguments are provided by the client in the GameConnection method `setConnectArgs`.

### Syntax

```
onConnect( con , name [ , arg1 , ... , arg14 ]  )
```

| | |
|---|---|
| con | A client connection. |
| name | A string containing the player's name. |
| arg1 | Up to 14 optional arguments containing any values, as provided by the client using `setConnectArgs`. |
| ... | |
| arg14 | |

### Example Implementation

```
function GameConnection::onConnect( %clientConn , %name , %str , %dex , %con )
{
   // Add this client to clientGroup
   if( !isObject( clientGroup ) )
   {
      new SimGroup( clientGroup );
   }

   clientGroup.add( %clientConn );

   %clientConn.name = %name;

   // Assumes these extra args were provided using a call to setConnectArgs()
   %clientConn.strength     = %str;
   %clientConn.dexterity    = %dex;
   %clientConn.constitution = %con;
}
```

### See Also

onConnectionAccepted, setConnectArgs

---

## GameConnection::onConnectionAccepted

### Purpose
The onConnectionAccepted callback is called by the *engine* on the client side and serviced by *script* on the client side (servicing meaning defining what happens during the callback) after the server accepts the client's connection request.

### Syntax
```
onConnectionAccepted( con )
```
con          A server connection.

### Example Implementation
```
function GameConnection::onConnectionAccepted( %serverConn )
{
    echo( %serverConn , " successfully connected to server." );
}
```

### See Also
onConnect

---

## GameConnection::onConnectionDropped

### Purpose
The onConnectionDropped callback is called by the *engine* on the client side and serviced by *script* on the client side (servicing meaning defining what happens during the callback) when the server drops this client. If a reason for the drop is given, it will be supplied in the reason argument.

### Syntax
```
onConnectionDropped( con , reason )
```
con          A server connection.

reason       A string containing the reason why the server dropped this client.

### Example Implementation
```
function GameConnection::onConnectionDropped( %serverConn, %reason )
{
    echo( "Server dropped the connection because: " , %reason );
}
```

### Notes
1. The client automatically deletes its server connection after calling onConnectionDropped, so you don't need to write code to manually delete it.

### See Also
delete, onDrop

---

## GameConnection::onConnectionError

### Purpose
The onConnectionError callback is called by the *engine* on the client side and serviced by *script* on the client side (servicing meaning defining what happens during the callback) when some kind of fatal *error* is seen on that connection.

## Syntax

onConnectionError( con , error )

| | |
|---|---|
| con | A server connection. |
| error | A string containing a description of the error. |

## Example Implementation

```
function GameConnection::onConnectionError( %serverConn, %error )
{
   echo( "This connection [" , %serverConn ,
        "] has encountered, an error: " , %error );
}
```

## Notes

1. The client automatically deletes its server connection after calling `onConnectionError`, so you don't need to write code to manually delete it.

---

## GameConnection::onConnectionTimedOut

### Purpose

The `onConnectionTimedOut` callback is called by the *engine* on the client side and serviced by *script* on the client side (servicing meaning defining what happens during the callback) when that connection times out. This may occur if the network connection to the server is severed, if the server crashes or shuts down.

### Syntax

onConnectionTimedOut( %clientConn  )

| | |
|---|---|
| %con | A client connection. |

### Example Implementation

```
function GameConnection::onConnectionTimedOut( %serverConn  )
{
   echo("The server connection has timed out." );
}
```

### Notes

1. The client automatically deletes its server connection after calling `onConnectionTimedOut`.

---

## GameConnection::onConnectRequest

### Purpose

The `onConnectRequest` callback is called by the server on a client connection whenever a client tries to connect to the server.

This callback must return a value that will indicate whether the client can connect or whether it is being rejected.

To allow a client to connect, simply return a NULL-string (""); otherwise return a string containing the rejection reason. (See example implementation.)

### Syntax

error = onConnectRequest( con , address , name )

| | |
|---|---|
| con | A client connection. |
| error | A string containing the reason a connection is to be rejected, or a NULL-string, indicating the connection will be accepted. |

address          A string containing the address of the client. Valid addresses contain both an IP address (A.B.C.D) and a port number (P): "A.B.C.D:P". The elements of an IP address may each be between 0 and 255, while ports can be between 1000 and 65536.

name             A string containing the name of the player (client.)

### Example Implementation
```
function GameConnection::onConnectRequest( %clientConn, %address, %name )
{

   // Check for too many players
   //
   if( clientGroup.getCount() > $Pref::Server::MaxPlayers )
   {
      return("CR_SERVERFULL");
   }

   // Do whatever other checks you need
   //


   // Return "" to signify an accepted connection.
   return "";
}
```

### Notes
1. To write this callback correctly, you must specify a return value. Return "" if the connection is to be accepted; otherwise return a string containing the reason the connection was refused.
2. If the engine automatically rejects a request, this callback does not get called. Table B.1.2 lists some automatic rejection reasons and the messages that go with them.

### See Also
onConnectRequestRejected

---

## GameConnection::onConnectRequestRejected

### Purpose
The onConnectRequestRejected callback is called by the engine on the client side and serviced by script on the client side (servicing meaning defining what happens during the callback) when a connection attempt has been rejected. The engine always supplies the reason for this rejection. In the callback, you can decode the reason.

### Syntax
```
onConnectRequestRejected( con , reason )
```
con              A server connection.

reason           A string containing the reason the connection was rejected.

### Example Implementation
```
function GameConnection::onConnectRequestRejected( %serverConn , %reason )
{
   switch$( %reason )
   {
   case "CHR_PASSWORD":
      if ($Client::Password $= "")
```

```
            %error = "Server requires a password.";
        else
            %error = "Incorrect password.";

    default:
        %error = "Connection error.  Please try another server.  " @
                 "Error code: ( " @ %reason @ " )";
    }
    error( %error );
}
```

**Notes**

1. Connection attempts may be rejected for a number of reasons, some of them automatic. Table B.1.2 lists some automatic rejection reasons and the messages that go with them.
2. The client automatically deletes its server connection after calling `onConnectRequestRejected`, so you don't need to write code to manually delete it.

**See Also**

onConnectRequest

---

**Table B.1.2**
Connection request rejection reasons and messages.

| Rejection Message | Description |
|---|---|
| CHR_GAME | This server is not playing the same game as the client. (Returned automatically by engine.) |
| CHR_PASSWORD | The server has specified a non-NULL value for the global $Pref::Server::Password and the client did not supply a proper password using the setJoinPassword method. (For more information on the $Pref::Server::Password global, see Chapter 4.) (Returned automatically by engine.) |
| CHR_PROTOCOL_GREATER CHR_PROTOCOL_LESS | The client connection protocol is higher/lower than the server. (Returned automatically by engine.) |
| CR_INVALID_ARGS | The client is attempting to send too many extra connection arguments. (Returned automatically by engine.) |
| Other | Any other value can be returned manually from the onConnectRequest() callback as a string. The strings and the meanings of these strings are up to you. |

---

**GameConnection::onConnectRequestTimedOut**

---

**Purpose**

The `onConnectRequestTimedOut` callback is called by a client on its server connection when a connection attempt times out. Clients will attempt to connect to a server four (4) times, waiting 2500 milliseconds between attempts. If no response is received by the end of the last attempt, this callback is called.

**Syntax**

onConnectRequestTimedOut( con )

con     A server connection.

**Example Implementation**

```
function GameConnection::onConnectRequestTimedOut( %serverConn )
{
    echo( %serverConn , " failed to reach the server." );
}
```

**Notes**

1. The client automatically deletes its server connection after calling `onConnectRequestTimedOut`, so you don't need to write code to manually delete it.

2. To modify the retry count of 4 attempts, you can change the "ConnectRetryCount" constant found in the file NetInterface.cc.

3. To modify the delay time of 2500 milliseconds, you can change the "ConnectRetryTime" constant found in the file NetInterface.cc.

## GameConnection::onDataBlocksDone

### Purpose
The `onDataBlocksDone` callback is called by a client on its server connection when it has received the last of the datablocks that the server will be transmitting for the current level/mission.

### Syntax
```
onDatablocksDone( con , sequence )
```

con — A client connection.

sequence — An integer value used for bookkeeping by the standard Torque scripts to determine if a datablock is part of the current set.

### Example Implementation
```
function GameConnection::onDatablocksDone( %clientConn , %sequence )
{
    // Various accounting code
}
```

### See Also
`onDataBlockObjectReceived`

### Notes
1. This callback is an exception to the callbacks as a method rule. Unlike all of the other callbacks that are methods of `GameConnections`, this callback is simply a function. (See the definition above for clarification.)

## onDataBlockObjectReceived

### Purpose
The `ondatablockObjectReceived` callback is called on a client every time a datablock is received.

### Syntax
```
onDatablockObjectReceived( index , total )
```

con — A server connection.

index — An integer value specifying the index of the current datablock that has been received. (Index values number from 0 to total-1.)

total — An integer value specifying the total number of datablocks that will be transmitted.

### Example Implementation
```
function onDatablockObjectReceived( %index, %total )
{
    echo( %index , " of ", %total , " total datablocks received");
}
```

**See Also**
onDataBlocksDone

---

## GameConnection::onDrop

**Purpose**

The onDrop callback is called by the server on a client connection when that connection has been deleted by the server.

**Syntax**

```
onDrop( con , reason  )
```

con               A client connection.

reason            A string containing the reason the connection was dropped.

**Example Implementation**

```
function GameConnection::onDrop( %clientConn , %reason  )
{
   echo("Client ", %clientConn, " dropped for reason: ", %reason );
}
```

---

## GameConnection::setLagIcon

**Purpose**

The setLagIcon callback is called by the client on its server connection whenever that connection is quiescent (not receiving packets) for longer than $Pref::Net::LagThreshold milliseconds, which is by default 400 milliseconds.

**Syntax**

```
setLagIcon( con , lagging )
```

con               A server connection.

lagging           A boolean value indicating that the connection is lagging (1) or is no longer lagging (0).

**Example Implementation**

```
function GameConnection::setLagIcon( %serverConn, %lagging )
{
   if( %lagging )
   {
     // Enable lag notification for the player
   }
   else
   {
     // Disable previously enabled lag notification
   }
}
```

**Notes**

1. This is a courtesy callback that allows game developers to provide feedback when a connection is slow or bad by displaying a lag icon to the user. Other than that, the callback has no functional purpose.

# B.1.4 GameConnection related NetObject Methods

| Method | Description |
|---|---|
| clearScopeToClient | Undoes the results of a call to scopeToClient. |
| getGhostID | Gets the ghost index (on server) for a ghost on a client. |
| scopeToClient | Forces this object to always be ghosted for a specific client. |
| setScopeAlways | Forces this object to always be ghosted to all clients. |

## clearScopeToClient

### Purpose
Use the clearScopeToClient method to stop this object from always being ghosted for a specific client. This undoes the effects of a previous call to scopeToClient.

### Syntax
obj.clearScopeToClient( con );

obj              An server object (any NetObject-derived object).

con              A client connection.

### Example Call
```
// Stop forcing this object to be 'in scope' for this client.
%curObj.clearScopeToClient( %client );
```

### See Also
scopeToClient

## getGhostID

### Purpose
Use the getGhostID method to get the server's client connection ghost index from a ghost (on the client).

### Syntax
id = obj.getGhostID( con );

obj       An server object (any NetObject-derived object).

id        An integer value representing the ghost index for the ghost this method was called on. If the object is not a ghost, −1 is returned instead.

con       A client connection.

### Example Call
```
%index = %ghostObject.getGhostID();
echo( "This ghost object ", %ghostObject, " has the ghost index ", %index ,
      " on the server's client connection." );
```

### See Also
GameConnection::getGhostID,          GameConnection::resolveGhostID,          GameConnection::
resolveObjectFromGhostIndex

## scopeToClient

### Purpose
Use the scopeToClient method to force an object to always be in scope for a specified client connection.

**Syntax**

```
obj.scopeToClient( con );
```

obj                 An server object (any `NetObject`-derived object).

con                A client connection.

**Example Call**

```
// Force this client to always render this object. (Always in scope.)
%curObj.scopeToClient( %client );
```

**See Also**

```
clearScopeToClient, setScopeAlways
```

---

### setScopeAlways

**Purpose**

Use the `setScopeAlways` method to force an object to be ghosted (`SCOPE_ALWAYS`) on all clients.

**Syntax**

```
obj.scopeToClient( );
```

obj                 An server object (any `NetObject` derived object.)

**Example Call**

```
// Force this object to always be ghosted for all clients
%curObj.setScopeAlways( );
```

**See Also**

```
scopeToClient
```

## B.2 Servers

## B.2.1 Server Methods

| Method | Description |
|---|---|
| allowConnections | Enables (disables) external network connections. |
| cancelServerQuery | Cancels and drops any outstanding queries. |
| getServerCount | Returns the number of game servers found by the last call to queryMasterServer(). |
| queryLanServers | Searches for game servers on a local-area network, matching a specified set of attributes. |
| queryMasterServer | Searches for game servers on the Internet, matching a specified set of attributes. |
| querySingleServer | Refreshes data for one server at a specific address. |
| setServerInfo | Retrieves the information from a specified server in the "found server list" and places this information in a series of $ServerInfo::* globals. |
| startHeartbeat | Starts a heartbeat to advertise this game server to any known master servers (as defined by the master server list). (See Section 4.2.4 for more info on this list.) |
| stopHeartbeat | Stops a previously started heartbeat. |
| stopServerQuery | Cancels and marks as "done" any outstanding queries. |

## allowConnections

**Purpose**
Use the `allowConnections` method to enable (or disable) external connections to this game.

**Syntax**
`allowConnections( enable );`

`enable`    A boolean value, specifying whether to enable (`true`) or disable (`false`) external network connections.

**Example Call**
```
// Allow LAN and Internet connections
allowConnections( true );
```

## cancelServerQuery

**Purpose**
Use the `cancelServerQuery` function to cancel a previous `query*()` call.

**Syntax**
`cancelServerQuery();`

**Example Call**
`cancelServerQuery();`

**See Also**
`queryLANServers, queryMasterServer, querySingleServer`

## getServerCount

**Purpose**
Use the `getServerCount` function to determine the number of game servers found on the last `queryLANServers` or `queryMasterServer` call.

**Syntax**
`count = getServerCount();`

`count`    An integer value between 0 and N, where N is the number of servers found in the last `queryLanServers()` or `queryMasterServer()` call.

**Example Call**
```
// Determine how many game servers were found in the last query
%numServers = %getServerCount();
```

**See Also**
`queryLANServers, queryMasterServer, setServerInfo`

## queryLanServers

**Purpose**
Use the `queryLANServers` function to establish whether any game servers of the required specifications (see syntax) are available on the local area network (LAN).

## Syntax

```
queryLanServers( port, flags, gameType, missionType, minPlayers, maxPlayers,
                 maxBots, regionMask, maxPing, minCPU, filterFlags );
```

| | |
|---|---|
| port | An integer value between 1000 and 65536 specifying the port to search for servers on. |
| flags | Not used. Set to 0. |
| gameType | A string specifying a game type to search for. Setting this to "ANY" matches all game types. |
| missionType | A string specifying a mission type to search for. Setting this to "ANY" matches all mission types. |
| minPlayers | An integer specifying the minimum player count to match. Set this to 0 to disable. |
| maxPlayers | An integer specifying the maximum player count to match. Set this to a high value (9999) to disable. |
| maxBots | An integer specifying the maximum AI controlled player count to match. Set this to a high value (9999) to disable. |
| regionMask | Not used. Set to 0. |
| maxPing | An integer specifying the maximum allowed ping time. Set to 0 to disable. |
| minCPU | An integer specifying the minimum allowed CPU speed. Set to 0 to disable. |
| filterFlags | A bit mask (see Table B.2.1) specifying specific server features to match against. Set to 0 to disable. |

## Example Call

```
// Find all LAN servers that are using port 2800
queryLanServers(2800,0,"ANY","ANY",0,9999,9999,0,0,0,0);
```

## See Also

getServerCount, queryMasterServer, setServerInfo, stopServerQuery

---

## queryMasterServer

### Purpose

Use the queryMasterServer function to query all master servers in the master server list and to establish whether they're aware of any game servers that meet the specified requirements, as established by the arguments passed to this function.

### Syntax

```
queryMasterServer( flags, gameType, missionType, minPlayers, maxlayers,
                   maxbBots, regionMask, maxPing, minCPU, filterFlags );
```

| | |
|---|---|
| flags | Not used. Set to 0. |
| gameType | A string specifying a game type to search for. Setting this to "ANY" matches all game types. |
| missionType | A string specifying a mission type to search for. Setting this to "ANY" matches all mission types. |
| minPlayers | An integer specifying the minimum player count to match. Set this to 0 to disable. |
| maxPlayers | An integer specifying the maximum player count to match. Set this to a high value (9999) to disable. |
| maxBots | An integer specifying the maximum AI controlled player count to match. Set this to a high value (9999) to disable. |
| regionMask | An integer values specifying the master server region to search. |
| maxPing | An integer specifying the maximum allowed ping time. Set to 0 to disable. |
| minCPU | An integer specifying the minimum allowed CPU speed. Set to 0 to disable. |
| filterFlags | A bit mask (see Table B.2.1) specifying specific server features to match against. Set to 0 to disable. |

### Example Call

```
// Find all game servers that are currently advertising on
// the master servers in our master server list
queryMasterServer(0,"ANY","ANY",0,9999,9999,2,0,0,0);
```

## Notes

1. In order for this function to do anything, we need to specify a master server list. This list may contain one or more master server addresses and is usually specified in the file " ~ /server/defaults.cs".

```
// Region Number : IP Address : Port Number
$pref::Master[0] = "2:192.168.123.15:28002";
$pref::Master[1] = "2:192.168.123.2:28002";
...
```

## See Also

getServerCount, queryLANServers, setServerInfo, startHeartbeat, stopServerQuery

---

**Table B.2.1**

filterFlags.

| bitmask | Description |
| --- | --- |
| 0x1 | Only match dedicated servers. |
| 0x2 | Only match servers that don't require a password. |
| 0x4 | Only match Linux servers |
| 0x80 | Engine version must match exactly. |

---

## querySingleServer

## Purpose

Use the querySingleServer function to requery a previously queried server, where the previous query could be either queryLANServers or queryMasterServer.

## Syntax

```
querySingleServer( address [ , flags ] );
```

| address | A string containing the address of a server to refresh. These addresses are of the form "A.B.C.D: Port", where A..D are values in the range [0,255] and Port is in the range [1000,65536]. |
| --- | --- |
| flags | Not used. This argument is a remnant that no longer has a purpose. |

## Example Call

```
// Refresh the information from the first server found in our last query.
SetServerInfo( 0 );
querySingleServer( $ServerInfo::Address );
```

## See Also

getServerCount, queryLANServers, queryMasterServer, setServerInfo, stopServerQuery

---

## setServerInfo

## Purpose

Use the setServerInfo function to retrieve all of the data for the server at index in our found server list and place that data in the $ServerInfo::* globals. (See Table B.2.2.)

## Syntax

```
success = setServerInfo( index );
```

| success | A boolean value specifying that data was found and extracted (true) or that no data was found (false). |
| --- | --- |
| index | An integer value specifying the  entry in the found server list to extract data from. |

## Appendices

### Example Call
```
// Print the addresses of all servers located in the last query.
for( %count = 0; %count < getServerCount() ; %count++)
{
    setServerInfo( %count );
    echo("Address for server ", %count, " is: ", $ServerInfo::Address );
}
```

### See Also
`getServerCount`, `queryLANServers`, `queryMasterServer`, `querySingleServer`

---

### Table B.2.2
`$ServerInfo::*` *globals.*

| global | Description |
| --- | --- |
| `$ServerInfo::Status` | Current status for this server. |
| `$ServerInfo::Address` | Address for this server including IP and port.<br>Ex: `"192.162.123.1:10000"` |
| `$ServerInfo::Name` | Server name. |
| `$ServerInfo::GameType` | Type of game currently playing. |
| `$ServerInfo::MissionName` | Name of current mission (map name). |
| `$ServerInfo::MissionType` | Type of current mission. |
| `$ServerInfo::State` | An informational message relaying the state of this server. |
| `$ServerInfo::Info` | Info string describing server. |
| `$ServerInfo::PlayerCount` | Number of players currently attached to server. |
| `$ServerInfo::MaxPlayers` | Max players allowed on server. |
| `$ServerInfo::BotCount` | Number of bots acting as players on server. |
| `$ServerInfo::Version` | Version number of server. |
| `$ServerInfo::Ping` | PING latency for serer in milliseconds. |
| `$ServerInfo::CPUSpeed` | Frequency of server host machine in MHz. |
| `$ServerInfo::Favorite` | 1 if this is a favorite; 0 otherwise. |
| `$ServerInfo::Dedicated` | 1 if this server is running dedicated; 0 otherwise. |
| `$ServerInfo::Password` | 1 if this server requires a password; 0 otherwise. |

---

## startHeartbeat

### Purpose
Use the `startHeartbeat` function to start advertising this game server on any master servers in the master server list.

### Syntax
```
startHeartbeat();
```

### Example Call
```
// Start advertising this server on the Internet
startHeartbeat();
```

### Notes
1. In order for this function to do anything, we need to specify a master server list. This list may contain one or more master server addresses and is usually specified in the file " ~ /server/defaults.cs".

```
// Region Number : IP Address : Port Number
```

```
$pref::Master[0] = "2:192.168.123.15:28002";
$pref::Master[1] = "2:192.168.123.2:28002";
...
```

**See Also**
queryMasterServer, stopHeartbeat

---

## stopHeartbeat

**Purpose**
Use the stopHeartbeat function to stop advertising this game server to any master servers on the master server list.

**Syntax**
stopHeartbeat();

**Example Call**
```
// Stop advertising this server on the Internet
stopHeartbeat();
```

**See Also**
queryMasterServer, startHeartbeat

---

## stopServerQuery

**Purpose**
Use the stopServerQuery function to cancel any outstanding server queries and mark them as "done".

**Syntax**
stopServerQuery();

**Example Call**
stopServerQuery();

**See Also**
queryLANServers, queryMasterServer, querySingleServer

---

# B.3 Communication

# B.3.1 Command Functions

| Function | Description |
|---|---|
| commandToClient | Send a command to a client for execution. |
| commandToServer | Send a command to a server for execution. |

---

## commandToClient

**Purpose**
Use the commandToClient function to remotely execute a named command on a specified server.

### Syntax

```
commandToClient( con , command [ , ... ] );
```

con                           A client connection.

command                   A string or tag specifying the command to execute on the client.

...                             Additional optional string or tag arguments.

### Example Call

```
// Execute the command "DoSomething" on all clients in ClientGroup
%count = ClientGroup.getCount();
for (%i = 0; %i < %count; %i++)
{
   %clientConn = ClientGroup.getObject(%i);
   commandToClient( %clientConn , "DoSomething" );
}
//
// The above code will attempt to execute the following function on each
// client found in the SimGroup ClientGroup
//
function clientCmdDoSomething( )
{
   // Does something
}
```

### Notes

1. Notice that the actual command to be executed on the client is named `clientCmdCOMMAND`, where `COMMAND` is the command string/tag passed to `commandToClient`.

### See Also

```
commandToServer
```

---

## commandToServer

### Purpose

Use the `commandToServer` function to remotely execute a named command on the server.

### Syntax

```
commandToServer( con , command [ , ... ] );
```

con                           A server connection.

command                   A string or tag specifying the command to execute on the server.

...                             Additional optional string or tag arguments.

### Example Call

```
// Execute the command "DoSomething" on the server
commandToServer( "DoSomething" );

//
// The above code will attempt to execute the following function on
// server.  The first argument to this function is always the ID of
// the client that issued the command.
//
function serverCmdDoSomething( %client )
{
```

```
    // Does something
}
```

**Notes**

1. Notice that the actual command to be executed on the server is named serverCmdCOMMAND, where COMMAND is the command string/tag passed to commandToServer.

**See Also**

commandToClient

# B.3.2 TCPObject Methods

| Method | Description |
|--------|-------------|
| connect | Attempt to connect to another TCPObject. |
| disconnect | Flush any outstanding sent data on a TCPObject connection and then close it. |
| listen | Listen on a port for connection attempts. |
| send | Send messages on an existing TCPObject connection. |

## connect

**Purpose**

Use the connect method to connect to another TCObject at a specified address, where that address is generally given in the form: "A.B.C.D:Port". A..D are integers in the range [0,255], and the Port value is an integer in the range [1000,65536].

**Syntax**

```
tcpobj.connect( address );
```

tcpobj       A TCPObject.

address      An address and port in one of three standard forms. (See notes.)

**Example Call**

```
// Connect locally on port 5000
new TCPObject( TCPClient );
TCPClient.connect("localhost:5000");
```

**Notes**

1. In addition to supporting numeric Internet Protocol (IP) addresses, the engine also supports host names and the use of the localhost address. The latter address type connects on the computer's loopback address, "127.0.0.1".

   - %tcpobj.connect( "www.garagegames.com:5000" );
   - %tcpobj.connect( "localhost:5000" );

**See Also**

disconnect

## disconnect

**Purpose**

Use the disconnect method to flush any outstanding sent data on an open TCPObject connection and then close that connection.

**Syntax**

```
tcpobj.disconnect();
```

```
tcpobj          A TCPObject.
```

**Example Call**
```
// Flush and close the TCPClient connection
TCPClient.disconnect("localhost:5000");
```

**Notes**
1. A TCPObject connection can buffer data (to be sent). By calling the disconnect() method on the object that is buffering the sends, you can safely flush that data to the TCPObject at the other end of the connection before closing the connection.

**See Also**
```
connect
```

---

## listen

**Purpose**
Use the listen method to start listening for connections on a specified port.

**Syntax**
```
tcpobj.listen( port );
```
```
tcpobj          A TCPObject.
```
```
port            An integer value in the range [1000,65536], specifying the port for this TCPObject to listen on.
```

**Example Call**
```
// Create a server object and listen for connection requests on port 5000
new TCPObject( TCPServer );
TCPServer.listen(5000);
```

---

## send

**Purpose**
Use the send method to transmit data across an established TCPObject connection.

**Syntax**
```
tcpobj.send( ... );
```
```
tcpobj          A TCPObject.
```
```
...             Any number of strings or numeric values separated by commas.
```

**Example Call**
```
// Send some data on an established connection
TCPClient.send("Hello", "this", "is bob!\n" );
```

**Notes**
1. Any data sent without a terminating new-line (\n) character will be buffered until a new-line is sent, or until disconnect() is called on this end of the connection.

**See Also**
```
disconnect
```

# B.3.3 TCPObject Callbacks

| Callback | Called when ... |
|---|---|
| onConnected | ... this TCPObject successfully connects to another TCPObject. |
| onConnectFailed | ... this TCPObject fails to connect to another TCPObject. |
| onConnectRequest | ... another TCPObject requests a connection with this TCPObject. |
| onDisconnect | ... this TCPObject is disconnected from another TCPObject. |
| onDNSFailed | ... a connection attempt using a host name fails to find the numeric IP equivalent. |
| onDNSResolved | ... a connection attempt using a host name successfully finds the numeric IP equivalent. |
| onLine | ... this TCPObject receives data from another TCPObject. |

## TCPObject::onConnected

**Purpose**
This callback is called when this TCPObject successfully connects to another TCPObject.

**Syntax**
```
onConnected( tcpobj );
```
 tcpobj          A client TCPObject instance.

**Example Implementation**
```
function TCPClient::onConnected( %this )
{
}
```

## TCPObject::onConnectFailed

**Purpose**
This callback is called when this TCPObject fails to connect to another TCPObject.

**Syntax**
```
onConnectFailed( tcpobj );
```
 tcpobj          A client TCPObject instance.

**Example Implementation**
```
function TCPClient::onConnectFailed( %Obj )
{
}
```

## TCPObject::onConnectRequest

**Purpose**
This callback is called when another TCPObject requests a connection with this TCPObject.

**Syntax**
```
onConnectRequest( tcpobj , addrBuf , idBuf );
```
 tcpobj          A server TCPObject instance.
 addrBuf         The address of the client trying to connect to this server.

Appendices

idBuf       An engine-supplied value use to create the connection if the server accepts it.

**Example Implementation**
```
function TCPServer::onConnectRequest( %Obj , %addrBuf , %idBuf )
{
    new TCPObject( TCPProxyConnection , %idBuf );
}
```

**Notes**
1. The engine assumes that a connection will be allowed and creates an identifier for it (idBuf).
2. If the server callback does decide to allow the connection, it simply creates a new TCPObject to act as a proxy for the connection and passes in the idBuf as the second argument in the creation command.
3. Server objects are only responsible for catching connection requests and creating proxy connections. All communications occur between clients and proxies.

## TCPObject::onDisconnect

**Purpose**
This callback is called when this TCPObject is disconnected from another TCPObject.

**Syntax**
```
onDisconnect( tcpobj );
```
tcpobj       A client TCPObject instance.

**Example Implementations**
```
// Called when proxy disconnects
function TCPClient::onDisconnect( %Obj )
{
}

// Called when client disconnects
function TCPProxyConnection::onDisconnect( %Obj )
{
}
```

**Notes**
1. This callback is only ever called as the result of a call to disconnect(). Simply deleting the connection will not call this.

## TCPObject::onDNSFailed

**Purpose**
This callback is called when a connection attempt using a host name fails to find the numeric IP equivalent.

**Syntax**
```
onDNSFailed( tcpobj );
```
tcpobj       A client TCPObject instance.

**Example Implementation**
```
function TCPClient::onDNSFailed( %Obj )
{
}
```

---

## TCPObject::onDNSResolved

**Purpose**

This callback is called when a connection attempt using a host name successfully finds the numeric IP equivalent.

**Syntax**

```
onDNSResolved( tcpobj );
```

 tcpobj        A client TCPObject instance.

**Example Implementation**

```
function TCPClient::onDNSResolved( %Obj )
{
}
```

---

## TCPObject::onLine

**Purpose**

This callback is called when this TCPObject receives data from another TCPObject.

**Syntax**

```
onLine( tcpobj , line );
```

 tcpobj        A client TCPObject instance.

 line         A string containing any value as transmitted by the TCPObject..

**Example Implementation**

```
// Called when the client sends data to the proxy
function TCPProxyConnection::onLine( %Obj , %line )
{
    echo("TCPProxyConnection::onLine( " @ %Obj @ " , " @ %line @ " ) " );
}
```

**Notes**

1. Both proxies and clients can send and receive data, so both sides of the connection (proxy and client) should implement this callback if they want to receive data.

# B.3.4 HTTPObject Methods

HTTPObject inherits all of the methods from TCPObject, so please look at the previous sections for details on those methods. In addition, HTTPObject adds two new methods, get and post.

| Method | Description |
| --- | --- |
| get | Send data request to a web server. |
| post | Send data to a web server. |

---

## get/post

**Purpose**

Use the get method to request data from a web server.
Use the post method to send data to a web server.

**Syntax**

```
httpobj.get( address, requestURI [ , query] );
```

```
httpobj.post( address, requestURI , query, post );
```
| | |
|---|---|
| `httpobj` | An HTTPObject. |
| `address` | A suitable address pointing to the web server. Ex: "IP:www.myserver.com:80" |
| `requestURI` | A string containing the path to a PHP file on the server. |
| `query` | A string containing a query to run on the server. Optional for get(). |
| `post` | The data to send in a `post` call. |

## B.3.5 HTTPObject Callbacks

HTTPObject inherits all of the callbacks from TCPObject, so please look at the previous sections for details on those methods.

## B.4 Torque AI

## B.4.1 `AIPlayer` Methods

| Method | Description |
|---|---|
| `clearAim` | Stop aiming. |
| `getAimLocation` | Get the current aim location. |
| `getAimObject` | Get the current aim object. |
| `getMoveDestination` | Get the current move destination. |
| `setAimLocation` | Set a new aim location. |
| `setAimObject` | Set a new aim object. |
| `setMoveDestination` | Set a new move destination. |
| `setMoveSpeed` | Set move speed between 0% and 100%. |
| `stop` | Stop moving. |

### `clearAim`

**Purpose**

Use the `clearAim` method to stop aiming at an object/location. After calling this method, the bot will look in its default forward direction.

**Syntax**
```
bot.clearAim();
```
| | |
|---|---|
| `bot` | An `AIPlayer` object. |

**Example Call**
```
%bot.clearAim();
```

**See Also**
`setAimLocation`, `setAimObject`

---

## getAimLocation

**Purpose**

Use the getAimLocation method to get the current location (position) the bot is aiming at.

**Syntax**

location = bot.getAimLocation();

location          A string containing an "X Y Z" world position, representing the last position the bot was aiming at.

bot               An AIPlayer object.

**Example Call**

```
// Find out where out bot is looking
%lookPosition = %bot.getAimLocation();
```

**Notes**

1. If this bot was never assigned an aim object or location, then this method returns an invalid position.

2. If this bot was assigned an aim location and that aim was subsequently cleared, this method will still return the old aim position.

3. If this bot is currently aiming at an object, this method will return that object's current position.

**See Also**

setAimLocation, setAimObject, getAimObject

---

## getAimObject

**Purpose**

Use the getAimObject method to get the ID of the current ShapeBase object the bot is aiming at.

**Syntax**

object = bot.getAimObject();

object            An integer value equal to an object ID, or -1 if the bot is not aiming at an object.

bot               An AIPlayer object.

**Example Call**

```
// Get the current target object ID
%targetID = %bot.getAimObject();
```

**See Also**

getAimLocation, setAimLocation, setAimObject

---

## getMoveDestination

**Purpose**

Use the getMoveDestination method to get the bot's current move destination.

**Syntax**

dest = bot.getMoveDestination();

dest              A string containing an "X Y Z" world-position representing the bot's last assigned move destination.

bot               An AIPlayer object.

**Example Call**

```
// Get the bot's current move destination
```

```
%moveDest = %bot.getMoveDestination();
```

**Notes**

1. If a move destination has not been assigned to this bot, this method returns "0 0 0".

**See Also**

```
setMoveDestination
```

---

### setAimLocation

**Purpose**

Use the `setAimLocation` method to make the bot continuously aim at a world position.

**Syntax**

```
bot.setAimLocation( location );
```

bot            An `AIPlayer` object.

location       A string containing an "X Y Z" world position.

**Example Call**

```
// Aim at bob's position
%bot.setAimLocation( %bob.getPosition() );
```

**Notes**

1. Once an aim location is set, the bot will continue to aim at that position.

**See Also**

```
getAimLocation, getAimObject, setAimObject
```

---

### setAimObject

**Purpose**

Use the `setAimObject` method to make the bot continuously aim at the position of any valid ShapeBase object plus an optional offset.

**Syntax**

```
bot.setAimObject( object [ , offset ] );
```

bot            An `AIPlayer` object.

object         A valid `ShapeBase` object name or ID.

offset         A string containing and "X Y Z" offset.

**Example Call**

```
// Aim 20 world units above bob's position
%bot.setAimObject( %bob , "0 0 20.0" );
```

**Notes**

1. Setting the aim object to an invalid object ID (such as 0) clears the aim, but until a new aim location is assigned, or until `clearAim()` is called, the bot's head will stay in the position it was in while last aiming.

2. Once an aim object is set, the bot will continue to track that object's position.

**See Also**

```
getAimLocation, getAimObject, setAimLocation
```

---
**setMoveDestination**
---

### Purpose
Use the `setMoveDestination` method to start the bot moving toward a new world position.

### Syntax
`bot.setMoveDestination( dest [ , slowDown = false ] );`

bot        An `AIPlayer` object.

dest       A three-element string containing an "X Y Z" vector, representing a world position. (Each element is a floating-point value.)

slowDown    An optional boolean value (defaults to `false`) specifying that this bot should slow down when it gets close to the move destination.

### Example Call
```
// Move to target position.
%pos = %target.getPosition()
%bot.setMoveDestination( %pos );
```

### Notes
1. `setMoveDestination` ignores the Z-value in destination vectors, so it can be left at 0.0 in all cases.

### See Also
`getMoveDestination`

---
**setMoveSpeed**
---

### Purpose
Use the `setMoveSpeed` method to adjust the overall movement speed for this bot from a speed of 0.0 (0%) to 1.0 (100%).

### Syntax
`bot.setMoveSpeed ( speed );`

bot        An AIPlayer object.

speed      A floating-point value between 0.0 and 1.0 controlling the overall speed of the bot.

### Example Call
```
// Move at 50% overall rate (in any movement direction)
%bot.setMoveSpeed( 0.5 );
```

### Notes
1. See B.4.3 for datablock parameters affecting `AIPlayer` movement rates.

---
**stop**
---

### Purpose
Use the `stop` method to cause the bot to stop moving in the direction of its current destination. Barring outside influences, the bot will slow and then come to a halt.

### Syntax
`bot.stop();`

bot        An AIPlayer object.

**Example Call**

```
%bot.stop();
```

**Notes**

1. Calling stop does not clear the move destination; it just sets an internal flag telling the bot that it is stopped.

**See Also**

```
setMoveDestination
```

# B.4.2 AIPlayer Callbacks

| Method | Description |
|---|---|
| onMoveStuck | Called when the bot has an assigned move destination, but has ceased to move (at all). |
| onReachDestination | Called when the bot reaches its last assigned move destination. |
| onTargetEnterLOS | Called when the bot has an assigned object and that object moves into line-of-sight. |
| onTargetExitLOS | Called when the bot has an assigned object and that object moves out of line-of-sight. |

## onMoveStuck

**Purpose**

Use the onMoveStuck callback to direct the bot's next action when it gets stuck while moving toward an assigned destination.

**Syntax**

```
onMoveStuck( DB , bot );
```

DB              The bot's current datablock.

bot             The bot that this callback is being called on.

**Example Call**

```
// Clear move destination if bot gets stuck
function PlayerData::onMoveStuck( %DB, %bot )
{
    %curPos = %bot.getPosition();
    %bot.setMoveDestination( %curPos );
}
```

**Notes**

1. This callback doesn't work well because any movement, even a little jitter, will cause the AIPlayer "is stuck" check to come back as `false`.

**See Also**

```
setMoveDestination
```

## onReachDestination

**Purpose**

Use the onReachDestination callback to tell a bot what to do when it has reached its last assigned destination.

**Syntax**

```
onReachDestination( DB , bot );
```

DB                  The bot's current datablock.

```
bot                 The bot that this callback is being called on.
```

**Example Call**
```
// Move to a random new location (within a limited area)
//
function PlayerData::onReachDestination( %DB, %bot )
{
   // Generate random X and Y destination values
   %X = getRandom( 0 , 20 );
   %Y = getRandom( 0 , 20 );

   // Move to this new random destination
   %bot.setMoveDestination( %X SPC %Y SPC "0.0" );
}
```

**See Also**
```
getMoveDestination, setMoveDestination, stop
```

## onTargetEnterLOS

**Purpose**
Use the onTargetEnterLOS callback to tell the bot what to do when a target object has moved (back) into the bot's line of sight (LOS).

**Syntax**
```
onTargetEnterLOS( DB , bot );
```
```
DB                  The bot's current datablock.
bot                 The bot that this callback is being called on.
```

**Example Call**
```
// Start shooting as soon as the bot sees its target
//
function PlayerData::onTargetEnterLOS( %DB, %bot )
{
   // Pull trigger on weapon in slot 0 and hold it down
   %bot.setImageTrigger( 0 , true );
}
```

**Notes**
1. LOS can be blocked by any object (or the terrain) with a valid collision- or LOS-mesh.
2. This callback is called as soon as a newly assigned target object is in LOS for the first time.
3. This callback is called once, every time LOS is reestablished.

**See Also**
```
onTargetExitLOS
```

## onTargetExitLOS

**Purpose**
Use the onTargetExitLOS callback to tell the bot what to do when a target object has moved out the bot's line-of-sight (LOS).

**Syntax**
```
onTargetExitLOS( DB , bot );
```
DB                  The bot's current datablock.

bot                The bot that this callback is being called on.

**Example Call**
```
// Stop shooting when the bot loses sight of its target
//
function PlayerData::onTargetExitLOS( %DB, %bot )
{
    // Release trigger on weapon in slot 0
    %bot.setImageTrigger( 0 , false );
}
```

**Notes**
1. LOS can be blocked by any object (or the terrain) with a valid collision- or LOS-mesh.
2. This callback is called once, every time LOS is lost.

**See Also**
```
onTargetEnterLOS
```

# B.4.3 Useful `PlayerData` Fields

| Field/Category | Description |
| --- | --- |
| **Forward and Backward Motion** | |
| maxForwardSpeed | Maximum forward velocity in world units per second. |
| maxBackwardSpeed | Maximum backward velocity in world units per second. |
| **Sideways Motion** | |
| maxSideSpeed | Maximum sideways velocity in world units per second. |
| **General Horizontal Motion** | |
| horizMaxSpeed | Maximum horizontal velocity on ground, in air, or in water. |
| horizResistFactor | Delta factor used to determine how much of horizResistspeed is removed from current velocity. |
| horizResistSpeed | Velocity at which horizontal resistance kicks in. |
| **Jumping** | |
| jumpDelay | Forced delay between jumps (in ticks). |
| jumpForce | Force applied to player on jump. Should be less than 40,000 * mass. |
| jumpEnergyDrain | Drain this many energy points for every jump. |
| jumpSurfaceAngle | Cannot jump if surface angle is equal to or greater than this many degrees. |
| maxJumpSpeed | Cannot jump if running faster than this. |
| minJumpEnergy | If the player's current energy is below this value, jumping is disabled. |
| minJumpSpeed | A minimum velocity below which jumping is disabled. |
| **Running** | |
| runForce | Accelerate player by this much per tick as a result of a move (command). Should be less than 40,000 * mass. |
| runSurfaceAngle | Cannot accelerate if surface angle equal to or greater to this many degrees. |
| **Upward Motion** | |
| upMaxSpeed | Maximum velocity allowed in the positive *z* direction. |

| Field/Category | Description |
|---|---|
| upResistFactor | Delta factor used to determine how much of upResistSpeed is removed from current velocity. |
| upResistSpeed | Velocity at which vertical resistance kicks in. |
| **Underwater Motion** | |
| maxUnderwaterForwardSpeed | Maximum underwater forward velocity in world units per second. |
| maxUnderwaterBackwardSpeed | Maximum underwater backward velocity in world units per second. |
| maxUnderwaterSideSpeed | Maximum underwater sideway velocity in world units per second. |

# B.4.4 `AIWheeledVehicle` Methods

| Method | Description |
|---|---|
| getMoveDestination | Get the current move destination. |
| setMoveDestination | Set a new move destination. |
| setMoveSpeed | Set move speed between 0% and 100%. |
| setMoveTolerance | Set move tolerance between 0.0 and infinity. |
| stop | Stop moving. |

### getMoveDestination

**Purpose**
Use the `getMoveDestination` method to get the wheeledbot's current move destination.

**Syntax**
```
dest = wheeledbot.getMoveDestination();
```
| dest | A string containing an "X Y Z" world-position representing the wheeledbot's last assigned move destination. |
|---|---|
| wheeledbot | An `AIWheeledVehicle` object. |

**Example Call**
```
// Get the wheeledbot's current move destination
%moveDest = %wheeledbot.getMoveDestination();
```

**Notes**
1. If a move destination has not been assigned to this wheeledbot, this method returns "0 0 0".

**See Also**
`setMoveDestination`

### setMoveDestination

**Purpose**
Use the `setMoveDestination` method to start the wheeledbot moving toward a new world position.

**Syntax**
```
wheeledbot.setMoveDestination( dest [ , slowDown = false ] );
```
| wheeledbot | An `AIWheeledVehicle` object. |
|---|---|
| dest | A three-element string containing an "X Y Z" vector, representing a world-position. (Each element is a floating point value.) |

slowDown        An optional boolean value (defaults to `false`) specifying that this wheeledbot should slow down when it gets close to the move destination.

**Example Call**
```
// Move to target position.
%pos = %target.getPosition()
%wheeledbot.setMoveDestination( %pos );
```

**Notes**
1. `setMoveDestination` ignores the Z-value in destination vectors, so it can be left at 0.0 in all cases.

**See Also**
```
getMoveDestination
```

---

## setMoveSpeed

**Purpose**
Use the `setMoveSpeed` method to adjust the overall movement speed for this `wheeledbot` from a speed of 0.0 (0%) to 1.0 (100%).

**Syntax**
```
wheeledbot.setMoveSpeed ( speed );
```
wheeledbot        An `AIWheeledVehicle` object.

speed        A floating-point value between 0.0 and 1.0 controlling the overall speed of the `wheeledbot`.

**Example Call**
```
// Move at 50% overall rate (in any movement direction)
%wheeledbot.setMoveSpeed( 0.5 );
```

**Notes**
1. See appendix sections B.4.6 through B.4.9 for datablock parameters that affect wheeled vehicle movement rates.

---

## setMoveTolerance

**Purpose**
Use the `setMoveTolerance` method to tell this wheeledbot how close it has to be to its move destination before calling the `onReachDestination()` callback.

**Syntax**
```
wheeledbot.setMoveTolerance( tolerance );
```
wheeledbot        An `AIWheeledVehicle` object.

tolerance        A floating point value in the range [ 0.0 , infinity ).

**Example Call**
```
// Fire onReachDestination() callback as soon as wheeledbot is within
// 5.0 world units of destination
setMoveTolerance( 5.0 );
```

**See Also**
```
getMoveDestination, setMoveDestination
```

---

## stop

### Purpose
Use the `stop` method to cause the wheeledbot to stop moving in the direction of its current destination. Barring outside influences, the wheeledbot will slow and then come to a halt.

### Syntax
```
wheeledbot.stop();
```
wheeledbot         An `AIWheeledVehicle` object.

### Example Call
```
%wheeledbot.stop();
```

### Notes
1. Calling stop does not clear the move destination; it just sets an internal flag telling the wheeledbot that it is stopped.

### See Also
`setMoveDestination`

# B.4.5 AIWheeledVehicle Callbacks

| Method | Description |
|---|---|
| onMoveStuck | Called when the wheeledbot has an assigned move destination, but has ceased to move (at all). |
| onReachDestination | Called when the wheeledbot reaches its last assigned move destination. |

---

## onMoveStuck

### Purpose
Use the `onMoveStuck` callback to tell the wheeledbot what to do when it gets stuck while moving toward an assigned destination.

### Syntax
```
onMoveStuck( DB , wheeledbot );
```
DB         The wheeledbot's current datablock.
wheeledbot         The wheeledbot that this callback is being called on.

### Example Call
```
// Clear move destination if wheeledbot gets stuck
function AIWheeledVehicle::onMoveStuck( %DB, %wheeledbot )
{
    %curPos = %wheeledbot.getPosition();
    %wheeledbot.setMoveDestination( %curPos );
}
```

### Notes
1. This callback doesn't work well because any movement, even a little jitter, will cause the `AIWheeledVehicle` "is stuck" check to come back as `false`.

### See Also
`setMoveDestination`

## onReachDestination

**Purpose**

Use the `onReachDestination` callback to tell the wheeledbot what to do when it has reached its last assigned destination.

**Syntax**

```
onReachDestination( DB , wheeledbot );
```

| | |
|---|---|
| `DB` | The wheeledbot's current datablock. |
| `wheeledbot` | The wheeledbot that this callback is being called on. |

**Example Call**

```
// Move to a random new location (within a limited area)
//
function AIWheeledVehicle::onReachDestination( %DB, %wheeledbot )
{
   // Generate random X and Y destination values
   %X = getRandom( 0 , 20 );
   %Y = getRandom( 0 , 20 );

   // Move to this new random destination
   %wheeledbot.setMoveDestination( %X SPC %Y SPC "0.0" );
}
```

**See Also**

`getMoveDestination, setMoveDestination, stop`

# B.4.6 Useful Movement/Physics `VehicleData` Fields

| Method | Description |
|---|---|
| `massCenter` | The vehicle's rigid body center of mass. |
| `maxSteeringAngle` | Maximum attainable steering angle, measured in radians. Steering angles are restricted to values between 0.0 and this angle. |
| `mass` | The vehicle's mass. |

# B.4.7 Useful Movement/Physics `WheeledVehicleData` Fields

| Method | Description |
|---|---|
| `engineBrake` | Floating-point value specifying how much the engine brakes when the engine is not engaged. |
| `engineTorque` | Floating-point value specifying the power of the engine. |

# B.4.8 Useful `WheeledVehicleSpring` Fields

| Method | Description |
|---|---|
| `antiSwayForce` | Force that acts to dampen lateral sway introduced when wheels opposite each other are extended at different lengths. |
| `damping` | Dampening force that counteracts the spring's force. |
| `force` | The force of the spring. Spring forces act straight up and are applied at the spring's root position, which is defined in the vehicle's shape. |

| Method | Description |
|---|---|
| length | The length of suspension travel from the root position. |

## B.4.9 Useful WheeledVehicleTire Fields

| Method | Description |
|---|---|
| kineticFriction | A floating-point value used in the physical simulation to represent the tire's surface friction when it is slipping. Affects steering, acceleration, and braking. |
| lateralDamping | A floating-point value used to dampen lateral tire forces. |
| lateralForce | A floating-point value determining left-right tire force/friction. Affects steering. |
| lateralRelaxation | A floating-point value used to relax lateral tire forces. |
| logitudinalRelaxation (misspelled in engine) | Measures the relaxing force applied against longitudinal forces generated by the tire. |
| longitudinalDamping | A floating-point value used to dampen longitudinal tire forces. |
| longitudinalForce | A floating-point value determining forward-backward tire force/friction. Affects acceleration and braking. |
| staticFriction | A floating-point value used in the physical simulation to represent the tire's surface friction when it is not slipping. Affects steering, acceleration, and braking. |

## B.4.10 AIConnection Methods

Please note that AIConnection is a grandchild of GameConnection, so you can refer to the GameConnection section for additional methods and callbacks that will also be associated with this class.

| Method | Description |
|---|---|
| getFreeLook | Check whether this connection is currently in free-look mode. |
| getMove | Get the value of a specified move parameter. |
| getTrigger | Get the value of a specified trigger number. |
| setFreeLook | Set this connection's free-look mode. |
| setMove | Set the value of a specified move parameter. |
| setTrigger | Set the value of a specified trigger number. |

### getFreeLook

**Purpose**

Use the getFreeLook method to check whether the current connection is in free-look mode.

**Syntax**

```
isFreeLook = con.getFreeLook();
```

| isFreeLook | A boolean value, set to true if the connection is in free look mode, and false otherwise. |
|---|---|
| con | A server connection. |

**Example Call**

```
// Check whether connection is in free-look mode
%isFreeLook = %conn.getFreeLook();
if( %isFreeLook )
    echo("In free-look mode");
else
    echo("Not in free-look mode");
```

**See Also**
setFreeLook

---

## getMove

**Purpose**
Use the getMove method to get the move setting for a specified move type

**Syntax**
setting = con.getMove( field   );

setting   A floating-point value within an acceptable range for the specified move type.

con       A server connection.

field     A string containing a move type.

**Move Types and Ranges**
x — Translation input in X-plane, with range [ -1.0 , 1.0 ].
y — Translation input in Y-plane, with range [ -1.0 , 1.0 ]
z — Translation input in Z-plane, with range [ -1.0 , 1.0 ]
yaw — Rotation input about Z-axis, with range [ -pi , pi ]
pitch — Rotation input about X-axis, with range [ -pi , pi ]
roll — Rotation input about Y-axis, with range [ -pi , pi ]

**Example Call**
```
// Check the current yaw setting
%yaw = con.getMove( "yaw" );
echo("Current yaw setting is: ", %yaw;
```

**See Also**
getTrigger, setMove, setTrigger

---

## getTrigger

**Purpose**
Use the getTrigger method to get the current value for specified trigger.

**Syntax**
trigger = con.getTrigger( triggerNum );

trigger        A boolean value representing the state of the specified trigger.

con            A server connection.

triggerNum     An integer value between 0 and 6 specifying the trigger to check.

**Example Call**
```
// See if the connection's (Player) is jumping
%jumping  = %conn.getTrigger( 2 );
if( % jumping )
   echo("Connection controlled player object is jumping");
else
   echo("Connection controlled player object is not jumping");
```

**See Also**
getMove, setMove, setTrigger

## setFreeLook

### Purpose
Use the `setFreeLook` method to set the current connection to free-look mode.

### Syntax
`con.setFreeLook( isFreeLook );`

con                         A server connection.

isFreeLook                  A boolean value. If `true`, free-look will be enabled; otherwise it will be disabled.

### Example Call
```
// Stop free-looking
%conn.setFreeLook ( false );
```

### See Also
`getFreeLook`

## setMove

### Purpose
Use the `setMove` method to set a move type for the control object connected to this `AIConnection`.

### Syntax
`con.setMove( field , value );`

con                 A server connection.

field               A string containing a move type.

value               A floating-point value within an acceptable range for the specified move type.

### Move Types and Ranges
x — Translation input in X-plane, with range [ -1.0 , 1.0 ].
y — Translation input in Y-plane, with range [ -1.0 , 1.0 ]
z — Translation input in Z-plane, with range [ -1.0 , 1.0 ]
yaw — Rotation input about Z-axis, with range [ -pi , pi ]
pitch — Rotation input about X-axis, with range [ -pi , pi ]
roll — Rotation input about Y-axis, with range [ -pi , pi ]

### Example Call
```
// Move forward at full-speed
%conn.setMove( "y" , 1.0 );
```

### See Also
`getMove, getTrigger, setTrigger`

## setTrigger

### Purpose
Use the `setTrigger` method to set or clear a trigger in the current control object for this connection.

### Syntax
`con.setTrigger( trigger , set );`

con                 A server connection.

trigger             An integer value between 0 and 6 representing on of the seven triggers.

set                    A boolean value. If `true`, this trigger is enabled/set/depressed; otherwise, it is disabled/unset/released.

**Example Call**
```
// Make the connection's control object jump (if it is a player)
%conn.setTrigger( 2 , true );
```

**See Also**
getMove, getTrigger, setMove

# B.5 Container and Raycasting

## B.5.1 Container and Raycasting Functions

### Listed Alphabetically

| Function | Description |
|---|---|
| containerBoxEmpty | Checks for absence of objects matching a specified type mask within the bounds of a variable-sized cube. |
| containerFindFirst | Initializes search query for a bounding cube search and returns first object found matching type mask. |
| containerFindNext | Returns next object found in search started with containerFindFirst. |
| containerRayCast | Checks for the presence of an object matching a specified type mask along a ray cast between a given starting position and ending position. |
| containerSearchCurrDist | Returns a value for the last object found using containerSearchNext, equal to the distance between the center of that object and the center of the current search area. |
| containerSearchCurrRadiusDist | Returns a value for the last object found using containerSearchNext, equal to the distance between the center of the current search area and the nearest point on that object. |
| containerSearchNext | Returns the ID of the next object in the search container of objects found by the last call to initContainerRadiusSearch. |
| initContainerRadiusSearch | Initiates a bounding-sphere (radius) search for all objects matching a specified type mask within a given radius of a specified world position. |

### Listed by Task

| Task | Function(s) |
|---|---|
| Cast a ray between two points and find the first object matching a specified type mask. | containerRayCast |
| Determine whether area in the game world enclosed by a bounding cube is empty of any objects matching a specific type mask. | containerBoxEmpty |
| Find all objects in the game world matching a particular type mask within a bounding cube. | containerFindFirst, containerFindNext |
| Find all objects in the game world matching a particular type mask within a bounding sphere. | containerSearchCurrDist, containerSearchCurrRadiusDist, containerSearchNext, initContainerRadiusSearch |

---

## containerBoxEmpty

---

### Purpose

Use the `containerBoxEmpty` function to determine whether a cubic area in the world is empty of any and all objects matching a specified type.

### Syntax

```
isEmpty = containerBoxEmpty( mask , center , xRadius [ , yRadius , zRadius ] );
```

| | |
|---|---|
| `isEmpty` | A boolean value specifying whether the tested box was empty (`true`) or not empty (`false`). |
| `mask` | An integer value specifying a type mask. Any objects matching this mask will be found if they are inside the search box. |
| `center` | A string specifying the center of the search area. |
| `xRadius` | A floating-point value specifying the X-radius of the box. |
| `yRadius` | An optional floating-point value specifying the Y-radius of the box. If not specified, this value is assumed to be equal to xRadius. |
| `zRadius` | An optional floating-point value specifying the Z-radius of the box. If not specified, this value is assumed to be equal to xRadius. |

### Example Call

```
// See if there are any vehicles within 20 world units of this player.
%pos = %player.getWorldBoxCenter();
%found = containerBoxEmpty( $TypeMasks::VehicleObjectType , %pos , 20.0 );
if(%found)
   echo("Found a vehicle near the player!");
else
   echo("No vehicles found near the player!");
```

---

## containerFindFirst

---

### Purpose

Use the `containerFindFirst` function to initialize a cube search for objects matching a specified type mask. This function returns the first object in the search container created by this search.

### Syntax

```
object = containerFindFirst( mask , location, xRadius , yRadius , zRadius );
```

| | |
|---|---|
| `object` | An integer value representing the ID of the first object found by this search, or 0 if no objects were found. |
| `mask` | An integer value specifying a type mask. Any objects matching this mask will be found if they are inside the search cube. |
| `location` | A string specifying the center of the search area. |
| `xRadius` | A floating-point value specifying the X-radius of the search cube. |
| `yRadius` | A floating-point value specifying the Y-radius of the search cube. |
| `zRadius` | A floating-point value specifying the Z-radius of the search cube. |

### Example Call

```
// Find all vehicles in a flattened cubic area around the player.
%pos = %player.getWorldBoxCenter();

// Find the first vehicle
%obj = containerFindFirst( $TypeMasks::VehicleObjectType ,
                           %pos , 20.0 , 20.0 , 0.0);
while( isObject( %obj ) )
```

```
{
   %objPos = %obj.getPosition();
   echo("Found vehicle at position: ", %objPos );

   // Find the next vehicle
   %obj = containerFindNext();
}
```

**See Also**
containerBoxEmpty, containerFindNext, containerSearchCurrDist, containerSearchCurrRadiusDist

---

## containerFindNext

### Purpose
Use the containerFindNext function to get the next object in the search container created by the last call to containerFindFirst.

### Syntax
object = containerFindNext();

object     An integer value representing the ID of the next object in the search container, or 0 if no objects are left in the container.

### Example Call
```
// Find all vehicles in a flattened cubic area around the player.
%pos = %player.getWorldBoxCenter();

// Find the first vehicle
%obj = containerFindFirst( $TypeMasks::VehicleObjectType ,
                           %pos , 20.0 , 20.0 , 0.0);
while( isObject( %obj ) )
{
   %objPos = %obj.getPosition();
   echo("Found vehicle at position: ", %objPos );

   // Find the next vehicle
   %obj = containerFindNext();
}
```

### See Also
containerBoxEmpty, containerFindFirst, containerSearchCurrDist, containerSearchCurrRadiusDist

---

## containerRayCast

### Purpose
Use the containerRayCast function to see whether an object matching the specified mask type is positioned along a ray starting at startPos and ending at endPos. One object may (optionally) be marked for exemption during this search.

### Syntax
object = containerRayCast( startPos , endPos , mask [ , exempt ] );

object          An integer value representing the ID of the nearest object found along the ray.

startPos       A string containing an "X Y Z" position to start the raycast at.

endPos              A string containing an "X Y Z" position to end the raycast at.

mask                An integer type mask used to specify which object type(s) to find.

exempt              An optional object ID for a single object that will be exempted during the raycast.

### Example Call
```
// Search for all objects within 10 world units of the front of the player
%start = %player.getWorldBoxCenter();
%direction = %player.getForwardVector();
%end = vectorScale( %direction, 10 );
%end = vectorAdd( %start , %end );
%hit = containerRayCast( %start , %end , -1 , %player );
```

### See Also
ContainerBoxEmpty, containerFindFirst, containerFindNext

---

## containerSearchCurrDist

### Purpose
Use the containerSearchCurrDist function to get the distance between the last retrieved search object's center and the center of the search area.

### Syntax
```
distance = containerSearchCurrDist();
```

distance    A floating-point value representing the distance from the last retrieved search object and the center of the search area. If there is no valid search object, this will be set to 0.0.

### Example Call
```
// Determine how far away the last search object was from the center
// of the search area.
%distance = containerSearchCurrDist();
```

### See Also
containerFindFirst, containerFindNext, containerSearchCurrRadiusDist, containerSearchNext, initContainerRadiusSearch

---

## containerSearchCurrRadiusDist

### Purpose
Use the containerSearchCurrRadiusDist function to get the distance between the search center and a point on the last retrieved search object's collision mesh, where that point represents the closest point on the collision mesh to the search area center (as specified in the last call to initContainerRadiusSearch).

### Syntax
```
distance = containerSearchCurrRadiusDist();
```

distance    A floating-point value representing the distance between the center of the last search area and a point on the last retrieved search object. The point, in this case, is the nearest point on the objects collision mesh to the center of the search area.

### Example Call
```
// Find nearest-point (to center of search) area on last retrieved search object
%distance = containerSearchCurrRadiusDist();
```

**See Also**
containerFindFirst, containerFindNext, containerSearchCurrDist, containerSearchNext, initContainerRadiusSearch

---

## containerSearchNext

**Purpose**
Use the containerSearchNext function to find the next object in the current search container as defined by the last call to initContainerRadiusSearch.

**Syntax**
```
object = containerSearchNext();
```

object    An integer value representing the ID of the next object in the search container, or 0 if no objects are left in the container.

**Example Call**
```
// Find all TSStatic objects within 15 world units of the player.
%pos = %player.getWorldBoxCenter();
initContainerRadiusSearch( %pos , 15 , $TypeMasks:StaticObjectType );

while( isObject( %curObject = containerSearchNext() ) )
{
   // Do something with the object %curObject
}
```

**See Also**
containerSearchCurrDist, containerSearchCurrRadiusDist, initContainerRadiusSearch

---

## initContainerRadiusSearch

**Purpose**
Use the initContainerRadiusSearch function to find all objects matching a specified mask within a specified sphere.

**Syntax**
```
initContainerRadiusSearch( centerPos , radius , mask );
```

centerPos    A string containing the "X Y Z" position that represents the center of the search sphere.
radius       A floating-point value representing the center of the search sphere.
mask         An integer type mask specifying the kinds of objects to match.

**Example Call**
```
// Find all TSStatic objects within 15 world units of the player.
%pos = %player.getWorldBoxCenter();
initContainerRadiusSearch( %pos , 15 , $TypeMasks:StaticObjectType );

while( isObject( %curObject = containerSearchNext() ) )
{
   // Do something with the object %curObject
}
```

**Returns**
No return value.

**Notes**

1. This search is static. That is, it will find all objects within the specified radius and then the found objects can be retrieved with ContainerSearchNext. To find new objects, you will have to reinitialize the search.

**See Also**

containerSearchCurrDist, containerSearchCurrRadiusDist, containerSearchNext

# B.5.2 Type Masks

| Mask | Matches Object Types (Classes) |
|---|---|
| $TypeMasks::CameraObjectType | Camera |
| $TypeMasks::CorpseObjectType | (Dead) Player<br>See Note 1 below. |
| $TypeMasks::DamagableObjectType | Any object initialized (in C++) as being damagable |
| $TypeMasks::DebrisObjectType | Debris |
| $TypeMasks::EnvironmentObjectType | Lightning, ParticleEmitter, Sky, Sun |
| $TypeMasks::ExplosionObjectType | Explosion |
| $TypeMasks::GameBaseObjectType | GameBase (and children) |
| $TypeMasks::InteriorObjectType | InteriorInstance |
| $TypeMasks::ItemObjectType | Item |
| $TypeMasks::MarkerObjectType | Marker |
| $TypeMasks::PhysicalZoneObjectType | PhysicalZone |
| $TypeMasks::PlayerObjectType | Player and AIPlayer |
| $TypeMasks::ProjectileObjectType | Projectile |
| $TypeMasks::ShapeBaseObjectType | ShapeBase (and children) |
| $TypeMasks::StaticObjectType | StaticObject |
| $TypeMasks::StaticRenderedObjectType | fxFoliageReplicator, fxLight, fxRenderObject, fxShapeReplicator, fxSunLight, InteriorInstance, sgDecalProjector, Terrain, TSStatic, volLight |
| $TypeMasks::StaticShapeObjectType | StaticShape |
| $TypeMasks::StaticTSObjectType | FlyingVehicle, fxFoliageReplicator, fxLight, fxRenderObject, fxShapeReplicator, fxSunLight, HoverVehicle, Item, Precipitation, sgDecalProjector, sgMissionLight, TSStatic, volLight, WheeledVehicle |
| $TypeMasks::TerrainObjectType | Terrain |
| $TypeMasks::TriggerObjectType | Trigger |
| $TypeMasks::VehicleObjectType | FlyingVehicle, HoverVehicle, WheeledVehicle |
| $TypeMasks::VehicleBlockerObjectType | VehicleBlocker |
| $TypeMasks::WaterObjectType | WaterBlock |

Note 1: A Player object is automatically marked as dead by the engine if its current damage is greater than or equal to its maximum damage.

## B.6 Basic Engine Coding

## B.6.1 Torque Data Types

Below you will find a comparative list of Torque data types, ANSI-C types, and `fieldTypes`. This list is provided to help you with a couple different programming problems.

First, for general coding, you should use a Torque type instead of an ANSI-C type.

Second, when you register globals and class members with the console, it is necessary to specify a fieldType. The following list includes all known fieldTypes and correlates them to the type of data they are meant to help register. Please note, if you find yourself needing to register a non-class data type with no matching fieldType, you may use any fieldType with a matching bit width. For example, a U32 has no matching fieldType, but can be registered using the TypeS32 fieldType.

| Torque Data Type | ANSI-C Type | fieldType |
|---|---|---|
| BitSet32 | n/a | TypeFlag |
| Box3F | n/a | TypeBox3F |
| ColorF | n/a | TypeColorF |
| ColorI | n/a | TypeColorI |
| F32 | float | TypeF32 |
| Vector <F32> | Vector <float> | TypeF32Vector |
| F64 | double | n/a |
| GuiControlProfile | n/a | TypeGuiProfile |
| MatrixF | n/a | TypeMatrixRotation (just the AngAxisF part) |
| MatrixF | n/a | TypeMatrixPosition (just the position part) |
| n/a | char * (SimObject name) | TypeSimObjectName |
| n/a | enum | TypeEnum (see EnumTable class) |
| n/a | Vector <bool> | TypeBoolVector |
| n/a | bool | TypeBool |
| Point2F | n/a | TypePoint2F |
| Point2I | n/a | TypePoint2I |
| Point3F | n/a | TypePoint3F |
| Point4F | n/a | TypePoint4F |
| Polyhedron | n/a | TypeTriggerPolyhedron |
| RectF | n/a | TypeRectF |
| RectI | n/a | TypeRectI |
| S16 | signed short | n/a |
| S32 | signed int | TypeS32 |
| Vector <S32> | Vector <signed int> | TypeS32Vector |
| S8 | signed char | TypeS8 |
| SimObject* | n/a | TypeSimObjectPtr |
| StringTableEntry | const char * | TypeString |
| StringTableEntry | const char * | TypeFilename |
| StringTableEntry | const char * | TypeCaseString |

| Torque Data Type | ANSI-C Type | fieldType |
|---|---|---|
| U16 | `unsigned short` | n/a |
| U32 | `unsigned int` or `unsigned long` | `(use TypeS32)` |
| U8 | `unsigned char` | `(use TypeS8)` |
| UTF16 | `unsigned short` | n/a |
| UTF32 | `unsigned int` | `(use TypeS32)` |
| UTF8 | `char` | `(use TypeS8)` |
| WayPointTeam | n/a | `TypeWayPointTeam` |

## B.6.2 Torque Standard Library

Below you will find a list of ANSI-C functions and their corresponding Torque Standard Library functions. Please be aware that some ANSI-C functions have multiple specialized Torque Standard Library variants.

| ANSI-C Function | Torque Standard Library Function |
|---|---|
| `atob` | `bool dAtob(const char *str)` |
| `atof` | `float dAtof(const char *str)` |
| `atoi` | `int dAtoi(const char *str)` |
| `fflush(stderr)` | `int dFflushStderr()` |
| `fflush(stdout)` | `int dFflushStdout()` |
| `free` | `void dRealFree(void* p)` |
| `isalnum` | `bool dIsalnum(const char c)` |
| `isalpha` | `bool dIsalpha(const char c)` |
| `isdigit` | `bool dIsdigit(const char c)` |
| `isspace` | `bool dIsspace(const char c)` |
| `malloc` | `void* dMalloc(int_size)` |
| `malloc` | `void* dRealMalloc(dsize_t s)` |
| `memcmp` | `S32 dMemcmp(const void *ptr1, const void *ptr2, unsigned len)` |
| `memcpy` | `void* dMemcpy(void *dst, const void *src, unsigned size)` |
| `memmove` | `void* dMemmove(void *dst, const void *src, unsigned size)` |
| `memset` | `void* dMemset(void *dst, S32 c, unsigned size)` |
| `printf` | `void dPrintf(const char *format, ...)` |
| `sprintf` | `int dSprintf(char *buffer, dsize_t bufferSize, const char *format, ...)` |
| `sscanf` | `int dSscanf(const char *buffer, const char *format, ...)` |
| `strcat` | `char* dStrcat(char *dst, const char *src)` |
| `strcat` | `char* dStrcatl(char *dst, dsize_t dstSize, ...)` |
| `strcat` | `UTF8* dStrcat(UTF8 *dst, const UTF8 *src)` |
| `strchr` | `char* dStrchr(char *str, int c)` |
| `strchr` | `char* dStrrchr(char *str, int c)` |
| `strchr` | `const char* dStrchr(const char *str, int c)` |
| `strcmp` | `int dStrcmp(const char *str1, const char *str2)` |
| `strcmp` | `int dStrcmp(const UTF16 *str1, const UTF16 *str2)` |
| `strcmp` | `int dStrcmp(const UTF8 *str1, const UTF8 *str2)` |
| `strcpy` | `char* dStrcpy(char *dst, const char *src)` |
| `strcpy` | `char* dStrcpyl(char *dst, dsize_t dstSize, ...)` |
| `strcspn` | `dsize_t dStrcspn(const char *str, const char *set)` |
| `stricmp` | `int dStricmp(const char *str1, const char *str2)` |
| `strlen` | `dsize_t dStrlen(const char *str)` |
| `strlwr` | `char* dStrlwr(char *str)` |

| ANSI-C Function | Torque Standard Library Function |
|---|---|
| strncat | char* dStrncat(char* dst, const char* src, dsize_t len) |
| strncmp | int dStrncmp(const char *str1, const char *str2, dsize_t len) |
| strncpy | char* dStrncpy(char *dst, const char *src, dsize_t len) |
| strncpy | char* dStrncpy(UTF8 *dst, const UTF8 *src, dsize_t len) |
| strnicmp | int dStrnicmp(const char *str1, const char *str2, dsize_t len) |
| strrchr | const char* dStrrchr(const char *str, int c) |
| strspn | dsize_t dStrspn(const char *str, const char *set) |
| strstr | char* dStrstr(char *str1, char *str2) |
| strstr | char* dStrstr(const char *str1, const char *str2) |
| strtok | char* dStrtok(char *str, const char *sep) |
| strupr | char* dStrupr(char *str) |
| tolower | char dTolower(const char c) |
| toupper | char dToupper(const char c) |
| vprintf | int dVprintf(const char *format, void *arglist) |
| vsprintf | int dVsprintf(char *buffer, dsize_t bufferSize, const char *format, void *arglist) |

# B.6.3 Torque Math Library

Below you will find a list of ANSI-C math functions and their corresponding Torque Math Library functions. Please be aware that some ANSI-C functions have multiple specialized Torque Standard Library variants.

To access any of these functions, simply include "math/mMath.h" in your code.

| ANSI-C Function | Torque Math Library Function |
|---|---|
| abs | S32 mAbs(const S32 val) |
| acos | F32 mAcos(const F32 val) |
| acos | F64 mAcos(const F64 val) |
| asin | F32 mAsin(const F32 val) |
| asin | F64 mAsin(const F64 val) |
| atan | F32 mAtan(const F32 x, const F32 y) |
| atan | F64 mAtan(const F64 x, const F64 y) |
| ceil | F32 mCeil(const F32 val) |
| ceil | F64 mCeilD(const F64 val) |
| cos | F32 mCos(const F32 angle) |
| cos | F64 mCos(const F64 angle) |
| fabs | F32 mFabs(const F32 val) |
| fabs | F64 mFabs(const F64 val) |
| fabs | F64 mFabsD(const F64 val) |
| floor | F32 mFloor(const F32 val) |
| floor | F64 mFloorD(const F64 val) |
| fmod | F32 mFmod(const F32 val, const F32 mod) |
| fmod | F64 mFmodD(const F64 val, const F64 mod) |
| log | F32 mLog(const F32 val) |
| log | F64 mLog(const F64 val) |
| pow | F32 mPow(const F32 x, const F32 y) |
| pow | F64 mPow(const F64 x, const F64 y) |
| sin | F32 mSin(const F32 angle) |
| sin | F64 mSin(const F64 angle) |
| sincos | void mSinCos(const F32 angle, F32 &s, F32 &c) |

| ANSI-C Function | Torque Math Library Function |
|---|---|
| sincos | void mSinCos(const F64 angle, F64 &sin, F64 &cos) |
| sqrt | F32 mSqrt(const F32 val) |
| sqrtd | F64 mSqrtD(const F64 val) |
| tan | F32 mTan(const F32 angle) |
| tan | F64 mTan(const F64 angle) |
| tanh | F32 mTanh(const F32 angle) |
| tanh | F64 mTanh(const F64 angle) |

The following is a short list of additional utility math functions provided by Torque.
To access any of these functions, simply include "math/mMath.h" in your code.

| Torque Math Library Utility Function | Action |
|---|---|
| S32 mClamp(S32 val, S32 low, S32 high); | val clamped to [low,high] |
| F32 mClampF(F32 val, F32 low, F32 high); | val clamped to [low,high] |
| void mCross(const F64* a, const F64* b, F64* res) | res = a X b |
| void mCross(const F32* a, const F32* b, F32 *res) | res = a X b |
| Point3F mCross(const Point3F &a, const Point3F &b) | a X b |
| void mCross(const Point3D &a, const Point3D &b, Point3D *res) | res = a X b |
| void mCross(const Point3F &a, const Point3F &b, Point3F *res) | res = a X b |
| F64 mDegToRad(F64 d) | d * pi/180.0 |
| F32 mDegToRad(F32 d) | d * pi/180.0 |
| F64 mDot(const Point3D &p1, const Point3D &p2) | p1 . p2 |
| F32 mDot(const Point3F &p1, const Point3F &p2) | p1 . p2 |
| S32 mMulDiv(S32 a, S32 b, S32 c); | (a * b) / c |
| U32 mMulDiv(S32 a, S32 b, U32 c); | (a * b) / c |
| F64 mRadToDeg(F64 r) | r * 180.0/pi |
| F32 mRadToDeg(F32 r) | r * 180.0/pi |

## B.6.4 StringTable Methods

| Method | Description |
|---|---|
| hashstring | Hash string into U32. |
| hashstringn | Hash string of given length into U32. |
| insert | Insert new entry into string table, optionally testing for case. |
| insertn | Insert new entry of given length into string table, optionally testing for case. |
| lookup | Search for entry in string table, optionally testing for case. |
| lookupn | Search for entry of given length in string table, optionally testing for case. |

**hashstring, hashstringn**

**Purpose**
Use these methods to build a (U32) hash value based on the contents of a string. The second variant of this method can truncate the string to a specified length.

**Syntax**
```
#include "core/StringTable.h"
static U32 hashString(const char* in_pString);
static U32 hashStringn(const char *in_pString, S32 len);
```

```
const char *in_pString
```
A pointer to a character string specifying the string for which to calculate a hash value.
```
S32 len
```
A signed integer specifying the maximum length of in_pString. Strings longer than this will be truncated.

**Example Call**
```
// Generate a hash for the string "hello world"
U32 helloHash = StringTable->hashString( "hello world");
```
**Returns**
Returns a U32 value equivalent to a hash of the specified string.

---

## insert, insertn

**Purpose**
Use these methods to insert a new entry into the string table. Both variants provide a case-sensitive comparison option, and the second variant of this method can truncate the string to a specified length.

**Syntax**
```
#include "core/StringTable.h"
StringTableEntry insert(const char *string, bool caseSens = false);
StringTableEntry insertn(const char *string, S32 len, bool caseSens = false);
```
```
const char *string
```
A pointer to a character string specifying the string to be inserted.
```
bool caseSens
```
An optional boolean specifying whether to use case-sensitive comparison.
```
S32 len
```
A signed integer specifying the maximum length of string. Strings longer than this will be truncated.

**Example Call**
```
// Add the entry "hello world" into the string table, ignoring case
StringTable->insert( "hello world" );
```
**Returns**
Returns a const char * containing the new entry.

---

## lookup, lookupn

**Purpose**
Use these methods to find an entry in the string table. Both variants provide a case-sensitive comparison option, and the second variant of this method can truncate the string to a specified length.

**Syntax**
```
#include "core/StringTable.h"
StringTableEntry lookup(const char *string, bool caseSens = false);
StringTableEntry lookupn(const char *string, S32 len, bool caseSens = false);
```
```
const char *string
```
A pointer to a character string specifying the string to be found.
```
bool caseSens
```
An optional boolean specifying whether to use case-sensitive comparison.
```
S32 len
```
A signed integer specifying the maximum length of string. Strings longer than this will be truncated.

**Example Call**
```
// Find an entry in the string table matching "heLLo WorLD" (ignore case)
StringTableEntry hello = StringTable->lookup( "heLLo WorLD" );
```

**Returns**
Returns a const char * containing the entry, or NULL.

# B.7 Game Class Coding

## B.7.1 Con Namespace Macros

| Macro | Description |
|---|---|
| ConsoleFunction | Used to create new console functions using C++. |
| ConsoleMethod | Used to create new console methods using C++. |
| ConsoleStaticMethod | Used to create new static console methods using C++. |

### ConsoleFunction

**Purpose**
Use the ConsoleFunction macro to create and expose new console functions using C++.

**Syntax**
```
#include "console/console.h"
ConsoleFunction(name, returnType, minArgs, maxArgs, usage1)
```

| name | An unquoted string containing the name of the new console function to create. |
|---|---|
| returnType | The return type for this new console function. |
| minArgs | The minimum number of arguments this function will take. May be any value 1 or greater. |
| maxArgs | The maximum number of arguments this function will take. If set to 0, this function can accept an infinite number of arguments; otherwise it should be set to minArgs or greater. |
| usage1 | A quoted string (const char *) containing a short description of the function and its usage. The null-string ("") is acceptable. |

**Example Call**
```
// Create a string comparison function in the console.
//
ConsoleFunction( strcmp, S32, 3, 3,
                 "strcmp(string1, string2) - Case-sensitive string compare." )
{
   return dStrcmp( argv[1], argv[2] );
}
```

**Notes**
1. This macro creates a declaration header; you must supply the body that follows it.
2. This macro supplies two variables to the body code that you place after it (listed in the following table).

| Automatic Variables | |
|---|---|
| S32 argc | A signed integer specifying the count of the arguments being passed to this method. |
| const char **argv | A pointer to a character string containing an array of const char * arguments. |

## `ConsoleMethod`

### Purpose
Use the `ConsoleMethod` macro to create and expose new console methods using C++.

### Syntax
```
#include "console/console.h"
ConsoleMethod(className, name, returnType, minArgs, maxArgs, usage1)
```

| | |
|---|---|
| `className` | An unquoted string containing the name of the C++ class this method is associated with. |
| `name` | An unquoted string containing the name of the new console method to create. |
| `returnType` | The return type for this new console method. |
| `minArgs` | The minimum number of arguments this method will take. This may be any value 2 or greater. |
| `maxArgs` | The maximum number of arguments this function will take. If set to 0, this method can accept an infinite number of arguments; otherwise, it should be set to minArgs or greater. |
| `usage1` | A quoted string (const char *) containing a short description of the method and its usage. The null-string ("") is acceptable. |

### Example Call
```
// Create a new console method: foo();
//
// Called in console like this: %obj.foo();
//
ConsoleMethod(myClass, foo, void, 2, 2, "obj.foo()")
{
    Con::printf("You called %s on object ID %d", argv[0], argv[1] );
}
```

### Notes
1. This macro creates a declaration header; you must supply the body that follows it.
2. This macro supplies three variables to the body code that you place after it (listed in the following table).

| Automatic Variables | |
|---|---|
| `SimObject *object` | A pointer to the object this method is called on. |
| `S32 argc` | A signed integer specifying the count of the arguments being passed to this method. |
| `const char **argv` | A pointer to a character string containing an array of const char * arguments. |

## `ConsoleStaticMethod`

### Purpose
Use the `ConsoleStaticMethod` macro to create and expose new static console methods using C++. Static console methods can be called without an instance of the class this method is associated with.

### Syntax
```
#include "console/console.h"
ConsoleStaticMethod(className, name, returnType, minArgs, maxArgs, usage1)
```

| | |
|---|---|
| `className` | An unquoted string containing the name of the C++ class this method is associated with. |
| `name` | An unquoted string containing the name of the new console method to create. |
| `returnType` | The return type for this new console method. |
| `minArgs` | The minimum number of arguments this method will take. This may be any value 1 or greater. |

maxArgs   The maximum number of arguments this method will take. If set to 0, this method can accept an infinite number of arguments; otherwise it should be set to `minArgs` or greater.

Exception: If `minArgs` is 1, `maxArgs` should be 2 or greater.

usage1   A quoted string (const char *) containing a short description of the method and its usage. The null-string ("") is acceptable.

**Example Call**
```
// Create a new static console method: bar();
//
// Called in console like this: myClass::bar();
//
ConsoleStaticMethod(myClass, bar, void, 1, 2, "obj.bar()")
{
   if( argc == 2 )
   {
      Con::printf("You called %s on object ID %d", argv[0], argv[1] );
   }
   else
   {
      Con::printf("You called %s, but no instance of this class exists!",
                  argv[0] );
   }
}
```

**Notes**
1. This macro creates a declaration header; you must supply the body that follows it.
2. This macro supplies three variables to the body code that you place after it (listed in the following table).

| Automatic Variables | |
|---|---|
| `SimObject *object` | A pointer to the object this method is called on. |
| `S32 argc` | A signed integer specifying the count of the arguments being passed to this method. |
| `const char **argv` | A ponter ti a character string containing an array of const char * arguments. |

## B.7.2 Con Namespace Functions

| Function | Description |
|---|---|
| `Con::addVariable` | Register a C++ global as a console global. |
| `Con::errorf` | Print an error message to the console. |
| `Con::evaluate` | Compile and evaluate a script file using C++. |
| `Con::evaluatef` | Compile and evaluate a string of script using C++. |
| `Con::execute` | Call a console function or method using C++. |
| `Con::executef` | Call a console function or method using C++. |
| `Con::getArgBuffer` | Get buffer space to pass an argument to `Con::execute` and to `Con::executef`. |
| `Con::getBoolVariable` | Get the value of a named boolean console global. |
| `Con::getFloatArg` | Get buffer space to pass a floating-point argument to either `Con::execute` or `Con::executef`. |
| `Con::getFloatVariable` | Get the value of a named floating-point console global. |
| `Con::getIntArg` | Get buffer space to pass an integer argument to either `Con::execute` or `Con::executef`. |

| Function | Description |
|---|---|
| `Con::getIntVariable` | Get the value of a named integer console global. |
| `Con::getLocalVariable` | Get the value of a named console local. |
| `Con::getReturnBuffer` | Get buffer space to return arbitrary string data from a console function/method. |
| `Con::getVariable` | Get the value of a named console global. |
| `Con::isFunction` | Determine if a named function exists in the console. |
| `Con::printf` | Print a normal message to the console. |
| `Con::removeVariable` | Unregister a previously registered C++ global. |
| `Con::setBoolVariable` | Set the value of a named boolean console global. |
| `Con::setFloatVariable` | Set the value of a named floating-point console global. |
| `Con::setIntVariable` | Set the value of a named integer console global. |
| `Con::setLocalVariable` | Set the value of a named console local. |
| `Con::setVariable` | Set the value of a named console global. |
| `Con::warnf` | Use to print a warning message to the console. |

| TaskAssociated | Function(s) |
|---|---|
| Register or unregister a C++ global as console global. | `Con::addVariable, Con::removeVariable` |
| Call console function/method from C++. | `Con::execute, Con::executef` |
| Check whether named console function exists from C++. | `Con::isFunction` |
| Execute console script from C++. | `Con::evaluate, Con::evaluatef` |
| Get buffer space to pass data in a call to `execute` or `executef`. | `Con::getFloatArg,` `Con::getIntArg` |
| Get buffer space to pass data in a call to `execute` or `executef`, or to return to the console. | `Con::getArgBuffer` |
| Get/Set console local/global variable using C++. | `Con::getBoolVariable, Con::getFloatVariable,` `Con::getLocalVariable, Con::getVariable,` `Con::setBoolVariable, Con::setFloatVariable,` `Con::setLocalVariable, Con::setVariable` |
| Print message to console from C++. | `Con::errorf, Con::printf, Con::warnf` |

## Con::addVariable

### Purpose
Use the `Con::addVariable` function to register a C++ global as a console global.

### Syntax
```
#include "console/console.h"
bool addVariable(const char *name, S32 type, void *pointer);
```
| `const char *name` | A pointer to a character string containing the name of global as it should be created in the console. |
| `S32 type` | A signed integer spedifying the type of variable for this global (see Section B.6.1). |
| `void *pointer` | A pointer to the C++ global that is to be registered. |

### Example Call
```
// Expose global that controls decal rendering
Con::addVariable("$pref::decalsOn", TypeBool, &smDecalsOn);
```

**Notes**
1. You can specify the console global name with or without a dollar ($) symbol. TGE will add one for you if you don't.

**Returns**
Returns `true` if the add succeeded.

**See Also**
`Con::removeVariable`

---

## Con::errorf, Con::printf, Con::warnf

**Purpose**
Use the `Con::errorf`, `Con::printf`, and `Con::warnf` functions to print error, normal, and warning messages (respectively) to the console from within C++ code.

**Syntax**
```
#include "console/console.h"
void errorf(const char *fmt,...)
void printf(const char *fmt,...)
void warnf(const char *fmt,...)
```

| | |
|---|---|
| `const char *fmt` | A pointer to a character string that describes the format to be used. |
| `...` | A format string of arguments depending on the format string. |

**Example Call**
```
// Print Hello World as an error string to the console.
Con::errorf( "%s\n" , "Hello World!" );
```

**Notes**
1. For additional information on variable format strings, please refer to an ANSI-C reference for the `printf()` function.

---

## Con::evaluate, Con::evaluatef

**Purpose**
Use the `Con::evaluate` and `Con::evaluatef` functions to compile and evaluate TorqueScript scripts from within C++ code.

**Syntax**
```
#include "console/console.h"
const char *evaluate(const char* string, bool echo = false,
                     const char *fileName = NULL);
const char *evaluatef(const char* fmt, ...);
```

| | |
|---|---|
| `const char* string` | A pointer to a character string containing the script code to be evaluated. |
| `bool echo` | Print the script to the console if this is true. |
| `const char *fileName` | A pointer to a charcater string containing a (path and) file name to save the compiled version of the script to. |
| `const char* fmt` | A pointer to a charcater string containing a format string that describes the script to be evaluated. |
| `...` | Arguments depending on the format string. |

**399**

**Example Call**
```
// Evaluate a simple script
const char *result;
result = Con::evaluate("vectorAdd(\"1 2 3\", \"1 2 3\");");
Con::printf("%s\n", result); // prints "2 4 6" to console

// Evaluate same script using variable substitution
const char *result;
result = Con::evaluatef("vectorAdd(\"%d %d %d\", \"%d %d %d\");",1,2,3,1,2,3);
Con::printf("%s\n", result); // prints "2 4 6" to console
```

**Notes**

1. For additional information on variable format strings, please refer to an ANSI-C reference for the `printf()` function.

**Returns**

Returns the results of the evaluation as pointer to a string.

**See Also**

`Con::execute, Con::executef`

---

## Con::execute, Con::executef (console function variants)

**Purpose**

Use the `Con::execute` and `Con::executef` functions to call a console function from within C++ code.

**Syntax**
```
#include "console/console.h"
const char *execute(S32 argc, const char* argv[]);
const char *executef(S32 argc, ...);
```

| | |
|---|---|
| `S32 argc` | A signed integer specifying the number of arguments to pass this function or method. |
| `const char *argv[]` | An array of pointers to character strings, each containing an argument. The first argument is assumed to be the console function name. |
| `...` | A variable list of arguments, each of which must be of the type `const char *`. The first argument is assumed to be the console function name. |

**Example Call**
```
// Execute simple function call
const char *args[2] = {"echo", "hello world"};
Con::execute(2,args); // prints "hello world" to console

// Execute same function call using variable arguments
Con::executef(2, "echo", "hello world" ); // prints "hello world" to console
```

**Returns**

Returns any results from the call or a NULL-string ("") if there were no results.

**See Also**

`Con::evaluate, Con::evaluatef`

## Con::execute, Con::executef (console method variants)

### Purpose
Use the Con::execute and Con::executef functions to call a console method on this object from within C++ code.

### Syntax
```
#include "console/console.h"
const char *execute(SimObject *object, S32 argc, const char *argv[]);
const char *executef(SimObject *, S32 argc, ...);
```

| | |
|---|---|
| SimObject *object | A pointer to the object on which to execute this method. |
| S32 argc | A signed integer specifying the number of arguments to pass this function or method. |
| const char *argv[] | An array of pointers to character strings, each containing an argument. The first argument is assumed to be the console method name. |
| ... | A variable list of arguments, each of which must be of the type const char *. The first argument is assumed to be the console method name. |

### Example Call
```
// Execute simple method call
const char *args[1] = { "dump" };
Con::execute(object, 1, args); // calls dump() on this SimObject

// Execute same method call using variable arguments
Con::executef(object, 1, "dump" ); // calls dump() on this SimObject
```

### Notes
1. For additional information on variable format strings, please refer to an ANSI-C reference for the printf() function.

### Returns
Returns any results from the call or a NULL-string ("") if there were no results.

### See Also
Con::evaluate, Con::evaluatef

## Con::getArgBuffer, Con::getFloatArg, Con::getIntArg

### Purpose
Use this group of functions to get buffer space for passing an argument to the Con::execute* functions.

### Syntax
```
#include "console/console.h"
char *getArgBuffer(U32 bufferSize);
char *getFloatArg(F64 arg);
char *getIntArg   (S32 arg);
```

| | |
|---|---|
| U32 bufferSize | An unsigned integer specifying the size of the requested buffer in bytes. |
| F64 arg | A double-precision floating-point value to be placed in the return buffer. |
| S32 arg | A 32-bit signed integer to be placed in the return buffer. |

### Example Call
```
// Stuff the floating-point 3.14159 into a buffer for passing to execute*()
char *buf  = Con::getFloatArg( (F64) 3.14159 );
```

## Notes

1. The last two functions will create a buffer just large enough to hold the floating-point or signed integer value and do the equivalent of a dSprintf() of that value into the buffer before returning it.

## Returns

| | |
|---|---|
| Con::getArgBuffer | Blank buffer, bufferSize bytes in length. |
| Con::getFloatBuffer | Variable-length containing dSprintf() version of arg. |
| Con::getIntBuffer | Variable-length containing dSprintf() version of arg. |

## See Also

Con::execute, Con::executef, Con::getFloatArg, Con::getIntArg

---

## Con::getBoolVariable, Con::getFloatVariable, Con::getIntVariable, Con::getLocalVariable, Con::getVariable

### Purpose

Use this group of functions to get the value of some console local or global variable as specified in name.

| Function | Gets console variable type |
|---|---|
| Con::getBoolVariable | Global boolean (bool). |
| Con::getFloatVariable | Global floating-point (F32). |
| Con::getIntVariable | Global integer (S32). |
| Con::getLocalVariable | Local variable of any type. |
| Con::getVariable | Global variable of any type. |

### Syntax

```
#include "console/console.h"
bool getBoolVariable (const char* name, bool def = false);
F32  getFloatVariable(const char* name, F32 def = .0f);
S32  getIntVariable  (const char* name, S32 def = 0);
const char* getVariable(const char* name);
```

| | |
|---|---|
| const char* name | A pointer to a character string containing the name of the console global variable to get. |
| bool def | A boolean variable specifying the default value to be returned if the named variable is not found. |
| F32 def | A floating-point variable specifying the default value to be returned if the named variable is not found. |
| S32 def | A signed integer variable specifying the default value to be returned if the named variable is not found. |

### Example Call

```
// Check whether full-screen mode is set.
bool isFullScreen = Con::getBoolVariable("$pref::Video::fullScreen");
```

### Returns

Returns the value of the console global or a default value (if the variable is not found), except for Con::getVariable(), which returns NULL if the variable is not found.

### See Also

Con::setBoolVariable, Con::setFloatVariable, Con::setIntVariable, Con::setLocalVariable, Con::setVariable

## Con::getReturnBuffer

**Purpose**

Use the Con::getReturnBuffer function to get buffer space to return an arbitrary length string data from a console function or method.

**Syntax**

```
#include "console/console.h"
char *getReturnBuffer(U32 bufferSize);
```

U32 bufferSize        An unsigned integer specifying the size of the buffer (in bytes) to return.

**Example Call**

```
// Get a return buffer and return this object's scale in it
char *returnBuffer = Con::getReturnBuffer(256);
const VectorF & scale = object->getScale();
dSprintf(returnBuffer, 256, "%g %g %g", scale.x, scale.y, scale.z);
return(returnBuffer);
```

**Notes**

1. The engine handles deleting this buffer, so you can just create it, use it, and forget it.

**Returns**

Returns a buffer of the specified length (in bytes).

**See Also**

Con::getArgBuffer, getFloatArg, getIntArg

## Con::isFunction

**Purpose**

Use the Con::isFunction function to determine whether a named function exists in the console.

**Syntax**

```
#include "console/console.h"
bool isFunction(const char *fn);
```

const char *fn        A pointer to a character string containing the name of the console function to search for.

**Example Call**

```
// Check to see that the echo() function exists
bool isFunction = Con::isFunction( "echo" );
if(isFunction)
   Con::printf("echo() exists?\n");
else
   Con::printf("echo() doesn't exist?\n");
```

**Returns**

Returns true if the specified console function exists.

**See Also**

SimObject::isMethod

## Con::removeVariable

### Purpose
Use the `Con::removeVariable` function to unregister a previously registered C++ global.

### Syntax
```
#include "console/console.h"
bool removeVariable(const char *name);
```
`const char *name`     A pointer to a character string containing the name of the persistent variable to unregister.

### Example Call
```
// Remove a global variable previously exposed as $myDummyVar
Con::removeVariable( "$myDummyVar" );
```

### Returns
```
Returns true if the variable could be removed.
```

### See Also
```
Con::addVariable
```

## Con::setBoolVariable, Con::setFloatVariable, Con::setIntVariable, Con::setLocalVariable, Con::setVariable

### Purpose
Use these functions to set console global variables of various types (listed in the following table).

| Function | Sets console variable type |
| --- | --- |
| `Con::setBoolVariable` | Global boolean (bool). |
| `Con::setFloatVariable` | Global floating-point (F32). |
| `Con::setIntVariable` | Global integer (S32). |
| `Con::setLocalVariable` | Local variable of any type. |
| `Con::setVariable` | Global variable of any type. |

### Syntax
```
#include "console/console.h"
void setBoolVariable (const char* name, bool var);
void setFloatVariable(const char* name, F32 var);
void setIntVariable  (const char* name, S32 var);
void setLocalVariable(const char *name, const char *value);
void setVariable(const char *name, const char *value);
```
`const char* name`     A pointer to a character string containing the name of the console global variable to set.
`bool var`     A boolean value to place in the console global variable.
`F32 var`     A floating-point value to place in the console global variable.
`S32 var`     A signed integer value to place in the console global variable.
`const char* value`     A pointer to a character string to place in the console global variable.

### Example Call
```
// Set the  full-screen mode global to true
Con::setBoolVariable( "$pref::Video::fullScreen", true );
```

**Returns**
No return value.

**See Also**
Con::getBoolVariable, Con::getFloatVariable, Con::getIntVariable, Con::getLocalVariable,
Con::getVariable

# B.7.3 ConsoleObject Macros

| Macro | Description |
|---|---|
| addNamedField | Exposes class member as a persistent field in the console. |
| addNamedFieldV | Exposes class member as a persistent field in the console and attaches validator. |
| DECLARE_CONOBJECT | Generates declaration code for exposing class in console. |
| IMPLEMENT_CO_DATABLOCK_V1 | Generates definition code for exposing SimDataBlock class in console. |
| IMPLEMENT_CO_NETOBJECT_V1 | Generates definition code for exposing Netobject class in console. |
| IMPLEMENT_CONOBJECT | Generates definition code for exposing ConsoleObject class in console. |
| Offset | Calculates offset of a class's member variable. |

---

### addNamedField, addNamedFieldV

**Purpose**
Use these macros to expose a class member as a persistent field in the console. Additionally, addNamedFieldV
registers the field with a validator.

**Syntax**
```
#include "console/consoleObject.h"
addNamedField(fieldName, type, className)
addNamedFieldV(fieldName, type, className, validator)
```

| | |
|---|---|
| fieldName | The name of the class member to expose. Persistent field is given same name. |
| type | Type specifier for this global (see Section B.6.1). |
| className | Name of class containing member. |
| validator | Pointer to a validator class instance. |

**Example Call**
```
// Add a field to ExplosionData
addNamedField(lightStartColor, TypeColorF, ExplosionData);

// Add a validated field to ExplosionData
// (lightStartRadius can take value between 0 and MaxLightRadius)
addNamedFieldV(lightStartRadius, TypeF32, ExplosionData,
            new FRangeValidator(0, MaxLightRadius));
```

**See Also**
addField, addFieldV, Offset

---

### DECLARE_CONOBJECT

**Purpose**
Use the DECLARE_CONOBJECT macro to declare the code needed to expose/register a class with the console for use
in scripts.

## Appendices

### Syntax

```
#include "console/consoleObject.h"
DECLARE_CONOBJECT(className)
```

className          Name of the class to declare as a console class.

### Example Call

```
// Generate declaration code to expose a new SimDataBlock class to the console
DECLARE_CONOBJECT( mySimDataBlock );
```

### Notes

1. Requires call to one of these macros (in the source file for this class): IMPLEMENT_CO_DATABLOCK_V1, IMPLEMENT_CO_NETOBJECT_V1, IMPLEMENT_CONOBJECT.

### See Also

IMPLEMENT_CO_DATABLOCK_V1, IMPLEMENT_CO_NETOBJECT_V1, IMPLEMENT_CONOBJECT

---

## IMPLEMENT_CO_DATABLOCK_V1, IMPLEMENT_CO_NETOBJECT_V1, IMPLEMENT_CONOBJECT

### Purpose

Use these macros to implement (define) the code needed to expose/register a class with the console for use in scripts.

| MACRO | Use for classes of this type |
|---|---|
| IMPLEMENT_CONOBJECT | ConsoleObject (and children) |
| IMPLEMENT_CO_NETOBJECT_V1 | NetObject (and children) |
| IMPLEMENT_CO_DATABLOCK_V1 | SimDataBlock (and children) |

### Syntax

```
#include "console/consoleObject.h"
IMPLEMENT_CONOBJECT(className)
IMPLEMENT_CO_NETOBJECT_V1(className)
IMPLEMENT_CO_DATABLOCK_V1(className)
```

className          Name of the class to implement as a console class.

### Example Call

```
// Generate definition code to expose a new SimDataBlock class to the console
IMPLEMENT_CO_DATABLOCK_V1( mySimDataBlock );
```

### Notes

1. Requires call to DECLARE_CONOBJECT macro in header file.
2. The higher-level implementation macros supersede the lower-level macros.
- For example, if you create a NetObject-derived class, use IMPLEMENT_CO_NETOBJECT_V1 instead of IMPLEMENT_CONOBJECT, even though your class is a grandchild of ConsoleObject.

### See Also

DECLARE_CONOBJECT

---

## Offset

### Purpose

Use the Offset macro to calculate the offset of a class's member variable.

**Syntax**
```
#include "console/consoleObject.h"
Offset(fieldName,className)
```
| | |
|---|---|
| fieldName | Name of the class member to calculate offset for. |
| className | Name of class containing this member. |

**Example Call**
```
// Calculate offset of a class member
U32 byteOffset = Offset( mySimDataBlock , dummyVar );
Con::printf(" mySimDataBlock.dummyVar exists at byte-offset %d\n, byteOffset );
```

**See Also**
```
addField, addFieldV
```

# B.7.4 ConsoleObject Methods

| Method | Description |
|---|---|
| addDepricatedField | Blocks the console (scripts) from creating a dynamic field with this name. |
| addField | Exposes a class member as a persistent field in the console. |
| addFieldV | Exposes a class member as a persistent field in the console and attaches a validator. |
| addGroup | Adds a new field group to this class. Members exposed as persistent fields after this point are added to the group. |
| endGroup | Stops adding fields to the last-added field group. |
| getClassName | Gets this class's name. |
| removeField | Unregisters a previously registered class member. |
| setField | Sets the value of a named field. |

---

## addDepricatedField

**Purpose**
Use the addDepricatedField method to block scripts from creating a dynamic field (attached to this class) with the specified name.

**Syntax**
```
#include "console/consoleObject.h"
static void addDepricatedField(const char *fieldName);
```
const char *fieldName    A pointer to a character string containing the name of a persistent field.

**Example Call**
```
void GuiControl::initPersistFields()
{
   // ...
   addDepricatedField("Modal"); // Disallow use of Modal field
   // ...
}
```

**Returns**
No return value.

**See Also**
```
removeField
```

---

## addField

### Purpose
Use the `addField` method to expose a class member as a persistent field in the console.

### Syntax
```
#include "console/consoleObject.h"
static void addField(const char *   in_pFieldname,
                     const U32      in_fieldType,
                     const dsize_t  in_fieldOffset,
                     const U32      in_elementCount = 1,
                     EnumTable     *in_table       = NULL,
                     const char    *in_pFieldDocs  = NULL);
static void addField(const char    *in_pFieldname,
                     const U32      in_fieldType,
                     const dsize_t  in_fieldOffset,
                     const char    *in_pFieldDocs);
```

| | |
|---|---|
| `const char *in_pFieldname` | A pointer to a character string containing the name to assign to a persistent field. |
| `const U32 in_fieldType` | An unsigned integer indicatng the type specifier for this global (see Section B.6.1). |
| `const dsize_t in_fieldOffset` | Offset of member in class. |
| `const U32 in_elementCount` | An unsigned integer specifying the number of elements to expose. (Arrays only.) |
| `EnumTable *in_table` | A pointer to an enumerated table translation class. (Translates names to enum values and vice versa.) |
| `const char *in_pFieldDocs` | A pointer to a character string containing a description of the field. |

### Example Call
```
void GuiControl::initPersistFields()
{
    // ...

    // Expose mClassName member as class field in console
    addField( "class",
              TypeString,
              Offset(mClassName, GuiControl),
              "Script Class of object."
            );
    // ...
}
```

### Returns
No return value.

### See Also
`Offset, removeField`

---

## addFieldV

### Purpose
Use the `addFieldV` method to expose a class member as a persistent field in the console and attach a validator.

**408**

**Syntax**
```
#include "console/consoleObject.h"
static void addFieldV(const char    * in_pFieldname,
                      const U32       in_fieldType,
                      const dsize_t in_fieldOffset,
                      TypeValidator * v,
                      const char    * in_pFieldDocs = NULL);
```

| | |
|---|---|
| `const char *in_pFieldname` | A pointer to a charcater string containing the name to assign to a persistent field. |
| `onst U32 in_fieldType` | An unsigned integer indicating the type specifier for this global (see Section B.6.1). |
| `const dsize_t in_fieldOffset` | Offset of member in class. |
| `TypeValidator * v` | A pointer to a validator class instance. |
| `const char *in_pFieldDocs` | A pointer to a charcater string containing a description of the field. |

**Example Call**
```
// Add a validated field to ExplosionData
// (lightStartRadius can take value between 0 and MaxLightRadius)
addFieldV( "lightStartRadius",
           TypeF32,
           Offset(lightStartRadius, ExplosionData),
           new FRangeValidator(0, MaxLightRadius),
         );
```

**Returns**
No return value.

**See Also**
```
Offset, removeField
```

---

## addGroup, endGroup

**Purpose**
Use these methods to add (open) and then to subsequently end (close) a field-group specifier for organizing (grouping) fields together. All fields added between matching calls to `addGroup` and `endGroup` will be listed together in the world editor inspector.

**Syntax**
```
#include "console/consoleObject.h"
static void addGroup(const char* name, const char* docs = NULL);
static void endGroup(const char* name);
```

| | |
|---|---|
| `const char* name` | A pointer to a charcater string containing the name of the group. |
| `const char* docs` | A pointer to a charcater string containing a description of the group. |

**Example Call**
```
// Add group named Parent
addGroup("Parent"); // Open the group

// addField*() statements here ...

endGroup("Parent"); // Close the group
```

**Returns**
No return value.

**See Also**
addField, addFieldV, addNamedField, addNamedFieldV

---

## getClassName

**Purpose**
Use the getClassName method to get the class's name.

**Syntax**
```
#include "console/consoleObject.h"
const char *getClassName() const;
```

**Example Call**
```
// Store object ID and class name in buffer
dSprintf(buf, bufLen, "%d: %s", pObject->getId(), pObject->getClassName());
```

**Returns**
Returns a pointer to a string containing the object's class name.

---

## removeField

**Purpose**
Use the removeField method to unregister a previously registered class member.

**Syntax**
```
#include "console/consoleObject.h"
static bool removeField(const char *in_pFieldname);
```
` const char *in_pFieldname`    A pointer to a character string containing the name of the field to unregister.

**Example Call**
```
void TerrainBlock::initPersistFields()
{
   // ...

   removeField("position");  // Remove position field
}
```

**Returns**
Returns true if the field could be removed.

**See Also**
addDepricatedField, addField, addFieldV, addNamedField, addNamedFieldV

---

## setField

**Purpose**
Use the setField method to set the value of a named field.

**Syntax**
```
#include "console/consoleObject.h"
```

```
bool setField(const char *fieldName, const char *value);
```
const char *fieldName      A pointer to a character string containing the name of the field to set.

const char *value      A pointer to a character string containing the value to assign to the named field.

### Example Call
```
bool GuiInspectorGroup::onAdd()
{
  // ...

  // Set initial padding field value to 1.0
  mStack->setField( "padding", "1.0" );

  // ...
}
```

### Notes
1. Unlike failed assignments in the console, using this function to assign a field that does not exist will not create that field. The assignment will just fail.

### Returns
Returns `true` if the field could be set. If this returns `false`, it means the field did not exist (and was not created).

### See Also
```
SimFieldDictionary::getFieldValue,SimFieldDictionary::setFieldValue,SimObject::getDataField,
SimObject::setDataField
```

## B.7.5 Sim Namespace Macros

| Macro | Description |
| --- | --- |
| DECLARE_CONSOLETYPE | Generates declaration code for a new console type. Also declares `get` and `set` methods for this type. |
| IMPLEMENT_CONSOLETYPE | Generates implementation (definition) code for a new console type. |
| IMPLEMENT_GETDATATYPE | Generates implementation (definition) code for a new console type's `get` method. |
| IMPLEMENT_SETDATATYPE | Generates implementation (definition) code for a new console type's `set` method. |

### DECLARE_CONSOLETYPE

### Purpose
Use the DECLARE_CONSOLETYPE macro to generate declaration code for a new console type. Also declares `get` and `set` methods for this type.

### Syntax
```
#include "console/simBase.h"
DECLARE_CONSOLETYPE(T);
```
T      Name of the new console class.

### Example Call
```
// Declare the ExplosionData console type
DECLARE_CONSOLETYPE(ExplosionData)
```

### See Also
```
DECLARE_CONOBJECT, IMPLEMENT_CO_DATABLOCK_V1, IMPLEMENT_CO_NETOBJECT_V1, IMPLEMENT_CONOBJECT,
IMPLEMENT_CONSOLETYPE, IMPLEMENT_GETDATATYPE, IMPLEMENT_SETDATATYPE
```

---

### IMPLEMENT_CONSOLETYPE

**Purpose**

Use the IMPLEMENT_CONSOLETYPE macro to generate implementation (definition) code for a new console type.

**Syntax**

```
#include "console/simBase.h"
IMPLEMENT_CONSOLETYPE(T);
```

T       Name of the new console class.

**Example Call**

```
// Implement the ExplosionData console type
IMPLEMENT_CONSOLETYPE(ExplosionData)
```

**See Also**

DECLARE_CONOBJECT, DECLARE_CONSOLETYPE, IMPLEMENT_CO_DATABLOCK_V1, IMPLEMENT_CO_NETOBJECT_V1, IMPLEMENT_CONOBJECT, IMPLEMENT_GETDATATYPE, IMPLEMENT_SETDATATYPE

---

### IMPLEMENT_GETDATATYPE, IMPLEMENT_SETDATATYPE

**Purpose**

Use these macros to generate implementation (definition) code for a new console type's get and set methods.

**Syntax**

```
#include "console/simBase.h"
IMPLEMENT_GETDATATYPE(T);
IMPLEMENT_SETDATATYPE(T);
```

T       Name of the new console class.

**Example Call**

```
// Implement get and set methods for new ExplosionData console type
IMPLEMENT_GETDATATYPE(ExplosionData)
IMPLEMENT_SETDATATYPE(ExplosionData)
```

**See Also**

DECLARE_CONOBJECT, DECLARE_CONSOLETYPE, IMPLEMENT_CO_DATABLOCK_V1, IMPLEMENT_CO_NETOBJECT_V1, IMPLEMENT_CONOBJECT, IMPLEMENT_CONSOLETYPE

## B.7.6 Sim Namespace Functions

**Table B.7.1**

*Sim namespace function descriptions.*

| Function | Description |
| --- | --- |
| Sim::findObject | Finds a SimObject based on a passed name or numeric ID. |
| Sim::getCurrentTime | Get the current simulation time. |
| Sim::getDataBlockGroup | Gets the named SimGroup "DataBlockGroup". |
| Sim::getRootGroup | Gets the named SimGroup "RootGroup". |

## Sim::findObject

**Purpose**
Use the `Sim::findObject` functions to find a `SimObject` based on a passed name or numeric ID.

**Syntax**
```
#include "console/simBase.h"
SimObject* findObject(U32 id);
SimObject* findObject(const char *name);
```

| | |
|---|---|
| `U32 id` | Sim ID of `SimObject` to find. |
| `const char *name` | String containing name of SimObject to find. |

**Example Call**
```
// Find first GameBase object named "BOB"
GameBase *obj = dynamic_cast<GameBase*>( Sim::findObject( "BOB" ) );
```

**Returns**
Returns a `SimObject` pointer to the object found by the search, or `NULL` if no object matching the search criteria was found.

**See Also**
`Sim::findObject` (templates)

---

## Sim::findObject (TEMPLATES)

**Purpose**
Use the `Sim::findObject` templated functions to find a `SimObject` based on a passed name or numeric ID. Generates code necessary to assign the address of the found object to a pointer that you provide (T*&t).

**Syntax**
```
#include "console/console.h"
bool findObject(SimObjectId id, T*&t);
bool findObject(const char *name, T*&t);
```

| | |
|---|---|
| `SimObjectId id` | Sim ID of `SimObject` to find. |
| `const char *name` | A pointer to a character string containing the name of the `SimObject` to find. |
| `T*&t` | A pointer to a `SimObject` or a child of SimObject. NULL if no object was located. |

**Example Call**
```
// Find first GameBase object named "BOB"
GameBase *obj = NULL;
Sim::findObject( "BOB" , obj );
```

**Notes**
1. Remember, these templates generate the code needed to assign an object ID into any suitable `SimObject`-derived class pointer, making these variants of `Sim::findObject()` much easier to use than the other predefined ones.

**Returns**
Returns `true` if the object could be found.

**See Also**
`Sim::findObject`

---

## Sim::getCurrentTime

**Purpose**

Use the Sim::getCurrentTime function to get the current simulation time.

**Syntax**

```
#include "console/simBase.h"
U32 getCurrentTime();
```

**Example Call**

```
// Get the current simulation time
U32 curTime = Sim::getCurrentTime();
```

**Notes**

1. Simulation time is the time elapsed since the engine started running and is measured in milliseconds.

**Returns**

Returns the current simulation time.

---

## Sim::getDataBlockGroup

**Purpose**

Use the Sim::getDataBlockGroup function to get a pointer to the "DataBlockGroup" SimGroup.

**Syntax**

```
#include "console/simBase.h"
SimDataBlockGroup *getDataBlockGroup();
```

**Example Call**

```
// Grab the SimGroup that contains all datablocks
SimGroup *group = Sim::getDataBlockGroup();
```

**Notes**

1. The group returned by this function contains all of a game's datablocks.

**Returns**

Returns a pointer to the special SimGroup "DataBlockGroup".

**See Also**

```
Sim::getRootGroup
```

---

## Sim::getRootGroup

**Purpose**

Use the Sim::getRootGroup function to get a pointer to the "RootGroup" SimGroup.

**Syntax**

```
#include "console/simBase.h"
SimGroup* getRootGroup();
```

**Example Call**

```
// Grab the SimGroup that contains all game objects
SimGroup *group = Sim::getRootGroup();
```

**Notes**
1. The group returned by this function contains all of a game's SimObjects and all other special SimGroups including "DataBlockGroup".

**Returns**
Returns a pointer to the special SimGroup "RootGroup".

**See Also**
`Sim::getDataBlockGroup`

# B.7.7 SimObject Methods

| Method | Description |
|---|---|
| assignName | Assigns a new name to the current SimObject. |
| deleteObject | Deletes the current SimObject. |
| getDataField | Gets the value of a named field. This can be a persistent or a dynamic field. |
| getFieldDictionary | Gets a pointer to this SimObject's field dictionary. |
| getId | Gets the ID of this SimObject. |
| getIdString | Gets the ID of this SimObject as a string. |
| getInternalName | Gets the internal name of this SimObject. |
| getName | Gets the name of this SimObject. |
| getType | Gets the type (mask) of this SimObject. |
| isDeleted | Checks to see if this SimObject has been deleted. |
| isMethod | Check to see if the specified method is associated with this SimObject. |
| isProperlyAdded | Checks to see if the onAdd() callback was called for this SimObject. |
| isRemoved | Checks to see whether the onRemove() callback was called for this SimObject. |
| registerObject | Registers this object with the simulation. |
| setDataField | Sets any dynamic or persistent field in this SimObject to a specified value. |
| setId | Sets this SimObject's ID. |
| setInternalName | Sets this SimObject's internal name. |
| unregisterObject | Unregisters this SimObject with the simulation. |

## assignName

**Purpose**
Use the `assignName` method to assign a new name to this SimObject.

**Syntax**
```
#include "console/simBase.h"
void assignName(const char *name);
```
`const char *name`  A pointer to a character string containing a name for the current object.

**Example Call**
```
// Actual snippets of engine code that create the RootGroup SimGroup
//
// in SimBase.h
enum SimObjectConstants
{
   // ...
```

```
    RootGroupId = 0xFFFFFFFF,
};
//
// in SimManager.cc
gRootGroup = new SimGroup();
gRootGroup->setId(RootGroupId);
gRootGroup->assignName("RootGroup");
```

**Returns**

No return value.

**See Also**

getName

---

## deleteObject

**Purpose**

Use the deleteObject method to delete this SimObject.

**Syntax**

```
#include "console/simBase.h"
void deleteObject();
```

**Example Call**

```
// Delete all NetConnection objects
NetConnection *walk = NetConnection::getConnectionList();
while(walk)
{
    NetConnection *next = walk->getNext();

    walk->deleteObject();

    walk = next;
}
```

**Notes**

1. This method automatically unregisters the SimObject before deleting it.

**Returns**

No return value.

**See Also**

unregisterObject

---

## getDataField

**Purpose**

Use the getDataField method to get the value of a named field.

**Syntax**

```
#include "console/simBase.h"
const char *getDataField(StringTableEntry slotName, const char *array);
```

 StringTableEntry slotName        String table entry specifying the field name to search for.

```
const char *array
```
A pointer to a character string containing an integer array index. If the field is not an array, pass NULL in this argument.

**Example Call**
```
// Print this class' datablock field name
char * dbName = myObject->getDataField( StringTable->insert( "datablock" ),
                                        NULL );
Con::printf("Datablock == %s ", dbName );
```

**Notes**
1. The field can be persistent or dynamic.

**Returns**
Returns a pointer to a character string containing the value of the named field, or a NULL string ("") if the field was not located.

**See Also**
```
ConsoleObject::setFieldValue,        setDataField,        SimFieldDictionary::getFieldValue,
SimFieldDictionary::setFieldValue
```

---

## getFieldDictionary

**Purpose**
Use the getFieldDictionary method to retrieve a pointer to this SimObject's field dictionary.

**Syntax**
```
#include "console/simBase.h"
SimFieldDictionary * getFieldDictionary();
```

**Example Call**
```
// Code to get field dictionary (in ConsoleMethod() definition)
SimFieldDictionary *dict = object->getFieldDictionary()->printFields(object);
```

**Returns**
Returns a pointer to this SimObject's field dictionary.

---

## getId, getIdString

**Purpose**
Use these methods to get the ID of this SimObject as a numeric value or as a string.

**Syntax**
```
#include "console/simBase.h"
U32 getId();
const char* getIdString();
```

**Example Call**
```
// Store object ID and class name in buffer
dSprintf(buf, bufLen, "%d: %s", pObject->getId(), pObject->getClassName());

// or

// Store object ID and class name in buffer
dSprintf(buf, bufLen, "%s: %s", pObject->getIdString(), pObject->getClassName());
```

**Returns**

Returns the simulation ID of this object as either an integer value or as a pointer to a string containing this value.

**See Also**

```
registerObject, setId
```

---

## getInternalName, getName

**Purpose**

Use these methods to get the internal or external name of this SimObject.

**Syntax**

```
#include "console/simBase.h"
StringTableEntry getInternalName();
const char* getName();
```

**Example Call**

```
// Print this object's internal and external names to the consoleFunction
Con::printf( "Obj name: %s has internal name:%s\n",
             getName(), getInternalName() );
```

**Returns**

Returns either a string table entry referencing this objects internal name or a pointer to a character string containing this objects externally visible name.

**See Also**

```
assignName, registerObject, setInternalName
```

---

## getType

**Purpose**

Use the getType method to get the type mask for this SimObject.

**Syntax**

```
#include "console/simBase.h"
U32 getType();
```

**Example Call**

```
// Check if this object is a vehicle
if( getType() & VehicleObjectType )
   Con::printf("This object is a vehicle.\n");
else
   Con::printf("This object is NOT a vehicle.\n");
```

**Returns**

Returns a bitmask which may be comprised of any combination of the following type bitmasks.

Type Bitmasks

| | | |
|---|---|---|
| AIObjectType | InteriorMapObjectType | StaticRenderedObjectType |
| AtlasObjectType | InteriorObjectType | StaticShapeObjectType |
| CameraObjectType | ItemObjectType | StaticTSObjectType |
| CorpseObjectType | MarkerObjectType | TerrainObjectType |
| DamagableItemObjectType | PhysicalZoneObjectType | TriggerObjectType |
| DebrisObjectType | PlayerObjectType | VehicleBlockerObjectType |

## Type Bitmasks

| | | |
|---|---|---|
| DecalManagerObjectType | ProjectileObjectType | VehicleObjectType |
| EnvironmentObjectType | ShadowCasterObjectType | WaterObjectType |
| ExplosionObjectType | ShapeBaseObjectType | |
| GameBaseObjectType | StaticObjectType | |

## isDeleted, isProperlyAdded, isRemoved

### Purpose
Use these methods to test the following aspects of this object.

| Method | Aspect(s) Tested |
|---|---|
| isDeleted | This SimObject is marked for deletion (and has been unregistered). |
| isProperlyAdded | The onAdd() callback has been called for this object, and it has been registered with the simulation. |
| isRemoved | The onRemove() callback has been called for this SimObject and it has been removed from the simulation, but not necessarily marked for deletion. |

### Syntax
```
#include "console/simBase.h"
bool isDeleted();
bool isProperlyAdded();
bool isRemoved();
```

### Example Call
```
// Don't delete if this object has already been marked for deletion.
if(!obj->isDeleted())
   delete obj;
```

### Notes
1. If an object has been marked for deletion, you should not use it. It will eventually be deleted by TGE.
2. If an object has been removed (from simulation), but not marked for deletion, you can still use it and even put it back into the simulation.

### Returns
Returns true if the tested aspect is valid.

## isMethod

### Purpose
Use the isMethod method to check if the specified console method is associated with this SimObject.

### Syntax
```
#include "console/simBase.h"
bool SimObject::isMethod( const char* methodName )
```
`const char* methodName`   A pointer to a character string containing the name of the method to check for.

### Example Call
```
// Does this SimObject support dump()?
if( !isMethod( "dump" ) )
   Con::errorf("This object does not support dump()?");
```

**Returns**
Returns `true` if the specified method is associated with this object.

**See Also**
`Con::isFunction`

---

## registerObject

**Purpose**
Use the `registerObject` method to register this SimObject with the simulation. Each of the four versions of this method assign an ID and name differently.

**Syntax**
```
#include "console/simBase.h"
```

| | | |
|---|---|---|
| `bool registerObject();` | automatically | none |
| `bool registerObject(U32 id);` | as specified | none |
| `bool registerObject(const char *name);` | automatically | as specified |
| `bool registerObject(const char *name, U32 id);` | as specified | as specified |

`U32 id`      An unsigned integer specifying the ID to assign to the new SimObject before registering it with the simulation.

`const char *name`      A pointer to a charcater string containing the name to assign to the new SimObject.

**Example Call**
```
// Write alternate code for creating and registering "RootGroup" SimGroup
//
// Actual code in SimManager.cc
//
//    gRootGroup = new SimGroup();
//    gRootGroup->setId(RootGroupId);
//    gRootGroup->assignName("RootGroup");
//    gRootGroup->register();
//
// Simpler code:
//
gRootGroup = new SimGroup();
gRootGroup->register( "RootGroup", RootGroupId );
```

**Returns**
Returns `true` if the registration succeeded.

**See Also**
`deleteObject`, `isProperlyAdded`, `unregisterObject`

---

## setDataField

**Purpose**
Use the `setDataField` method to set a persistent or dynamic field belonging to this SimObject to a specified value.

**Syntax**
```
#include "console/simBase.h"
void setDataField(StringTableEntry slotName, const char *array,
```

```
                      const char *value);
```
StringTableEntry slotName          String table entry specifying the field name to change.

const char *array          A pointer to a character string containing an integer array index. If the field is not an array, pass NULL in this argument.

const char *value          A pointer to a character string containing the value to set the field to.

## Example Call
```
// Lock this object so it can't be edited in the Inspector
setDataField( StringTable->insert("locked", false), NULL, "false" );
```

## Returns
No return value.

## See Also
ConsoleObject::setFieldValue, SimFieldDictionary::getFieldValue, SimFieldDictionary::setFieldValue, getDataField

---

## setId

### Purpose
Use the setId method to set this SimObject's ID.

### Syntax
```
#include "console/simBase.h"
void setId(SimObjectId id);
```
SimObjectId id          A pointer to a character string containing the new ID for this SimObject.

### Example Call
```
// Actual snippets of engine code that create the RootGroup SimGroup
//
// in SimBase.h
enum SimObjectsConstants
{
   // ...
   RootGroupId = 0xFFFFFFFF,

};
//
// in SimManager.cc
gRootGroup = new SimGroup();
gRootGroup->setId(RootGroupId);
gRootGroup->assignName("RootGroup");
```

### Returns
No return value.

### See Also
isFirstPerson, registerObject

---

## setInternalName

### Purpose
Use the setInternalName method to set this SimObject's internal name.

### Syntax
```
#include "console/simBase.h"
void setInternalName(const char* newname);
```
const char* newname        New internal name for this SimObject.

### Example Call
```
// Set this object's internal name to buddy
setInternalName( "buddy" );
```

### Returns
No return value.

### See Also
```
isFirstPerson
```

---

## unregisterObject

### Purpose
Use the `unregisterObject` method to unregister this SimObject with the simulator.

### Syntax
```
#include "console/simBase.h"
void unregisterObject();
```

### Example Call
```
// Unregister every object in "RootGroup"
for (SimSetIterator obj(Sim::getRootGroup()); *obj; ++obj)
{
    SimObject* sobj = dynamic_cast<SimObject*>(*sobj);

    if (sobj)
    {
        sobj->unregisterObject();
    }
}
```

### Returns
No return value.

### See Also
```
isDeleted, isRemoved, registerObject
```

# B.7.8 SimFieldDictionary Methods

| Method | Description |
| --- | --- |
| assignFrom | Copies all field names and their values from a source field dictionary to this one. |
| getFieldValue | Gets the value of a named field in this dictionary. |
| printFields | Prints the names and values of all fields in a specified SimObject's dictionary to the console. |
| setFieldValue | Sets the value of a named field in this dictionary, creating it if the field is not already present. |

---

## assignFrom

### Purpose
Use the `assignFrom` method to copy all field names and their values from a source field dictionary to this one.

### Syntax
```
#include "console/simBase.h"
void assignFrom(SimFieldDictionary *dict);
```
 `SimFieldDictionary *dict`          A pointer to a source field dictionary.

### Example Call
```
// Assign field values from SimObject "Billy" to SimObject "Bob"
SimObject *srcObj = Sim::findObject( "Billy" );
SimObject *dstObj = Sim::findObject( "Bob" );
SimFieldDictionary * billyDictionary = NULL;

SimFieldDictionary * bobDictionary = NULL;

if( srcObj && dstObj )
{
   billyDictionary = srcObj->getFieldDictionary();
   bobDictionary   = dstObj->getFieldDictionary();

   bobDictionary->assignFrom( billyDictionary );
};
```

### Returns
No return value.

---

## getFieldValue

### Purpose
Use the `getFieldValue` method to get the value of a named field in this dictionary.

### Syntax
```
const char *getFieldValue(StringTableEntry slotName);
```
 `StringTableEntry slotName`          String table entry specifying the name of the field to retrieve.

### Example Call
```
// See if billy has any friends and give him some if he doesn't
//
SimObject *obj = Sim::findObject( "Billy" );
SimFieldDictionary * billyDictionary = NULL;
char *friends = NULL;
StringTableEntry friendsField = StringTable->insert( "friends" );

if( obj )
{
   billyDictionary = obj->getFieldDictionary();

   friends = billyDictionary->getFieldValue( friendsField );

   if( !friends )
```

```
    {
        Con::printf("Billy has no friends!  Poor billy...\n");

        billyDictionary->setFieldValue( friendsField , "Bob" );

        Con::printf("Billy has one friend: %s\n" , friends );
    }
    else
    {
        Con::printf("Billy has these friends: %s\n" , friends );
    }
};
```

**Returns**
Returns a pointer to a string containing the value of the specified field, or a NULL-string ("") if the field does not exist.

**See Also**
```
ConsoleObject::setFieldValue,    setFieldValue,           SimFieldDictionary::getFieldValue,
SimFieldDictionary::getFieldValue, SimObject::getDataField, SimObject::setDataField
```

---

## printFields

**Purpose**
Use the `printFields` method to print the names and values of all fields in a specified SimObject's dictionary to the console.

**Syntax**
```
void printFields(SimObject *obj);
```
` SimObject *obj`       A pointer to the SimObject that owns the field dictionary to be dumped.

**Example Call**
```
// Dump all of the fields assigned to Billy to the console
SimObject *obj = Sim::findObject( "Billy" );
SimFieldDictionary * billyDictionary = NULL;
char *friends = NULL;
StringTableEntry friendsField = StringTable->insert( "friends" );

if( obj )
{
    billyDictionary = obj->getFieldDictionary();

    billyDictionary->printFields();
};
```

**Returns**
No return value.

---

## setFieldValue

**Purpose**
Use the `setFieldValue` method to set the value of a named field in this dictionary, creating it if the field is not already present.

**Syntax**
```
#include "console/simBase.h"
void setFieldValue(StringTableEntry slotName, const char *value);
```
StringTableEntry slotName          A string table entry specifying the name of the field to set.

const char *value                  A pointer to a character string containing the new value for the named field.

**Example Call**
```
// See if billy has any friends and give him some if he doesn't
//
SimObject *obj = Sim::findObject( "Billy" );
SimFieldDictionary * billyDictionary = NULL;
char *friends = NULL;
StringTableEntry friendsField = StringTable->insert( "friends" );

if( obj )
{
   billyDictionary = obj->getFieldDictionary();

   friends = billyDictionary->getFieldValue( friendsField );

   if( !friends )
   {
      Con::printf("Billy has no friends!  Poor billy...\n");

      billyDictionary->setFieldValue( friendsField , "Bob" );

      Con::printf("Billy has one friend: %s\n" , friends );
   }
   else
   {
      Con::printf("Billy has these friends: %s\n" , friends );
   }
};
```

**Returns**
No return value.

**See Also**
```
ConsoleObject::setFieldValue,    getFieldValue,    SimFieldDictionary::getFieldValue,
SimFieldDictionary::getFieldValue, SimObject::getDataField, SimObject::setDataField
```

## B.7.9  NetObject Methods

To use any of these methods, you must include "sim/netObject.h" in your code.

| Method | Description |
| --- | --- |
| bool isClientObject(); | Returns true if this object is on the client. |
| bool isGhost(); | Returns true if this is a ghost of a server object. |
| bool isGhostable(); | Returns true if this is a server object and this object can be ghosted. |
| bool isGhostAlways(); | Returns true if this is a server object and this object is always ghosted. |
| bool isScopeable(); | Returns true if this is server object that is ghostable and not set to be always in scope. |

| Method | Description |
|---|---|
| `bool isScopeLocal();` | Returns `true` if this is a server object that is ghostable and is set to local scope. |
| | If `true`, this object will always be in scope on the client connection that owns it. |
| `bool isServerObject();` | Returns `true` if this object is on the server. |

# B.7.10 Stream References

This reference lists a significant number, but not all, of the streaming methods. These methods are listed both by data type/class and alphabetically (separated between header files). Furthermore, the first list of stream methods annotates methods that support optimization.

To use this reference most efficiently, first find and select a stream method that supports the operation you need from the data type- or class-ordered list. Then, go to the alphabetical list to find the syntax for the method, as well as the header file it comes from.

Note that individual game classes will often supply their own specialized streaming classes. If you don't find exactly what you need here, please examine the class (and parent classes for that class) that you are streaming.

| Data Type / Class | Streaming Methods (bold indicates optimized) |
|---|---|
| `bit(s)` | `readBits`, `writeBits` |
| `bool` | `read`, `readFlag`, `write`, `writeFlag` |
| `char[]` / `U8[]` | `read`, `readLine`, `readLongString`, `readSTString`, `write`, `writeLine`, `writeLongString` |
| `char[256]` | `readString`, `writeString` |
| `ColorF` | `read`, `write` |
| `ColorI` | `read`, `write` |
| `F32` | `read`, `readFloat`, **`readSignedFloat`**, `write`, `writeFloat`, **`writeSignedFloat`** |
| `F64` | `read`, `write` |
| Math classes (except `AngAxisF`) | `mathRead`, `mathWrite` |
| `MatrixF` | `readAffineTransform`, `writeAffineTransform` |
| `Point3F` | **`clearCompressionPoint`**, **`dumbDownNormal`**, **`readCompressedPoint`**, **`readNormalVector`**, **`readNormalVector`**, **`setCompressionPoint`**, **`writeCompressedPoint`**, **`writeNormalVector`**, **`writeNormalVector`** |
| `S16` | `read`, `write` |
| `S32` | `read`, **`readSignedInt`**, `write`, **`writeSignedInt`** |
| `S8` | `read`, `write` |
| `U16` | `read`, `write` |
| `U32` | `read`, `readClassId`, **`readCussedU32`**, **`readRangedU32`**, `write`, `writeClassId`, **`writeCussedU32`**, **`writeRangedU32`** |

**Alphabetic Streaming Method Listing (w/ Arguments)**

```
#include "core/bitStream.h"
        void clearCompressionPoint()
        Point3F dumbDownNormal(const Point3F& vec, S32 bitCount)
        void readAffineTransform(MatrixF*)
        void readBits(S32 bitCount, void *bitPtr)
        S32 readClassId(U32 classType, U32 classGroup)
        void readCompressedPoint(Point3F* p, F32 scale = 0.01f)
        U32 readCussedU32()
        bool readFlag()
        F32 readFloat(S32 bitCount)
```

**Alphabetic Streaming Method Listing (w/ Arguments)**

```
        void readNormalVector(Point3F *vec, S32 bitCount)
        void readNormalVector(Point3F *vec, S32 angleBitCount, S32 bitCount)
        U32 readRangedU32(U32 rangeStart, U32 rangeEnd)
        F32 readSignedFloat(S32 bitCount)
        S32 readSignedInt(S32 bitCount)
        void readString(char stringBuf[256])
        void setCompressionPoint(const Point3F& p)
        void writeAffineTransform(const MatrixF&)
        void writeBits(S32 bitCount, const void *bitPtr)
        void writeClassId(U32 classId, U32 classType, U32 classGroup)
        void writeCompressedPoint(const Point3F& p,F32 scale = 0.01f)
        void writeCussedU32(U32 val)
        bool writeFlag(bool val)
        void writeFloat(F32 f, S32 bitCount)
        void writeNormalVector(const Point3F& vec, S32 bitCount)
        void writeNormalVector(const Point3F& vec, S32 bitCount)
        void writeRangedU32(U32 value, U32 rangeStart, U32 rangeEnd)
        void writeSignedFloat(F32 f, S32 bitCount)
        void writeSignedInt(S32 value, S32 bitCount)
        void writeString(const char *stringBuf, S32 maxLen=255)
```
**#include "math/mathIO.h"**
```
        bool mathRead(Stream& stream, mathClassName* b)
        bool mathWrite(Stream& stream, const mathClassName& p)
```
**#include "core/stream.h"**
```
        bool read(ColorF*)
        bool read(ColorI*)
        bool read(type * val)
        bool read(const U32 in_numBytes,  void* out_pBuffer)
        void readLine(U8 *buffer, U32 bufferSize)
        void readLongString(U32 maxStringLen, char *stringBuf)
        void readString(char stringBuf[256])
        const char *readSTString(bool casesens = false)
        bool write(const ColorF&)
        bool write(const ColorI&)
        bool write(type val)
        bool write(const U32 in_numBytes, const void* in_pBuffer)
        void writeLine(U8 *buffer)
        void writeLongString(U32 maxStringLen, const char *string)
        void writeString(const char *stringBuf, S32 maxLen=255)
```

# B.7.11  GameBase Methods

| Method | Description |
|---|---|
| getControllingClient | Get a pointer to the client connection that controls this GameBase object. |
| getDataBlock | Get a pointer to the GameBaseData instance assigned to this GameBase object. |
| setControllingClient | Assign a new client connection as the controlling client for this GameBase object. |
| setDataBlock | Assign a new datablock to this GameBase object. |

---

## getControllingClient

### Purpose
Use the `getControllingClient` method to get a pointer to the client connection that controls this `GameBase` object.

### Syntax
```
#include "console/gameBase.h"
GameConnection *getControllingClient()
```

### Example Call
```
// Check to be sure this object has a controlling client and if not,
// assign the local client as its controlling client.
if ( GameConnection * gc = getControllingClient() )
{
   // Do some work on this object
}
else
{
   GameConnection *localClient = getLocalClientConnection();

   setControllingClient( localClient );
}
```

### Returns
Returns a pointer to this object's controlling client, or NULL if this object is not currently controlled by a client.

### See Also
`setControllingClient`

---

## getDataBlock

### Purpose
Use the `getDataBlock` method to get a pointer to the GameBaseData instance assigned to this GameBase object.

### Syntax
```
#include "console/gameBase.h"
GameBaseData *getDataBlock()
```

### Example Call
```
// Swap billy's and bob's datablock pointers
GameBase *billy = NULL;
GameBase *bob = NULL;

Sim::findObject( "Billy" , billy );
Sim::findObject( "Bob" , bob );


if( billy && bob )
{
   GameBaseData *tmp = bob->getDatablock();

   if( !bob->setDatablock( billy->getDatablock() ) )
   {
```

**428**

```
        Con::errorf("Bob won't swap!\n");
    }

    if( !billy->setDatablock( tmp->getDatablock() ) )
    {
        Con::errorf("Billy won't swap!\n");
    }
}
```

**Returns**
Returns the datablock assigned to this object, or NULL if no datablock has been assigned yet.

**See Also**
setDataBlock

## setControllingClient

**Purpose**
Use the setControllingClient method to assign a new client connection as the controlling client for this GameBase object.

**Syntax**
```
#include "console/gameBase.h"
void setControllingClient(GameConnection *client);
```
 GameConnection *client          A pointer to a new controlling client to assign to this GameBase object.

**Example Call**
```
// Check to be sure this object has a controlling client and if not,
// assign the local client as its controlling client.
if ( GameConnection * gc = getControllingClient() )
{
   // Do some work on this object
}
else
{
   GameConnection *localClient = getLocalClientConnection();

   setControllingClient( localClient );
}
```

**Returns**
No return value.

**See Also**
getControllingClient

## setDataBlock

**Purpose**
Use the setDataBlock method to assign a new datablock to this GameBase object.

**Syntax**
```
#include "console/gameBase.h"
bool setDataBlock(GameBaseData* dptr);
```

```
GameBaseData *dptr          A pointer to a new datablock to assign to this GameBase object.
```

**Example Call**
```
// Swap billy's and bob's datablock pointers
GameBase *billy = NULL;
GameBase *bob = NULL;

Sim::findObject( "Billy" , billy );
Sim::findObject( "Bob" , bob );


if( billy && bob )
{
   GameBaseData *tmp = bob->getDatablock();

   if( !bob->setDatablock( billy->getDatablock() ) )
   {
      Con::errorf("Bob won't swap!\n");
   }

   if( !billy->setDatablock( tmp->getDatablock() ) )
   {
      Con::errorf("Billy won't swap!\n");
   }
}
```

**Returns**
Returns `true` if the assignment worked.

**See Also**
`getDataBlock`

# Index